MODELS OF ACHIEVEMENT

Reflections of Eminent Women in Psychology

VOLUME 3

Edited by

Agnes N. O'Connell
Montclair State University

2001

LAWRENCE ERLBAUM ASSOCIATES, PUBLISHERS
Mahwah, New Jersey   London

Copyright © 2001 by Agnes N. O' Connell.
All rights reserved. No part of this book may be reproduced in any form, by photostat, microfilm, retrieval system, or any other means, without prior written permission of the publisher.

Lawrence Erlbaum Associates, Inc., Publishers
10 Industrial Avenue
Mahwah, NJ 07430

Cover design by Kathryn Houghtaling Lacey

Library of Congress Cataloging-in-Publication Data

(Revised for Vol. 3)
Models of achievement : Reflections of eminent women in psychology, Volume 3, edited by Agnes N. O' Connell

Includes bibliographical references and indexes.
1. Women psychologists—United States—Biography.
2. Psychology—United States—History—20th century.
3. Sex discrimination in psychology—United States.
I. O' Connell, Agnes N.   II. Russo, Nancy Felipe, 1943–
BF109.A1M6 1983   150¢.88042   82-23583
ISBN 0-231-05312-6 (v. 1: alk. paper)
ISBN 0-231-05313-4 (pbk.: v. 1)
ISBN 0-8058-0083-2 (L. Erlbaum Associates: v. 2)
ISBN 0-8058-0322-X (pbk)
ISBN 0-8058-3556-3c (V. 3)
ISBN 0-8058-3557-1 (pbk)

Books published by Lawrence Erlbaum Associates are printed on acid-free paper, and their bindings are chosen for strength and durability.

Printed in the United States of America
10 9 8 7 6 5 4 3 2 1

Contents

Reviewers and Affiliations *ix*

Foreword *xiii*
Janet Taylor Spence

Preface *xvii*
Agnes N. O'Connell

PART I
General Introduction

Chapter 1
Partners in Progress: Illuminating a New Vision of Women in Psychology 3
Agnes N. O'Connell

PART II
Historical and Social Contexts

Chapter 2
A Century of Contrasts: Historical and Social Contexts of the 20th Century 13
Agnes N. O'Connell

PART III
Autobiographical Perspectives

Chapter 3
Frances Mitchell Culbertson, 1921–   *29*

Chapter 4
Patricia M. Bricklin, 1932–   *45*

Chapter 5
Frances Degen Horowitz, 1932–   *63*

Chapter 6
Norine G. Johnson, n/a   *79*

Chapter 7
Sandra Wood Scarr, 1936–   *97*

Chapter 8
Dorothy W. Cantor, 1937–   *113*

Chapter 9
Diane J. Willis, 1937–   *125*

Chapter 10
Elaine Hatfield, 1937–   *135*

Chapter 11
Phyllis A. Katz, 1938–   *149*

Contents

Chapter 12
Linda M. Bartoshuk, 1938– *169*

Chapter 13
Patricia Keith-Spiegel, 1939– *185*

Chapter 14
Kay Deaux, 1941– *201*

Chapter 15
Judith E. N. Albino, 1943– *219*

Chapter 16
Margaret W. Matlin, 1944– *239*

Chapter 17
Pamela Trotman Reid, 1946– *255*

Chapter 18
Jeanne Brooks-Gunn, 1946– *275*

Chapter 19
Diane F. Halpern, 1947– *293*

Chapter 20
Janet Shibley Hyde, 1948– *307*

Chapter 21
Lillian Comas-Díaz, 1950– *329*

PART IV
Achievement Patterns in the 20th Century

Chapter 22
Profiles and Patterns of Achievement for 53 Eminent Women: Synthesis and Resynthesis 3   343
Agnes N. O'Connell

Index   *421*

Note. Birth year not available for publication at Dr. Johnson's request.

Reviewers for *Models of Achievement, Volume 3*

The Editor and Autobiographers are grateful to the following for their reviews of one or more manuscripts.

Jeff Adams, Widener University
Robin P. Arnold, Philadelphia, Pennsylvania
Mary Brabeck, Boston College
Barry Bricklin, Wayne, Pennsylvania
Pamela Brown, Widener University
Jan Culbertson, Oklahoma University Health Sciences Center
Kimberly Carr, Ball State University
Cindy Clement, University of Hawaii
Elinor Cowling, Xerox Corporation
Jennifer Detta, Ball State University
Valerie Duffy, University of Connecticut and Yale University
Katie Fast, Yale University
Nicole Friedman, California School of Professional Psychology
Michi Fu, California School of Professional Psychology
Charles Gallagher, Widener University
Rochel Gelman, University of California–Los Angeles
Shirin Ghazanfari, SUNY–Geneseo

Meryl Ginsberg, California School of Professional Psychology
Nathaniel Glasser, Widener University
Sam Glucksberg, Princeton University
Katharine Gompers, Illinois School of Professional Psychology
Diane Gooding, University of Wisconsin-Madison
Adele Eskeles Gottfried, California State University at Northridge
Brad Greenspan, Widener University
Nicole Greenspan, Widener University
Tamar Hammer, Widener University
Cheryl Helman, Widener University
Mary Anne O'Connell Hone, River Edge, New Jersey
Frederick M. Jacobsen, George Washington University
Melissa Katter, SUNY-Geneseo
Gwendolyn Puryear Keita, American Psychological Association
David H. Kelly, Montclair State University
Mary Beth Kenkel, California School of Professional Psychology
Jennifer Kleinman, Emory University
Mary L. LaMay, Loma Linda University
Jean Lau Chin, CEO Services, Newton, Massachusetts
Linwood Lewis, Sarah Lawrence College
Robin Lett, Ball State University
Erendida Lopez-Garcia, The Wright Institute
Dana Martin, CUNY Graduate Center
Andrew McMeekan, Widener University
Maria Murguia, University of Wisconsin-Madison
Brian T. O'Connell, St. Joseph's Hospital, Albuquerque, New Mexico
Suzanne Ouellettte, CUNY Graduate Center
Asimin W. Panayoutou, Massachusetts School of Professional Psychology
Connell F. Persico, California School of Professional Psychology
Natalie Porter, California School of Professional Psychology
Stephen A. Ragusea, State College, Pennsylvania
Richard L. Rapson, University of Hawaii
Alisa Robinson, American Liver Foundation

Reviewers

Scott Romeika, Widener University
Renee Saris, Ball State University
Monica Schneider, SUNY-Geneseo
Louise Silvern, University of Colorado-Boulder
Joan Nahmie Smith, Denver, Colorado
Charles Sommerfield, Yale University
Derek Snyder, Florida State University-Tallahassee
Abigail Stewart, University of Michigan-Ann Arbor
Ira Sugarman, Montclair State University
Susan Tabb, Widener University
George P. Taylor, Atlanta, Georgia
Nina Thomas, Morristown, New Jersey
Leslie Throckmorton-Belzer, Ball State University
Lori Van Wallendael, University of North Carolina-Charlotte
Heather Wallach, University of Rochester Medical Center
Richard A. Weinberg, University of Minnesota
Jennifer Wrangham, Ball State University
Sue R. Zalk, CUNY Graduate Center

Foreword

No particular event marked psychology's almost precipitous "discovery of women." But it was clearly in the mid-to-late 1960s that under the influence of a rising feminism and the Civil Rights Movement, women began to have a visible impact on the discipline of psychology and its professional organizations. One of the early indicators of women psychologists' willingness to question their prior treatment was the appearance of articles in which lesser women's status in the field was documented. It ranged from data showing a marked preference of investigators (most of them male) for employing men rather than women in their research, the tendency of faculty members to list male graduate students as junior authors in their research publications but to thank female graduate students for their help in a footnote, and, of course, the scarcity of women psychologists in academia and leadership positions in general.

On the heels of these early publications came articles devoted to understanding women and their position in our society such as, for example, assessment of women's and men's stereotypes about women's characteristics versus those of men and beliefs about appropriate sex roles for men and women (the use of the word *gender* to designate socially constructed as opposed to biologically rooted phenomena had yet to be introduced), along with development of novel theories to replace old ideas about men and women, such as the temperamental qualities purportedly responsible for women's failure to achieve. From being topics that were all but ignored, publications related to gender and the psychology of women began to grow rapidly in the late 1960s and early 1970s. Initially, gender-related research (most of which was done by women) was generally regarded as not quite respectable, and at best, not as serious or important as other areas of study (attitudes that have largely but not fully disappeared). But it was at least possible to get such studies published. Outlets expanded dramatically in 1975 with the appearance of the journal, *Sex Roles*, with Phyllis Katz as editor, and in 1976, of the *Psychology of Women Quarterly*, published by Division 35 (Psychology of Women) of the American Psychological Association (APA) with Georgia Babledelis as editor.

APA also began to discover its many women members in the late 1960s, and its Boards and Committees made self-conscious efforts to nominate women for various positions in the governance structure. Women began to be elected to leadership positions, and collectively, became a major political force within the APA and in other professional organizations as well. These developments were due in part to the large pool of talented women psychologists who were available and eager to take advantage of these new opportunities.

Academia, however, was slower to respond to the changes taking place in societal attitudes and practices. Among other obstacles to women's entry into academic positions were anti-nepotism rules and the unspoken understanding that for PhD couples, positions were offered to the husband with efforts being made to tuck the wife somewhere else. The overall result was a small number of women in psychology departments (and academia in general). My own experience was quite typical. After earning my PhD in 1949, I was hired at Northwestern University as (I later learned) an "experiment." The experiment was apparently a success—at least I was promoted. However, after I left that department (to get married and take a nonacademic position because of anti-nepotism), it was years before another woman was appointed. Some time later, in 1969, when I joined the Department of Psychology at the University of Texas, I was again the only woman on the faculty. Just as it did elsewhere, that situation only gradually changed over the next 10 to 15 years. (I am pleased to report that by the time I retired in 1997, the department had 10 women on the faculty, distributed throughout the academic ranks.)

Quite obviously, the years from approximately 1965 to 1975 or 1980 were ones of almost revolutionary significance for the political and occupational position of women within the field and the emergence of gender as a legitimate and important area of inquiry. The group of eminent women whose autobiographies appear in this volume were players in this transformational period in the history of psychology. As their chapters attest, they were leaders in bringing about the transformation and the beneficiaries of the new opportunities it opened up. The personal stories these women tell are rich and varied, and the accomplishments they report are wide-ranging. Their achievements illustrate what those of us who entered the field before 1960 could hardly have imagined 40 years ago: By the end of the century, women were elected to high office in professional organizations, they were appointed to the upper levels of college administration, and women psychologists came closer and closer to equaling and surpassing men in their intellectual leadership in the science and the profession.

The autobiographical chapters in this volume provide valuable information and insights to historians about what went on in women's lives during those remarkable years in the history of the field. As examples of the progress women have made and continue to make, these chapters should also bring encouragement to students of psychology and the younger members of our discipline, and provide models for them to emulate.

The transformation that has taken place in American psychology since the early 1960s did not arise from a vacuum but out of historical contexts within both the discipline and American society at large. In Chapter 2, Agnes O'Connell, editor of this volume, provides such an account. In this chapter, she presents an overview of the major events of the 20th century, the place of women within society and legislation relevant to women, and finally, an outline of the history of changes in women's roles in psychology's major professional organizations. This chapter is an invaluable summary, particularly to those unfamiliar with these historical events: where women psychologists were at the beginning of the 20th century and how they came to be where they were at the end.

In each of the previous volumes, O'Connell, herself a recognized model of achievement, wrote a concluding chapter in which she provided content analyses of the themes within the lives and careers of the women included in the volumes. The last chapter of the current volume is an even more ambitious undertaking. In it, O'Connell presents an in-depth content analysis of the personal and professional lives of all 53 women represented in the three volumes of *Models of Achievement: Reflections of Eminent Women in Psychology*, reporting similarities and differences in their family backgrounds and their personal and professional life histories. Most important, these analyses identified transhistoric trends and patterns for these 20th-century eminent women. As an original and unique piece of scholarship that fills in gaps in our knowledge, this chapter commands attention from a wide audience, ranging from colleagues with a serious interest in gender to undergraduate women who aspire to become our future colleagues. On a personal level, it pleases me that I have gone from one of a few women to one of many, and I envy those young women who are just beginning.

—*Janet Taylor Spence*
Dennis, Massachusetts

Preface

My work on eminent women's lives, careers, and contributions to psychology has been a central focus of my professional life for more than a quarter of a century. The foundation for this work began to emerge while I was a doctoral student at Rutgers University (1971–1974) and was shaped by serving as chair of the Task Force on Women Doing Research for the Division of the Psychology of Women (now the Society for the Psychology of Women) of the American Psychological Association (APA). As head of this Task Force, I organized and chaired a series of workshops at regional and national conventions in 1976–1977. These workshops underscored the need to preserve the contributions of women to the field of psychology and the need to increase the visibility of strong, resilient role models for the acculturation of women into nontraditional occupational roles. The Task Force on Women Doing Research published the findings of these workshops in a report on "Gender-Specific Barriers to Research in Psychology" (O'Connell et al., 1978) and recommended that the stories of eminent women in psychology be made known.

Acting on this recommendation and in an effort to bring information about the lives of women in psychology to as many colleagues and students as quickly as possible, I organized and chaired a symposium in 1979 devoted to reflections of eminent women in the discipline. The first APA Symposium on Eminent Women in Psychology featured Mary Ainsworth, Margaret Hubbard Jones, Molly Harrower, and Mary Henle (their expanded and revised autobiographies are in Volume 1 of *Models of Achievement*).

It did not occur to me when initiating these symposia that I would be celebrating women's achievements and authoring and editing books about these achievements and the contexts in which they were made in this new millennium. The first symposium originated an important annual tradition at the convention and a significant new subfield, the history of women in psychology. This subfield preserves and celebrates women's lives and strengths, their widespread participation, substantial contributions, impact, and heritage in APA, the field of psychology, and the larger society.

The response to the 1979 symposium was so positive that in 1980 I asked Nancy Russo (Bernstein & Russo, 1974) to act as discussant; she continued in that capacity (and as co-author and co-editor) on a regular basis for more than a decade.

To further celebrate and preserve women's life stories and contributions, I served as senior author and editor of several publications in the 1980s and 1990s beginning with *Eminent Women in Psychology* (O'Connell & Russo, 1980) that contained seven biographies. The first two volumes of *Models of Achievement: Reflections of Eminent Women in Psychology* (O'Connell & Russo, 1983, 1988) each contained 17 autobiographies and chapters on historical and social context and on similarities and differences among the women. *Women in Psychology* (O'Connell & Russo, 1990) contained 36 biographies assessing the contributions of women to psychology and society written by me (2 biographies) but predominantly by such distinguished colleagues (34 biographies) as Ludy T. Benjamin, Jr. and Stephanie A. Shields, Florence L. Denmark and Nancy Felipe Russo, Laurel Furumoto, Harrison G. Gough, Howard E. Gruber, Lewis P. Lipsitt and Dorothy H. Eichorn, Elizabeth Scarborough, M. Brewster Smith, and Michael Wertheimer. *Women's Heritage in Psychology* (O'Connell & Russo, 1991) delineated women's contributions by selected subfields.

In 1992, for the celebration of the APA Centennial and again in 1996 for the 50th Anniversary Celebration of the APA Divisions, I developed and presented (with Louise Vetter) an exhibit at the APA annual meetings consisting of brief biographies and photographs of approximately 100 eminent women in psychology.

Preserving the lives and achievements of women psychologists and illuminating women's roles, experiences, and contributions in shaping the field of psychology across the centuries is crucial in the exploration of how knowledge in the field has developed and been used. These works facilitate understanding of the impact of societal and historical context on the evolution of psychology and on women's lives. They define how, despite substantial hardships, the contributions of women psychologists are interwoven with the evolution of all subfields of psychology, beginning with the field's early roots.

The cumulative reflections and assessments of eminent women provide a major knowledge base for the study of the historical evolution of psychology and the study of women's lives in the 20th century.

Simultaneously, these reflections and assessments render a sense of heritage and purpose and serve as a source of inspiration. These works increase the visibility of distinguished women and their contributions, provide needed role models, and serve as a catalyst for change.

There exists a great and continuing demand for knowledge about women's contributions in psychology especially from the perspective of the women themselves. More than a dozen years have intervened between the publication of Volumes 2 and 3 of *Models of Achievement*. In these intervening years, I have continued to organize, chair, and sometimes serve as discussant of the annual APA symposium. Volume 3 presents expanded, comprehensive, and revised autobiographies of a selection of 19 women who presented brief autobiographical sketches at the Eminent Women Symposium at the annual meetings of APA, approaching and crossing into the third millennium.

In response to the frequent requests of students, the eminent women in Volume 3 represent a predominantly younger cohort—contemporary role models who were born and earned their doctorates in the mid-20th century. In addition to responding to reader demand for information about younger, more contemporary women, the autobiographies in this volume shed light on historical phenomena that have affected lives, opportunities, and achievements.

The content analyses of these autobiographies delineate historic and transhistoric, epoch and time-specific profiles of eminent women in psychology. Individually and collectively the three volumes of *Models of Achievement: Reflections of Eminent Women in Psychology* yield invaluable perspectives on women's lives and careers in psychology and in society in the 20th century. Volume 3 renders current, expansive perspectives and comparisons not present in the earlier two volumes.

Models of Achievement, Volume 3 is a resource for libraries and researchers and is appropriate as a required or supplementary text for courses and seminars in the psychology of women, gender roles, history of psychology, personality, life-span development, counseling, career development, and women's studies. In addition, the descriptions of the creative, productive, and professionally rewarding interactions among colleagues of both sexes found in these autobiographies provide knowledge, wisdom, and inspiration for a wide and diverse range of readers.

The work of preserving a history of psychology that includes the vision of women as psychologists and serves as a source of inspiration has received encouragement and support from many sources including numerous APA divisions, especially the Society for General Psychology, the Society for the Teaching of Psychology, the Division of

Developmental Psychology, the Society for Personality and Social Psychology, the Society for the Psychological Study of Social Issues, the Division of the History of Psychology, and the Society for the Psychology of Women; Psi Chi, the National Honor Society in Psychology; and APA groups including the Committee on Women in Psychology, the Board of Social and Ethical Responsibility, and the Board of Ethnic Minority Affairs.

The Foreword by the distinguished Janet Taylor Spence, past president of both the American Psychological Association and the American Psychological Society (her autobiography appears in Volume 2), is deeply appreciated. Thanks go to Georgia Babladelis, Elizabeth Scarborough, and the late Virginia Staudt Sexton, whose encouragement made the early work on eminent women possible, to Nancy Felipe Russo for her contributions to the earlier volumes, and to colleagues, students, and the many reviewers who encouraged the publication of Volume 3. Thanks also go to Larry Erlbaum and his staff, especially Sara Scudder.

A special acknowledgment goes to the illustrious contributors who expanded and revised their autobiographies with patience and cooperation. The assistance of Beatrice Truica in preparing the index and Michelle Thorpe and Catherine Philley in preparing the demographic tables is gratefully acknowledged. Library and empirical research, content analyses, preparation and writing of integrative chapters of this book were made possible by the Faculty Scholarship Incentive Program of Montclair State University.

—Agnes N. O'Connell
Montclair State University

REFERENCES

Bernstein, M. D., & Russo, N. F. (1974). The history of psychology revisited: Or, up with our foremothers. *American Psychologist, 29*, 130–134.

O'Connell, A. N., Alpert, J., Richardson, M. S., Rotter, N., Ruble, D. N., & Unger, R. K. (1978). Gender-specific barriers to research in psychology: Report of the Task Force on Women Doing Research—APA Division 35, *Journal Supplement Abstract Service: Catalog of Selected Documents in Psychology* (MS No. 1753) 8.

O'Connell, A. N., & Russo, N. F. (Eds.). (1980). Eminent women in psychology: Models of achievement [Special issue]. *Psychology of Women Quarterly, 5*(1).

Preface

O'Connell, A. N., & Russo, N. F. (Eds.). (1983). *Models of achievement: Reflections of eminent women in psychology* (Vol. 1). New York: Columbia University Press.

O'Connell, A. N., & Russo, N. F. (Eds.). (1988). *Models of achievement: Reflections of eminent women in psychology* (Vol. 2). Hillsdale, NJ: Lawrence Erlbaum Associates.

O'Connell, A. N., & Russo, N. F. (Eds.). (1990). *Women in psychology: A bio-bibliographic sourcebook.* Westport, CT: Greenwood.

O'Connell, A. N., & Russo, N. F. (Eds.). (1991). Women's heritage in psychology: Origins, Development, and future directions [Special APA Centennial issue]. *Psychology of Women Quarterly, 15*(4).

PART I

GENERAL INTRODUCTION

CHAPTER 1

Agnes N. O'Connell

Partners in Progress: Illuminating a New Vision of Women in Psychology

Agnes N. O'Connell

The purpose of *Models of Achievement: Reflections of Eminent Women in Psychology* is to present a new way of thinking about, and looking at, women—as partners in the evolution and progress of the field. This new conceptualization and vision can be brought into sharp focus by preserving and illuminating the often unacknowledged and undervalued accomplishments of women in the field. The major growth of psychology in America occurred in the 20th century, but from the very beginning of the field in the 19th century, women have been partners in its progress. A full picture of the generation of knowledge in the field requires the realization that the fundamental contributions of women psychologists are interwoven with the evolution of psychology. In the early years of the discipline, women often were silent partners, lacking recognition for their noteworthy contributions. As the years passed, women's diverse and excellent contributions became more and more difficult to ignore. Recognition increased—first as subordinate or junior partners then more and more as equal partners. At the beginning of the 21st century, although women have made substantial and significant contributions, recognition as full partners in the complex evolution and progression of the field has yet to be acknowledged.

The autobiographies and analyses contained in these volumes provide an important knowledge base for the study of the historical evolution of psychology and the study of women's lives in the 20th century. They respond to the historical neglect of women's lives and contributions and give these remarkable women the opportunity to define and interpret their experiences in their own words. From these autobiographies and accomplishments, a new concept and vision of women in psychology materializes. Simultaneously, illuminating a new vision of women in psychology sheds light on vital role models of achievement.

Although the number of women psychologists in the field is increasing, there are still too few in senior positions. Tenured full professors in graduate and undergraduate departments continue to be predominantly men (76%), whereas untenured lecturers continue to be women (81%) (APA Research Office, 1999a, 1999c). According to the Task Force on the Changing Gender Composition of Psychology (Pion, et al., 1996), a shift in the gender composition of the field will occur in this third millennium. When that shift occurs, it is likely that tenure and seniority for many more women will not be far behind. Until that transition, strong role models of achievement and knowledge of eminent women's lives and careers can help alleviate the isolation of women professionals who may feel that they are competing alone against insurmountable odds (O'Connell et al., 1978). According to Elizabeth Douvan (1974), for a young woman to see her own aspirations realized in other women's lives can be a crucial support at times of stress when she might otherwise decide that her aspirations are too difficult to attain. Wisdom and inspiration are contained in the lives and careers of these eminent women and in the varied combinations of perseverance, determination, resourcefulness, dedication, humility, humor, and achievement apparent in their autobiographies.

In *Models of Achievement, Volume 3*, the new way of thinking and envisioning women is shaped by women old enough to have achieved eminence but generally younger than the women whose autobiographies are contained in the earlier two volumes. In comparison to the earlier volumes (O'Connell & Russo, 1983, 1988), 18 of the 19 women in this volume were born between 1932 and 1950 and earned their doctorates between 1959 and 1979; 12 of the 17 women in the second volume were born between 1915 and 1936 and earned their doctorates between 1942 and 1967; 13 of the 17 women in the first volume were born between 1897 and 1913 and earned their doctorates between 1917 and 1939.

Distinctive criteria for choosing the women in this volume include outstanding and unusual contributions to various areas of psychology and society in the 20th century and the strong potential for continuing to make such contributions in the 21st. Other defining criteria include a sustained record of achievement over a significant period of time, achievement that has withstood the clarifying filter of time; being a pioneer, an innovator, a leader, or an expert. These are women of great creative achievement whose lives do not follow the beaten path. They are women whose indomitable spirit makes the pursuit of challenge and achievement possible in the face of discrimination, humiliation, trivialization, and other barriers.

Their families of origin range from wealthy and professional to poor and disadvantaged. The women have experienced sexism, racism, poverty, exclusion, and issues of acculturation in their educational and professional pursuits and in their daily lives. These barriers were overcome with courage, resilience, and grace. Obstacles did not keep them from making extraordinary contributions in academe, industry, and government. Their work in theory, research, or practice and in traditional, emerging, or innovative areas reaches the highest standards of excellence. These women are scholars, researchers, clinicians, leaders, educators, activists, policymakers, and so much more. Their personal lives embody a cross-section of lifestyles in the 20th and early 21st centuries; they are single, married and childless, married with children, single parents, and grandmothers.

They are multidimensional in purposes and goals and certainly in charge of their lives. Each is unique in her definition of fulfillment and the specific configuration of her choices, but each possesses the remarkable strength, talent, resiliency, and flexibility to influence as well as be influenced by her surroundings.

Historical and cultural events shaped the availability and content of opportunities for these women. The affluence that followed World War I was followed by deprivation during the Great Depression. World War II brought educational and employment opportunities for women, but its aftermath brought professional retrenchment. It was not until the civil rights and women's movements of the 1960s and 1970s that new breakthroughs were made, and women in psychology were instrumental in forging them. In the last quarter of the 20th century, women made major strides in education. In 1976, women earned 32.8% of PhD doctorates in psychology; that percentage reached 66.6% by 1997 (APA Research Office, 1999b; Keita, Houston, Wisnieski, & Cameron, 1999). The impact of these strides and the gains of the 1960s and the 1970s are particularly evident in the autobiographies presented in this volume. With the growth of the field, women enjoyed improved occupational participation, yet decades after the resurgence of the women's movement, equality of access and opportunity is yet to be realized (Pion et al., 1996).

Since its formation in 1892, nine women have achieved the distinction of serving as APA president, two since the mid 1990s: Dorothy

Cantor (1996) and Norine G. Johnson (2001). Their autobiographies are contained in this volume. In the 1970s and 1980s, five women achieved this distinction: Anne Anastasi (1972), Leona E. Tyler (1973), Florence L. Denmark (1980), Janet Taylor Spence (1984), and Bonnie R. Strickland (1987). Their autobiographies are contained in Volume 2 of *Models of Achievement* (O'Connell & Russo, 1988); Spence also wrote the Foreword for the present volume. The two women who served as APA president in the early 20th century were Mary Whiton Calkins (1905) and Margaret Floy Washburn (1921). Their biographies are contained in *Eminent Women in Psychology* (O'Connell & Russo, 1980) and more extensively in *Women in Psychology: A Bio-Bibliographic Sourcebook* (O'Connell & Russo, 1990).

In contrast to the few women presidents in APA's long history, 6 of the first 11 presidents of the American Psychological Society (APS), established in 1988, were women: Janet Spence (1988–1989), Marilynn Brewer (1993–1995), Sandra Scarr (1996–1997), Kay Deaux (1997–1998), Elizabeth Loftus (1998–1999), and Elizabeth Capaldi (1999–2000) (American Psychological Society, 1999). The autobiographies of Scarr and Deaux are contained in this volume. Spence has the unique distinction of serving both the APA and the APS as president. In academe, few women have served as university presidents; the autobiographies of two of them, Judith E. N. Albino and Frances Degen Horowitz, are in this volume.

The women whose autobiographies are in this volume have made multiple contributions in too many areas of psychology to identify here, but some highlights illustrate the richness of the contents of the material that follows. These eminent women have been instrumental in developing new areas in psychology, illuminating controversial areas, and advancing existing areas. Patricia Bricklin was a pioneer in media psychology; Frances Culbertson in international psychology; Linda Bartoshuk in the study of psychophysics of the sense of taste; Lillian Comas-Díaz, Pamela Trotman Reid, and Diane Willis in the study of minority populations; Albino in health psychology; Elaine Hatfield in the study of love, equity theory, and emotional contagion. Patricia Keith-Spiegel was instrumental in developing a code of ethics for psychologists. The research of Diane Halpern, Janet Hyde, and Scarr shed light on the nature/nurture debate. Bricklin, Cantor, Comas-Díaz, Culbertson, Johnson, Keith-Spiegel, and Willis have advanced clinical, counseling, and school psychology; Halpern and Margaret Matlin, cognitive psychology; Jeanne Brooks-Gunn, Cantor, Culbertson, Horowitz, Johnson, Phyllis Katz, Reid, Scarr, and Willis, developmental psychology; Albino, Bartoshuk, Deaux, Hyde, Matlin, and Willis, experimental psychology; Albino, Brooks-Gunn, Cantor, Comas-Díaz, Deaux, Hyde, Johnson, Katz, Keith-Spiegel, Matlin, and

Reid, the psychology of women and gender issues; Hyde, psychometrics; Bartoshuk and Matlin, sensation and perception; Deaux, Hatfield, and Katz, social psychology; and Albino, Bricklin, Cantor, Horowitz, Johnson, Keith-Spiegel, and Willis, techniques of assessment, evaluation, and training.

It is clear that a new way of thinking about and perceiving women encourages equality of access, opportunity, and recognition. The concept and perception of women as partners in progress, as exemplars, as fully functioning, competent, capable contributors to psychology and to society illustrated in these volumes are crucial for a future marked by equality, excellence, and progress.

These autobiographies provide an incentive for achieving these goals now and in the future. To clarify the context and contents of these autobiographies, this book employs three levels of analysis: the universal for all women; the group for women in psychology (and by extension for other professional women); and the individual for a particular person. The universal level is presented in an overview chapter on the historical and social context of the 20th century, the context for women, and the context for women and the field of psychology. The group level is presented in a chapter examining similarities and differences in the lives and careers of the 19 eminent women; further comparisons are made between the women in this volume and the 34 eminent women in the two earlier volumes to delineate transhistoric and time-specific trends and patterns. The distinguished women themselves present the individual level in their autobiographies.

The autobiographies in these volumes provide a history of the development of psychology through the lens of women who contributed to its progress in the 20th century as well as a history of the development of their lives and careers.

The autobiographies and analyses are a source of knowledge, wisdom, and inspiration for men and women and for the field of psychology. It is hoped that these volumes will be the catalyst for a revolution of concept and vision, a new way of thinking about and looking at women in psychology and in society, and a new conceptualization, perception, and recognition of women as partners in progress across time.

REFERENCES

American Psychological Society. (1999). *Board of Directors 1999–2000.* [Online]. Available: http//www.psychological science.org/about_board.htlm.

APA Research Office. (1999a). *Data on education and employment—Doctorate (gender and rank)* [Online]. Available: http://research.apa.org/doc14.html.

APA Research Office. (1999b). *Data on education and employment—Doctorate (tenure and gender)* [Online]. Available: http://research.apa.org/doc15.html.

APA Research Office. (1999c). *Demographic shifts in psychology* [Online]. Available: http://research.apa.org/gen1.html.

Douvan, E. (1974). The role of models in women's professional development. *Psychology of Women Quarterly, 1*, 5–20.

Keita, G. P., Houston, S., Wisnieski, & Cameron, L. (1999). *Women in the American Psychological Association.* Washington, DC: American Psychological Association.

O'Connell, A. N., Alpert, J., Richardson, M. S., Rotter, N., Ruble, D. N., & Unger, R. K. (1978). Gender-specific barriers to research in psychology: Report of the Task Force on Women Doing Research—APA Division 35. *Journal Supplement Abstract Service: Catalog of Selected Documents in Psychology* (MS No. 1753) 8.

O'Connell, A. N., & Russo, N. F. (Eds.). (1980). Eminent women in psychology: Models of achievement [Special issue]. *Psychology of Women Quarterly, 5*(1).

O'Connell, A. N., & Russo, N. F. (Eds.). (1983). *Models of achievement: Reflections of eminent women in psychology.* New York: Columbia University Press.

O'Connell, A. N., & Russo, N. F. (Eds.). (1988). *Models of achievement: Reflections of eminent women in psychology* (Vol. 2). Hillsdale, NJ: Lawrence Erlbaum Associates.

O'Connell, A. N., & Russo, N. F. (Eds.). (1990). *Women in psychology: A bio-bibliographic sourcebook.* Westport, CT: Greenwood.

Pion, G. M., Mednick, M. T., Astin, H., S., Hall, C. I., Kenkel, M. B., Keita, G. P., Kohout, J. L., & Kelleher, J. C. (1996). The shifting gender composition of psychology. *American Psychologist, 51*, 509–528.

PART II

HISTORICAL AND SOCIAL CONTEXTS

CHAPTER 2

Agnes N. O'Connell

A Century of Contrasts: Historical and Social Contexts of the 20th Century

Agnes N. O'Connell

THE 20TH CENTURY: A PANORAMIC VIEW

A new century and a new millennium call for looking forward to the possibilities of the future and for building on the richness of the past. The 20th century provided the historical and social context for a substantial part of the lives and careers of the 19 eminent women in this volume. Historical analyses of the 20th century reveal that it has been one of extraordinary change and progress, filled with conflict and contrasts for the general population, women, and the field of psychology.

The 20th century has seen major technological and information revolutions that have brought the country and the world closer together. Global distances have shrunk and the people of the world are readily reachable face-to-face or via the media and the Internet. Space ships have orbited the earth and astronauts have walked on the moon.

A century of valiant movements that fought for peace, justice, and equality, the 20th century at the same time has been one of the most devastating in terms of lives lost through world and regional wars, genocide, and hunger. It has also been one of the most innovative in science and technology. Nuclear medicine has made huge advances in health care while nuclear weapons have caused massive destruction.

The first 50 years witnessed two world wars, the rise of fascism and communism, the holocaust, a major depression, the start of the Cold War, the suffragette movement, and significant economic reforms. The next 50 years saw the demise of communism in the Soviet Union, the fall of the Berlin Wall in Germany, the Korean War, the Vietnam War, endless outbreaks of regional wars, civil rights activism, the resurgence of the women's movement, extended life expectancy, and a global economy.

WOMEN IN THE 20TH CENTURY: LANDSCAPES AND PORTRAITS

At the turn of the 20th century, women were engaged in scientific advances and in the suffragette movement for equality and justice. Marie Curie, the brilliant scientist, received the Nobel Prize in Physics. Elizabeth Cady Stanton and Susan B. Anthony, leaders of the suffragette movement, continued to champion women's rights while Alice Paul organized the National Woman's Party to conduct a more militant strategy. On August 26, 1920, 72 years after the first Women's Rights Convention at Seneca Falls, New York, the 19th amendment was ratified and 26 million women of voting age gained the right to vote (First National Women's Conference, 1978).

Some 10 years later, during the Great Depression, legislation restricted employment of married women; there was strong public disapproval of married women working when men were unable to find employment (First National Women's Conference, 1978). Universities adopted anti-nepotism rules that in application, often kept wives in professional couples from employment in the same institutions as their husbands. Although the percentage of working women was relatively static between 1900 and 1940, the percentage changed dramatically during World War II. Wartime needs required women's employment. "Rosie the Riveter" became a national symbol (First National Women's Conference, 1978). Most of the women whose autobiographies are in this volume were born in the 1930s and 1940s. Between 1940 and 1960, the number of working women and the proportion of working wives increased significantly (Rotella, 1998).

In 1953, Simone deBeauvoir's extraordinary book, *The Second Sex*, a scholarly and historical analysis of the inferior status of women, was published in the United States. The inferior status of Black women had led to the founding in 1935 of the National Council of Negro Women in New York with Mary McLeod Bethune as its first president. Two decades later, Rosa Parks, a Black seamstress, refused to give up her bus seat to a White man and was arrested, touching off the 1956 Montgomery, Alabama bus boycott (First National Women's Conference, 1978). The research of psychologists Mamie Clark (1917–1983) and her husband Kenneth on self-concept and identity in Black children was cited in the 1964 Supreme Court decision in *Brown v. the Board of Education* to desegregate schools. In 1996, 40 years after the bus boycott, Rosa Parks was awarded the Presidential Medal of Freedom (Blankenship, Bezdek, & Ruth, 1998).

As the wife of a sitting president in the midst of the Great Depression and World War II (1933–1945), Eleanor Roosevelt turned her 12 years in the White House into a model of activism and humanitarianism. In 1961, she chaired President Kennedy's Commission on the Status of Women (First National Women's Conference, 1978). Legislation that responded to the needs for equality and justice followed in the 1960s and 1970s, the decades of the doctorate for most of the eminent women in this volume. In 1963 and 1972, the Equal Pay Act made wage discrimination based on sex illegal—equal pay for equal work. In 1964 and 1970, Title VII of the Civil Rights Act made it illegal to discriminate on the basis of race, sex, religion, or national origin in hiring, assignment, compensation, promotion, and termination of employees; it also authorized affirmative action. In 1972, Title IX of the Amendment to the Education Act prohibited sex discrimination (against students and employees) in any educational program or activity receiving federal financial assistance (APA Report of the Task Force on the Changing Composition of Psychology, 1995). In 1997, more than 100,000 women participated in intercollegiate athletics—a fourfold increase since 1981. In 1995, women comprised 37% of college student athletes, compared to 15% in 1972 (Riley & Cantu, 1997).

The frustration and disappointments of women in the 1950s were captured and analyzed in Betty Friedan's best-selling book, *The Feminine Mystique* (1963), that described the social pressures that limited women's roles to wives and mothers. This book served as a catalyst, setting in motion the resurgence of the Women's Movement in the late 1960s and the 1970s.

Further legislative instruments of social change followed. In 1978, The Women's Educational Equity Act provided education equity for women in the United States and the Pregnancy Discrimination Act required employers to treat disabilities arising from pregnancy and birth the way they would treat any other disability (APA Report of the Task Force, 1995). According to Gose (1997), women constitute 56% of students in U.S. colleges and universities. Employed mothers have become the norm with 62% of mothers of preschoolers and 77% of mothers with children between 6 and 17 years (Matlin, 2000) in the workforce. Women who work full time earn 74% of the median annual salary of men (World Almanac, 1999). The wage gap persists even when such factors as occupation, education, and experience are taken into account (Matlin, 2000).

Women's larger percentage of the population was not evident in the country's highest offices nor in their representation in U.S. state and national legislatures. In 1984, Geraldine A. Ferraro was chosen to run for vice president of the United States. She was the first woman to run for that office on a major party ticket (Blankenship, Bezdek, & Ruth, 1998). The Democratic candidate for president lost, however, and she did not serve as vice president. In 1999, women in state legislatures held one in four seats, more than at any time in history. On the national level they comprised 12% of Congress, up 2% from 1992 (Ford Foundation Report, 2000). In contrast women hold 39% of national legislative seats in the Nordic countries (Sweden, Norway, Finland, Denmark, and Iceland; Ford Foundation Report, 2000). Sandra Day O'Connor became the first woman and the 102nd U.S. Supreme Court Justice in 1981; Ruth Bader Ginsburg, the second in 1993 (Read & Witlieb, 1992). Madeleine Albright, a naturalized citizen, was the first woman to serve as U.S. Secretary of State in 1997 (Blankenship, Bezdek, & Ruth, 1998). It is clear that much remains to be done.

THE 20TH CENTURY, WOMEN, AND PSYCHOLOGY: MULTIPLE SNAPSHOTS

The century in the field of psychology and the APA, now one of the world's largest professional associations, fostered steady growth in the early years then rapid expansion between 1915 and 1945 when the number of psychologists in APA grew from approximately 300 to 4,173 (Capshew, 1999). An even more rapid expansion followed in the 55 years after the end of World War II. At the turn of the 21st century, 83,096 fellows, members, and associates were registered in APA (APA Membership Register, 2000).

During the early years, psychologists Helen Thompson Woolley (1874–1947) and Leta Stetter Hollingworth (1886–1939) used their scientific skills to refute myths about women's abilities and nature. Karen Horney (1885–1952) and Clara Thompson (1893–1958) challenged classical psychoanalysis and stressed the importance of interpersonal and cultural processes. Horney developed her own theory and founded the Association for the Advancement of Psychoanalysis. Charlotte Buhler (1893–1974) developed humanistic psychology, preceding Abraham Maslow who is widely considered the movement's founder. Edna Heiderbreder's (1890–1985) classic book, *Seven Psychologies* (1933), provided a detailed exposition and analysis of the deep structure of seven systems of psychology (O'Connell & Russo, 1990).

Two women, Mary Calkins (1905) and Margaret Washburn (1921), served as APA presidents during those early years when the membership was 162 and approximately 400, respectively (O'Connell & Russo, 1990). During the 1920s and 1930s, increasing numbers of women were making careers in psychology, and by the 1930s, approximately one third of the APA membership were women (Walsh, 1985). One fifth of the psychologists listed in the 1938 edition of *American Men of Science* were *women*. Early in World War II (1941), the National Council of Women Psychologists was formed to further the war effort and promote opportunities for women psychologists. The expectation that women psychologists would replace men in colleges and clinics was not fully realized because of "sex prejudice" (Walsh, 1985). By 1959, the organization had become the International Council of Psychologists, a leading, international organization open to men as well as women. Frances M. Culbertson served as president of this organization, 1979–1980. Her autobiography is in this volume.

Little or no recognition was given to women psychologists in the 1950s and 1960s with two notable exceptions: In 1966 Nancy Bayley received the APA Distinguished Scientific Contributions Award for her important work in developmental psychology and in 1968 Eleanor Gibson received the same award for her contributions to perceptual learning (Russo, O'Connell, & Deacon, 1990). Yet, such recognition remained rare. Most of the women in this volume earned their doctorates in the 1960s and 1970s.

Approximately 35 women and men who objected to the sexism within APA and the field of psychology founded the Association for Women Psychologists in 1969 (name changed to the Association for Women in Psychology in 1970). According to the by-laws, among the purposes of the new organization were "to insure equality of opportunity for women and men within the profession of psychology" and "to establish facts and explode myths" about sex differences (Tiefer, 1991, p. 638). In 1970, an APA Task Force was charged with studying the status of women. It later became the Committee on Women in Psychology "to ensure that women achieve equality as members of the psychological community" (Keita, Houston, Wisnieski, & Cameron, 1999) and made the recommendation that an APA Division on the Psychology of Women (Division 35) be established.

In 1973, the APA Division on the Psychology of Women (name changed to the Society for the Psychology of Women in 1999) was established in response "to pressures relating to the status of women in psychology" and "to promote the research and study of women" (Mednick & Urbanski, 1991, p. 651). Of the 52 divisions of APA, this is the fifth largest with 3,378 members in 1998 (Keita et al., 1999). Those who served as president of the division include Pamela Trotman Reid

(1991–1992), Janet Shibley Hyde (1993–1994), Norine G. Johnson (1994–1995), and Phyllis Katz (1999–2000); their autobiographies are in this volume. The first president was Elizabeth Douvan (1973–1974). Early in the 1970s, courses on the psychology of women became an important part of the academic curriculum and still are. Researchers began to question the generalizability of earlier research that excluded women; research on women flourished in the last decades of the 20th century.

In 1998, women comprised 47.7% of APA membership, 41.6% of the Board of Directors and 35.5% of the Council of Representatives; the same percentages in 1988 were 37.1%, 33.3%, and 27.8%, respectively (Keita et al., 1999). Women's participation in APA governance fluctuated; in 1975 there were no women on the Board of Directors and just one in 1979. Among the women who have served on the Board of Directors after 1966 (Keita et al., 1999) are Anne Anastasi (1969–1973), Leona Tyler (1966–1968, 1972–1974), Dorothy Eichorn (1970–1972), Janet T. Spence (1976–1978, 1983–1985), Florence Denmark (1977–1978, 1979–1981), Patricia Bricklin (1987–1989), Sandra Scarr (1988–1989), Judith Albino (1990–1994), Dorothy Cantor (1991–1993, 1995–1997), and Norine Johnson (1997–1999, 2000–2002). The autobiographies of Bricklin, Scarr, Albino, Cantor, and Johnson are in the present volume. Serving as editor of APA journals was long the prerogative of men. In 1979, 4.2% of the editors of these prestigious professional journals were women; in 1996 the percentage was 15.2%. Sandra Scarr was editor of the APA journal *Developmental Psychology* in 1981. Increasing the participation of women continues to be a priority of the Committee on Women in Psychology in the 21st century (Keita et al., 1999).

Fellow status in APA honors psychologists who have made "outstanding and unusual contributions to the field." In 1998, 23% of all fellows were women, i.e., 2.6% of all women in APA were fellows, whereas 7.8% of men were, not significantly different from 1988 when 17.7% of all fellows were women, 2.8% of all women and 7.8% of all men were fellows (Keita et al., 1999). Thus, at the end of the 20th century, the extraordinary contributions of women to the field of psychology were still inadequately recognized and undervalued by their primary professional organization.

By the turn of the 21st century, APA had established 52 functioning divisions of specialties in science and practice. The divisions with the highest representations of women were: Psychology of Women (97.3%), Developmental Psychology (57.2%), Psychoanalysis (56.6%), Society for the Psychological Study of Ethnic Minority Issues (55.8%), Society of Pediatric Psychology (54.5%), Clinical Psychology (53.9%), and Media Psychology (51.4%). Divisions that focus on psychotherapeutic practice (Divisions of Clinical Psychology, Counseling Psychology, Psychotherapy, Psychoanalysis, and Psychologists in Independent Practice) are among the largest with approximately 3,000 or more members and divisions of other health provider subfields, not far behind (APA Membership Register, 2000). Myriad outstanding women, too numerous to name them all here, who have provided leadership and innovation in clinical and counseling psychology include Martha Bernal, Patricia Bricklin, Dorothy Cantor, Lillian Comas-Díaz, Frances Culbertson, Erika Fromm, Norine Johnson, Mildred Mitchell, Carolyn Payton, Bonnie Strickland, Leona Tyler, and Diane Willis. The autobiographies of Bricklin, Cantor, Comas-Díaz, Culbertson, Johnson, and Willis are in this volume.

In 1988, research-oriented members of APA disenchanted with the health provider aspects of the organization established the American Psychological Society (APS), "To promote, protect, and advance the interests of scientifically oriented psychology in research, application, and the improvement of human welfare" (American Psychological Society, 1998). Among the many founding women members were Dorothy Eichorn, Sandra Scarr, and Bonnie Strickland. Sandra Scarr (1996–1997) and Kay Deaux (1997–1998) served as president of this new organization; their autobiographies are in this volume.

Of all new PhD recipients in psychology, 57% earned degrees in the health service subfields: clinical, counseling, and school; 43% earned new PhDs in a variety of research fields (APA Research Office, 1999c). In 1976, 32.8% of PhD recipients in psychology were women; in 1984 for the first time, 50.1% were women. In 1997, 66.6% of PhD recipients in psychology were women with the largest percentages in the subfields of Developmental (79.1%), School (78.6%), Educational (73.3%), Clinical (71.1%), Counseling (64.7%), Social (64.2%), Psychometrics (63.6%), and General Psychology (63.3%; Keita et al., 1999). Of the doctoral recipients in 1997, men were more likely to be employed full time (78%) than women (65%; Kohout & Wicherski, 1999). Between 1973 and 1997, the proportion of psychologists in academic settings declined and the proportion in business/industry increased (APA Research Office, 1999a). Nonetheless, despite the fact that approximately two thirds of new doctoral recipients in psychology were women, at the end of the 20th century, only 35% of full-time faculty at U.S. colleges and universities were women (Matlin, 2000) and men were more likely to be tenured and in the highest ranks (APA Research Office, 1999b, 2000; National Science Foundation, 1998). Minority faculty were also less likely to be tenured or at the rank of full professor (National Science Foundation, 1998). In 1993, racial and ethnic minority men and women represented approximately 9% of all full-time faculty (Murray & Williams, 1999). Analyses of full-time employed psychology PhDs in academic settings indicated that 50% of the men were at the rank of full professor, whereas 25% of the women were; women's median salaries were 86% that of men's (APA Task Force on the Changing Composition of Psychology, 1995). These disadvantaged statuses in the academy and in salary differentials have a long history and, at the end of the 20th century, were not resolved.

The subfields that are most often chosen by current PhD recipients range from those that began the century to those that have evolved during the century. Human development has been a focus of psychologists since the beginning with many women making notable contributions. Nancy Bayley (1899–1994), one of the first to introduce life-span development as a frame of reference for research, developed the internationally used Bayley Scales of Mental and Motor Development, widely recognized as one of the best standardized measures of infant development. Barbel Inhelder (1913–), Jean Piaget's chief collaborator for 48 years, produced 12 volumes on cognitive development, 7 with Piaget. Inhelder pioneered the application of genetic epistemology to the study of mental deficiency, cross-cultural research, and the field of learning. Her work was essential in the "cognitive revolution," especially in developmental psychology. Eleanor Gibson (1910–), best known for her studies with the visual cliff, demonstrated the primacy of depth perception. Through extending the concepts of ecological psychology to the study of perceptual development in infancy, she established an entire field. Bernice Neugarten (1916–) founded, and made ground-breaking contributions to, the academic field of adult development and aging. Eleanor Maccoby's (1917–) highly productive career in developmental psychology spans some 60 years. Her research and methodological contributions illuminated the socialization of young children and the critical dimensions of their social behavior. Her reviews of gender differences have significantly influenced the direction and content of future research. Other early contributors include Mary Ainsworth, Jacqueline Goodnow, Frances Graham, Myrtle McGraw, Lois Murphy, Lillian Troll, and many others. Later in the century, Jeanne Brooks-Gunn, Diane Halpern, Frances Horowitz, Margaret Matlin, Pamela Trotman Reid, Sandra Scarr, and Diane Willis are among the women who have made noteworthy contributions to cognitive development, developmental psychology, and related fields; their autobiographies are in this volume.

Experimental, social, and industrial/organizational psychology have early roots in psychology with many notable women who have advanced this work including Judith Albino, Linda Bartoshuk, Kay Deaux, Denmark, Gibson, Elaine Hatfield, Hollingworth, Lillian Gilbreth, Marie Jahoda, Phyllis Katz, Christine Ladd-Franklin, Martha Mednick, Patricia Cain Smith, Carolyn Sherif, Spence, Strickland,

and Woolley. The autobiographies of Albino, Bartoshuk, Deaux, Hatfield, and Katz are in this volume.

The work in personality, the self, motivation, ethics, and testing began early in the century and has been advanced by the substantial contributions of multitudes of women. Anne Anastasi (1908–), the most prominent living woman in psychology, recipient of the U.S. Presidential National Medal of Science, and author of numerous classic works (Sexton & Hogan, 1990) heads the long list of notable women that includes Bayley, Charlotte Buhler, Calkins, Else Frenkel-Brunswik, Anna Freud, Florence Goodenough, Ravenna Helson, Heidbreder, Horney, Janet Hyde, Patricia Keith-Spiegel, Jane Loevinger, Spence, Strickland, Thelma Thurstone, and Tyler among others. The autobiographies of Hyde and Keith-Spiegel are in this volume.

Later in the century, the subfield that focuses on the study of the growing field of cultural diversity and is represented by APA Division 45, the Society for the Psychological Study of Ethnic Minority Issues, emerged. In 1995, Blacks, Hispanics, and American Indians were 23%, Asians 3%, of the U.S. population according to the National Science Foundation (1998). Women constituted 51% of the population and 22% of the total science and engineering labor force. In 1997, people of color earned 13.9% of new doctorates in psychology, a significant increase over the comparable percentage of 7.5% in 1977 (APA Research Office, 1999b). Pioneering women of color who have made substantial contributions to the field of psychology include Martha Bernal, the first Mexican-American woman to receive the doctorate in psychology in 1962 and innovator in the study of cross-cultural development; the aforementioned Mamie Clark; Lillian Comas-Díaz, an innovator and leader in the study of people of color, cultural, cross-cultural, and international issues; Ruth Howard (Beckham), the first Black woman to receive a doctorate in psychology in 1934 and a pioneer in the study of triplets and adolescents; Carolyn Payton, the first woman and first Black to serve as Director of the U.S. Peace Corps and leader in minority issues; Pamela Trotman Reid, a leader in the study of the intersections of gender, race, ethnicity, and class and in the study of African American women and children; Diane Willis, a major contributor to clinical and pediatric child psychology and to the study of American Indian children. The autobiographies of Comas-Díaz, Reid, and Willis are in this volume.

The major impact of women psychologists on the evolution, development, and transformation of the discipline of psychology and its organizations, and how their contributions have shaped intellectual history and contributed to societal policies, are all part of women's integral heritage in the field and in society (O'Connell & Russo, 1980,

1983, 1988, 1990, 1991; Stevens & Gardner, 1982). This reality was not fully nor widely acknowledged by the end of the 20th century.

In examining the past century, it is clear that in society and in the field of psychology, women made progress. This progress needs to be protected and advanced in the 21st century.

In many ways, the field of psychology was a microcosm, reflecting and being reflected by the larger society during the 20th century. Women in both venues fought an uphill, difficult battle for equality of access, opportunity, and renown. Substantial hard fought gains were made by, and for, women in psychology as well for women in U.S. society. The 20th century was marked by advances and retrenchments, progression, regression, and evolution of the field and of society, moving toward global perspectives and considerations. Building on the richness of the 20th century, we are armed to move forward in the 21st century to better understandings of ourselves and others, generating superior theories and applications, becoming better healers and advocates of primary prevention and psychological health, working more effectively for peace, justice, equality, and full acceptance of the diversity and creativity amongst us in this challenging scientific and technological world that we inhabit.

REFERENCES

American Psychological Association. (1995, October). *Report of the Task Force on the Changing Composition of Psychology*. Washington, DC: Author.

APA Membership Register. (2000). Washington, DC: American Psychological Association, vii-viii.

APA Research Office. (1999a). *Changes in employment: PhD psychologists: 1973, 1983, 1993, 1997* [Online]. Available: http://research.apa.org/doc11.html.

APA Research Office. (1999b). *Data on education and employment: General* [Online]. Available: http://research.apa.org/gen1.html.

APA Research Office. (1999c). *New PhDs in psychology by subfield: 1997* [Online]. Available: http://research.apa.org/doc16.html.

APA Research Office. (2000). *Data on education and employment: Doctoral.* Available: http://research.apa.org/doctoral.html.

American Psychological Society Membership Directory. (1999). Washington, DC: American Psychological Society.

Blankenship, K., Bezdek, A., & Ruth, S. (1998). Update: The process continues. In S. Ruth (Ed.), *Issues in feminism* (pp. 505–509). Mountain View, CA: Mayfield.

Capshew, J. H. (1999). *Psychologists on the march: Science, practice, and professional identity in America, 1929–1969.* New York: Cambridge University Press.

De Beauvoir, S. (1953). *The second sex.* New York: Knopf.

The First National Women's Conference. (1978, March). *An official report to the President, the Congress and the people of the United States.* Washington, DC: National Commission on the Observance of International Women's Year, U. S. Department of States, 1978.

Ford Foundation Report. (2000, Winter). *A special issue on women: Now it's a global movement.* New York: Ford Foundation.

Friedan, B. (1963). *The feminine mystique.* New York: Norton.

Gose, B. (1997, May 23). Minority enrollments rose in 1995, a study finds. *Chronicle of Higher Education,* p. A38.

Heidbreder, E. (1933). *Seven psychologies.* New York: Century.

Keita, G. P., Houston, S., Wisnieski, & Cameron, L. (1999). *Women in the American Psychological Association.* Washington, DC: American Psychological Association.

Kohout, J., & Wicherski, M. (1999). 1997 *Doctorate employment survey.* Available: http:research.apa.org/des97contents.html.

Matlin, M. W. (2000). *The psychology of women* (4th ed.). New York: Harcourt.

Mednick, M. T. & Urbanski, L. L. (1991). The origins and activities of APA's Division of the Psychology of Women. In A. N. O'Connell & N. F. Russo (Eds.), Women's heritage in psychology: Origins, development, and future directions [Special APA Centennial issue]. *Psychology of Women Quarterly,* 15(4), 651–663.

Murray, T. M., & Williams, S. (1999, April). *Analyses of data from graduate study in psychology: 1997–1998.* Washington, DC: APA Research Office. Available: http://research.apa.org/grad98contents.html

National Science Foundation. (1998). *Women, minorities, and persons with disabilities in science and engineering.* Available: http://www.nsf.gov/sbe/srs/nsf99338/hilight.html.

O'Connell, A. N. & Russo, N. F. (1980). Eminent women in psychology: Models of achievement [Special issue]. *Psychology of Women Quarterly,* 5(1).

O'Connell, A. N., & Russo, N. F. (Eds.). (1983). *Models of achievement: Reflections of eminent women in psychology* (Vol. 1). New York: Columbia University Press.

O'Connell, A. N., & Russo, N. F. (Eds.). (1988). *Models of achievement: Reflections of eminent women in psychology* (Vol. 2). Hillsdale, NJ: Lawrence Erlbaum Associates.

O'Connell, A. N. & Russo, N. F. (1990). *Women in psychology: A bio-bibliographic sourcebook.* Westport, CT: Greenwood.

O'Connell, A. N., & Russo, N. F. (Eds.). (1991). Women's heritage in psychology: Origins, development, and future directions [Special centennial issue]. *Psychology of Women Quarterly,* 15(4).

Read, P. J. & Witlieb, B. L. (1992). *The book of women's firsts.* New York: Random House.

Riley, R. W., & Cantu, N. V. (1997, June). *Title IX: 25 Years of progress.* Washington, DC: U.S. Government Printing Office.

Rotella, E. J. (1998). Women and the American economy. In S. Ruth (Ed.), *Issues in feminism* (pp. 346-389). Mountain View, CA: Mayfield.

Russo, N. F., O'Connell, A. N., & Deacon, M. (1990). Selected award-winning contributions. In A. N. O'Connell & N. F. Russo (Eds.), *Women in psychology: A bio-bibliographic sourcebook* (pp. 361–377). Westport, CT: Greenwood.

Sexton, V. S., & Hogan, J. D. (1990). Anne Anastasi (1908). In A. N. O'Connell & N. F. Russo (Eds.), *Women in psychology: A biobibliographic sourcebook* (pp. 13–22). Westport, CT: Greenwood.

Stevens, G., & Gardner, S. (1982). *The women of psychology* (Vol. II). Cambridge, MA: Schenkman.

Tiefer, L. (1991). A brief history of the Association for Women in Psychology. In A. N. O'Connell & N. F. Russo (Eds.), Women's heritage in psychology: Origins, development, and future directions [Special APA Centennial issue]. *Psychology of Women Quarterly, 15*(4), 635–649.

Walsh, M. R. (1985). Academic professional women organizing for change: The struggle in psychology. *Journal of Social Issues, 41,* 17–27.

World almanac and book of facts, 1999. (1998). Mahwah, NJ: World Almanac Books.

NOTES

1. The autobiographies of Ainsworth, Clark, Howard (Beckham), McGraw, Mitchell, Murphy, and Sherif are in O'Connell and Russo (1983).
2. Biographies of Anastasi, Bayley, Buhler, Calkins, Denmark, Frenkel-Brunswik, Gibson, Gilbreth, Goodenough, Goodnow, Heidbreder, Helson, Hollingworth, Horney, Inhelder, Jahoda, Ladd-Franklin, Maccoby, Sherif, Spence, Strickland, Thurstone, Tyler, and Washburn are in O'Connell and Russo (1990).
3. Autobiographies of Anastasi, Bernal, Denmark, Eichorn, Fromm, Graham, Mednick, Payton, Smith, Spence, Strickland, Troll, and Tyler are in O'Connell and Russo (1988).

PART III

AUTOBIOGRAPHICAL PERSPECTIVES

CHAPTER 3

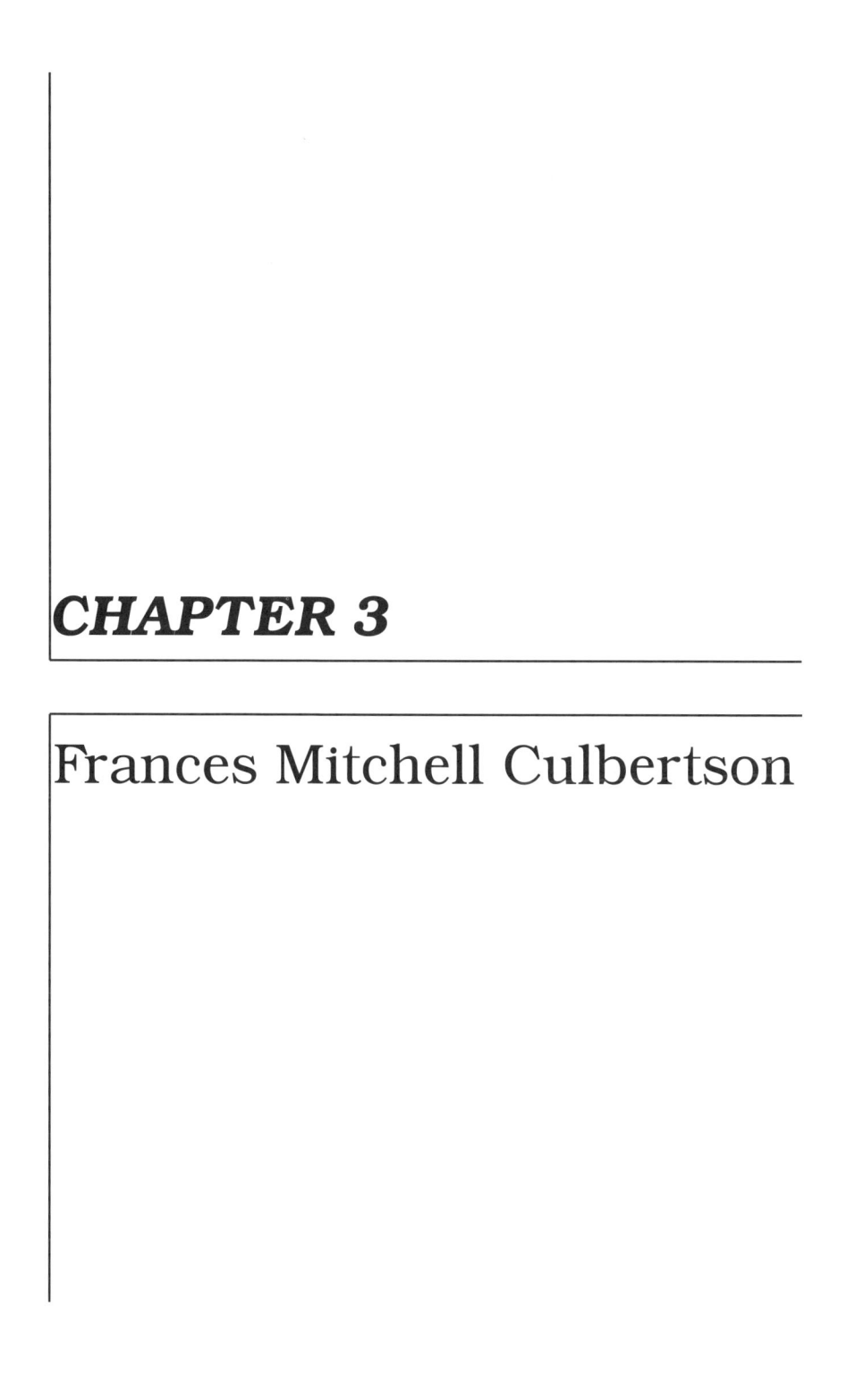

Frances Mitchell Culbertson

Photographer: Leidner Studio.

Frances Mitchell Culbertson

Learn little maiden, till you grow old;

Learning is better than silver or gold;

Silver or gold may vanish away;

But a good education will never decay.

—(Anonymous)

CHILDHOOD AND ADOLESCENT YEARS

I was born January 31, 1921, in the Deaconess Hospital for Women, in Boston, Massachusetts, the youngest of three children. I was fortunate in my birthplace, since Boston was—and is—a city where education and cultural activities are available and valued. Thus, the message in the short poem quoted above, which I learned in kindergarten, reflects the significant influences and themes of my life.

My parents were Russian Jewish immigrants, uneducated, and poor. They met and were married in Paris, a most romantic story. When my father entered this country and was greeted by an immigration official, a discussion ensued and my father's name was changed from David Uchitelle to David Mitchell. I presume the immigration official could not understand my father and chose a name closest to what my father had uttered.

My father was initially employed as a tailor at Hart, Schaffner, and Marx, a prominent men's clothing manufacturer. Dissatisfied with his working conditions, he eventually left to become an independent businessman, as well as a union organizer. My mother, Goldie Fishman, was a daily domestic worker and a housewife.

My parents came to the United States because they believed the "streets were paved with gold," a fantasy that did not prove true for them. Although they worked very hard, they always had a very limited income. My recollections of my early years are filled with memories of deprivation. Life was a major struggle for us, and hunger was not uncommon, but the major necessities of life were provided to us through the good offices of public health institutions, social agencies, and philanthropic organizations. The personnel of these organizations was predominately female, and these women represented outstanding role models of "helping" people. Because of their humanitarian interventions, there were financial and nurturing influences in our lives that helped to ease the worries of daily living.

Some of my earliest and fondest memories are of public health nurses, librarians, and teachers. Because I was undernourished, the threat of tuberculosis became a major concern. In nursery school, I was required to rest for 2 hours a day after lunch while the other children were out on the playground. During these interludes, public health nurses read aloud to me, and this quickly became my favorite activity.

The neighborhood librarian reinforced my love of being read to, and the desire to learn to read. From the time I was 4 years old, as soon as I was allowed to go to the library myself, she befriended me and saved special books for me. Just me! I would go each day, pick up my books, "read them," and hasten back the next day for the new delights she had in store for me.

My older brothers also reinforced my love of reading. As they did their homework assignments, they would sit with me, pretending that I, too, was doing homework. I had a little desk and a chair, in a special place in the "victrola room." I can still recall very clearly the RCA record player with the dog on the inside of the cover. Every day, I would sit there for hours, reading to myself and to the dolls that surrounded me. Playing school was an almost daily activity. My relatives often commented to my mother that I was born to be a teacher, and of course I heard and remembered these observations.

In the fifth grade, I had a teacher, Miss Ryan, who also became a significant role model for me. She was a "Boston Brahmin," which meant that she was very wealthy and belonged to the Boston Junior League. Traditionally, members of this organization have contributed time, money, and effort to people in economically deprived communities.

Miss Ryan donated her teaching time to help my impoverished neighborhood. She was an exceptional teacher. And for a poor, one might even say neglected child, she created a school environment that was a place of joy. Her classroom was an accepting, rewarding, and cozy haven. Despite the fact that there were 50 children in the class, Miss Ryan's influence turned us into a very cohesive group. She would bring flowers from her garden to the classroom and tell us about them. Then, recognizing that our familiarity with flowers was limited to dandelions, she taught us how to make dandelion necklaces. She introduced us to places far outside our small world. We learned about Mexico, Canada, France, England, and many other countries. I was fascinated by these discussions, and I believe that my interest in international psychology had its seeds sown in this classroom.

On Fridays, Miss Ryan would appear resplendent in long, flowing dresses, ready to go to her Junior League teas after class. The children's eyes always widened on these days as we "oohed and aahed" at this beautifully dressed woman. Near the end of the school year, she announced that she was to be married and that we were all invited to her wedding. On the appointed day, her chauffeured car came down our streets, picking up each of the children from her class to attend her wedding. What an event that was for us! I still relish the memory of Miss Ryan's wedding when I recall it. However, what is more significant for me is the wedding itself opened a world to me I never knew existed.

I was a very apt student as well as "teacher's pet" throughout my elementary and high school years. I ended these years as a class officer, on the honor roll, having distinguished myself as a commercial (business) major, and full of sadness about leaving my comforting and rewarding home away from home.

REVIEW OF EARLY YEARS

Looking back over my early years, I am cognizant that the poem's message of learning was nurtured and reinforced by the women who entered my life, such as the public health nurses, the librarian, and my teacher, Miss Ryan. In these early years, I learned three things from the beginning: (a) that learning was an important activity for me; (b) that to excel in learning yielded very positive rewards; and (c) that women were important change agents for me.

EARLY ADULT YEARS

At high school graduation, I was not really ready to leave the protected world of adolescence and school and face the world of work. However, it was essential that I obtain a paying job immediately since my family continued to be poor and needed money for daily expenses. In line with the expectations of the times, I had prepared myself for employment in business. I learned the skills required to be a secretary, a bookkeeper, and a sales person. Although I was perceived by my teachers to be an exceptionally gifted student, none of them ever counseled me to follow any route other than the one for which I had prepared myself. And in my family, there never was any question that upon graduation I would go to work, even though my brothers were directed toward a college education.

At this time another major event occurred that had an impact on me. My mother died, very suddenly, from uremic poisoning, and I was left to care for my father. Shortly after high school graduation, I became a caretaker, a housekeeper, and a wage earner.

My first job was in a local candy store, Sunday's Candies. The owner, Mr. Caplow, was a graduate of Harvard University and had earned a master's degree in business. He viewed his three shops as a huge enterprise where all the business principles he had learned at Harvard were to be implemented. Interviewing for this job, I was given an intelligence test, a manual dexterity test, a number of personality tests, and a "behind the counter how I would look with a white coat" test. I was truly impressed when I was hired among a large and competitive pool of applicants.

A unique feature of the candy store was that Harvard University students were employed evenings. I developed good friendships with many of these students and was invited to many of the social events on the Harvard campus. At these gatherings, where I was the only non-college student, I began to realize the importance of continuing my education, and dissatisfaction with my mundane job grew rapidly. I wanted to be something more than a "candy girl," something more worthy.

I decided to apply to the Boston City Hospital for a position as a laboratory technician. I had met Mayor James Curley when my father was a labor union organizer. This acquaintanceship eased my way into being admitted to the hospital's Medical Technology Training Program, a paid program. After my year of training there, I found employment at the Harvard Medical School Hematology Research Laboratory, located in the Beth Israel Hospital. This research laboratory was under the direction of Dr. Benjamin Alexander, an internationally known hematologist. My first published research paper on thiamine metabolism resulted from this position (Alexander, Culbertson, & Landwehr, 1945).

While I was employed in the Harvard Medical School Hematology Research Laboratory, my father died and I went to live with the family of a friend. Out of the blue I received a letter stating that I had been granted a fully-paid, 4-year scholarship to whatever school I chose to attend. I found out that I owed this spectacular windfall to one of my Sunday's Candies friends, Dr. Edward Blackman, who had submitted my name to the Edward's Scholarship Fund of Boston. Dr. Blackman had earned his PhD in general studies and humanities from Harvard University and later taught at Michigan State University in the Humanities Department. How he obtained my school records, I do not know, and he never would tell me. With Dr. Blackman's support and encouragement, I accepted the Edwards Scholarship Fund offer. I applied to the University of Michigan because of its outstanding Biochemistry Department. I was accepted as a biochemistry major and arrived at Ann Arbor in 1944.

My freshman year was a nightmare. I had never had algebra, trigonometry, calculus, chemistry, or physics, and writing themes was absolutely not in my repertoire of academic skills. My first major trauma occurred when I submitted my first theme paper in an English composition class. The professor, aghast at what I had written, called me in and posed some sharp questions about why I was attending college. I returned to the dormitory in tears, wondering if I was going to survive. I confided my fears to two much younger fellow students. They insisted that I could learn the necessary skills. Under the tutelage of these two generous young women, I completed my English class, earning an A+, and was exempted from the requirement to enroll in additional composition classes. The English professor was duly impressed.

In the second semester of the freshman year, I was required to choose a social science course. Introductory psychology was one of the choices available. This proved to be a most stimulating course. My success in that course led me to enroll in experimental psychology. At the end of the term, the professor, Dr. John Shepard, asked me to become his laboratory assistant. My good grades, enthusiasm for the laboratory exercises, and my maturity were most certainly factors that led to his request. This honor was the impetus that prompted me to change my major to psychology.

During my junior year I met John Culbertson, one of the many discharged World War II servicemen who were returning to college to complete their studies. John, who had been a pilot during the war, soon became a central figure in my life, and we made plans to be married upon completion of our undergraduate degrees.

In my senior year I was chosen to be class assistant to Dr. Norman R. F. Maier. Dr. Maier had earned his PhD from the University of Michigan in 1928. He had journeyed abroad in 1947 to study with Wolfgang Kohler and his gestalt psychology colleagues. Gestalt psychology is often referred to as the psychology of perception. Dr. Maier returned to the University of Michigan in 1931 and remained there for the rest of his career. He is known for his theoretical work in the field of reasoning, frustration–aggression, and human relations.

As graduation approached, I was about to marry John and was looking for ways to support my husband while he pursued graduate studies in economics. When Dr. Maier learned that I was considering sales or clerical work as a source of income, he roared, "NO WAY! You are a very good student. I will find you employment and you will enter graduate school." And that is what I did. We married in 1947 and we both enrolled in graduate programs, I in psychology and he in economics. At that time, this was a rare occurrence. Very few couples pursued graduate study at the same time.

Social psychology was developing as a major course of study on the campus and all the important academic and research faculty in the field were coming to Ann Arbor. Due to the efforts of Dr. Theodore Newcomb, the Survey Research Center from the U.S. Department of Agriculture was transferred to the University of Michigan bringing Drs. Rensis Likert and Angus Campbell into our midst. Dr. Likert is especially known for the "Likert scales," which are often used in social science research. Dr. Kurt Lewin, universally accepted as the founder of modern social psychology, was to join the faculty that year but, unfortunately, he died before he could make the move. Nevertheless, his Group Dynamics and Action Research colleagues did make the transfer, greatly enriching this area of study. The influx of more and more outstanding social psychologists convinced me that this was an exciting field, and with Dr. Maier's guidance and encouragement, I declared social psychology as my graduate major.

In my first semester of graduate school, Dr. Helen Peak, one of the very few women professors in academia at that time, was my instructor in introductory social psychology. Dr. Peak was one of the founding members of the National Council of Women Psychologists (NCWP), which later became the International Council of Women Psychologists (ICWP) and, ultimately, the International Council of Psychologists (ICP). At the first class meeting, Dr. Peak announced that all women in her class who wished to achieve high grades must join the ICP. This was a tongue-in-cheek comment, because I was the only woman in the course. Of course I signed up for membership immediately. This simple act was my initiation into international psychology. This simple act has affected my entire life. On receipt of the first newsletter, I was bitten by the "international" bug, and it became an important variable in everything I did and still do. I often wonder if the studying of international places in the 5th grade with Miss Ryan was the seeding of these interests.

I completed my Master of Science degree in social psychology and continued in the social psychology doctoral program. When my husband and I finished our preliminary examinations and were working on our thesis topics, we decided we had experienced enough of campus life. Our plan was for John to find a job that would permit us to live more comfortably while we completed our respective dissertations. When John obtained a position with the Federal Reserve Board, we left Ann Arbor and moved to Washington, DC.

The dissertation topic I had chosen originally had to be discarded because I could not obtain subjects for my planned research, so I had to develop a completely different thesis. I chose to study modifying emotionally held attitudes through role playing. My husband was a wonderful contributor to this project. To ensure that the data were not contaminated by my participation, John administered the questionnaires before and after the initial phase. He continued his assistance in a number of ways, meanwhile working on his own thesis at the same time. When I gave birth to twins, John and Joanne in 1951, both of our academic efforts slowed dramatically. I was not able to complete my PhD until 1955. Two years later, my dissertation was first published (Culbertson, 1957).

At that time I was completely involved with family life and had no intention of working outside the home. One evening when we were entertained at the home of one of John's colleagues, I met Dr. Emma Layman, a research psychologist at Children's Hospital who offered me a part-time position researching pica behaviors of low-income children. I accepted, but within a month after I joined Dr. Layman's project, my husband received a teaching position offer at the University of Wisconsin-Madison. We decided to return to the academic world and in September, 1957 we moved to Madison.

REVIEW OF EARLY ADULT YEARS

In reviewing my early adult years, I have become aware of how willing I am to accept new learning experiences when they present themselves, and this "openness" has led to many opportunities. I am also aware that my desires and abilities for new learning experiences and my attainment of good levels of knowledge have been the path to the successful life that my parents only dreamed of. I maintained my interest in international psychology although my non-academic responsibilities limited my participation in this area. Last, I believe my experiences during this period taught me the importance of mentoring and networking with others in pursuing professional goals.

MIDDLE AND LATE ADULT YEARS

When we arrived in Madison, I was already the mother of three children, John, Joanne, and Lyndall who were born in Washington, DC, and a fourth child, Amy, who was to be born very shortly. My family responsibilities were paramount to me at this time. Also, academic employment was not available to me because the Madison campus had a nepotism rule that prevented me from teaching in the same college as my husband. I therefore concentrated solely on his career as a professor of economics.

Our family settled into a faculty housing area called University Houses, which was a wonderful place. It clustered together all the newly arrived faculty members, allowing us to get to know one another and become friends. An old Michigan associate, Dr. Leonard Berkowitz, lived there with his family, as did Dr. Maressa Orzack, an experimental psychologist who had studied at Columbia University. Dr. Orzack and I shared a desire to remain active in our professions, and we often had friendly conversations about how we would ultimately accomplish this goal.

About a year after we arrived in Madison, I met Dr. Harvey Stevens, whose work was primarily in the field of mental retardation. Dr. Stevens had just been appointed Director of Wisconsin Central Colony and Training School, a new facility for severely developmentally-disabled children and adolescents. I was pleased by his proposal that I develop a research laboratory for his new facility, but with four young children, I did not feel that full-time employment was feasible. A short time later, I made a counter proposal to Dr. Stevens of a job-sharing arrangement with Dr. Maressa Orzack. Dr. Stevens was amenable to our plan, and we began employment the following week. There is no doubt in my mind that this arrangement, instituted in the late 1950s, was one of the earliest job-sharing plans ever developed by and for women psychologists.

I worked with Dr. Orzack to establish a research arm at the Wisconsin Central Colony and Training Institute. While working on this project, a representative of the State of Wisconsin asked if I would be willing to return to the university for training as a clinical child psychologist, a specialty in very short supply. The state proposed to pay my expenses for retraining, as well as a stipend that would provide for babysitting and other major expenditures. I found this offer very attractive, particularly because my research job had a limited term of employment.

Thus it was that in 1959 I returned for postdoctoral training as a clinical psychologist at the University of Wisconsin-Madison. It was a wonderful 2 years of retooling. I had taken a number of clinical psychology credits at Michigan, purely out of interest in the field, so that I had a good background for this undertaking. Dr. Barclay Martin was my clinical psychology training mentor at the University of Wisconsin, and Dr. Rudy Mathias was my mentor at the Wisconsin Diagnostic Center for Children and Adolescents. When I finished the program in 1961, I went to work for the Wisconsin Diagnostic Center.

In 1965, my husband was invited to be a visiting economist at the University of California-Berkeley, and our family headed west for a year. By now a confirmed working mother, I contacted Dr. Margaret Singer of the National Institute of Mental Health (NIMH), who was engaged in a research project involving schizophrenogenic communication. Dr. Singer hired me to work with her on a part-time basis during our stay in California.

On our return to Madison, I was offered an Acting Chair position in the psychology section of the Child Psychiatry Department at the University of Wisconsin-Madison. I remained in that position until my husband was again invited to Berkeley in 1967.

When our second year at Berkeley ended and we returned to Madison, I joined the Madison Public School System as a school psychologist. Dr. Myron Seeman, the Chief School Psychologist, felt that it was important to have a clinical psychologist on the team. My experience in this area led to an invitation to become a member of the Psychology Department at the University of Wisconsin-Whitewater, which was developing a new program in school psychology. Although the offer was very attractive to me, I approached it with trepidation, because it involved a demanding 1-hour commute from my Madison home. However, my husband was extremely supportive, and together we practiced the drive until I was comfortable with it.

I became a professor of psychology at the University of Wisconsin-Whitewater in 1968. I held this position for 20 years, and was the Director of the School Psychology program for most of that time. The department, when I joined it, included only two women professors: Dr. Charlotte Christner, and Alice Schoof, M.S. in psychology. Dr. Christner was a very supportive colleague and was a strong resource for me. As Chair of the Psychology Department, she was always available to listen and to offer help when I needed it. It was she, during those years at Whitewater, who encouraged and enabled me to pursue both my national and international interests.

In 1970, at a meeting of the American Psychological Association, I met Dr. Frances Mullen, Assistant Superintendent of Schools, in charge of Special Education with the Board of Education of the Chicago School System. Dr. Mullen was a founder of the National Council of Women Psychologists (NCWP) and a former president of the International Council of Women Psychologists (ICWP). In 1976, she became the Secretary-General of the International Council of Psychologists (ICP). She was always a strong influence and a valued colleague to me, so much so, that I have dedicated a book to her (Culbertson, 1990).

One of the happenings that led to my being recognized as an exceptional international psychologist was the work that Dr. Mullen and I accomplished during my elective years in the International Council of Psychologists in gaining membership into the United Nations (UN) as a Non-Governmental Organization. From 1974 to 1979, we worked diligently on the acceptance of our application as a Non-Governmental Organization with the United Nations. It was during my presidency that the application was finally accepted. This was a highly significant event for our organization and an honor during my presidency. It must be recognized that the International Council of Psychologists is, to the best of my knowledge, the first psychological organization with many U.S. members to receive this honor. To this day, we are actively involved and play a role in many of the decisions made by this august body. Today, we have representatives to the UN in New York City, Geneva, Switzerland, and Vienna, Austria, and they continue to play an important role in the organization's functions and decisions.

As my four children grew up and my family obligations became less restrictive, I became more personally involved in the International Council of Psychologists (ICP). I was elected to a number of committees and to the Board of Directors. I became Secretary in 1977 and President in 1979. My presidential year coincided with the United Nations Year of the Child. I invited Dr. Estafania Aldaba-Lim, a representative from the Philippines and chair of the United Nations Year of the Child, to be our guest speaker. She arrived in her national costume and gave an inspired address. Dr. Aldaba-Lim and I became friends and continue to maintain contact to this day.

In 1974, Dr. Frances Mullen and Dr. Calvin Catterall, a Professor of Special Education at Ohio University, founded the International School Psychology Association (ISPA), at the Vierjahrzeiten Hotel in Munich, Germany. I was invited to attend this meeting and become one of the founding members. It was at this seminal meeting that I initiated Project Share, which continues to this day. Project Share links professional psychologists around the world, permitting them to share their world of work, their social activities, and even their homes for short periods (Culbertson, 1977). This has been a lively and successful program, counting among its members many national and international organizations including the American Psychological Association (APA), the International Association of Applied Psychology (IAAP), and the Society of Inter-American Psychology (SIP).

I continue to be active in the International Council of Psychologists (ICP) and support it in any way I can. In addition, I am deeply involved in international activities within the American Psychological Association (APA). I served as founding member and Chair of the International School Psychology Committee, APA, Division 16 (School Psychology), and Chair of the APA Committee on International Relations in Psychology. I was a founding member and Council Representative of the Division of International Psychology (a new APA division). Currently, I am President of the Applied Gerontology Division of the International Association of Applied Psychology (IAAP) and a member of the IAAP Executive Board.

I have presented research papers at international conferences since 1972. Most recently, I have presented research findings on stresses, strains, and coping styles of women around the world, and mental health of professional women internationally at meetings of the International Council of Psychologists and the International Applied Psychology Associations in England, France, Spain, Portugal, Taiwan, Japan, and the United States. This visibility in the professional arena resulted in my election to the prestigious Executive Board of the International Association of Applied Psychology.

In the international domain, I work assiduously in mentoring women psychologists from developing countries because they are less likely to be recognized for their research endeavors or given opportunities to travel. This mentoring consists of helping them with research projects, involving them in my research projects, and assisting them in their efforts to obtain funds for travel to conventions. Culbertson, et al. (1992) is a representative publication of this mentoring.

I retired from the University of Wisconsin-Whitewater in 1988 and moved into private practice—to practice what I had preached, you might say. I joined Mental Health Associates. Today, my clinical focus is in hypnotherapy with children, adolescents, and adults, especially women. Recently, I changed my research directions to include resilience behaviors of aging women around the world. This activity is a new journey to me.

REVIEW OF MIDDLE AND LATE YEARS

In my middle and later years, I have concentrated on increasing involvements in professional organizations and serving them in a variety of official capacities. These activities have brought me into contact with a number of dedicated international and national psychologists who have been inspiring role models for me. I have reached a point in my life where I hope to serve as a role model to others. The rewards and recognitions I have received are related to my life-long enthusiasm for learning, to a willingness to accept new challenges, and to an openness to the contributions of colleagues and friends. These are the values I have carried into my middle and later years that I am trying to pass on to others.

As I summarize my life's travels in the field of psychology, it seems that I was very fortunate to have been in the right place at the right time. I was fortunate to be one of the early women to become involved in international psychology. I was fortunate to be a participant in founding an international organization. I was one of the early women psychologists to develop an international internship program for school psychology students. Finally, I was an early ambassador and mentor in international psychology, having begun my affiliation in 1948.

I was honored to be recognized for my international work in clinical and school psychology by the Brazilian Clinical Psychology Association. The American Psychological Association and its members have honored me with several awards: (a) the APA Award for Distinguished Contribution to the International Advancement of Psychology, for my work worldwide with women, adolescents, and children; (b) recognition as an eminent woman psychologist at an APA symposium and this volume; and (c) the presentation of a career award from APA, Division 52, International Psychology, for years of outstanding contribution to international psychology.

None of this work could have been accomplished without the support and encouragement of my husband, John Culbertson, an internationally recognized economist in the field of world trade and money and banking. I was also fortunate to have the affection and cooperation of my four children: John D. Culbertson, PhD, Economics, University of Wisconsin-Madison, an economic consultant in Washington, DC; Joanne D. Culbertson, MS Public Policy, Harvard University, who works for the National Science Foundation in Washington, DC; Lyndall G. Culbertson Surgal, BA Music, University of Wisconsin-Madison, a graphic artist and musician in New York City; and Amy L. Culbertson, MS Counseling, University of Wisconsin–Madison, a management consultant with the Army Research Institute in Washington, DC.

I became internationally minded, I believe, in Miss Ryan's fifth-grade class and have never deviated from that interest. Although I was supported by both men and women along my career path, women had major roles in "paving my streets with gold." Miss Ryan planted the seeds of internationalism, and Dr. Peake opened the door to international interests. Dr. Mullen pulled me into action and international leadership roles. Dr. Christner created the avenues for my international endeavors during my academic years of teaching.

As the future unfolds, I hope I can continue to learn, develop theories, engage in research, and provide strategies and avenues of learning of resilient behaviors for disadvantaged people around the world, especially aging women. In looking back at my career, I've learned that mentors and mentoring were necessary elements of my success. I now know that by mentoring my international and national women colleagues, I can honor and repay those who mentored me.

REFERENCES

Alexander, B., Culbertson, F., & Landwehr, G. (1945). Studies of thiamine metabolism in man. Thiamine and pyrimadine excretion with special reference to the relationship between injected and excreted thiamine in normal and abnormal subjects. *Journal of Clinical Investigation, 15,* 294–303.

Culbertson, F. M. (1957). Modification of an emotionally-held attitude through role playing. *Journal of Abnormal and Social Psychology, 54,* 231–235.

Culbertson, F. M. (1977). Project Share, 1977. *Communique, National Association of School Psychologists, 5,* 114.

Culbertson, F. M. (1990). *Voices in international school psychology: A memorial tribute to Frances A. Mullen.* Madison, WI: Twenty-First Century Press.

Culbertson, F. M., Comunian, A. L., Farence, S., Fukuhara, M., Halpern, E., Miao, E.S.-C.Y., Muhlbauer, V., O'Roark, A., & Thomas, A. (1992). Stresses, strains, and adaptive responses in professional women: Cross-cultural reports. In U. Gielen, L. L. Adler, & N. A. Milgram (Eds.), *Psychology in international perspective* (pp. 281–298). Amsterdam: Swets & Zeitlinger B. V.

REPRESENTATIVE PUBLICATIONS

Culbertson, F. M. (1974). An effective, low-cost approach to the treatment of disruptive children. *Psychology in the Schools, 22,* 183–187.

Culbertson, F. M. (1975). Average students' needs and perceptions of school psychologists. *Psychology in the Schools, 12,* 191–196.

Culbertson, F. M. (1977). The trainer's group in school psychology—International. *International Flash, Supplement of International Psychologist, 19,* 2.

Culbertson, F. M. (1977). State of school psychology. *The Wisconsin School Psychologist, January,* 3–4.

Culbertson, F. M. (1977). The search for help of parents of autistic children or beware of professional "group think." *Journal of Clinical Child Psychology, 6,* 63–65.

Culbertson, F. M. (1978). Average students' needs and perceptions of school psychologists. *Contemporary school psychology: Selected readings for psychology in the schools.* Vrandon, VT: J. L. Carroll.

Culbertson, F. M. (1982). Autistic children and public school education. *School Psychology International, 2,* 27–30.

Culbertson, F. M. (1983). International school psychology—Cross cultural perspectives. In T. Kratochwill (Ed.), *Advances in school psychology* (pp. 45–82). Mahwah: Lawrence Erlbaum Associates.

Culbertson, F. M. (1985). *Voices in international school psychology: A memorial tribute to Calvin Caterall.* Madison, WI: Twenty-First Century Press.

Culbertson, F. M. (1985). Frances M. Culbertson. *Revue de Psychologie Appliquee, 35,* 2.

Culbertson, F. M. (1987). Graphic characteristics on the Draw-a-Person Test for identification of physical abuse. *Journal of Art Therapy, 4,* 30–33.

Culbertson, F. M. (1989). A four-step hypnotherapy model for Gilles de la Tourette's Syndrome. *American Journal of Clinical Hypnosis, 31,* 242–251.

Culbertson, F. M. (1990). Relaxation strategies for the school-aged child. In P. Keller & S. Heyman (Eds.), *Innovations in clinical practice: A source book* (pp. 183–192). Sarasota, FL: Professional Resource Exchange, Inc.

Culbertson, F. M. (1998). Hypnotherapy with the elderly. In W. J. Matthews, & J. H. Edgette (Eds.), *Current thinking and research in brief therapy* (pp. 137–160). Philadelphia, PA: Taylor & Francis.

Culbertson, F. M., & Feral, C. (1989). Pattern analysis of Wechsler Intelligence Scale for Children-Revised profiles of delinquent boys. *Journal of Clinical Psychology, 45,* 651–660.

Culbertson, F. M., & Gunn, R. (1966). Comparison of the Bender-Gestalt Test and the Frostig Test in several clinical groups of children. *Journal of Clinical Psychology, 22,* 439–443.

Culbertson, F. M., & Hatch, A. (1990). Relaxation strategies with an anxious school-aged child. *Psychotherapy in Private Practice, 8,* 33–40.

Culbertson, F. M., & Marganona, E. A. (1983). Mexican and United States' students' attitudes toward the aged. *International Journal of Group Tensions, 3,* 42–56.

Culbertson, F. M., Reilly, D., & Barclay, J. (1977). The current status of competence-based training, Part 1: Validity, reliability, logistical, and ethical issues. *Journal of School Psychology, 15,* 68–74.

Culbertson, F. M., & Rimm, S. (1980). Cross-cultural validation of GIFT, an instrumentation of creativity. *The Journal of Creative Behavior, 14,* 272–273.

Culbertson, F. M., & Wille, C. (1978). Relaxation training as a reading remediation tool for school-aged children. *Canadian Counsellor, 2,* 128–131.

Spielberger, C., & Culbertson, F. M. (1996). Assessment of anger in school-aged children. In C. D. Spielberg & I. G. Sarason (Eds.), *Stress and emotion* (pp. 193–201). Washington, DC: Taylor & Francis.

CHAPTER 4

Patricia M. Bricklin

Photographer: Alan L. Fox.

Patricia M. Bricklin

The opportunity to do a life review sometimes occurs near the end of a person's life. The opportunity to consider these issues at a time when you are active and still very much engaged with life, both personally and professionally, is both an honor and somewhat frightening. It is an honor to consider the possibility that you have made contributions to the field of psychology that are having an impact and may be enduring. It is frightening for the very same reasons.

I have considered my life to be a series of transitions and occasional transformations that are continuously and dynamically integrating the personal and the professional. My personal life is about being a wife, mother, and extended family member, a friend and a citizen of smaller and larger communities. My professional life has focused and continues to focus on learning and related emotional disorders in children, adolescents, young adults and their families; bringing psychology to the public through the media and popular press; legal and ethical issues in the regulation of the profession; the role of professional organizations as advocates for both the profession and the public interest; and the evolution of professional education and training in professional psychology.

I believe the integration of the personal and the professional has been critical in my development and is evident from my earliest years.

EARLY YEARS

My earliest memories are being Irish Catholic and surrounded by the mystery of church and the magic of music. I grew up in a family of musicians. Operas, symphonies, and songs of all sorts were ever present. I remember that at 4 years of age my grandmother took me to the local radio station to sing Brahms Lullaby on the Saturday morning children's hour. (Singing on the radio and singing in shows became a regular part of my life up to and including early graduate school.)

I was an only child and my mother worked as a caseworker for the American Red Cross. My Grandmother was the love of my life and she filled me with love and Irish stories, e.g., Tales of Brian Beru, the first Irish King. She told me that I was descended from him and should consider myself Princess Pat. I was special, she said, an only child and a Princess.

It was only when I started kindergarten that I realized being special also meant not having a father. My father, Gregor M. McIntosh, was a soldier in World War I who died from war incurred disabilities. I never knew him.

My immediate family was my grandmother, Mary Ellen Treanor Nicholson, and my mother, Agnes Crompton McIntosh. Although my life was rich with love, music, books, and intellectual stimulation, part of me longed for a large noisy intact family, with lots of brothers and sisters and lots going on. I found that "dream" family in a house across the street, a large orthodox Jewish family whose youngest daughter became my best friend. Participation in the life of that family enriched my life in many ways, an appreciation for the varieties of religious experience, the model of an integrated family, and my first introduction to psychology as a profession (an older sister and her husband were in the mental health field). I believe these years from the time I was 6 until I went away to college at 16 set the stage for my later personal and professional life. I became a psychologist, married a man who was Jewish and happily absorbed into his loving family, and together we produced the "noisy, lively" family I had desired.

My Catholic education at St. Angela Hall and St. Ursula Academy in Toledo, Ohio and later at St. Joseph College in Emmitsburg, Maryland was outstanding. The nuns, Sister Lelia and Sister Justa, daily provided intellectual challenges and encouraged questioning, such as *Why? What? How?* However, this very special educational experience also sent mixed messages of: "You can be whatever you choose" but also "Be whatever the role for women prescribes." In addition, the World War II climate of my late childhood and early adolescence projected the feeling of a country working together, with teamwork, optimism and new roles for women that added to a personal dissonance of which I was yet unaware.

It was a summer job that ultimately turned into a lifetime work that gave direction to my life and formed my commitment to children with special needs.

The Matthews School in Baltimore, Maryland was a small residential school for children 3 to 12 with physical, cognitive, and emotional difficulties. These children and the director of the school, Helen Matthews, a dedicated school psychologist and former student of Lightner Witmer, were my inspiration and Helen was my mentor motivating me to consider graduate school in psychology. In addition, the children and the families with whom I worked provided the real motivation for my interest in psychology. I got no support for this idea from my mother, who was strongly against graduate degrees for women, stating firmly that it would reduce my chances to marry by a significant degree.

It was not until much later that I understood that my mother's motivation was to spare me from replicating her life—a life without a partner where she had to work to support herself and a child (me) and give up (she believed) a promising singing career. At the time I did not argue or try to change my mother's mind about further education. I simply proceeded toward my goal.

I sometimes wonder if I had truly understood her concerns, I might have done something different. I don't believe so.

GRADUATE SCHOOL, MARRIAGE, CHILDREN AND EARLY CAREER

Getting into graduate school was another matter. Although I was permitted to take graduate courses at the Johns Hopkins University while I was working at the Matthews School after college graduation, applying for acceptance into the PhD program was a different experience.

The professor who interviewed me told me my grades were fine, my test scores acceptable, and my letters of recommendation excellent but I was a woman. "If you were ugly," he said, "and I thought you would never marry, I might consider accepting you. However, you will marry and have children. We cannot invest time and energy in you and let you take the place of a man who will use his education while you will not." With this he got up and left the room. Although this could not happen overtly today, there was no recourse at the time!

Temple University, in Philadelphia, was different. They admitted me first to the masters program and then the PhD program. At that time, the best child-oriented psychology experience was in the Reading Clinic, a part of the Department of Psychology. Here I found the integration of clinical work and remedial education I had been seeking. At that time, the Reading Clinic founded by Emmett Betts, an educational psychologist and reading expert, was famous worldwide and attracted clients and graduate students from all over the country. These were exciting times as the field of reading and learning disabilities evolved. I was fortunate to have several fine mentors and role models during this period (Marjorie Johnson, Roy Kress, Jules Abrams, and Paul Daniels, psychologists, educators, and reading specialists).

In graduate school I met my husband, Barry Bricklin, a clinical psychologist to be. We married and during the course of completing my dissertation we had two sons, Brian and Scott. Doing a dissertation in precomputer days with a baby and a two-year-old was a challenge.

These were challenging times in general; the women's movement, civil rights, civil rights for the handicapped, the Vietnam War, and the development of rock and roll all affected both our professional and personal lives. As Brian and Scott approached schoolage, our two daughters, Carol and Alisa, were born. This was a joyful and busy time, both personally and professionally. In addition to my role as wife and mother of four growing children, I was consulting to two schools for children with language-learning disabilities, expanding the learning therapy paradigm and developing a parent education/counseling model.

In my own young adult professional and personal development, a series of transformations (marriage and motherhood, combined with my 1950s and early 1960s concept of these roles) occurred side by side with my increased participation as a young professional psychologist, a transitional experience slowly building event by event. This created subtle conflicts and dissonance of which I was then unaware—the need to be a perfect wife and mother; perfectly competent psychologist; passive, compliant wife and mother; and assertive psychologist. A subsequent unplanned and highly unlikely series of experiences provided the opportunity to become aware of this personal/professional dissonance and transform it to a syntonic whole.

THE MEDIA: CHALLENGE AND RISK

In 1965, I was invited to appear on a popular daily radio program that interviewed guests and then took calls from listeners. With some reluctance, I accepted the invitation and found to my surprise that I actually enjoyed the experience and found it a real challenge to simply and clearly communicate psychological information in nontechnical language. I did not know it, but this particular program spot was being used to audition psychologists for a continuing program. At that time, each of the CBS-owned stations throughout the country planned to have its own daily psychology program.

Shortly after my appearance on the show, I received a call from the program director of the station asking me to come in for an interview. In that interview, he explained the potential program format and asked me if I would be interested. In the course of our discussion, I told him that my husband, Barry, was also a psychologist. At this point we began to explore the option of doing the program as a husband/wife professional couple. In subsequent conversations and interviews, my husband and I discussed the pros and cons of such a venture—the potential ethical and communication dilemmas and challenges. Until that time, as far as we knew, psychologists in the media were few- and not-too-well-received by their peers. At the same time, the opportunity to do a responsible and thoughtful job and explore new avenues for professional psychology was there. We decided to take the risk. We began 5 years of daily radio that started as half-hour programs and were extended to an hour and a half as they grew in popularity. This was followed by a year of daily television, and finally a weekly radio program that extended into the 1980s.

As psychologists in the media before media psychology existed as a legitimate area of concentration for psychologists, we found ourselves confronting a number of personal, professional, and ethical issues for which clear guidelines did not exist. These issues revolved around working as a team, our responsibilities to the profession of psychology, ethical dilemmas, our responsibilities to our listeners, and the organization and communication of psychological content (Bricklin, 1984).

WORKING AS A TEAM

Up to this point, Barry and I had worked as independent professionals, each with our own areas of expertise. My practice primarily involved school consultation and problems of children, whereas he focused more on adults. Our area of overlap was the family, although our perspective and points of intervention were different. We had, of course, consulted with each other but had never really worked together.

Balancing our individual communication styles and our individual patterns of professional intervention within the context of our existing personal relationship required mutual effort and adjustment. We served as both information-giving psychologists and husband/wife and parent role models to a huge listening audience. This caused us to examine not only our effectiveness as cocommunicators, but also the nature of our personal relationship and the kind of marriage/family role model we projected. Both of us had grown up with fairly traditional views of men and women in family relationships. Although we viewed ourselves as professional equals, there was initially a power differential in our personal relationship with each other and my view of our respective roles in the family.

The absence of men on a day-to-day basis, together with my grandmother's and mother's view of them, allowed me to develop an unrealistic expectancy of the power of men and their controlling strength in personal relationships. This personal/professional dissonance initially affected both the information we provided to listeners as well as the roles we projected. Certainly, it affected our therapeutic work outside of the media. The gradual evolution of our relationship as equal professional and personal partners created a transformational influence on my work with children, parents, teachers, and later in organizational contexts.

RESPONSIBILITY TO THE PROFESSION

In our media work, we considered two major questions in this connection—questions still being debated by others. First, *should* psychologists be involved in the media at all, particularly in listener participation programs? Second, is it possible for psychologists to participate in such programs in a professionally responsible and ethical manner that enhances psychology? Both of us believed that this was possible, and the intervening years seemed to support this view. Initially, the attitudes of our peers were variable. All of the ethical committees of the various local and state psychological associations, together with the various medical and psychiatric societies, reviewed audiotapes of our programs for possible professional and ethical lapses. Most professional organizations at that time believed it was impossible for a professional to be ethical on a "call in" program. To their surprise, they found no ethical violations.

Although already highly sensitive to ethical and professional responsibility, this early constant monitoring by our peers certainly sharpened our awareness and gave us early first-hand experience with peer review. Our more frequently asked questions by listeners were: "My therapist says I should…. What do you think I should do?" or "My therapist says…. What docs he/she mean?" Questions such as these provided us with the opportunity to reaffirm the nature of the therapist–client relationship and encourage client–therapist communication to a point of honesty far beyond what seemed to exist at the time.

It was also clear that it would have been unethical and professionally irresponsible for us to use our media recognizability as a mechanism for increasing our own independent practices. In response to the frequently asked question: "How can I get to see you?" we would offer other appropriate sources of referral information.

ETHICAL DILEMMAS

Pressure from some of our advertising sponsors to be spokespersons for their products was a recurrent ethical issue, as well as who or what sorts of products or services were appropriate as sponsors for professional psychologists.

However, the most difficult and continuous dilemma for us was the ethical principle, which, at that time, prohibited personal advice in the media. For the most part, we helped to provide our listeners with the kind of information on which they could base an informed decision. We worked through questions and answers, analogies and illustrations, to clarify unclear or distorted points or feelings in the way of intelligent decision making. However, from time to time *not* to give personal advice would, in our opinion, have been unethical and irresponsible. One of many incidents dramatically illustrates this point.

A mother called us and claimed her teenaged daughter had told her repeatedly she wanted to kill herself. She asked: "Is this serious? Should I get her help?" We answered, "Absolutely yes, as soon as possible" and reiterated that every suicide attempt should be taken seriously. Specific referral sources were offered, and an off-the-air follow-up phone call was arranged to make certain that appropriate professional help was contacted.

RESPONSIBILITY TO OUR LISTENERS

In addition to the "personal advice" dilemma, the preceding anecdote illustrated some of the basic considerations of responsibility to the listener. In the broadest ethical sense, the need to balance the ethical principles of autonomy (the right of the person to self-direction) and beneficence (motivation to do what is best for a person—to help others) was ever present. At times they conflicted just as they sometimes do in independent psychotherapeutic practice.

Communicating information accurately and clearly to diminish the opportunities for distortion was always a primary aim and responsibility. Providing our listeners with access to a network of appropriate referral sources was clearly a continuing responsibility. We introduced our listeners to the concept that a number of different professional disciplines delivered mental health services, the differences among them and the concept of psychologists as autonomous providers of service. An informal survey of community and organization referral sources at that time indicated an increase in contacting and using available mental health and remedial education services. A considerable number of individuals indicated that the reason for their initial contact with the agency or professional had been information we provided.

We keenly felt the responsibility for providing the opportunity for follow-up to determine the extent to which information received was accurately interpreted and useful. It was in the interest of accurate informational follow-up that we began to write and have the station distribute several informational booklets, for example, *Helping Your Young Child To Learn*, (Bricklin, B. & Bricklin, P., 1966).

HOW TO ORGANIZE AND COMMUNICATE PSYCHOLOGICAL CONTENT

The total lack of visual feedback in our contact with listeners and callers contributed to our considerable attention to developing more effective listening skills. We found ourselves more clearly able to attend to a caller's tone, rhythm, and sensory representation modes beyond the actual verbal content of the communication. These listening skills, finely tuned in situations where there was no visual feedback, have been invaluable in other areas of my professional life.

The constant interaction with listeners helped us to sharpen and organize our thinking. The circumstances of peoples' lives were clearly very different and the wording of their questions often varied. Yet, it appeared to us that there actually were only a finite number of questions to which all of us were seeking answers. We began to develop a response paradigm that provided the context for our "on-the-air" information. The focus of the program through the early 1970s was family- and child-centered. We created a "family council" mechanism for strengthening family organization, and within this context, developed what we believed to be critical foundation skills in family interaction and functioning. These included communicating without blame, non-adversarial methods for getting people to take a closer look at themselves, setting effective limits, and developing independence. These foundation skills and strategies to implement them are reported in *Strong Family, Strong Child* (Bricklin, B. & Bricklin, P., 1970b), *Improving Your Child's Learning Ability* (Bricklin, B. & Bricklin, P., 1970a) and *Reducing Negative Behavior* (Bricklin, B. & Bricklin, P., 1968), booklets and books growing out of our organization of "on air" information.

Over the years, we noted an increase in public awareness and sophistication about psychology and a shift in our "on-the-air" callers from emphasis on child and family to a focus on the self and personal relationships. Again, a response paradigm developed. A growing notion that the human nervous system is just not constituted for ease in long-term monogamous relationships led to the conceptualization of four natural "enemies" of marriage or of any long-term intimate relationship. These enemies were conceived as outgrowths of the human condition and not necessarily as "sickness" or pathology. They included dependency needs or that each person secretly expects to get more than he or she gives, the illusory expectation that marriage can bring a sense of personal meaning, that people become irrationally blaming too easily, and that people falsely expect marriage to consistently engender excitement without personal effort.

These ideas were formalized in another book, *Conquering the Natural Enemies of Marriage* (Bricklin, B. & Bricklin, P., 1977). There was considerable cross-fertilization in our ongoing media experiences and our individual therapeutic practices. Our ideas were critically scrutinized by both our professional colleagues and our listeners. This kind of ongoing review and comment was incredibly valuable. Our notions about therapy and specific therapeutic strategies underwent dramatic shifts as a direct result of our media work. My continuing work on the transformational self-concept shift necessary in working with children who had learning disabilities, their families, and teachers, uses many of the strategies developed during this period, including the Bricklin Inner Shouting Technique developed by Barry, which enables an individual to "mourn" and "accept" an unchangeable event.

In 1981, because of other commitments, we completed our media work. The opportunity for the personal and professional transformation that the media experience provided for me created the context for my intense involvement in professional activities. Specifically, I had the personal experience of public accountability for professional activity, including direct and visible wrestling with issues of ethical competence, clarity of communication, and effectiveness of service. There were risks and difficulties. However, the very real experience of making a difference as a dual advocate for psychology and consumers of psychological services has enormously influenced my subsequent involvement in licensing and credentialling activities, as well as other professional and consumer issues.

LICENSURE AND CREDENTIALLING

From 1965 to 1972, Pennsylvania psycholgists worked actively to have a licensing law enacted. Although Barry and I arranged for our radio station general manager to present several editorials on the need for licensing as public protection, we were, at that time, ethically unable to use our radio influence personally for professional guild interests.

The governor signed the bill into law in May, 1972, but not before it had been amended to permit psychologists with less than doctoral level credentials to be licensed for full independent practice. Two lessons were learned from this event; one quickly and one very slowly. The first was a political lesson in the importance of monitoring votes and the necessity for effective lobbying even at the last minute. The second, I learned as a member of the first licensing board appointed by the governor. The prime mandate for any regulatory board is to protect the public and interpret and implement the law. There is no place for guild advocacy on licensing boards. This was my first experience with the interface of psychology and law, the implications, possibilities and inhibitions of legal language. These encounters with the legal aspects of regulating our profession have been challenging, frustrating, and raised many questions.

Writing regulations to interpret Pennsylvania's psychology licensing law required a careful look at possible language to specifically interpret the more general language of the law. The more precise the language, the less room for interpretation; the less specific the language, the more room for interpretation. Which does the best job of protecting the public? This is not easy or sometimes even possible to answer.

As a woman, I was struck by the frequent unfairness to women in licensing requirements. Requirements for full-time educational, internship, and supervised experiences had a particularly negative impact on women who elected to have careers and children. I worked hard to change these regulations and was ultimately successful in my own state.

The relationship of the required education and training in psychology to an individual's competence in the practice of psychotherapy is difficult to establish. This is a troubling issue. Antilicensing persons frequently use the example of effective psychotherapists without the required education and training credentials as a reason for abolishing licensing laws.

I suspect that the relationship between education and training and competence has not been established because we have not asked the right questions or looked in the right places. Is it possible that one of the critical decisions in competence is not "how to" but "when to," for example, *when* to warn, *when* to break confidentiality, *when* to intervene directly, *when* not to respond, *when* to refer, and so on. The factors involved in decisions of "when" seem to depend more on broad generic education and training than the technological skills of "how."

In my early years on the Board, I was also particularly alarmed at the revictimization of women in disciplinary hearings, and I worked hard to minimize the opportunities for this and to humanize the entire licensing process. Mobility and scope of practice issues in licensing are important for all practicing psychologists and currently often act as barriers to individual psychologists. Can you move easily from one state to another? Can you practice in one state doing what you do in another state? At my own state level and at the national level as a president of the Association of State and Provincial Psychology Boards (ASPPB), I have worked to reduce some of these barriers. Progress is slow.

Over the years as a licensing Board member and for the past several years as its Chair, I have become convinced that our methods of credentialling and consumer protection, although flawed, are both necessary and better than no statutory regulation. Increased consumer protection through better education of the consumer to make informed choices about professional services, as well as improved enforcement procedures to prevent continued professional misuse of power, ought to be high priorities for regulatory boards, and the profession in general.

I believe very strongly that the licensing and regulatory issues we debate in the abstract as if they were absolutes are not so simply right or wrong. In the day-to-day review of applicants for licensure, in the handling of complaints and making decisions relative to possible unethical, incompetent, and illegal practice, these issues are no longer abstract. They are part of the personal and professional life of individual aspiring psychologists, already licensed psychologists, and their clients. The resulting discussions on the issues are no longer so clear; they are permeated with shades of gray on all sides.

Thus, although we try to talk about and deal with issues in regulation as if they were black or white, this is just not so in our current state of definitions of education, experience, ethics, and competence. Although this may not be the easiest approach from a legal perspective, perhaps we should stop and truly appreciate the many variations in the shades of gray in our profession and its applications, continuing in our step-by-step fashion to clarify the richness of that shading.

PROFESSIONAL ORGANIZATION INVOLVEMENT

I had never been an organizational person until one day in 1970. I attended a meeting and left the room momentarily during the election of officers. I returned to find myself secretary of the clinical division of the Pennsylvania Psychological Association (PPA). I did not have any real interest in organizational involvement, but one or two issues provided the necessary intriguing hooks. I became the first woman president of the Philadelphia Society of Clinical Psychologists and ultimately President of the PPA. I made personal contact with other state psychological association officers and the American Psychological Association (APA) and began to discover an entire network of professional psychologists concerned and active in similar interests. This kind of support network more than anything else provided the impetus for my continued organizational involvement.

It was legislative activity at the state level that helped to resolve one lingering conflict for me. Working on public interest issues such as programs and services for children, child abuse, and adolescent and family programs always seemed right to me. Working on guild issues to advance the profession initially seemed self-serving and therefore not always quite right. At that time on the national scene, psychologists were increasingly achieving recognition as autonomous providers and many states had "Freedom of Choice" laws. In Pennsylvania, this became our highest priority. As president and later as legislative coordinator, I worked with others for successful passage of this legislation. When we succeeded I felt particularly gratified because this effort for freedom of choice represented to me in one single issue advocacy both for the consumer and the profession. My transformation as a political person was complete. My advocacy conflict was resolved and I now see most issues—managed care, parity, prescriptive authority, services for children and families, child abuse, professional education and training, specialization in psychology—all as both guild and public interest issues. For more than 30 years in APA and other organizations, this view has allowed me to work comfortably from an advocacy perspective on many of these issues.

In my later work on the APA Insurance Trust, I also found there was a differential impact on women of various kinds of insurance, rates and liability coverage (as well as on other groups such as gays and lesbians), and that this differential impact was an important guild and consumer issue needing attention. Much has been accomplished. I currently work on prescriptive authority for psychologists in many places (state, licensing, APA, exam development, etc.) and I do this for two major reasons. It's a guild/scope of practice, issue for psychologists, and a consumer issue for women and children who are often the victims of overmedication. I believe psychologists can do better for them.

In the course of my professional organization advocacy work there have been big lessons and small lessons learned along the way that I continue to find useful.

1. The first small lesson is "Stay in the room" or, if you leave, you'd better be prepared for what may happen in your absence. This is true both literally and figuratively.
2. The second small lesson is "Know when not to talk." I learned this lesson during a hearing on an important legislative matter where I had testified. Our lobbyist had told me he had a guarantee of a majority vote on our issue. An opponent of the bill arose to deliver a tirade against the

bill with distorted information attacking psychology. I started to jump up to respond to the attacks. Our lobbyist pulled me down saying "When you're sure you've got the votes, keep still." This is also true both literally and figuratively.
3. The third small lesson concerns the importance of "conversations that never took place!" In my capacity as Chair of the Licensing Board, I had a conversation one night with the governor's legal counsel, the night before the governor was to sign a bill important to psychology. He told me the governor would not sign the bill and explained the reason. We worked on ways to ensure that what the governor feared would happen if he signed the bill, would not happen. He said he would see what he could do and shortly called me back to say the governor would sign the bill. He ended the conversation with "Remember, we never had these conversations." The governor did sign the bill into law and what he feared never did happen.

I have noted over the years in other venues how many decisions are made and actions taken during "conversations that never took place."

So remember the Bricklin Small Lessons Learned Along the Way: (a) Stay in the Room; (b) Keep still when you've got the votes; and (c) Be mindful of the importance of conversations that never took place.

In all my work at community, state and national levels, the committed dedicated people with whom I've worked have been role models, mentors, and friends. The opportunity to participate as part of this network of concerned and knowledgeable professionals on matters that will affect our profession and the consumers of our services *now*, as well as in the *future*, has been and is a humbling, powerfully moving, sometimes frightening, and always transforming experience. This was the *big* lesson learned along the way.

PROFESSIONAL PSYCHOLOGY EDUCATION AND TRAINING

Since the early 1970s, I have been involved in one way or another with professional graduate education; at Temple University and the Johns Hopkins University training teachers, reading and learning specialists and other school specialists to work with special needs children; at Hahnemann University, and now at the Widener University Institute for Graduate Clinical Psychology, educating and training future psychologists for an uncertain but I believe exciting future. It is in this work that I find an opportunity to integrate and link the other aspects of my professional life. Professional organization advocacy, licensing and credentialling issues, ethics, media work, writing and my work in assessment, intervention and consultation with children, adolescents, teachers, parents in an ecological context, all come together in my work with students. They are my inspiration.

My commitment to them is rooted in my commitment to the future of professional psychology. It has been a privilege to be part of the movement to develop professional programs offering the PsyD degree. Thanks to the vision of Jules C. Abrams, my longtime mentor, I believe we are the oldest PsyD program in the country and the first to have a joint JD/PsyD and PsyD/MBA program. Through my work with the National Council of Schools and Programs in Professional Psychology, both as one of its past presidents, and in other capacities. I am committed to work and advocate for a doctoral level education and training model in professional psychology that is current, relevant to the needs of the 21st century, and grounded in the science of the profession. I am also committed to the continued development, viability, and expansion of the profession of psychology to ensure the availability of positions for our graduates. I am currently serving on a number of future-oriented committees, one especially concerned with training, examination and credentialling issues necessary to expand the scope of practice of psychologists.

It is hard to measure or represent a professional life spent primarily in service and advocacy with the traditional benchmarks of success—research and publications. It would be possible, I guess, to look at professional awards, honorary doctoral degrees and other recognitions received. Although these are certainly important to me, I would rather measure my life by my family, the many successful psychologists, teachers, and reading specialists I have trained and who still check in from time to time, the numbers of licensed psycholgists who feel comfortable enough to call me with legal and ethical questions, and the many people I still meet in unlikely places who say "I remember you and Barry from the radio or TV. I raised my children listening to you" or "You helped me through a very difficult time."

CONCLUSIONS

Working on what has turned out to be the two themes of my life—commitment to service and being in tune with the music of life, I see that my family is the drum and bass line that establishes the "beat" of my life:

Barry for his support, his incredible contributions to clinical psychology in the custody areas, and his communication of the importance of risk taking. Our sons, the two rock musicians, talented singers, songwriters with CDs and music on movie soundtracks who communicate the joys and burdens of talent and what it takes to pursue a dream. Our daughters, one a talented administrative assistant to the director of a clinical psychology program, full of integrity, loyalty, commitment to service who manages with care and skill and is a better psychologist than all of us. The other daughter, who represents the future of psychology, a PsyD and an almost PhD who followed in her parents' career footsteps and did it "her way," representing new service roles for psychology in the navy.

I believe that the integration of the personal and professional transitions and transformations of life is critical.

Marriage, parenting, the media, professional practice, teaching, professional organizations, and licensing and credentialling activities are the important experiences that to date have provided the transitions and transformations of my life. When I think about this, I realize that experience with each of them is part of each of my days ending as Barry and I usually do with a late night dinner where we mutually regenerate.

There are times when family matters have their ups and downs, when graduate students are not challenged and excited, when parents of the child with learning disabilities continue to believe he is stupid, when issues in professional psychology seem unsolvable, when no one cheers the rock musicians, when an applicant has failed the licensure exam by one point and the candles at our late night dinner don't burn so brightly—but not often and not all at once. Most nights the candles burn brightly indeed.

REFERENCES

Bricklin, B., & Bricklin, P. (1966). *Helping your young child to learn*. Philadelphia, PA: WCAU, CBS Radio.

Bricklin, B., & Bricklin, P. (1968). *Reducing negative behavior*. Philadelphia, PA: WCAU, CBS Radio.

Bricklin, B., & Bricklin, P. (1970a). *Improving your child's learning ability*. Philadelphia, PA: WCAU, CBS Radio.

Bricklin, B., & Bricklin, P. (1970b). *Strong family-strong child*. New York: Delacorte.

Bricklin, B., & Bricklin, P. (1977). *Conquering the natural enemies of marriage*. Buckingham, PA: Buckingham.

Bricklin, P. (1984, Fall). Transitions and transformations. *Psychotherapy in Private Practice, 2*, 21–34.

REPRESENTATIVE PUBLICATIONS

Bricklin, B., & Bricklin, P. (1967). *Bright child-poor grades: The psychology of under-achievement*. New York: Delacarte.

Bricklin, B., & Bricklin, P. (1987). Obituary: Zygmunt A. Piotrowski (1904–1985). *American Psychologist, 42*, 261–262.

Bricklin, B., & Bricklin, P. (1999). Custody data as decision-theory information: Evaluating a psychological contribution by its value to a decision maker. *Clinical Psychology, 6,* 339–343.

Bricklin, P. (1961). Implementing the changing concepts in remediation. *International Reading Association Conference Proceedings, 6,* 67–70.

Bricklin, P. (1970). Counseling parents of children with learning disabilities. *The Reading Teacher, 23,* 331–338.

Bricklin, P. (1982). Self-concept, fear of failure and learning disability: An educational/therapeutic approach. *The Disabled Reader, 6,* 1.

Bricklin, P. (1983). Working with parents of learning disabled/gifted children. In L. Fox, et al. (Eds.), *The learning disabled/gifted child* (pp. 243–260). Baltimore: University Park Press.

Bricklin, P. (1984). An ecological approach to assessment. *Spectrum, 1.*

Bricklin, P. (1984). Learning disabilities and emotional disturbances: Critical issues in definition, assessment and service delivery. *Learning Disabilities, 3,* 141–156.

Bricklin, P. (1991). The concept of "Self as learner": Its critical role in the diagnosis and treatment of children with reading disabilities. *Journal of Reading, Writing, and Learning Disabilities International, 3,* 201–215.

Bricklin, P. (1993, May). When ethics are law. *The Pennsylvania Psychologist Quarterly,* 8–9.

Bricklin, P. (1998). Training psychologists for psychotherapy and other interventions with children. *Psychotherapy in Private Practice, 17,* 19–28.

Bricklin, P., & Gallico, R. (1986). Emotional disturbance. In K. Kavale, S. Forness, & M. Bender (Eds.), *Handbook of learning disabilities* (pp. 227–249). New York: Grune and Stratton.

Carlson, C., Tharinger, D., Bricklin, P., DeMers, S., Paavola, J. (1996). Health care reform and psychological practice in schools. *Professional Psychology: Research and Practice, 27,* 14–23.

DeLeon, P., Bennett, B., Bricklin, P. (1997). Ethics and public policy formulation: A case example related to prescription privilege. *Professional Psychology: Research and Practice, 28,* 518–525.

Newman, R., & Bricklin, P. (1990). Parameters of managed mental health care: Legal, ethical and professional guidelines. *Professional Psychology: Research and Practice, 22,* 26–35.

Tharinger, D., Lambert, N., Bricklin, P., Feshbach, N., Johnson, N., Oakland, T., Paster, V., Sanchez, W. (1996). Education reform: Challenges for psychology and psychologist. *Professional Psychology: Research and Practice, 27,* 24–33.

NOTE

1. Parts of this paper have been adapted from an earlier article, Bricklin, P. (1984, Fall). Transitions and transformations. *Psychotherapy in Private Practice, 2,* 21–34.

CHAPTER 5

Frances Degan Horowitz

Photographer: Don Hamerman.

Frances Degen Horowitz

I became a psychologist because I was deemed a troublemaker. The story of how this happened has its roots in the fact that after my graduation in 1954 from Antioch College, with a bachelor's degree and a major in philosophy, I received a Ford Foundation Fellowship to study for a master's degree in elementary education at Goucher College—a program that was a prototype for the eventual development of masters degrees aimed at encouraging liberal arts graduates to pursue the teaching of elementary school as a career.

A couple of months after marrying Floyd Horowitz in 1953, my husband and I made our way to Baltimore and to Goucher College. While he wrote, I studied to become an elementary school teacher. As the 1-year degree program was coming to its end, we decided to relocate to Iowa City, Iowa where my husband had been a member of the Writer's Workshop at the University of Iowa. He wanted to finish that degree and then pursue a doctoral degree in English literature. I applied to the Iowa City public school system and became a fifth-grade teacher at Lincoln School beginning in the fall of 1954.

Entering my fifth grade classroom and fresh from my master's degree, I saw one set of fifth grade readers. "What about those children who might not yet be reading at fifth grade level or those who might be reading at an advanced level?" "Not of concern," the principal said.

"We only use one set of readers in the fifth grade," he said.

"Why?" I asked. "Wouldn't it make sense to give a reading test and provide reading materials suitable to each child's assessed reading level?"

"We don't do reading groups for the fifth grade," he answered. I persisted and finally convinced the school psychologist that I should be allowed to give a reading test. As one might expect, there was a range of tested reading skills among these fifth graders that went from the second- to the eighth-grade level.

My request for appropriate reading material was granted, but only partially. They would provide the books for the children reading *below* grade level but not for those reading *above* grade level. The reason was that it would pose a problem next year for the sixth-grade teacher if the children in my class had read the sixth-grade books or higher level readers. I acquiesced and substituted other materials for the more advanced readers.

Such was my initial encounter with the Iowa City Public School system. Shortly thereafter, I requested days off for the Jewish holidays. There was no policy and no provision. I was one of only two Jewish personnel in the entire school system. I was given the days off but it was clearly a grudging concession.

A little later on, I proposed a field trip for the class. They didn't do that in the Iowa City schools, I was told, and my proposal was rejected. Then I suggested that the fifth graders in my class run a small school supply store on a co-op basis for the entire school. (I had worked in a consumer co-op milk dairy in Wyandotte, Michigan during two work division periods while at Antioch College.) I had the idea that the fifth graders would keep the supply store's books as a kind of mathematics project and, in the process, learn a little about money and economics. The school and neighborhood were not convenient to any stores; the children were always running out of pencils and paper. I thought a co-op school supplies store would be an opportunity for both a service and an instructional program. *This* request went to the school board. Was there a socialist in their midst? Denied.

My first year of teaching ended without any further incident that I can recall. But I was clearly marked and noted. Never mind that my teaching, actually, was successful and I truly enjoyed working with fifth-grade children.

As summer approached, I thought I would take advantage of the presence of the University of Iowa and enroll in some summer courses, but even the modest tuition was beyond our means until one of my teachers from Goucher College, Miss Esther Crane, on hearing I would not be taking any courses because of finances, sent me a check for $75, the cost for summer tuition. When I accepted with gratitude, I assured her I would pay it back. But she demurred. No need to pay her back.

She was sure I would do something similar for someone in the future when I could. And whenever I have been able to do so, I silently remember Miss Esther Crane and the moral IOU I am repaying.

I took two courses during that summer of 1955—one from Boyd McCandless, who was a developmental psychologist and the Director of the Iowa Child Welfare Research Station, and one from Gustav Bergman, the renowned logical positivist philosopher who taught, partially, in the psychology department. Summer over, I returned to teaching fifth grade.

During that second year, active in the Iowa City Teacher's Association, I became its President-elect (1955). (There was no union, but this rather benign organization was regarded with some suspicion by the school district's administration.) However, my appetite was whetted for more study. I decided to see if I could get into a doctoral program and, naturally, because I was a teacher, I thought of pursuing a doctoral degree in the School of Education at the University of Iowa.

Unbeknownst to me, the Superintendent of the Iowa City Schools was a close friend of the Dean of the School of Education. He told the Dean that it would be best not to accept me into the graduate program because I was a troublemaker.

Somehow Boyd McCandless caught wind of this, got in touch with me, and suggested I become a student at the Iowa Child Welfare Research Station. I had no idea that the Iowa Child Welfare Research Station was, at that time, one of the preeminent places to study child and developmental psychology. I had never taken an undergraduate course in psychology; I had never heard of Kenneth Spence, Charlie Spiker, or E. L. Lindquist, all luminaries in their time. I was only dimly aware of the various schools of thought in psychology. I had barely gotten through college math and was scared to death of the prospect of doing statistics.

But with the rejection from the School of Education in hand, if I wanted to continue to study, I had to accept Boyd McCandless' bold and kind invitation—an invitation that was accompanied by the offer of a full fellowship plus tuition.

Thus did chance and opportunity and Esther Crane's $75 come together for a troublemaker in a small university town that operated, in part, on a network of gossip. So it happened that I was to become a psychologist. Never intended it. Never sought it. Never coveted it. Chance and opportunity.

Iowa was then *the* center for the Hull-Spence variety of behaviorism and the Iowa Child Welfare Station represented a mixture of traditions—stimulus–response theory applied to child behavior, classic normative studies of language development, motor development, socialization, and ground-breaking approaches to natural observation, experimental manipulation, and statistical analyses.

Three years later—3 heady years later—having climbed the steepest learning curve I have ever experienced, I had my degree with an observational/experimental dissertation on the reinforcement value of peers as social stimuli for preschool children, having mastered the famed statistics courses of Paul J. Blommers, Everett Franklin Lindquist, and much more.

Boyd McCandless was a developmentalist interested in the process of early socialization. He was my mentor and friend and a great teacher. He was concerned to see me launch a career and advised me to write up my dissertation, for publication. Which I did, in two articles in *Child Development* (Horowitz, 1961, 1962).

Boyd McCandless stayed friend, mentor, and colleague. When he became the founding editor of APA's new journal, *Developmental Psychology*, he invited me on to its editorial board, along with all the then illustrious names of the field. I was barely 8 years past my degree.

Living in Iowa City, a Midwest community, albeit a university town, was an experience in itself. Being Jewish there was to be a stranger in a strange land, a theme that runs through much of my adult life. I had grown up in the Bronx in a neighborhood almost entirely Jewish and in the midst of an extended Degen family of aunts and uncles and cousins—my father's five brothers and sisters—full of Jewish tradition and holidays and rich in ethnic identity, with a good dose of wariness about all that was not Jewish.

It was thus natural that in Iowa City we made friends with fellow New Yorkers, Gerald and Eileen Siegel. Jerry was a doctoral student in speech pathology, studying in the University of Iowa's famed Speech Pathology Department of Wendell Johnson.

Chance and opportunity. When Jerry finished his degree he went further west to North Dakota and then was invited to go to Parsons, Kansas where the University of Kansas, under the aegis of its Bureau of Child Development and its director, speech pathologist Richard Schiefelbusch, was initiating some of the earliest of behavioral studies of children with retardation in an institution for the retarded. When Jerry went to Kansas, my husband and I were on our way to Oregon with our 9-week-old son and our dog, to Southern Oregon College and Oregon's rules prohibiting the employment of two members of the same family.

But I did do some teaching, I wrote up my dissertation for publication, and I got a grant from Sigma Xi to do some research (Horowitz, 1962). Toward the end of our first year in Oregon, Jerry recommended to Dick Schiefelbusch that I be invited to Parsons, Kansas on a summer research fellowship they had available. Eager for the research opportunity and delighted to be again with our friends, we relocated to Parsons, Kansas for the summer.

During that time, Dick Schiefelbusch took my husband and me to Lawrence, Kansas for a look around the campus of the University of Kansas. Chance and opportunity. For, unbeknownst to us, Dick Schiefelbusch was hatching a plan. He had his eye on me for joining him at the University of Kansas in the Bureau of Child Research. He had a good relationship with George Waggoner, legendary Dean of the University of Kansas' College of Arts and Sciences. Schiefelbusch arranged for my husband to visit with some of the people in the English Department. The university was expanding and Dick had ideas for grand schemes.

We went back to Oregon, unaware of any of this plotting. But in May of the next spring, a phone call from George Waggoner to my husband came with the offer of a position in the English department. I called Dick Schiefelbusch and asked him if there would be anything for me to do if we came. Kansas, too, had a nepotism rule. He said that something would work out. When we got there, Dick Schiefelbusch gave me a desk in the Bureau of Child Research and found somewhere $100 a month for me, effectively covering baby-sitting expenses. Our second son had been born just before we left Oregon.

It was 1961 when we went to Kansas. We intended to remain a few years and then move on somewhere else—there was the nepotism rule and perhaps we might go to a place where we would not again be strangers in a strange land. Dick encouraged me to apply for a Public Health Service Post-Doctoral Fellowship. It enabled me to embark on some research. There was talk that the nepotism ruling was going to be eliminated and within three years Kansas' nepotism rule was history, as they say.

Once this happened, interesting events began to unfold that led, ultimately, to my taking on the creation of what became the Department of Human Development and Family Life, fashioned according to a vision that I had outlined for Dean George Waggoner. The founding of this department involved an unbelievably fruitful partnership with the Bureau of Child Research and Richard Scheifelbusch.

When we finally left Kansas in 1991, we had spent the sum of 30 years at the University of Kansas and in Lawrence. In those 30 years my husband and I grew up professionally, we raised our family, and we became deeply involved in community. Over the course of those 30 years, I evolved as a behavioral scientist and psychologist.

Having studied at the University of Iowa, I was steeped in behaviorism and in the methodology of group design and analysis. So I think it a bit curious that soon after arriving in Kansas, I found my scientific interests gravitating toward issues related to individual differences—not the typical individual differences of assessment and testing, but individual differences in relation to how similar experiences and environments have differential impact on the development of different children.

Chance and opportunity again played a part. Piagetian theory was sweeping through the field of child development and with it a special focus on infants. But I was not so much interested in what I called the "gee whiz" study of infants, seeing what infants could do that we thought they could not do. Rather, I wanted to look at the individual differences in infants and how they responded to the environment and, ultimately, as my ideas developed, how matches between a child and his or her environment shaped development (Horowitz, 1969). I also grew more convinced of the necessity of a truly developmental approach where we would have to track these transactions developmentally if we were going to be able to explain developmental outcomes.

Realizing the importance of trying to study individual differences as early in life as possible, and with the federal research funding emphasis in the 1960s and 1970s on young children, I decided to develop an infant research laboratory. With a succession of excellent graduate student colleagues, we embarked on a series of somewhat parametric studies of infant visual attention and discrimination. While doing these studies, using the standard procedure of exposing a stimulus for a set period of time (20 seconds) it became clear that some of the babies looked at the stimulus for as long as it was presented, while others looked for a smaller number of seconds and seemed to be done with the stimulus.

I suggested we try leaving the stimulus on only for as long as the infant was looking. If the infant looked away for as much as 2 seconds, that would become the signal to move on to the next stimulus presentation. We called this strategy for studying infant visual attention the "infant control procedure"—letting the infant control the duration of the stimulus presentation. When we did this some infants were done with a stimulus after only 5 or 10 seconds; others looked for 20 or 30 seconds, sometimes a minute and even longer (Horowitz et al., 1972a, 1972b).

This permitted us to discover a very robust phenomenon that is now widely recognized: In the early months of life it was already to be seen that there are infants who are consistently short-lookers; there are infants who are consistently long-lookers. Refining the analyses even further, we demonstrated that the most reliable index of infant-looking behavior is the peak looking time during the infant control procedure (Horowitz, Tims, & McCluskey, 1974; Colombo & Horowitz, 1985).

The long- and short-looking characteristic increased my interest in pursuing individual differences research. I was looking for even earlier measures when, through chance and opportunity, made possible by being a part of the research associated with the federally funded Early

Childhood Research Laboratory program at Kansas, I came into association with pediatrician T. Berry Brazelton. Brazelton had used his superb clinical eyes to observe variations in newborn infant behavior. Picking up some of the items from the Graham-Rosenblith Scale and using his clinical intuition, he began to develop a systematic newborn observational strategy. I joined Arnie Sameroff, Ed Tronick, and several others to work with Brazelton to devise a reliable assessment, scale, using Brazelton's initial work. The result was the Neonatal Behavioral Assessment Scale, or the Brazelton Scale (Brazelton, 1973).

There were a number of challenges in developing this assessment. Defining the items and achieving reliability in the scoring of the items were clearly tasks to be done. Much more important, however, were the moral and philosophical issues that were involved. Here we were developing an assessment that could be done in the first month of life. Indeed, it can be done with a normal one-day-old infant. How might such an assessment be used and misused? Concerned about the potential misuse of a measurement scale for newborn infants we set out, deliberately, to make sure that it was not possible, from the way in which the items were set-up and scored, to derive a single number from the test. Indeed, we set out to make sure the scale was something of a psychometric nightmare. The definitions of optimal newborn behavior were organized so that for some items optimal was at the low end of the 9-point scoring scale; for others at the high end; for others in the middle.

We did this deliberately. I and the others involved did not wish to be party to creating an assessment that could produce a single number that could be assigned to an infant only a few days of age. We did not want to be party to creating an assessment that could be misused in the way so many psychometric instruments in our field have been.

All of us involved in the development of the scale agreed about preventing misuse by making it impossible to add up the individual scale scores, some of us feeling more passionate than others. But on some other matters we were not in agreement, specifically in relation to prediction. There were some who envisioned that performance on the Brazelton in the first few days of life would correlate with performance on something else in later months and years and be predictive of developmental outcome. Much of the thrust of testing and assessment has been for the purposes of prediction. Brazelton wanted very much for this evaluation to become part of the pantheon of predictive instruments.

I disagreed with this as a goal on theoretical grounds, and from the beginning expressed doubt and skepticism that the assessment would be ever predictive of anything of significance. I made sure, in true troublemaking form, to do so publicly and in writing at every opportunity. The theoretical basis for my position rested on my view that development is all about multiple variables functioning in a dynamic equation over time. From this perspective there is no reason to believe that a newborn assessment will have any long-term predictive value—except perhaps in the case of a severely compromised organism (Horowitz & Linn, 1982; Horowitz, Sullivan, & Linn, 1978).

Or put another way, developmental outcome is the result of complex variables operating over time in an equation—for example: A + B × C—taken to the nth power divided by D. If this equation is dynamic over time, a measure of "A" in this equation at birth would not permit you to predict later developmental outcome with any degree of confidence (Horowitz & Linn, 1982; Horowitz, Linn, & Buddin, 1983).

Developmental outcome, from my perspective, is not predictable unless you know the nature of a large number of the variables in the equation, how they interact, and how they will change over time both in absolute values and in relationship to one another. There are, of course, known conditions that constrain the functions of the equation. A child born with Down's syndrome is likely to have diminished intellectual development across the life span. Though even here, very targeted environmental intervention can ameliorate the degree of diminishment and some day physiological intervention may also be possible (Horowitz, 1984, 1985, 1987a, 1987b).

This brings me to what I consider my major interest and, potentially, contribution—being a voice on behalf of a model and theory of development that assumes developmental outcome, at any point, will ultimately be accounted for by an equation of interacting variables involving organismic or constitutional factors and experiential factors (Horowitz, 1987a, 1987b, 1990, 1992).

Please note that I use the words *organismic* and *constitutional* and not *genetic*. Organismic (or constitutional) refers to a package of variables that includes genes, biological functioning, and the effect of environmental variables on biological functioning, such as nutrition, toxins, radiation, alcohol, tobacco smoke, stress, abuse, disease, injury, physical insult, and more.

I consider an emphasis only on the genes in this constitutional package, and the ascribing of percentages to genetic influence quite wrong-headed and in our current context, socially irresponsible. I think current efforts to give percentages for genetic influences are socially irresponsible in the same way that I and others were socially irresponsible when we signed up with enthusiasm for the war on poverty in the 1970s (Horowitz, 1993).

As developmental psychologists engaged in that war, we were very certain of the power of the kinds of environmental interventions we specified to affect positively the developmental outcome of poor children. We were full of dreams about what we would and could accomplish and we promised much. Our zeal was driven by a naive environmentalism: Assuming more power for the few variables over which we had control than they and we possibly could have had; grand overgeneralizations that were not truly supportable by the science we knew.

In the end, we achieved much less than we thought we would. But also, in the end, this exercise of naive environmentalism did much damage to the nurture side of the nature–nurture debate. It claimed too much and could deliver too little. We over-promised what we could not possibly achieve. In doing so, we contributed to the discrediting of the environmental position and to paving the way for the credibility of an equally simplistic genetic model—a naive hereditarianism (Horowitz, 1996).

That genetic model is now in ascendance. Every-time someone discovers a gene for something, the headline proclaims it as one more piece of evidence for genetic determinism. At the same time, in the body of the article, one finds that the amount of variance that can be accounted for by the discovered gene is often modest. Nevertheless, there is a hunger out there for the kind of certainty that genetic determinism promises—a kind of simplicity that encourages those who would rather not support the difficult science that would help us understand the nature of the experiences and environments that interact with constitutional variables to determine developmental outcome. This attractive simplicity can contribute to a social zeitgeist in the United States, most especially, of ominous import (Horowitz, 2000).

In 1978, I delivered the Presidential address to Division 7 (APA's Division of Developmental Psychology) on individual differences. I proposed an early version of a model of development that eventually evolved into what I call the structural/behavioral model of development. In this model, an organismic/constitutional dimension interacts with an experiential dimension, with provision for a very complex set of combinations and permutations in different developmental domains at different periods of development.

I will leave out the complexities and convolutions. In every venue where I have discussed, used, or presented this model, I have been at pains to note that the organismic or, as I now prefer, the constitutional dimension, is *not* an equivalent of a genetic dimension. Yet several years ago when I was asked by two textbook writers for permission to reprint the model in their text, I discovered that they intended to change the label on the *constitutional* dimension of the model from *organismic* to *genetic*. Obviously, I did not give my permission.

Subsequently, the model was used in a variant form by one of the authors in an oral presentation—without attribution, I might add—to make the case for genetic determinism. I am amazed at how strong this drive is to fit the complexity of human development into a model that is balanced toward genetic determinism, although lip service in these discussions is usually given to environmental influence.

Yet the data are building in support of the kind of structural/behavioral model I have espoused, and I should note, for some aspects of Donald Hebb's (1949) original model related to learning and neurological organization. There is evidence being entered into the debate among those working in the context of a dynamical systems model. Some critical evidence is coming from studies in the neurosciences, especially those demonstrating that experience reorganizes the brain and neurological functioning. For example, learning to read, in children *and* in adults, produces demonstrable changes in neurological organization and functioning.

When asked to evaluate what I think will have been my contribution to child development and developmental psychology, I would cite the work I have done on infant attention and with the Neonatal Behavioral Assessment Scale. But, I would probably give more emphasis to my efforts to articulate a model and speak on behalf of a theory about development that recognizes the complexity of the interactions and transactions between constitutional and experiential variables in determining development outcomes (Horowitz, 2000).

Perhaps I might cite some of the roles I have played in our science: in writing, editing, fostering organizations, and giving leadership to the venues where we share our science. Some of it has been of the troublemaking kind by being a voice advocating against simplistic explanations, challenging prevailing formulations, using position and opportunity to make sure other voices of challenge would be heard, or provided a platform. Some of this troublemaking was subtle, some not. A lot of what I have done has been to take advantage of the chance and opportunity that was provided by people who have given me a hand along the way—often an almost unseen hand. In turn, I had the chance and opportunity to work with talented graduate students and post-doctoral students who became colleagues and friends.

Growing up, even into and past college, even up to the moment of entering graduate study in psychology, I never intended to be a psychologist. As a philosophy major at Antioch College, I thought of psychology as a very difficult subject. But coming to developmental psychology started me on journey that has led me, in some ways, back to philosophy, to the roots of ideas and systems of thought that shape how one thinks about science and its social construction. It is not exactly a grand tour ending up where one began, but in my case it has been a journey full of satisfaction, chance, and opportunity—most notably influenced by Miss Esther Crane's so very generous gift of $75 to someone in Iowa City, Iowa, deemed to have been a troublemaker.

REFERENCES

Brazelton, T., Freedman, D., Horowitz, F., Koslowski, B., Robey, M., Ricciuti, H., & Sameroff, A. (1973). *Neonatal Behavioral Assessment Scale.* London: Wm. Heinemann Books Ltd.

Colombo, J., & Horowitz, F. D. (1985). A parametric study of the infant control procedure. *Infant Behavior and Development, 8,* 117–121.

Hebb, D.O. (1949). *The organization of behavior.* New York: Wiley.

Horowitz, F. D. (1961). Latency of sociometric choice among preschool children. *Child Development, 32,* 235–242.

Horowitz, F. D. (1962). Incentive value of social stimuli for preschool children. *Child Development, 33,* 111–116.

Horowitz, F. D. (1962). The relationship of anxiety, self-concept, and sociometric status among fourth, fifth and sixth grade children. *Journal of Abnormal Social Psychology, 65,* 212–214.

Horowitz, F. D. (1969). Learning, developmental research, and individual differences. In L. P. Lipsitt & H. W. Reese (Eds.), *Advances in child development and behavior* (Vol. 4, pp. 84–126). New York: Academic Press.

Horowitz, F. D., Paden, L. Y., Bhana, K., & Self, P. (1972a). An "infant control" procedure for studying infant visual fixations. *Developmental Psychology, 7,* 90–92.

Horowitz, F. D., Paden, L., Bhana, K., Atchison, R., & Self, P. (1972b). Developmental changes in infant visual fixations to differing complexity levels among cross-sectionally and longitudinally-studied infants. *Developmental Psychology, 7,* 88–89.

Horowitz, F.D., Tims, S. M., & McCluskey, K.A. (1974). Duration of visual fixation to different black and white checkerboard stimuli. In F. D. Horowitz (Ed.), Visual attention, auditory stimulation and language discrimination in young infants. *Monographs of the Society for Research in Child Development, 39,* 116–120.

Horowitz, F. D., Sullivan, J. W., & Linn, P. (1978). Stability and instability in newborn infants: The quest for elusive threads. In A. Sameroff (Ed.), Organization and stability of newborn behavior: A commentary on the Brazelton Neonatal Behavioral Assessment Scale. *Monographs of the Society for Research in Child Development, 43,* 29–45.

Horowitz, F. D., Linn, P. L., & Buddin, B.J. (1983). Neonatal assessment: Evaluating the potential for plasticity. In T. B. Brazelton & B. Lester (Eds.), *New approaches to developmental screening of infants* (pp. 27–50). New York: Elsevier.

Horowitz, F. D., & Linn, P. L. (1982). The Neonatal Behavioral Assessment Scale. In M. Wolrich & D. K. Routh (Eds.), *Advances in developmental pediatrics* (Vol. 3, pp. 233–255). Greenwich, CT: JAI.

Horowitz, F. D. (1984). The psychobiology of parent-offspring situations. In L. P. Lipsitt & C.Rovee-Collier (Eds.), *Advances in infancy research* (Vol. 3, pp. 1–22). New York: Ablex.

Horowitz, F. D. (1985). *Making models of development.* Washington, DC: Zero to Three.
Horowitz, F. D. (1987a). *Exploring developmental theories: Toward a structural/behavioral model of development.* Hillsdale, NJ: Lawrence Erlbaum Associates.
Horowitz, F. D. (1987b). Targeting infant stimulation efforts: Theoretical challenges for research and intervention. In N. Gunzenhauser (Ed.), *Infant stimulation,* Pediatric Roundtable 13 (pp. 97–108). Skillman, NJ: Johnson & Johnson Baby Products Co.
Horowitz, F. D. (1990). Developmental models of individual differences. In J. Colombo and J. Fagan (Eds.), *Individual differences in infancy: Reliability, stability and prediction* (pp. 3–18). Hillsdale, NJ: Lawrence Erlbaum Associates.
Horowitz, F. D. (1992) The concept of risk: A reevaluation. In S. L. Friedman and M. D. Sigman (Eds.), *The psychological development of low birthweight children* (pp. 61–88). Norwood, N.J.: Ablex Publishing Corp.
Horowitz, F. D. (1993). Bridging the gap between nature and nurture: A conceptually flawed issue and the need for a comprehensive new environmentalism. In R. Plomin and G. E. McClearn (Eds.), *Nature, nurture and psychology* (pp. 341–353). Washington, DC: APA Books.
Horowitz, F. D. (1996). Facts, truth and social responsibility: Reflections of a developmental scientist. In Strozier, C. B. and Flynn, M. (Eds.), *Trauma and the self* (pp. 81–94). Savage, MD: Rowman and Littlefield Publishers, Inc.
Horowitz, F. D. (2000). Child Development & the PITS: Simple questions, complex answers and developmental theory. *Child Development, 70,* 1.

REPRESENTATIVE PUBLICATIONS

Colombo, J., Mitchell, D. W., O'Brien, M., & Horowitz, F. D. (1987). The stability of visual habituation during the first year of life. *Child Development, 58,* 474–487.
Horowitz, F. D. (Ed.) (1974). Visual attention, auditory stimulation and language discrimination in young infants. *Monographs of the Society for Research in Child Development, 39,* 5–6.
Horowitz, F. D., & Linn, L. P. (1984). Recent NBAS research –The use of the scale in research. In T. B Brazelton, *Neonatal Behavioral Assessment Scale* (pp. 97–104). Clinics in Developmental Medicine. Philadelphia, PA: Lippincott.
Horowitz, F. D., & O'Brien, M. (Eds.). (1985). *The gifted and the talented: Developmental perspectives.* Washington, DC: American Psychological Association.
Horowitz, F. D., & O'Brien, M. (1986). Developmental determinants and child health behavior: Research priorities. In N. Krasnegor, M. Cataldo, & J. D. Aresteh (Eds.), *Child health behavior: A behavioral pediatrics perspective.* New York: Wiley.
Horowitz, F. D. (1988). A Jewish woman in academic America. In S. Brehm (Ed.), *Seeing female: Reflections by women scholars* (pp. 53–65). Westport, CT: Greenwood Press.

Horowitz, F. D., & O'Brien, M. (1989). Children as futures: In the interest of the nation. *The American Psychologist, 44,* 441–445.
Horowitz, F. D., (1990). The multiple partnership: Scientist, university, agency and government. *The American Psychologist, 45,* 51–53.
Horowitz, F. D. (1990). Developmental models of individual differences. In J. Colombo & J. Fagen (Eds.), *Individual differences in infancy: Reliability, stability and prediction* (pp. 3–18). Hillsdale, NJ: Lawrence Erlbaum Associates.
Horowitz, F. D. (1992). John B. Watson's legacy: Learning and environment. *Developmental Psychology, 28* (pp. 360–367). Reprinted in R. D. Parke, P. A. Ornstein, J. J. Rieser, and C. Zahn-Waxler (Eds.), (1994). *A Century of Developmental Psychology.* Washington, D.C. (pp. 233–247).
Horowitz, F. D. (1995). The nature nurture controversy in social and historical perspective. In F. Kessel (Ed.), *Psychology, science, and human affairs: Essays in honor of William Bevan.* Boulder, CO: Westview Press.
Horowitz, F. D., & Haritos, C. (1998). The organization and the environment: implications for understanding mental retardation. In J. A. Burack, R. M. Hodapp, & E. Zigler (Eds.), *Handbook of mental retardation and development* (pp. 20–40). New York: Cambridge University Press.
Horowitz, F. D. (2000). Child development & the PITS: Simple questions, complex answers, and developmental theory. *Child Development, 70,* 1.
Spencer, M. B., & Horowitz, F. D. (1973). The effects of systematic social and token reinforcement on the modification of racial and color concept attitudes in black and white preschool children. *Developmental Psychology, 9,* 246–254.

CHAPTER 6

Norine G. Johnson

Photographer: unavailable.

Norine G. Johnson

FAMILY LORE: I'M GOING TO HELP THEM GET OUT

Just as the turning points in the lives of the women in my family shaped them, so did their responses to life's opportunities and tragedies shape my professional life. One of my family stories occurred when I was about 10. We were taking a Sunday family drive. It would have been the summer of 1945 or 1946 when having enough gasoline to put in a car was a new luxury. We lived by the White River in Indianapolis, Indiana, in a suburb built at the start of World War II. But that day, we were driving by the White River where it meandered downtown, and I saw some dark, threateningly looming structures across the river. I asked my parents what they were and was told they were "the projects." When I asked, "What are the projects?" my parents answered, "Where poor people live." According to family lore, I replied, "I'm going to help them get out."

WOMEN IN MY EARLY LIFE

I was born during the Depression. My parents would talk about choices, such as whether to make a payment on my father's newly acquired dental equipment or pay the electric bill. Until the day she died, my mother would not eat bananas or spaghetti, two foods on which she subsisted during the "hard years." But she also described how all of their friends would get together on Sundays, pool their money, buy a roast, pile the babies on the beds surrounded by coats so they wouldn't fall off, play cards, dance, and have a feast. My mother taught me that fun is an important part of life and can strengthen us during bad times.

Education was of prime importance in my family. Educating women was valued; my paternal great-grandmother was the 4th woman in Indiana to graduate college. My mother, Marie Collins Goode, was a college graduate, a journalist, a social worker, and later a teacher. She obtained her master's degree while I was in college. She modeled for me both the importance of getting an education and using it to help others. One of the places she taught was Fruitville, Florida, where the migrant workers would enroll their children just for the season. She went to their homes to work with them after school. She bought them books and clothes, and she invented new ways to make learning interesting. Following surgery when she was in her late seventies, she was admitted to a nursing home in Florida. I was there when the young receptionist came flying into the room and said, "I heard Marie Goode was here. She taught me how to write. I just wanted to say hello and thank her."

My father, Frank Oakes Goode, was a dentist who loved children. He used his plaster of paris equipment to make storybook characters like *Pinnochio* for his child patients. They would watch the toy being made while he worked on their teeth. Then, either he would paint it for them or the older ones would paint their own. My memory is that they always left smiling.

The most important woman to influence my life was my grandmother, Verna Gentry Collins Derby. When Verna was 28 years old in 1915, her husband, John Collins, was killed in an ambush. He was the sheriff in Berea, Kentucky and had arrested a man to breakup a feud. The man's brothers killed my grandfather. At 28, my grandmother had 4 children, ages 8 to 18 months, having married at age 16. She had home-making skills and little money. Her telling of her undiagnosed depression is chilling. "I was sitting at the kitchen table with the children. It was 6 months after John died. And I looked at the head of the table and he wasn't there. I had set a plate for him. I hadn't needed to cook because the neighbors would leave food at the back door. And I said to myself, "Verna, you silly fool, he's dead. Now get on with it."

My grandmother made the decision to go to nursing school in Louisville, Kentucky. I have a picture on my home office wall of my grandmother in her nursing uniform, and questions from her story have guided my career. How did she do that? Where do women with few material resources find the strength to persevere and succeed while maintaining families and friends? How can we as a society, as a profession, develop the knowledge base and skills to help young girls and women develop these strengths?

EDUCATION

I chose DePauw University in Greencastle, Indiana because of its outstanding liberal arts education and well-respected psychology department. For the first time, I became aware of gender discrimination. DePauw only accepted applications from women in the top third of their high school class whereas men applicants need only be in the top half. Scholarships were for men. Initially I was angry; later I was elected Vice President of the University Senate, and I tried to change some of the more egregious rules.

Skinner's (1953) work had a major impact on us as psychology students. I can still picture the "basketball court" we designed. Carolyn Uhlinger and I taught our rats to compete and score points by pushing silver balls into round holes at each end of a "court" to simulate opposing baskets. Others would come down to the psychology basement lab and cheer us on. One of the tenets I now take to leadership positions and my professional roles within psychology is that it is possible to work hard, do good, and have fun.

In my senior year, I took an honors course in the history of psychology with Felix Goodson that transformed me to another level in my love and appreciation of psychology. We met in a small, intimate setting with a fireplace. I remember the respect with which he treated our ideas. I still wanted to be a professional psychologist, but I now wanted to make a significant contribution to the science that underpinned our practice.

After leaving college, I married and put my plans for graduate school on hold while my husband built his career and we started a family. Being a supportive wife and a parent was extremely important to me. We moved 4 times, about every 18 months for 6 years to advance his business career. Cammarie was born in 1960 in Detroit, Michigan, and Kathryn in 1963 in Cleveland, Ohio. I was a full-time mom for the first 4 years of Cam's life, and the struggle balancing my professional life and parenting started when Kathie was 9 months. For me as a woman with a family, children, and later a mother to care for, integrating my personal and professional life was always difficult. In the beginning, the only way I could do it was by isolating the two parts of my life. When I was with my family, I didn't think about school and when I was in school or studying, I tried hard not to let thoughts and images of my family interrupt my concentration. I was equally dedicated to both and loved both with a passion.

I wanted to be a knowledgeable, skilled, clinical psychologist. I wanted to do psychotherapy and I also wanted to write books about the psychology of children. We had just moved back to the Detroit area, and I contacted old friends to advise me about graduate school. During the summer of 1964, I enrolled in the clinical psychology program at Wayne State University in Detroit, Michigan.

My friends recommended I talk to Professor Frank Auld who was chair of the Clinical Psychology Department at Wayne State University. He asked penetrating questions about what I wanted, what my experiences were, and how I might manage it all. I felt heard and supported. The program was planned so that students could work part time with all the doctoral classes occurring on Tuesdays and Thursdays. That fit perfectly with my desire to both parent and complete my doctorate. I was accepted as a student in the clinical psychology program and was awarded a National Institute of Mental Health scholarship that allowed me to pay for quality child care and my books. Perhaps most of all, the scholarship gave me confidence in my ability.

I received my doctorate in psychology in 1972 with a major in clinical psychology and a minor in child development. Carolyn Shantz, nee Uhlinger, my former DePauw rat basketball-playing friend, was a professor at the Merrill Palmer Institute of Child Development. Her teaching and the early works of Piaget (1952) had a significant influence on my specialization in child psychology.

I became immersed in the world of psychology. I studied each night from 10:00 p.m. until 2:00 a.m. after our children were in bed and the housework was done. I remember it was an unreal, encapsulated time. I enjoyed my children and their activities during the day and early evening. Also, I was being paid to do the intellectual tasks I loved most, study psychology, think about psychology, talk about psychology, ask psychological questions, and totally submerge myself in our research and literature.

I had an assessment practicum at Beth Israel Hospital in Detroit under the supervision of Lamar Gardner. He was a master clinician and a demanding teacher. He taught me the value of life-long learning. I now read everything I can get my hands on, and seek supervision or consultation before I start practicing in a new area. I also learned the importance of knowing when to deviate from protocol.

I was assigned to a recently self-admitted patient. I was expected to do a full battery, complete interview, Wechsler Adult Intelligence Scale, Rorschach, TAT, etc. However, Dr. Gardner pulled me aside and said, "Do not ask this man anything about his history other than 'Why now did you decide to come into the hospital?' Give him the Rorschach only but do no inquiries of responses." When I asked the patient this question, he replied, "It's the safest place in town for me tonight. I will be leaving in the morning." I administered the Rorschach as directed and left. As far as I know, that's the closest I've come to a member of the Mafia.

During my second year at Wayne, our third daughter, Margaret, was born. Her birth illustrates the survival technique of separating school and family. I went into the early stages of labor the morning of my last final that semester, analysis of variance. My husband and I went to the class and persuaded the professor to let me take the exam but in another room from the other students. After 3 hours, I turned in the exam and we went to the hospital. Margaret was born later than afternoon. I was tired but she was wonderful, healthy, and beautiful.

My master's and doctoral research involved looking at how children's perceptions of social cues are influenced by their past reinforcement histories. This research took me to the projects of Detroit and it was reminiscent of my early memories of Indiana. Reuben Barron, a social psychologist, was my dissertation advisor. I spent a summer mainly with the teens and in the youth center but also having coffee with their mothers. Toward the end of the summer, a new friend advised me to leave early and not come back. That night the riots started in Detroit and there were fires throughout the city.

After completing my course work and successfully passing the orals, my husband's employer transferred him again and we moved from Detroit to Cleveland, Ohio. Dr. Auld's colleague from Yale, Marvin Wasman, was the Director of Psychology at University Hospitals and offered me an APA-approved, NIMH-funded clinical internship with a specialization in child psychology.

At University Hospitals, I received top-quality training in child therapy, and I am particularly indebted to Ehud Koch for his talent in pushing me to excellence. His intolerance of mediocrity was balanced by his message that he knew you could do better. He also noticed my innovative side and encouraged its growth by asking me to stay on for a postinternship year. I was assigned as a consultant to pediatrics, neurology, and endocrinology departments. In that position I became the first "pediatric psychologist" at University Hospitals, although at that time psychology leaders such as Logan Wight were only starting to develop the concept of a discipline of pediatric psychology.

We saw over 200 patients a day in the clinics. I devised screening measures for depression, anxiety, parenting, and other psychological conditions and adapted them to the population. I learned how to succinctly consult with medical staff and received positive feedback for clear and concise formulations of the issues and pragmatic recommendations. After only 9 months, I left the position because my husband had accepted a job in Boston. I regretted leaving Cleveland, where the children were in schools that matched their individual needs, where we had lots of friends and a place in the community, and where I was thriving in an exciting innovative position.

CAREER DEVELOPMENT

Getting a new job was difficult. I knew no one in Boston. None of my mentors had talked to me about the importance of networking, and joining my national and state psychological associations. Using my survival technique of compartmentalizing family and profession, I took a year off to get everyone settled, found schools and community resources, explored historic Boston, met neighbors, and had lots of out-of-town visitors. Then I was ready to get a job. I took a position as the Director of Psychology at Kennedy Memorial Hospital for Children. Kennedy was a rehabilitation hospital with 100 inpatient beds, a day school from kindergarten through eighth grade, and unlimited outpatient potential and offered me an opportunity to expand on the skills I was developing in pediatric and clinical child psychology.

In addition to myself, the department consisted of one master's level psychologist and 25% of a Neurology Department secretary's time. When I left in 1988, 18 years later, the Psychology Department had 35 staff positions. All of the senior staff were licensed doctoral psychologists, and, the junior staff were former interns in postdoctoral positions. In the early years at Kennedy, the department was like a family. I'll always have fond memories of those days.

Seventy-five percent of the child patients, although they carried neurological diagnosis, today would be considered with DSM IV diagnoses of Post Traumatic Stress Disorder, conduct disorder, mood disorders, as well as Attention Deficient Hyperactivity Disorder, the autism spectrum, learning disabilities, seizure disorders, head trauma, Tourettes, etc. These children were also from our poorest neighborhoods and frequently came from disorganized homes.

I had the opportunity to "help out" this population and make a contribution consistent with the goals fostered by my early history. I set about quickly to change certain policies and procedures such as expanding visiting hours for parents and incorporating families into the nursing units and therapeutic programs. I developed and learned how a policy servicing the public's needs with fiscal responsibility starts a positive chain reaction.

We developed a full service psychological assessment program, including neuropsychology, medical units and school consultative services, and an integrated treatment program (ABCS Psychological Services) for children and families. ABCS integrated the major approaches—psychodynamic (affective), behavioral, cognitive, and family (systemic) for children with the multiple problems of our population.

Our training programs developed a national reputation and gave me the opportunity to become a teacher, like my mother, thus fulfilling one of my life goals. We offered organized practicum, APA-approved internship, and postdoctoral training experiences. Many staff members came as interns whereas others came as staff into newly created positions as we expanded into family psychology and neuropsychology. Most became leaders in Massachusetts psychology and have remained colleagues and friends: John Anderson, Elizabeth Baker, John Baker, Jim Barron, Charlie Brown, Jeff Colluci, Bob Coutu, Jack Jordan, Don Manthie, Roslin Moore, Leon Monnin, Marsha Padwa, and Jessica Wolfe, are a few. Mrs. Eleanor Jordan, Head Secretary, kept us going with her organizational skills and the humor of Emma Brombeck.

In 1975, another major opportunity occurred that gave me the knowledge base and tools to integrate business practices into my work and later organizational work, such as the American Psychological Association. I was accepted into a two-year continuing education program in Mental Health Administration and Planning, jointly sponsored by the Harvard Medical and Business schools and designed to train future commissioners of mental health. A colleague, Dr. Gersh Rosenbaum, a regional director for the Massachusetts Department of Mental Health and Retardation, recommended me for the program.

I also had the opportunity to develop a course unit titled, *Women Administrators*. As with Harvard's advanced programs, the content was outstanding and the opportunities for networking were excellent. But I was aware of gender biases. Another woman and myself commented on the limited number of women in the course and the lack of women administrators and women's issues in the material being covered. We were challenged to develop a module to be included in the course that formed the base of my later writing and continuing education presentations on business practices for women and women entrepreneurs.

In 1976, Dr. Robert Feldman, Chair of the Department of Neurology, Boston University Medical School, offered me a position as Clinical Assistant Professor that I still hold. I taught neurology, pediatric, and orthopedic medical students, interns and residents for more than 12 years. The Psychology Department had sufficient respect within the hospital so that we were consulted on major medical decisions involving admission, discharge, and treatment, including medication. Other appointments were Adjunct Faculty Member at the Massachusetts School of Professional Psychology from 1978 to 1988 and Adjunct Associate Professor in the Department of Counseling Psychology at Boston College from 1978 to 1981.

During this time, using new neuropsychological understandings of children my scholarly contributions included innovative approaches to assessment and treatment of children with emotional, physical, and/or learning disabilities. The hospital developed a continuing education program for the community, and I presented at state and national conferences. I also advocated through appointments to the regional and state mental health commissions for public policies that addressed the needs of children and their families.

Opportunities arose for me to actualize my life goals of empowering children, teaching, and improving financial resources. In January of 1988, I left Kennedy (now Franciscan Hospital for Children) to go into full-time private practice. Over the previous 10 years, I had built a small part-time practice. John Malloy, EdD, Director of Special Education, Braintree Public Schools had made me an offer I couldn't refuse. I used to advise students and interns that sometimes in your career, a train comes along that you can't afford to miss. This was my time to act on that philosophy.

In August of 1987, John Malloy asked, "Norine, if you could teach anything you wanted to all the special education administrators in southeast Massachusetts, what would that course look like?" I was on vacation, my mind was free and for 20 minutes, I talked about a dream program for children with neurological dysfunction that would allow them to go to school in their community instead of having to go to a hospital, residential home, or a day school.

When he called at the end of September, his message was short. "They like it but we need it in writing with dollars attached. Could you get it to me next Tuesday?" Two months later we signed a contract. I left the hospital with the exciting prospect of helping to move services for children into the community, doing so by teaching professionals in public schools the psychological principles we had developed for educating and treating children and their families.

When asked if it is scary to leave the security of a paid position for the uncertainty of self-employment, I describe the experience as walking off a challenging high cliff during total darkness and waking up to find oneself surrounded by fields of flowers, bright clouds, and sunshine. Even with the disruptive and disturbing effects of managed care on patient care, I have never regretted the decision to go into independent practice.

Being a psychologist has offered me many opportunities for multiple routes and branches in my career journey rather than a single, well-trodden path. Currently I have four psychology businesses, ABCS (Affect, Behavior, Cognition, Systems) Psych Resources, Access for Change, JPP (Johnson, Portnoy, & Pollack) Consultants: Business Practices for Professionals, and W2W, (Woman to Woman). The current form of ABCS Psychology Resources, an assessment, therapeutic and consultative service for families and educational systems, resulted from combining the training seminars developed as a result of Dr.

Malloy's request with the integrative assessment and treatment approach I had developed at Kennedy.

In 1997, I became an owner of Access for Change, an incorporated group practice that was designed to give us flexibility to meet the changing health care climate under managed care. The psychologists involved are John Anderson, Jean Lau Chin, Stanley Gross, and Marsha Padwa. My particular areas of interest are women and adolescent girls, using a partnership model of psychotherapy developed from the current research on valuing diversity and building strengths and integrating cognitive, feminist, and family therapy.

JPP Consultants: Business Practices for Professionals began in 1997 and offers consultation and continuing education to individuals and groups seeking to learn how to develop thriving professional practices. My partners are Sanford Portnoy and Ethan Pollack. Each brings a different perspective to the difficult challenges in the current health care climate. We have developed a unique approach linking practitioner autonomy, good client care, gender issues, and sound business practice.

W2W was incorporated in 1997 by women psychologists who are leaders in the field and dedicated to the development and dissemination of quality products specifically designed to build strengths, promote health, and enhance quality living for today's woman while having fun. The owners are Dorothy Cantor, Carol Goodheart, Sandra Haber, Ellen McGrath, Alice Rubenstein, Lenore Walker, Karen Zager, and myself.

MAJOR CONTRIBUTIONS AND ACHIEVEMENTS

One of the most important events in my professional life began when Judith Worell and I, during a APA Division 35 brainstorming, thought of a National Conference on Feminist Practice. This was heartedly endorsed by the division. For the next several years, a group of nine women, Mary Brabeck, Jean Lau Chin, Lucia Gilbert, Beverly Greene, Natalie Porter, Maryann Santos de Barona, Karen Wyche, Judith Worell, and myself worked to organize the highly successful and extremely satisfying National Conference on Education and Training in Feminist Practice at Boston College in 1993.

My first book, *Shaping the Future of Feminist Psychology* (Worell & Johnson, 1997), the product of that conference, was accepted as the second book in the APA Division 35 book series edited by Cheryl Travis. Working with Judith Worell and all of the wonderful women attending the conference was one of the major growth opportunities in my life. Several concepts came from the conference: that feminist practice is extensive and includes a breadth of interventions; that a feminist science and theory underpin feminist practice; that diversity is a primary value of feminist practice; and that there is a distinct, identifiable feminist process.

In August of 1995, I gave my presidential address for Division 35 on women's strengths from a feminist perspective (Johnson, 1995). This was influenced by many feminist writers on social constructionism, power, and resiliency (Gilligan,1982; Griscom, 1992; Hare-Mustin & Marecek, 1988; Unger & Crawford, 1992; Worell, 1992).

This experience was the beginning of a very productive period in my life where I was asked to give keynote addresses, invited addresses, and continuing education presentations on feminist practice by groups like the Committee on Equality of Professional Opportunity at the Southeastern Psychological Association, and the APA Division of Clinical Psychology, Section on Women. Taking a focus on strengths and integrating work from the foremothers of feminist therapy and women of color (Brodsky & Hare-Mustin, 1980); Chin, De la Cancela & Jenkins, 1993; Comas-Diaz & Greene, 1994; Worell & Remer, 1992; Wyatt, 1997), together with the recent work on the feminist theory and principles of feminist therapy from the national conference (Brabeck & Brown, 1998; Wyche & Rice, 1997) resulted in the development of a Strengths Inventory Assessment measure and the Partnership Model for treatment of women. This formed the basis for my next scholarly project.

Dorothy Cantor, during her APA Presidential year, seized the opportunity to "move an agenda critical to women." She appointed Karen Zager and myself to head an initiative on the development of girls during adolescence. Working with Dr. Zager on this project for three years confirmed for me the power of women working together, the support, honesty, and caring that can occur, and the intellectual growth that results in products that would never have existed otherwise.

Beyond appearance: A new look at adolescent girls (Johnson, Roberts, Worell, 1999) with section editors Jessica Henderson Daniel, Denise DeZolt, and Lyn Mikel Brown was one product of the task force. Dr. Zagar and Alice Rubenstein's trade book (in press) for adolescent girls and their mothers was another one. The products of the task force encompassed four themes which brought together the threads of my professional life: an emphasis on considering the strengths of adolescent girls; a developmental perspective; valuing diversity; and a reliance on research for guiding decisions and conclusions. Most of the work prior to our task force had focused on giving the public a wake-up call on the negative societal effects on adolescent girls (American Association of University Women, 1991; Maccoby, 1990; & Pipher, 1994.) An exception was a 1997 national study on adolescent health (Resnick et al., 1997).

THE WORK ON BUSINESS PRACTICES AND WOMEN ENTREPRENEURS

Since the early 1980s, I have written columns and articles for psychological organizations such as the Massachusetts Psychological Association, the Division of Independent Practice, and the Division of the Psychology of Women on business practices for psychologists. The thrust of my work in this area has several principles: There are stages of development of a career; one must have a business plan to thrive; there are gender differences that affect how one does the business part of professional practice; good business is good client care; and networking, partnerships and group practice are vital in today's health care climate.

I was deeply honored when my colleagues elected me as the American Psychological Association's President for 2001. As only the ninth woman elected as President in the Association's 112 years, it was an opportunity to influence the evolving American health care system toward one that better serves public needs and moves forward the diversity agenda, including gender. For our society, the changes in the health care scene are probably the biggest social public policy change in the last 20 years. Using the strength of psychology that comes when the diverse constituencies join with the public, community, and provider groups, I had the opportunity to address this important public and professional issue.

Convening an ad hoc council on the nation's health care needs enabled psychology to bring together our science and practice constituencies for the public interest and participate in this national debate. Another major initiative was to address challenges to psychology's education and training institutions coming out of my experiences as a training director, APPIC executive committee member, and member of the APA Committee on Accreditation. One of my top concerns had been the need to provide a better future for psychology students and graduates. A third presidential initiative was expanding opportunities for psychology science and practice. My election to the presidency was the result of a team effort, and the principles of feminist collaboration and process would guide my choices during my tenure.

Division 35, the Psychology of Women, has always been my home in APA. Ever since Bernice Lott found me standing alone at a Division social hour and introduced me to everyone she knew—which seemed like everyone—I have felt a place of friendship and collegiality within APA. There isn't space here to mention the number of outstanding women who have been part of my growth and development, but perhaps just mentioning some of the women who have been presidents of the division during those years will give a glimpse of the wealth of talent and dedication within the division: Janet Hyde, Phyllis Katz, Ellen Kimmel, Bernice Lott, Natalie Porter, Pam Reid, Melba Vasquez, Judith Worell, Jan Yoder, and Lenore Walker.

For almost 25 years I was involved in organized psychology. First, it was on the state level, serving on the Massachusetts Psychological Association's Board of Directors, as President from 1981 to 1983, and as APA Council Representative from 1985 to 1988 and 1995 to 1997. Gerry Koocher provided strong mentoring during my first year on the council. I was elected co-chair of the APA Finance Committee in 1987, when Charles Spielberger was Treasurer, and to the APA Board of Directors in 1997. During this time, I was a critical part in creating the financial policy that changed APA from an organization whose assets were threatened and shrinking to a financially solid association with major real estate holdings and a rich stock portfolio.

For the past several years, I have been honored to receive state and national recognition for my contributions to psychology. In 1998, the APA Committee on Women in Psychology honored me with the Distinguished Leader for Women in Psychology Recognition Award. That year, I was elected as a Distinguished Practitioner in the National Academy of Practice in Psychology. Previous awards and recognitions included election in 1991 as a Fellow in the American Psychological Association and the Ezra Saul Award in 1988 from the Massachusetts Psychological Association. In 1999, the Massachusetts Psychological Association presented me with the Career Contribution Award. My long-time friend and colleague, Gerald Koocher, wrote one of his funny and tear-bringing poems to commemorate the occasion.

INTEGRATING MY PERSONAL AND PROFESSIONAL LIFE

As I noted earlier, throughout most of my career, I used the survival technique of compartmentalizing family and profession. During my early, most intense family-raising years, often without knowing it, I was putting the pieces together, developing competencies in professional practice, expanding my knowledge base, and developing a network. At the same time I was ensuring that our children received quality education, took lessons, and that there were fun, quality family times. In the middle stage of my career, I was learning how to work with a range of patients, how to develop and implement organizational policies, the importance of good financial plans, and developing my own framework for viewing psychology practice. During this time my children had developed their own interests, friendships, and abilities, including sports, and turning our garage into a neighborhood theater. We expanded our family vacations to include exploring Mayan Indian sites, Machu Pinchu, and scuba diving.

My major publications have come late in my life and my career, which I hope will be an encouragement to other women who want to write but are blocked or can't find the time in their current schedules. Writing never came easy for me. Journal writing and poetry were passions but the process of writing something to be read by my colleagues was agonizing. I would procrastinate, and unless it was something demanded for a deadline, I frequently never delivered. Two factors changed that: my collegial relationships in the Division of the Psychology of Women and my husband, Wayne Woodlief. Wayne is a newspaper writer and he reinforced me with positive comments about my writing, editing that protected me from embarrassment, and specific questions that increased my clarity.

In the later part of my career, I had the opportunity to actualize this accumulated knowledge, these skills, and the joy of a bedrock of friends and colleagues. My family expanded to include sons-in-law, Charles Burlile, Matthew Fraidin, and Shane Wedge. Now I am also blessed to be a grandmother. Just as Verna Derby was to me, I hope to be a loving, strong grandmother to Kate Johnson Burlile, Max Collins Johnson Fraidin, and Taylor Johnson Wedge.

LASTING THEMES

The early influences from my family, the turning points and how they handled the tragedies and choices have shaped the themes and work of my professional life as a psychologist. The lasting themes of my career include: the intense desire to promote diversity and empower others, particularly the poor, children, adolescent girls, and women; the importance of financial management, program development, and network building to actualize the potential power of psychology for the public; the development of psychotherapeutic approaches that focus on strengths and partnership; and how, like my parents, you can have a feast when you collaborate with colleagues and friends.

REFLECTIONS

I love being a psychologist. I have worked with more than 900 clients in the course of my career and had the opportunity to learn while doing this important work. Involvement in the American Psychological Association has been an important part of my professional and personal life. I experience involvement as an opportunity to give back to psychology some small part of what I've received.

I think the contribution for which I will be most remembered is the focus on strengths. By focusing on strengths and using feminist process, I brought new frameworks to psychological practice with children, adolescent girls, and women. I also encouraged research opportunities in this new direction of inquiry. By focusing on psychology's strengths within our national organization, the American Psychological Association, I was able to bring the power of psychology to bear on a major issue of our time—quality health care for all. Like an architect, I built frameworks that others filled in so that together we built lasting structures.

REFERENCES

American Association of University Women. (1991). *Shortchanging girls, shortchanging America*. Washington, DC: American Association of University Women Educational Foundation.
Brabeck, M., & Brown, L. (1998). Feminist theory and psychological practice. In J. Worell & N. Johnson (Eds.), *Shaping the future of feminist psychology: Education, research, and practice* (pp. 15–36). Washington, DC: APA Press.
Brodsky, A. M., & Hare-Mustin, R. (1980). *Women and psychotherapy*. New York: Guilford Press.
Chin, J. L., De La Cancela, V. & Jenkins, Y. (1993). *Diversity in psychotherapy: The politics of race, ethnicity, and gender*. Westport, CN: Praeger.
Comas-Díaz, L. & Greene, B. (1994) *Women of color: Integrating ethnic and gender identities in psychotherapy*. New York: Guilford.
Gilligan, C. (1982). *In a different voice: Psychological theory and women's development*. Cambridge, MA: Harvard University Press.
Griscom, J. V. (1992). Women and power: Definition, dualism, and difference. *Psychology of Women Quarterly, 16*, 380–414.
Hare-Mustin, R. & Marecek, J. (1988). The meaning of difference: Gender theory, postmoderism, and psychology. *American Psychologist 43*, 455–464.
Johnson, N. G. (1995, August). *Feminist frames of women's strength: Visions for the future*. Presidential address to the Division of the Psychology of Women, presented at the annual convention of the American Psychological Association, New York, NY.
Johnson, N. G., Roberts, M. C., and Worell, J. (1999). *Beyond appearance: A new look at adolescent girls*. Washington, DC: American Psychological Association.
Maccoby, E. E. (1990). Gender and relationships: A developmental account. *American Psychologist, 45*, 513–520.
Piaget, J. (1952). *The origins of intelligence in children*. New York: International University Press.
Pipher, M. (1994). *Reviving Ophelia: Saving the selves of adolescent girls*. New York: Ballantine Books.
Resnick, M. D., Bearman, P. S., Blum, R. W., Bauman, K. E., Harris, K. M., Jones, J., Tabor, J., Beuhring, T., Sieving, R. E., Shew, M., Ireland, M., Bearinger, L. H., & Udry, J. R. (1997). Protecting adolescents from harm: Findings from the National Longitudinal Study on Adolescent Health. *Journal of the American Medical Association, 278*, 823–832.
Skinner, B. F.(1953). *Science and human behavior*. New York: Macmillan.

Unger, R., & Crawford, M. (1992). *Women and gender: A feminist psychology*. Philadelphia, PA: Temple University Press.

Worell, J. (Ed.). (1992). Women and power [Special Issue]. *Psychology of Women Quarterly, 16*, 4.

Worell, J., & Remer, P. (1992). *Feminist perspectives in therapy*. New York: Wiley.

Worell, J., & Johnson, N. G. (Eds.). (1997). *Shaping the future of feminist psychology: Research, education, and practice*. Washington DC: American Psychological Association.

Wyatt, G. (1997). *Stolen women: Reclaiming our sexuality, taking back our lives*. New York: Wiley.

Wyche, K. and Rice, J. (1997). Feminist therapy: From dialogue to tenets. In J. Worell and N. Johnson (Eds.), *Shaping the future of feminist psychology: Education, research, and practice* (pp. 57–71). Washington, DC: American Psychological Association.

REPRESENTATIVE PUBLICATIONS

Johnson, N.G. (1998–1999) Column: APA Doings for Women. *Psychology of Women Newsletter, 26(1)*, 6; *26(2)*, 6; *26(3)*, 6; *26(4)*, 6.

Johnson, N.G. (1994–1995). President's message. *Psychology of Women Newsletter, 21(4)*, 1-2; *22(1)*, 1-2; *23(2)*, 1-2; *23(3)*, 1-2; *23(4)*, 1-2.

Johnson, N.G. (1994). Health care industry in Massachusetts lays off hundreds of psychologists. *Massachusetts Psychological Association Quarterly*, May.

Johnson, N. G. (1986). Perspectives of an APA approved internship training director: The national conference on training clinical child psychologists. *The Clinical Psychologist, 39*.

Johnson, N. G. (1983). Plight of single parent families. In F. P. Jacob (Ed.), *Papers Read at the 19th Annual Convention of the Psychological Association of the Philippines*. Manila, Philippines: Psychological Association of the Philippines.

Johnson, N. G. (1981) Child/family therapy: A question of whom and when. *Family and Child Mental Health Journal, 7*, 130–137.

Johnson, N. G., Portnoy, S. M., & Pollack, E. (1999). Building, expanding, and enhancing a career in psychology. *Massachusetts Psychological Association Quarterly, 43*(3), 5.

Johnson, N. G., Portnoy, S. M., & Pollack, E. (1998). Professional practice partnerships: Maintaining autonomy. *Massachusetts Psychological Association Quarterly, 42*(1), 5.

Johnson, N. G., Portnoy, S. M., & Pollack, E. (1998). Professional practice partnerships: We is better than I. *Massachusetts Psychological Association Quarterly, 41*(4), 5.

Johnson, N. G., & Remer, P. (1997). Postdoctoral training in feminist psychological practice. In N. G. Johnson & J. Worell (Eds.), *Shaping the future of feminist psychology: Research, education, and practice* (pp. 203–225). Washington DC: American Psychological Association.

Johnson, N. G., & Roberts, M.C. (1999). Passage on the wild river of adolescence: Arriving safely. In N. G. Johnson, M. C. Roberts, & J. Worell (Eds.),

Beyond appearance: A new look at adolescent girls (pp. 3–18). Washington, DC: American Psychological Association.

Johnson, N. G. (1973). The effects of discrepancies in social reinforcement and different instructional sets on early adolescents' responses. *Dissertation Abstracts International,*

Worell, J., & Johnson, N. G. (1997). Introduction: Creating the future: Process and promise in feminist practice. In N. G. Johnson & J. Worell (Eds.), *Shaping the future of feminist psychology: Research, education, and practice* (pp. 1–14). Washington DC: American Psychological Association.

CHAPTER 7

Sandra Wood Scarr

Photographer: Phillip R. Scarr.

Sandra Wood Scarr

When I was born in August 1936, the nation was at the depths of the Great Depression. My parents were little affected, however, as my father, John Ruxton Wood, was a physician in the U.S. Army with a secure living. My mother, Jane Powell Wood, was a primary school teacher before her marriage in 1930, a holding pattern for many young women of her generation. Both parents were from proud southern families whose ancestors had emigrated from England to Virginia in the late 1600s. My mother's family moved on to eastern Tennessee with Daniel Boone in the 1720s where the Powells and Blackwells became prominent citizens. My father's family remained in Virginia, where they founded the Duke Tobacco Company and later Duke University.

Before my birth, my parents had spent 4 years in the Philippines, where they lived well, with several servants and an active social life in the officers' club. My mother was a club champion golfer and an excellent bridge player, my father a trophy-winning tennis player and good bridge companion. They traveled to China and collected beautiful furnishings that are with me today. My parents were a dashing young couple when they moved to Washington, DC, to begin a family.

CHILDHOOD

In the early years, Daddy was moved from the Washington Surgeon General's Office to do an advanced degree in biochemistry at Columbia University, in preparation for a lifelong career in medical research. In 1939, before we left Washington, my sister Joanne was born. Standing on a brick wall outside of Walter Reed Hospital, looking up at my mother's hospital window, is my earliest memory. With our nanny, Mary Jackson, in tow we moved to the New York suburbs, until the outbreak of World War II. In 1942, after a brief stay in Washington, my father was assigned to head the Army Research Laboratories at Edgewood Arsenal, MD, the chief chemical warfare post in the country.

From age 6 to 14, I lived in a large rambling house overlooking the Chesapeake Bay. In retrospect, it was an unusual childhood that varied from complete freedom to roam unsupervised around the army post to being choked with escaped tear gas from the chemical warfare plant. My sister and I watched German prisoners of war with armed guards at work in our yard. I didn't know that other American children didn't have gas masks and German gardeners. More than anything, I remember the many cocktail parties where my sister and I helped maids pass hors d'oeuvres and were introduced to the company, who came from many universities to help in the war effort.

I roamed with a gang of other kids whose parents were also confident they were perfectly safe without oversight. We rode bikes, climbed trees, skipped along the beach, and built forts in the woods. As junior members of the officers' club circle, we swam and played tennis and golf. Girls and boys still played together for much of the day. It's hard to imagine that such an idyllic child environment ever existed.

After the war, several parents decided the rural Maryland schools were not suitable for their children's education and organized a van to take us to private schools in Baltimore, an 80-mile round trip every day. In the seventh grade, my education was revolutionized. The Bryn Mawr School for Girls opened my young eyes to serious scholarship. I was so far behind! It took me nearly a year to catch up with Bryn Mawr's curriculum, but it set the standard for the remainder of my education.

My father was moved to the Army Surgeon General's Office in 1950, so we moved to Chevy Chase, a Washington suburb. Two years later, we were given quarters at Walter Reed when Daddy became head of the Army Institute of Research. My mother golfed and played bridge. My sister and I were enrolled at the National Cathedral School for Girls, an Episcopal Church school where we spent our high school years. It was a superb, classical education. We studied Latin, French, mathematics, English, history, and religion. There were no faddish courses on social sciences or how to write a driver's license application. I had the usual adolescent romances with boys from local all-male schools, and attended a large number of dances, movies, and picnics. I was sent to dancing school. More than anything, my mother wanted me to be popular with boys; girls were much less important, because, in her mind, women were defined by whom they married.

COLLEGE

For murky reasons, I decided to go from a Southern church school to the flaming liberal environment of Vassar College, which forever changed my life. I can only conclude that neither my parents nor I had any idea of what Vassar stood for—women's liberation—before the national Women's Movement was even formed. Being exposed to New York intellectuals and educated, northern Blacks was earthshaking.

I went to Vassar with a strong, rather well developed interest in psychology. My naïve version of psychology was "understanding people." Vassar's version of psychology was conditioned eye-blinks and maze running rodents. Sociology and anthropology represented the human side of the social sciences, so I migrated to these majors. I did research with Harriet Zuckerman, later a distinguished Professor of Sociology at Columbia University and foundation president. One project was on classmates' reproductive plans (most wanted four children) and another on Whittaker Chambers' case against Alger Hiss (like other liberals, we were wrong about Hiss's guilt).

After graduating from Vassar College in 1958, I had spent 10 formative years in all-women's education where I was strongly influenced, for better and for worse. On the upside, Cathedral School and Vassar College taught me to be assertive and self-confident. Leadership roles went, by default, to women, and I filled my share. Courage and outspokenness are assets that have served me well throughout my life. On the downside, commitment to a career put me at odds with my parents and often with husbands. For the generation of women educated in the 1950s, persistence in a full-time career after children were born was a source of stern disapproval. In the workplace, however, I became an early star.

My first real job was in a Family and Child Service agency, where I learned a lot about myself. The agency paid for me to go to graduate school part time. Graduate work in an intellectually vapid program told me I did not want to be a social worker, and trying to help poor, vulnerable people with individual therapy was depressing. What most clients needed were cash and community support. After a year I went to the National Institute of Mental Health as a research assistant in the Laboratory of Socio-Environmental Studies. There, I was totally happy working for Carmi Schooler on studies of hospitalized schizophrenics. He strongly encouraged me to go to graduate school in psychology. In 1960, I enrolled in the PhD program in social psychology at Harvard University.

GRADUATE SCHOOL

The atmosphere at Harvard was not exactly friendly to women graduate students. Gordon Allport told me that accepting women was a waste of valuable resources because we were unlikely to pursue serious academic careers. "Women just get married and rear children," he said. This was true for some, but surely not for all. At many universities, women were not considered for serious academic posts, and other women followed husbands and took whatever employment was available. I assured Professor Allport that *I* would pursue a serious career. Maybe his annoying challenge had some impact on my life-long persistence.

At Harvard I became interested in child development and genetics, a combination that continued throughout my career. My dissertation was a twin study of genetic differences in motivation, in which I traveled all over the Boston area testing 5 to 10-year-old identical and fraternal twin girls. Irving Gottesman, whose research on genetics of schizophrenia is well known, was my final advisor. At a time when naïve environmentalism was rampant—in fact, the only intellectual game in town—it was tough to claim that genes mattered to behavior, but I was perverse enough to take on the world.

In the early 1960s only a handful of intellectuals had interests in evolution and population genetics, which showed that in every population genetic variability was important in behavioral differences among individuals. How could this not be true for humans? As my dissertation research showed, there was indeed evidence of genetic variability in activity level and sociability among these very human Boston children (Scarr, 1966, 1969).

I was married in December of 1961 to a fellow graduate student in sociology, Harry Scarr. In December 1962, our son Phillip was born. I collected data for my dissertation half of the time and cared for Phillip the other half of the time, a schedule that continued until finishing the entire tome in 1964. I was always rather proud that I earned my PhD in 4 years, while getting married and having a child.

ACADEMIA

My first encounters with employment when my PhD was imminent were not encouraging. Because I already had a baby son, no one would recommend or hire me. I knocked on all the university doors in the Washington, DC area, where we moved after Harry took a postdoctoral job at NIMH. By sheer persistence, I talked my way into an interview with the Director of the Institute of Child Study at the University of

Maryland. He took me on for a part-time teaching position, which expanded to three-quarters and then a full-time assistant professorship over 2 years. I began research with a couple of other faculty members, and generally made myself useful. My son went to the university nursery school, and we had a full-time housekeeper—the first of many helpers who allowed me to pursue a real career. It was a rocky start for a mother with a Harvard PhD.

In 1966, my husband took a job in sociology at the University of Pennsylvania. I followed along, of course, and looked for employment in the area. That was the way things were done then. I landed a 1-year, halftime Visiting Assistant Professorship in Psychology at Penn, which made me a marginal faculty member, at best. I used the other half of the time to begin several research projects and write research grants. I shared an office with Randy Gallistel, a new PhD from Yale, who thought I was intellectually from outer space (genetics?). Twenty-five years later, Randy and I co-edited the American Psychological Society's journal, *Current Directions in Psychological Science*. He and his wife, Rochel Gelman, became my lifelong friends.

After the 1-year appointment in psychology, I was hired in Penn's Graduate School of Education, first as a lecturer and then as an Assistant Professor of Human Development. In addition to getting a research program underway with a large twin study of Black and White school children's achievement and IQ test scores and an observational study of infant fears (Scarr & Salapatek, 1970), it was time to have another child. Karen was born in June 1967, which gave me a summer to get her settled. In 1969 I was promoted to Associate Professor (with tenure), and Rebecca was born in July.

After Arthur Jensen's infamous 1969 *Harvard Education Review* article (Jensen, 1969) on genetics, social class, and racial differences in IQ, my research became trendy. Psychology Department faculty, who had previously not let me use their library, suddenly wanted me to speak at their gatherings. *Science* published two of my major articles (Scarr-Salapatek, 1971a, b). By comparing identical and fraternal twins' aptitude and school achievement scores, I showed that intellectual development was heavily influenced by genetic variability, but more so among advantaged than disadvantaged children. When opportunities abound, genetic differences shine through. When environmental opportunities are restricted, individuals do not have the chance to express their genetic individuality to the fullest extent, and individual differences are more influenced by the lack of environmental support. On average, Black children showed less genetic and more environmental influence than White children, meaning their opportunities to develop individuality were more restricted than those of Whites. This was a revolutionary way to think about the impact of environments on genetic expression in human behavior (Scarr-Salapatek, 1972).

At the same time, I collaborated with Margaret Williams, a neonatologist at Philadelphia General Hospital, who was in charge of the intensive care newborn nursery. She and I developed a protocol to stimulate prematurely born infants. Based on animal research on the beneficial effects of early stimulation on brain development and weight gain, we reasoned that preemies, confined for weeks and months to incubators, received virtually no early stimulation. Taking them out of isolettes to be rocked and exposed to music and human speech could provide beneficial effects. Our experiment assigned every other low birth weight infant to the stimulation nursery or to the control nursery, where they received the usual isolette treatment. We were the first to publish a real experimental study showing that the stimulated babies gained weight faster and left the hospital earlier than the others (Scarr-Salapatek & Williams, 1972, 1973). Within 10 years, taking preemies out of their isolettes became standard neonatal practice.

My career was in high gear. By mid-1970, I left my husband and Penn for the University of Minnesota—and another temporary position—with Philip Salapatek, who was hired as a tenured faculty member of the Institute of Child Development. We were married in December of 1972, and Stephanie was born in November of 1973.

After the first year at Minnesota, I earned a permanent position as Associate Professor in the Institute and was promoted to Professor in 1973. For the first time, I felt like a full-fledged member of academia, not just scraping along. My colleague, Rich Weinberg, with whom I have worked continually for more than 25 years, and I began the collaborative Minnesota Adoption Projects that made news all over the world. We received large research grants and were truly in heaven.

The Minnesota Transracial Adoption Project included 101 White families who had adopted Black children. This study was analogous to the animal cross-fostering studies that estimate the effects of genetic differences and rearing environments on behavioral development. We showed that these children, at the average age of 7 years, were performing far better on IQ tests than Black children reared in Black families in the same area of the country (Scarr & Weinberg, 1976, 1977a, 1977b, 1977c). We did not find that these young Black children had any genetic limitations to intellectual development, when given culturally appropriate learning opportunities.

In a much later follow-up study, however, when the transracial adoptees were 18 years of age, we found their intellectual and academic scores had declined to levels not very different from other Blacks in the surrounding area (Weinberg, Scarr, & Waldman, 1992). The reasons for this are unclear, as the adoptees could have been discriminated against, as other Blacks are, or they could have had some genetic limitations to later intellectual development. A cross-fostering study cannot speak to this controversy. The Transracial Adoption Project and its results were very unsettling, to put it mildly.

The Minnesota Adolescent Adoption Study focused on sources of individual differences among adoptive and biological families of comparable backgrounds. All of the adopted children were in their homes by 2 months of age. Two siblings in each family were currently between 16 and 22 years old. This study was designed to show the full impact of home rearing environments at the end of adolescence. We were very surprised by the results. The influence of home environments was, in fact, considerably *less* in this older sample than in younger samples of adoptees and biological siblings who had been studied (Scarr & Weinberg, 1978). Genetic differences were more prominent in the intelligence, school achievement, and personality test scores of these late adolescents than among younger children.

This result changed our whole way of thinking about how the environment works. Rather than the home environment having a cumulative impact across development, its influence in fact *wanes* from early childhood to adolescence. We began to think of how older children and adolescents make their own environments to a greater extent than younger ones by choosing activities that interest them, by choosing friends, and by the influences their own personal characteristics have on their interactions with others in the community. This thinking led to several papers on how people make their own environments (Scarr, 1992, 1993; Scarr & McCartney, 1983; Scarr & Weinberg, 1983). Over the years, Richard Weinberg and I have published about 50 journal articles together and never had a fight, a testament to his excellent temperament and character.

In 1974, after being paid a few hundred dollars a year less than my husband, by the Institute Director's design, federal affirmative action came along to review women's salaries. I received a 25% increase, to some male colleagues' consternation.

People often asked me how I did it—four young children and a full-time career. "Easy," I said. "Hire help, pay her well, and treat her right." Throughout much of my career, in each city, we had the same housekeeper, without whom I would never have been able to manage the household. For more than 30 years, I rarely ran the vacuum cleaner, shopped for groceries, or did the laundry. I did sometimes cook. My time at home was spent almost entirely with the family or working after hours on academic matters. Because I was reared in a household with help, even though my mother was not employed, I was not conflicted about paying someone else to do the housework while I worked full time elsewhere.

After a year at the Institute for Advanced Study in the Behavioral Science in 1976 to 1977, Yale University recruited me as Professor of Psychology, where I remained until 1983. At Yale, I developed a series of studies on early interventions to test theories about the impact of deliberate interventions on genetic variability. It was a time when the impact of *Head Start* was challenged, and other intervention programs were struggling to show any effects. Indeed, in Bermuda we found that only seriously disadvantaged children gain much from early interventions, because most families provide adequate environments to support their children's normal development (Scarr & McCartney, 1988). Similarly, in studies of child care centers, we found minimal to no effects of differences in quality of care, because nearly all child-care environments were adequate, and the children had families to provide learning opportunities as well (Deater-Deckard, Pinkerton & Scarr, 1996).

In 1983, I became Commonwealth Professor and Chair of the Psychology Department at the University of Virginia. The decision to move to Charlottesville was more a lifestyle change than a career choice (it's much prettier, more pleasant, and the schools are better in Charlottesville than in New Haven). By this time, my career was established, and it did not matter with what institution I was affiliated. I continued with research on family and child-care effects, with several unpopular papers on the minimal to null effects of differences in quality of child care, within a range of state regulated centers (Scarr, 1997, 1998). Family effects are always powerful determinants of children's intellectual and personal outcomes.

Note that inhumane, abusive, and neglectful home environments *do* have deleterious effects on children's development. We do not need any more research to show this is true! The debate over the past 2 decades, however, has centered on more subtle differences in a range of average to below average homes.

JOURNALS, CONSULTING, ASSOCIATIONS, AND AWARDS

While at Minnesota, I began a long career of editing journals. My classical education at the National Cathedral School and Vassar College paid off. (Writing and speaking in clear prose are art forms, not taken lightly in my schools. We were drilled on grammar and proper speech.) The first assignment was the APA Division 7 (Developmental) *Newsletter*, a modest start. In 1976, I became Associate Editor of the *American Psychologist*, and in 1981, Editor of the APA journal, *Developmental Psychology*. Finally, in 1991, I was the co-founding editor, with C. R. Gallistel, of *Current Directions in Psychological Science*, published by the American Psychological Society. I have loved journal editing because of the opportunity to influence what is read by colleagues and students—not only the content, but the clarity of communication.

Throughout my career, I have consulted often with government and nonprofit organizations and served on boards and committees of professional organizations. Giving psychology away and using community opportunities to train graduate students always seemed to me a mutually beneficial exchange. I had a 10-year consulting relationship with the Bermuda government that allowed me to take groups of (very lucky) students there several times a year to test children and consult on research projects. Other less exotic locales were Parent–Child Centers, *Head Start*, the Urban League, the National Institute of Mental Health, and so on. I served on so many dozens of university committees, notably finance, governance, and research administration, that they are a blur in my memory.

By 1977, I chaired the APA Committee on the Protection of Human Subjects in Research, as we drafted significant documents to implement congressional legislation governing human research. I was elected president in 1981 of APA Division 7, to the APA Council in 1985, and to the Board of Directors in 1988 (from which I resigned in 1990). In the Behavior Genetics Association, I was on the Board in 1973 and President in 1985. In the Society for Research in Child Development, I was on Governing Council from 1976 to 1983, Chair of the Finance Committee in 1987, and President in 1989. As a founding member of the American Psychological Society, I was elected to the Board in 1991 and as president in 1996. Being elected president of the organization I most admired coincided with leaving academia for the corporate world, which made it difficult for me to be a fully-involved leader.

Ethical concerns led me speak out on scientific issues about the impact of low-level lead exposure. Several studies had suggested that even very low levels of exposure could have negative effects on children's learning and social behavior. Claire Ernhart, Professor of Psychiatry at Case Western Reserve University, and I collaborated to review research on the effects of lead exposure. A federal court asked us to visit Herbert Needleman, Professor of Psychiatry at University of Pittsburgh, to examine his research records for their credibility, because the federal government was using them in a suit against several companies.

We found Needleman's research faulty (Ernhart & Scarr, 1991), which led us to report his misconduct to the NIH. Claire and I had to defend ourselves in the same federal court against Needleman and the U.S. Justice Department, who sought to suppress our findings. We were most fortunate to find David Geneson to defend us. David became a great friend and personal hero, who wrote an eloquent judgment for the court that science must be an open and honest process. Eventually, Needleman was found guilty of misrepresentation and had to retract research reports in the journals that published them.

The most painful part of this effort was the polarization of the psychological community over scientific truth versus alleged benefits to the underprivileged. Being a whistleblower is very difficult, even when you know you are ethically and scientifically correct (Ernhart, Scarr, & Geneson, 1993; Scarr, 1994).

Honors have been bestowed along the way. In 1988, APA gave me an award for Distinguished Contributions to Research in Public Policy, and in 1993, APS gave me the James McKeen Cattell Award for Distinguished Contributions to Applied Research. I was elected to the American Academy of Arts & Sciences in 1989; the Academy was founded by John Adams some 220 years ago to recognize intellectual achievements and to encourage intellectuals to serve the nation's public interest. I am proud to serve on the Academy's Council and Strategic Planning Committee.

THE CORPORATE WORLD

After 5 years as Chair of the Psychology Department at the University of Virginia, I began to branch out into other activities. In 1990, I joined the Board of Directors of KinderCare Learning Centers, Inc., the largest child care provider in the U.S., with more than 1,150 centers in 38 states. Being on a corporate board was a better education than any I had received since leaving Harvard. What a challenge to understand financial balance sheets and debt projections, corporate executives' vocabularies and strategic thoughts, and planning models. Other directors—investment bankers and corporation executives—taught me to think like a manager and be aware of the value added to shareholders and the bottom line by each decision. Being on the Board of a publicly traded company is a daunting responsibility. After participating in the lackadaisical, inefficient administration of universities, the KinderCare Board was enlightening and inspiring.

To my great surprise, the directors elected me Chairman of the Board in 1994. An even greater surprise came the following year, when the Board chose me to replace the Chief Executive Officer (CEO). Very suddenly I moved from the security of a major university psychology department to the rigors and risks of a corporate suite. I also had to retire from the University of Virginia, move to company headquarters in Alabama, and assume my new CEO role—overnight. For nearly 2 years, I worked harder and probably accomplished more than I had ever done before. Decisions about child-care policy could be carried out immediately. We could actually make differences in parent's and children's lives and see the results. It was exhilarating.

The poignant end of the story is that KinderCare was bought by Kohlberg, Kravis, and Roberts, a New York investment firm (they own Safeway, RJR Nabisco, and Bordens, among many other companies) in 1997. As always, they bring in their own management, so I was retired to greener pastures, but it was fun while it lasted.

RETIREMENT

After extensive consultation with family members, I surprised many friends by deciding to move to The Big Island in Hawaii. The children and I had vacationed there numerous times, and I knew it had many advantages over any other place in the world, and I have seen much of the world. So, here I am living in a tropical paradise, in the United States, working on community and political issues. My house is heavenly, with a pool and spa, right on the ocean front. I have developed an extensive orchid collection (they grow outdoors in the yard here, of course), and my house is full of blooming plants. It doesn't get better than this for me. My children and their families come at least annually to spend time in Hawaii, and I travel to visit them every few months. My sister, her family, and friends come as well. In August 1998, I became a certified scuba diver (later an advanced diver, and even a rescue diver), and now four other family members have joined me underwater. I also travel a lot, especially on cruise ships.

On reflection, the proudest achievement of my life is to have four happy, productive, adult children, and one adorable grandson (so far). They taught me so much about individual differences and the different paths that siblings take to become the best each can be. Among my four is a computer network engineer, an attorney, a biochemist, and an advertising executive. As they grew up, the children validated my twin and adoptive family research on the importance of genetic individuality.

I spent more than 30 years doing research and teaching psychology at major research universities. My academic career was interesting, rewarding, and varied, but that's enough of one career. My corporate sojourn could have lasted longer, but I would have soon burned out at the pace I had set. Hawaii feels very good to me after two exceedingly demanding careers. I am truly enjoying getting into politics and environmental groups and making a difference at local and state levels. Besides, it is refreshing to try new things, especially at an advanced age.

REFERENCES

Deater-Deckard, K., Pinkerton, R., & Scarr, S. (1996). Child care quality and children's behavioral adjustment: A four-year longitudinal study. *Journal of Child Psychology & Psychiatry, 37*(8), 937–948.

Ernhart, C. B. & Scarr, S. (1991, May). Report on the research of Dr. Herbert Needleman based on samples reported in the 1979 article in the *New England Journal of Medicine*. Federal Court Decision in the District Court for the District of Utah, Central Division, Civil Order No. 86-C-924.

Ernhart, C. B., Scarr, S., & Geneson, D. F. (1993). On being a whistleblower: The Needleman case. *Ethics and Behavior, 3*, 73–93.

Jensen, A. R. (1969). How much can we boost IQ and scholastic achievement? *Harvard Education Review, 39*, 1–123.

Scarr, S. (1966). Genetic factors in activity motivation. *Child Development, 37*, 663–673.

Scarr, S. (1969). Social introversion-extroversion as a heritable response. *Child Development, 40*, 823–832.

Scarr, S. (1992). Developmental theories for the 1990's: Development and individual differences. *Child Development, 63*, 1–19.

Scarr, S. (1994). Psychological science in the public arena: Three cases of dubious influence. *Scandinavian Journal of Psychology, 36*, 164–188

Scarr, S. (1997). Why variations in child care quality have little impact on children's development. *Current Directions in Psychological Science, 6*, 143–148.

Scarr, S. (1998). American child care today. *American Psychologist, 53*, 95–108.

Scarr, S. and McCartney, K. (1983). How people make their own environments: A theory of genotype->environment effects. *Child Development, 54*, 424–435.

Scarr, S. and McCartney, K. (1988). Far from home: An experimental evaluation of the mother–child home program in Bermuda. *Child Development, 59*, 531–543.

Scarr, S., & Salapatek, P. (1970). Patterns of fear development during infancy. *Merrill-Palmer Quarterly, 16*, 53–90.

Scarr, S., & Weinberg, R. A. (1976). IQ test performance of black children adopted by white families. *American Psychologist, 31*, 726–739.

Scarr, S., & Weinberg, R. A. (1977a). Intellectual similarities within families of both adopted and biological children. *Intelligence, 1*, 170–191.

Scarr, S., & Weinberg, R. A. (1977b). Rediscovering old truths, or a word by the wise is sometimes lost. *American Psychologist, 32*, 681–683.

Scarr, S., & Weinberg, R. A. (1977c). Nature and nurture strike (out) again. *Intelligence, 3*, 31–39.

Scarr, S., & Weinberg, R. A. (1978). The influence of "family background" on intellectual attainment. *American Sociological Review, 43*, 674–692.

Scarr, S. & Weinberg, R. A. (1983). The Minnesota adoption studies: Genetic differences and malleability. *Child Development, 54*, 260–267.

Scarr-Salapatek, S. (1971a). Unknowns in the IQ equation. *Science, 174*, 1223–1227.

Scarr-Salapatek, S. (1971b). Race, social class and IQ. *Science, 174*, 1285–1295.

Scarr-Salapatek, S. (1972). IQ: Methodological and other issues. *Science, 178*, 229–240.
Scarr-Salapatek, S., & Williams, M. L. (1972). A stimulation program for low birth weight infants. *American Journal of Public Health, 62*, 662–667.
Scarr-Salapatek, S., & Williams, M. L. (1973). The effects of early stimulation on low birth weight infants. *Child Development, 44*, 94–101.
Weinberg, R.A., Scarr, S., and Waldman, I.D. (1992). The Minnesota transracial adoption study: A follow-up of IQ test performance at adolescence. *Intelligence, 16*, 117–135.

REPRESENTATIVE PUBLICATIONS

Grotevant, H. D., Scarr, S., & Weinberg, R. A. (1977). Intellectual development in family constellations with adopted and natural children: A test of the Zajonc and Markus Model. *Child Development, 48*, 1699–1703.
Grotevant, H. D., Scarr, S., & Weinberg, R. A. (1977). Patterns of interest similarity in adoptive and biological families. *Journal of Personality and Social Psychology, 35*, 667–676.
Scarr, S. (1978). From evolution to Larry P., or what shall we do about IQ tests? *Intelligence, 2*, 325–342.
Scarr, S. (1981). *Race, social class and individual differences in IQ: New studies of old issues.* Mahwah, NJ: Lawrence Erlbaum Associates.
Scarr, S. (1981). Testing for children: Implications for assessment and intervention strategies. *American Psychologist, 36*(10), 1159–1166.
Scarr, S. (1984). *Mother Care/Other Care.* New York: Basic Books.
Scarr, S. (1985) Constructing psychology: Making facts and fables for our times. *American Psychologist, 40*, 499–512.
Scarr, S. (1988). Race and gender as psychological variables: Social and ethical issues. *American Psychologist, 43*, 56–59.
Scarr, S. (1997). How people make their own environments: Implications for parents and policy makers. *Psychology, Public Policy, and Law, 2*, 204–228.
Scarr, S. (1999). Freedom of choice for poor families. *American Psychologist, 54*, 144–145.
Scarr, S. (2000). Toward voluntary parenthood. *Journal of Personality, 68*(3).
Scarr, S., Phillips, D., and McCartney, K. (1989). Working mothers and their families. *American Psychologist, 44*(11), 1402–1409.
Scarr, S., Phillips, D., and McCartney, K. (1990). Facts, fantasies, and the future of child care in the United States. *Psychological Science, 1*, 26–35.
Scarr, S. & Vander Zanden, J. (1987). *Understanding Psychology* (4th ed.). New York: Random House.
Scarr, S., & Weinberg, R. A. (1978a). Attitudes, interests, and IQ. *Human Nature, 1*, 29–36.
Scarr, S., & Weinberg, R. A. (1978b). The rights and responsibilities of the social scientist: Reply to Oden and MacDonald's comment. *American Psychologist, 33*, 955–957.
Scarr, S., & Weinberg, R. A. (1980). Calling all camps! The war is over! *American Sociological Review, 45*, 859–864.

Scarr, S., Weinberg, R. A. (1981). The transmission of authoritarianism in families: Genetic resemblance in social-political attitudes? In S. Scarr, *Race, social class and individual difference in I.Q.* (pp. 399–427). Mahwah, NJ: Lawrence Erlbaum Associates.

Scarr, S., & Weinberg, R. A. (1986). The early childhood enterprise: Care and educaiton of the young. *American Psychologist, 41*(10), 1140–1146.

Scarr, S., Weinberg, R. A., & Levine, A. (1986). *Understanding development.* New York: Harcourt Brace.

Scarr, S., Weinberg, R. A., & Waldman, I. D. (1993). IQ correlations in transracial adoptive families: An eleven year follow up. *Intelligence, 17,* 541–555.

Scarr, S. & Yee, D. (1980). Heritability and educational policy; Genetic and environmental effects on IQ, aptitude, and achievement. *Educational Psychologist, 15,* 1–22.

CHAPTER 8

Dorothy W. Cantor

Photographer: Alan L. Fox.

Dorothy W. Cantor

In 1996, I had the honor of serving as the 105th (and eighth woman) President of the American Psychological Association (APA). My colleagues had given me the opportunity, albeit briefly, to chart a course for 155,000 psychologists! The first thing I did when elected was to call together an advisory group of some 36 women who were also eminent women in psychology to help me define my agenda. Clearly, I lead by consensus building. I greatly value the input of others, and I have tremendous respect for women and what we can achieve together.

My own career path to this point has been somewhat circuitous. I grew up in the Bronx, the only child of a substitute teacher and a lawyer, in a time when girls were raised to go to college and have a career in case (God forbid!) they ever had to work. My parents paid little attention to anything but my academic achievement, and fortunately, I was bright enough to get that attention. I learned very early to depend on myself and my own resources. I was also fortunate to be in a public school system that paid special attention to its gifted students, and I was able to benefit from what today would be called "enrichment programs" from the time I was in fifth grade. I also skipped several grades so that I graduated from high school at 16. I attended City College of New York (CCNY), not because my parents were unable to afford more than the tuition of $10 a semester, but because I was too young and insecure to leave home.

In 1957, I graduated from CCNY, summa cum laude, as an elementary school teacher. My mother, the teacher, had not particularly encouraged me, but that was one of the few careers I perceived as open to me. (The others were nurse and secretary.) I took a number of psychology courses and talked about going on to graduate school. However, I didn't for two reasons: I was still too insecure to think of breaking out of the mold and doing something so risky, and I got married the day after I finished my student teaching. I was 20-years old. I taught fifth grade for 2 years after graduating. When I was 22, my son was born and I "retired." That, too, was part of the expectation for young women and I always did what was expected of me. My daughter was born 3 years later.

I often describe the easy way in which my life evolved after that as "dumb luck." What I mean is that I had my children when I was comparatively young, again, as per what was expected of me. The serendipitous effect was to free me up very early from family–career conflicts. By the time I finished my doctoral work, 19 years after having graduated from CCNY, my children were 17 and 14, I was a lot more mature and a lot less insecure, and I had the energy and time to pursue my career with full focus. I had earned two masters degrees along the way, from Kean University of New Jersey, which subsequently honored me with a Distinguished Alumni Award (1995). The first was in Reading Education (1968), and the second was in School Psychology (1972). It took me 4 years to earn each of those degrees, because I pursued them almost entirely at night. My husband, Gerry, was somewhat ahead of his time, both how he encouraged me to pursue further education and how he made it possible for me to do so by assuming more of the share of childrearing than was customary for fathers at the time. He remains one of my most staunch supporters. When I earned my PsyD from the Graduate School of Applied and Professional Psychology (GSAPP) at Rutgers University in 1976, I told my husband that I'd have to work hard to catch up with my male peers who had not taken such a circuitous route to their degrees. Since then, he has asked me, "Have you caught up yet?" A few years ago, I finally recognized that they'd have to catch me!

A major theme of my development has been the integration of career and family. My experience has led me to value the concept of sequencing, that is, that women *can* do it all, but not all at once. I have seen that when we try to do it all at once, we may serve both our families and our careers, but our personal needs are disregarded. Even for those women who do not have the choice of "retiring" for the period of their children's early years, there is the possibility of focusing on one arena more than the other in order to save energy for themselves. When I stayed at home to raise my children, I didn't know that I had another choice. Women today are faced with a difficult choice, and no matter what choice they make, they are often left to deal with the guilt induced it. In our book, *Women in Power* (Cantor & Bernay, 1992), Toni Bernay and I talk about the two *DreamTracks* which women have: bride/mother and career/ambition and of the challenge of balancing the two.

To balance career and family, I took all of my graduate work at schools that were in close proximity to home. You can imagine my joy when the opening of the Rutgers Graduate School of Applied and Professional Psychology (GSAPP) Psy.D. program was announced. I could get there in 35 minutes. The new degree for professional psychologists sounded appropriate and exciting and it didn't occur to me that it might be risky. I also worked part time during most of my graduate education, but I worked in nearby schools so that my hours and vacations would coincide with those of my children. I was a reading teacher and then a school psychologist.

While a student at Rutgers, I met a number of people who were to have a major influence on my career and thinking. The first was Jack Bardon, my dissertation chairman. He had a view of school psychology as the true model of professional psychology because it encompassed all of the skills that psychologists have and could be applied in a variety of settings. It was he who suggested that although my interests might be varied, I concentrate my writing in one area so that I could develop a cohesive body of work. Equally important to me was a woman whom I met while a student. Helen Strauss is still my role model and the woman I'd have chosen to be my mother if I had a choice. Helen, who was already a licensed masters level psychologist, went back to school and completed her doctoral studies at the age of 55. Then she enrolled in a 7-year postdoctoral program in psychoanalysis. Even today at over the age of 80, she is still practicing full time, writing about the effects of aging on the therapist, and presenting widely on the subject. If ever I think of myself as too old to do something, I look at Helen Strauss and am reminded that we are never too old. Helen is the mother of 5 and grandmother of 11. Her family is always her priority.

Finally, while at GSAPP, I was exposed to a group of psychologists in independent practice who served as adjunct faculty and were collectively known as the "New Jersey Mafia." Morrie Goodman, Marv Metsky, Stan Moldawsky, Gene Shapiro and Bob Weitz were staunch advocates for psychology. They not only had been part of the Organizing Council that fought for the opening of the Professional School, but had been leaders of the battle for licensure and freedom of choice legislation in New Jersey and served in varying capacities in the APA. They encouraged the Rutgers students to join APA and the New Jersey Psychological Association (NJPA), and to become involved in advocacy to protect our professional interests. They stood ready to mentor any of us that showed an interest. For me, advocacy and leadership seemed to come naturally. My father had been the master of his Masonic Lodge, and since I was a child, I always seemed to become president of the groups in which I participated. I was even copresident of that first class at GSAPP.

From the time I finished my doctoral work, I began to serve on NJPA Committees. I was elected to the NJPA Board of Directors for the first time in 1979 and was President in 1986. I saw my overall goal as "making the world safe for psychology." I was concerned with such issues as incursions into the autonomy of practitioners, expanding the settings in which psychologists could practice, and improving our image in the public eye. Those issues led me to work in APA as well. My first APA assignment was to the Subcommittee on Professional Services Review, whose task was to revise the insurance industry's review system that was then the bane of psychology's existence. I was next elected to the Public Information Committee, and served as its chair. Concurrently, I was elected as member-at-large of the Board of the newly formed Division of Independent Practice and served as co-chair of public information for the Division of Psychoanalysis. In 1988, I was elected to the APA Council of Representatives by NJPA and to serve on the Committee for the Advancement of Professional Practice (CAPP). In both of those positions, I took a strong stand for the autonomy of practice, the protection of the confidentiality of the therapist/patient relationship, and the inclusion of psychologists as providers in health care plans. My colleagues on the Council of Representatives elected me to the Board of Directors in 1991. My goal was still to make the world safe for psychology, but as a member of the Board, I expanded my view to include the safety of the science of psychology and the education of psychologists. I felt productive as a member of the Board and enjoyed the opportunity to develop projects that were of particular importance to me. I introduced and chaired the Task Force on the Changing Gender Composition of Psychology, which produced a comprehensive case study, an Action Plan that is being overseen by the APA Committee on Women in Psychology (CWP), and an interdisciplinary conference involving other professions that are experiencing the same gender shift. The goals were to understand the phenomenon and maintain the status, prestige, and earning power of the professions as they became increasingly female. I also introduced and chaired the Task Force on Urban Initiatives, whose mission was to bring psychology's expertise and knowledge to bear on the problems in America's cities. It eventually became an APA standing committee.

I did not begin my service on the Board of Directors with the idea in mind that it would lead to the APA Presidency. However, in March of 1993, Norine Johnson asked me how I felt about running for the presidency. I told her that I was ambivalent. She replied, "That's not the response I want from my candidate." Norine's comment gave me the push I needed to make my decision. I realized that it would have been hypocritical for me to encourage women to take on leadership roles, and then to decline to seek the highest position in APA myself. Once I made the decision, I ran seriously and hard, committed to running twice if need be. It did take two campaigns before I won, but it was well worth it for the opportunity to influence the future of the profession.

When I completed my doctoral degree in 1976, I was still working as a school psychologist. I was impressed with the number of children referred to me who were children of divorce. With my newfound credibility as a doctoral level psychologist, I suggested to my principal that I organize a group for those children. I looked to the literature for guidance and discovered that there was hardly anything available at that time. That led to my first journal article and subsequently to my first book, *Divorced Parents and Their Children: A Guide for Mental Health Professionals* (Cantor & Drake, 1983), written with a Rutgers colleague, Ellen Drake. My work with divorced families led me to conceptualize divorce as a separation/individuation issue, and to particularly look at that in terms of women's development.

Consequently, when Toni Bernay, whom I met through APA, and who over the years has become my best friend and confidante, suggested that together we edit a book about women, I immediately agreed. That book, *The Psychology of Today's Women: New Psychoanalytic Visions* (Bernay & Cantor, 1986) is considered ground-breaking in that it examines women's development through the life cycle from a psychoanalytic perspective. In 1990, *Women as Therapists: A Multi-theoretical Casebook* (Cantor, 1990) that I edited, was published. *What Do You Want To Do When You Grow Up?* (Cantor, 2000), a trade-book about planning for living a productive life after retirement, was published in 2000. I am also involved in a project with seven other prominent women psychologists to bring other women our understanding of issues important to them, such as relationships, money, and balancing their lives. By being open to the world and people around me, I have found subjects about which to think and write.

I became licensed as a psychologist in 1978 and started an independent practice. I worked with children, adolescents and adults in psychoanalytically-oriented psychotherapy. I still see patients and supervisees 4 days a week and consider my practice to be home base. I have always reserved the fifth day for other professional activities. For several years after graduation, I served as Director of Continuing Education for GSAPP. My next position was as Director of Professional Affairs for NJPA, where my responsibilities included lobbying and advocacy, interfacing with other professional groups, and dealing with the insurance industry. Finally, in 1991, I realized that I had to set aside my one day out of the office for writing and APA-related activities.

In 1987, a wonderful merging of my interests in advocacy and women's issues occurred. Along with Toni Bernay and Lenore Walker, I was instrumental in founding Women in Psychology for Legislative Action(WPLA), a political action committee. One of its purposes is to acquaint women in Congress with our agenda, and we did that through an event on the Hill, in conjunction with the Congressional Caucus on Women's Issues.

I awoke early in the morning after one luncheon and thought, "What did those Congresswomen have growing up that I didn't have?" I realized that I had raised a research question. I thoughtfully waited until 10 a.m. EST before calling Toni Bernay in California and announcing to her that I had an idea for our next book. We excitedly developed the concept of interviewing women in high-elected office to find the answer to the question I had posed. We recognized that for the project to come to fruition, we would need an agent and a publisher. We had also learned that you begin with writing a proposal, and that until a publisher has indicated an interest, it is not a good idea to write a whole book.

At the time we began our project, there were only 27 women in Congress. To insure an adequate sample, we had to turn to another group of elected officials: women in the executive branch of state government. The result of our research is our seminal study, *Women in Power—The Secrets of Leadership* (Cantor & Bernay, 1992), that was published in March of 1992, in time for the election that was being called "The Year of the Woman." We learned a great deal about the messages young girls need to receive to take a leadership path in their lives, whether in politics or other arenas. The messages are:

1. You are loved and special.
2. You can do anything you want to do.
3. It's all right to take risks.
4. You can use and enjoy your Creative Aggression.
5. You are entitled to dream of greatness.

We developed the concept of the Leadership Equation, which states: Leadership = Competent Self + Creative Aggression + EmpathyPower. By a *Competent Self* we mean an indelible, positive self image that isn't erased in the face of challenge, confrontation, or failure. We define *Creative Aggression* as aggression used in the service of life and growth, which allows you to take initiative, speak out, lead others, express opinions, set goals, and insist on your rights. *EmpathyPower* is power as women define it; power to move an agenda, to help others, to get the job done. It is flexible, mediating, and inclusive, rather than "command and control."

I did not get the messages growing up, but I acquired them as a result of a good experience in psychoanalysis and from my mentors, colleagues, husband, and friends along the way. My therapy, subsequent to graduation from GSAPP, made it possible for me to recognize that what I had to say was worthwhile and to take the risk of putting my ideas out to be criticized and challenged. Thus, I learned to recognize my Competent Self and with that I was able to use my Creative Aggression. As a therapist, I strongly believe that the therapeutic experience can profoundly change our lives and that women whose upbringing did not include these valuable messages can internalize them later in life.

With our understanding of what women need to assume leadership, Toni and I are now training women in industry, as well as our colleagues in psychology. My dream is to see women in the leadership and policymaking positions in the APA in numbers proportionate to their representation in the organization. I am reminded of the prediction made by the Center for American Women and Politics at Rutgers University in the mid 1980s. They noted that at the rate we were progressing, it would take 410 years before women would be represented in Congress in proportion to their numbers in the general population. Similarly in psychology, I am concerned at this juncture that we will continue to elect fewer than one woman President of the APA every decade, as has been the case until now. We cannot be the majority of psychologists working in science, education or practice, and not be an integral part of the policymaking bodies that will determine the ways we work.

I brought EmpathyPower to my role as President of the APA. I see it as my intuitive leadership style, as it is for many women. I began by having a clear agenda. Not only did it include a focus on women's issues, but on the cities as well. I wanted to move the Association in the direction of translating our knowledge into public policy, contributing to solutions while enhancing our public image. I included the voices of as many of my colleagues as I possibly could, for advice, suggestions, brainstorming, and comfort. I wanted the members of the Association to know that I was accessible and interested in what they had to say.

APA CEO Ray Fowler dubbed my presidency, "The Cantor era of good feeling" because I worked hard and successfully to bring about cooperation between science and practice within APA and collaboration among disparate groups of mental health professionals. I convened a summit meeting of the presidents of nine national mental health associations. The biggest challenge to all of our practitioner members was the incursion of managed care into their work, interfering with their autonomy and their earning power, and with their patients' confidentiality. Our product, on behalf of consumers of mental health services was "Your Mental Health Rights," a document that defined those rights that must be available, regardless of the extant health care system.

The project that emerged from my Women's Advisory Group was the Task Force on Adolescent Girls, chaired by Norine Johnson and Karen Zager. Their first product, *Beyond Appearance: A New Look at Adolescent Girls* (Johnson, Roberts, & Worell, 1999) was published by APA books in 1999. It is a textbook that looks at girls' strengths and resiliencies. A trade book for adolescent girls and their parents was another outgrowth of the Task Force. The agenda created by the Task Force is being carried forward by the APA Committee on Children, Youth and Families.

With my term behind me, I am able to look back on it with pride and I have become comfortable with the notion of being eminent! I recognize that I have done something that few women in psychology have done, that I have made a difference and that many of my colleagues look to me with respect and admiration. I am proud that my colleagues in NJPA named me Psychologist of the Year in 1987, that I was admitted to the National Academies of Practice in 1989 and became an APA Fellow in the same year, that my colleagues in APA gave me a Heiser Award for Advocacy in 1993, that the Association for the Advancement of Psychology gave me its 1994 award for Outstanding Sustained Advocacy efforts, and that I was awarded the 1999 APA Award for Distinguished Contributions to Applied Psychology as a Professional Practice.

Since completing my term as President, I have joined the Board of the American Psychological Foundation and the APA Insurance Trust. Here I have new opportunities to broaden my own horizons while serving the needs of my psychologist colleagues. I am also proud to have been named to the Board of Trustees of the Rosalynn Carter Institute, which focuses on helping caregivers, an honor that has come to me as a result of my work with women's issues and with APA. I have learned that every activity that I undertake creates new avenues for me, not all of which I can pursue. Sometimes, I have to say no. It takes an ongoing effort to remember that I can't be involved in everything. I am currently contemplating the time in the near future when I will run for no more positions in APA. I want to be able to step aside and make way for leadership by the next generation, which I trust will include many more women.

The most important message I have for young women who look to me as a role model is that you must find balance in your life, treat yourself with respect and caring, and find successful ways of coping with the inevitable problems that arise. Some of the ways I manage are part of my personality and others I have acquired with experience. I am fortunate to work fast and to be highly organized.

Nine years ago I hired a part-time administrative assistant, a position that never seemed necessary in solo practice. Having a typist and an answering machine met my needs until then. I hire graduate students as research assistants for my writing projects. Learning to delegate more was a must. I also preserve my leisure and family time. I never work later than 10 p.m., in part because my brain just stops functioning at that hour and is only able to absorb television drama! I plan vacations at reasonable intervals throughout the year and my husband and I love to travel. Being away from the office, the phone, and my computer forces me to focus differently. I try diligently to exercise 3 times a week, not because I love it, but because since I had angioplasty in 1984, I know exercise is essential to my survival. The life-threatening illness also led me to clarify and confirm my values. I spend as much time as I can with my two children, Joshua (b. 1959), Laura (b. 1962), their spouses, and my 5 wonderful grandchildren, Brad (b.1985), Scott, and Andrew (b. 1988) Cantor; and Alex (b. 1989) and Molly (b. 1992) Cramer.

I have received many honors from my peers, including the election to the APA presidency. But the most rewarding honor came in June, 1995 from my grandson, Brad, who was then 9½ years old. He invited me to the closing ceremony of the enrichment program for gifted children that he participated in the local public school system. I did not know that each of the third graders was going to describe his or her heroes and heroines. Here is what Brad read:

> My grandmother, Oma, is my heroine. She grew up in the Bronx. She is very important and nice. And she is also very important to many people. She has written a couple of semi-famous books. One is *Women in Power*. I think she is one of the most important people I know. Oma is my heroine.

Nothing could be more meaningful and thrilling to me than to have the love and respect of my family, who are, as they always have been, my priority. I am really pleased to have found a way to balance my life and that I have not missed the joy and love of my husband, children, and grandchildren as I pursued my career path. My wish for my future is that it is long, healthy, and filled with the same pleasures, excitement, and caring that I have been blessed with up until now. I know there remain wonderful new adventures and challenges for me and I plan to take on as many as I can.

REFERENCES

Bernay, T., & Cantor, D. W. (Eds.). (1986). *The psychology of today's women: New psycholoanalytic visions.* Hillsdale, NJ: Analytic Press.
Cantor, D. W. (2000). *What do you want to do when you grow up?* New York: Little, Brown.

Cantor, D. W. (Ed.). (1990). *Women as therapists: A multi-theoretical casebook.* New York: Springer.
Cantor, D. W., & Bernay, T. (1992). *Women in power—The secrets of leadership.* Boston: Houghton-Mifflin.
Cantor, D. W., & Drake, E. A. (1983). *Divorced parents and their children: A guide for mental health professionals.* New York: Springer.
Johnson, N. G., Roberts, M. C. & Worell, J. (Eds.). (1999). *Beyond appearance—A new look at adolescent girls.* Washington, DC: APA Books.

REPRESENTATIVE PUBLICATIONS

Cantor, D. W. (1999). There is a future for professional psychology. In H. Kaley, M. Eagle, & D. L. Wolitzky (Eds.), *Psychoanalytic therapy as health care* (pp. 79–88). Hillsdale, NJ: Analytic Press.
Cantor, D. W. (1999). Ensuring the future of professional practice. *American Psychologist, 54*(11).
Cantor, D. W. (1998) Achieving a mental health Bill of Rights. *Professional Psychology: Research and Practice, 29*(3), 315–316.
Cantor, D. W. (1998). Patients' rights in psychotherapy. In G. P. Koocher, J. C. Norcross, & S. S. Hill (Eds.), *Psychologists desk reference.* New York: Oxford University Press.
Cantor, D. W. (1994). Memories of childhood abuse: Protecting our patients and ourselves. *Register Report, 20*(1), 27–28.
Cantor, D. W. (1992) Research and the practitioner. *New Jersey Psychologist, 42*(3), 21–23.
Cantor, D. W., & Moldawsky, S. (1985). Training for independent practice: A survey of graduate programs in clinical psychology. *Professional psychology: Research & practice, 16*(6), 768–772.
Cantor, D. W. (1983). Independent practice: Minding your own business. *Psychotherapy in Private Practice, 1*(1), 19–24.
Span, M. N., & Cantor, D. W. (1983). Caution: Joint custody. *New Jersey Family Lawyer, 2*(5), 88–89, 96.
Cantor, D. W. (1982). The psychologist as child advocate with divorcing families. *Journal of Divorce, 6*(2), 77–86.
Cantor, D. W. (1982). Divorce: Separation or separation–individuation? *American Journal of Psychoanalysis, 42*(4), 307–313.
Cantor, D. W. (1979). Divorce: A view from the children. *Journal of Divorce, 2*(4), 357–361.
Cantor, D. W. (1978). School-based groups for children of divorce. *Journal of Divorce, 1*(2), 183–187.
Cantor, D. W. & Spragins, A. (1977). Delivery of psychological services to hearing impaired children in elementary school. *American Annals of the Deaf, 122*(3), 330–336.

CHAPTER 9

Diane J. Willis

Photographer: The University of Oklahoma Health Sciences Photographic Services.

Diane J. Willis

Mother's Day has always been special, but more so because I was born on Mother's Day, May 9, 1937 in Tahlequah, Oklahoma. My father William "Bill" Pascal Willis was attending summer school at Northeastern State University in Tahlequah when he met an attractive, 16-year-old woman, Zelma Marie Bynum, who was to become his wife. Bill Willis, who had a master's degree in history, taught school for a period of time before taking over and buying a general merchandise store from his father-in-law, Herb Bynum. For 20 years, he ran successful grocery, hardware, and clothing stores before being tapped to run for the Oklahoma House of Representatives. My father had a distinguished career serving as Chair of Appropriations, Speaker of the House for three terms, and Chair of the Taxation and Revenue Committee.

He is the only House member to have a scholarship named after him and awarded to disadvantaged students at all 26 colleges and universities in Oklahoma. His name graces a mental health center, a vocational technical school, and a highway in Oklahoma.

My mother, Zelma Bynum Willis, bore seven children and ran a very successful clothing store in Tahlequah, Oklahoma. She was a generous merchant who often gave clothes to children at the local Methodist Home and to poor families who traded with her. Her name graces a child guidance center, and both of my parents have a room at Northeastern State University named after them.

My six younger siblings all reside in Tahlequah, and all have families. Joyce has three children, is retired from a career of teaching, and is now a successful real estate agent in the office of my sister, Billie. Billie also has three children, one of whom is a judge, and has a career as a real estate broker. Herb Bynum Willis was an accountant by training, who eventually headed a rural electric cooperative. He is deceased but he has a 13-year-old son, Herb Bynum Willis, Jr. My sister, Zelma, retired early from her career as an elementary school teacher and now works with her husband in their professional rodeo business. They have three children. William P. Willis, Jr. and H. Doak Willis are both attorneys who practice in Tahlequah. They each have two children. Thus, I have 14 wonderful nieces and nephews.

My paternal grandmother, Lula Wyatt Willis, was a member of the Kiowa tribe as was my father. I was fortunate to be able to interact with my Kiowa relatives since my father often took the family to Anadarko, OK, the heart of Kiowa country. All of my siblings were enrolled in the tribe, but only two of us have been active in Pow Wows, Indian family reunions, and celebrations. To be a member of the tribe one must have at least one-fourth Kiowa blood quantum. We can trace my Indian grandmother, Lula Wyatt, whose father, William Wyatt (my great grandfather) was related to Sir Francis Wyatt, the first Governor of Jamestown.

My grandfather, Herb Bynum, as well as my parents, had a very positive influence on me. They taught me a great deal about business and purchasing clothes for our store from the Merchandise Mart in Dallas, Texas. They taught me the value of hard work. As mentioned earlier, my mother modeled generosity and hard work. Later on, my father taught me the value of politics and how to accomplish getting legislation passed that could be helpful and of benefit to people. He was also very proud of his Indian heritage and passed along this pride and interest to me. As a result of his influence I have actively worked with tribes and the Indian Health Service to try to inspire the lives of American Indian children and families. In 1999, the Oklahoma Federation of Indian Women named me "Outstanding Indian Woman of the Year 2000."

I attended Northeastern State University in Tahlequah, Oklahoma, from 1955 to 1959, graduating in May of 1960 with a BS degree in biology and a minor in speech. I received my Medical Technology (ASCP) training at St. John's Hospital in Tulsa, Oklahoma, from January to December of 1960, and used this training while attending graduate programs. To fulfill a long time desire to attend a religious institution, I attended Southern Seminary in 1962 to 1963. From 1963 to 1965, I attended George Peabody College, where I received my MA degree in psychology. I then chose to transfer to the University of Oklahoma in 1965 and completed my PhD degree in experimental child psychology in 1970. After completing a 2-year post-doctoral fellowship in general clinical psychology at the University of Oklahoma Health Sciences Center, I became a licensed psychologist.

While active in youth work at my church, I often counseled students but felt limited in my knowledge base. So, I decided psychology would provide that knowledge base, and I transferred from Seminary to Peabody College. During my graduate work at George Peabody, Drs. Nicholas Hobbs, Susan Gray, Lloyd Dunn, and Sam Ashcroft were my mentors, and my love for developmental/clinical psychology and developmental disorders grew from their influence and guidance. Throughout my career, I have focused on children with developmental disorders, including children who have emotional, physical, and cognitive disabilities as a result of maltreatment. This is largely because of the influence of my mentors at George Peabody, who were nationally renowned for their work in the area of disabilities. Dr. Nicholas Hobbs, who was Chair of the Department of Psychology at Peabody, required all psychology graduate students to obtain a minor in special education, and this led me in the direction of clinical and developmental work within the field of psychology. Drs. Oscar Parsons and Logan Wright were my mentors at the University of Oklahoma Health Sciences Center, and they challenged me to publish, think as a scientist-practitioner, and be active in the American Psychological Association (APA).

My first psychology position was at the University of Oklahoma Health Sciences Center in the Department of Communication Disorders, where I taught two graduate psychology courses and ran a one-person psychology clinic for children with speech and hearing impairments. Practicum students worked with me in evaluating and treating children ages 2 to 12 years. At this time in 1975, the Society of Pediatric Psychology was established, and I was one of the founding members.

I resigned my faculty position in the Department of Communication Disorders in 1974 when I was offered a position in the Department of Pediatrics as Coordinator of Inpatient Pediatric Psychology Services. I remained the coordinator for 2 to 3 years and resigned to accept the position as Director of Psychological Services at the Child Study Center in the Department of Pediatrics. The position change was prompted by the fact that the inpatient coordinator position had become so busy that my work hours had expanded from 7:00 a.m. to 9:00 p.m. to meet the requests for consultations.

I could not obtain assistance for the consultations at that time, so I decided to accept the position at the Child Study Center (CSC) that had been offered to me twice before. Subsequently, the Chair of the Department of Pediatrics was pressured by the other pediatric faculty to hire two psychologists for consultation and liaison to the inpatient service at Children's Hospital. The pediatric faculty liked having a psychologist participate in rounds with them, as I had done routinely, and they liked having daily consults. Thus, my contributions were in establishing a format for referrals, same-day consults, and expanding a mental health component to teaching rounds for medical students, residents, and faculty. My mentor, Dr. Logan Wright, was one of the founders of the field of pediatric psychology in 1968. At the Health Sciences Center, he was Chair of the Section and coordinated outpatient services. During my tenure as Coordinator of Inpatient Pediatric Psychology Services and then as Director of Psychological Services at the CSC, I became Associate Editor of the Pediatric Psychology Newsletter for 1 year, and then I became editor (1973–1975).

Within a year, I developed the newsletter into a journal, and I was the first editor (1975–1976) of the *Journal of Pediatric Psychology (JPP)*. The first issues focused on special topics that had not received much press, but were nevertheless very important. Child abuse and neglect were the focus of one entire journal issue (Willis, 1976a), and this was published before the general public and professionals took much interest in the topic. Child neuropsychology was the topic for another issue (Willis, 1976b). With children showing up in hospitals injured, and physicians not recognizing the signs of child maltreatment, I felt that it was absolutely essential to train pediatric psychologists in this area. I resigned as editor of the *Journal of Pediatric Psychology* after 1 year, when I was elected President-elect of the Society of Pediatric Psychology. Shortly after this, I was also appointed editor of the *Journal of Clinical Child Psychology (JCCP)* from 1977 to 1982.

My major contributions early in my career were as founder and editor of JPP and developing JCCP into a peer-reviewed journal. In addition, while the Society of Pediatric Psychology was a young organization, I contributed to publicizing the new field and increasing both interest and membership in the organization through my role as editor of the expanded Newsletter for the society. During my tenure as president-elect and president of the Society, we voted to form a contract with a professional publisher for the journal, and soon the Society became financially solvent.

During my tenure as editor of JCCP, the journal began publishing timely and relevant research as well as clinical and advocacy articles. When I resigned as editor and became President of the Section on Clinical Child Psychology of Division 12 (1982–1983), my focus on training issues resulted in the Hilton Head Conference for Training in Clinical Child Psychology. Proceedings of the conference (Tuma, 1985) were published and used as a guide for training clinical child psychologists for the future. Reference is still made to the published proceedings from this conference.

I have also made contributions to psychology by focusing attention on the issue of child maltreatment. This work began with editing and developing the special issue of JPP on the topic in the 1970s, but extended to my service on the APA Board of Professional Affairs, and chairing the Task Force on Child Maltreatment for APA. This task force produced a report for publication as a special issue of JCCP in the 1990s (Willis, 1995) and a brochure on child abuse. While President of the Division of Child, Youth, and Family Services (Division 37) in the 1980s, I chaired a task force that resulted in a published text on prevention of child maltreatment (Willis, Holden, & Rosenberg, 1992). I also proposed and helped found the Section on Child Maltreatment within Division 37 in the 1990s. More recently, I guest edited a special violence issue for *Psychotherapy: Theory, Research, and Practice* (1991) and guest edited two book publications by APA on abstracts of child abuse publications (Willis, Bagwell, & Campbell, 1991; Willis, Broyhill, & Campbell, 1991).

I was fortunate to be one of two psychologists who were appointed to serve on the first U.S. Advisory Board on Child Abuse and Neglect (1989–1993), and to testify before the National Academy of Sciences on child abuse in 1992. I also testified before the U.S. Congress on the issue of child abuse within Indian country. The U.S. Advisory Board published four reports for Congress and all Board members contributed to the reports (U.S. Advisory Board, 1990, 1991, 1993). Several recommendations made by the Board became law through legislation that the Board proposed.

I received the Nicholas Hobbs Award from Division 37 for my contributions to child advocacy (1993). I also received the Distinguished Professional Contributions Award in 1996 from Division 12 for my long-standing clinical work and advocacy on behalf of children, and as a mentor–teacher. The Society of Pediatric Psychology presented me with a Distinguished Contributions Award in 1982 for my contributions as mentioned earlier, and the Oklahoma Psychological Association presented me with the Distinguished Psychologist Citation (1989) for my work on behalf of psychology. The first time the Karl Heiser Award was given by APA in 1992, I was one of the recipients to receive the award for my long-standing work on the former Committee for the Advancement of Psychology, and subsequently, the Association for the Advancement of Psychology.

LESSONS AND SUGGESTIONS

Looking back at my life, I believe I will be remembered as the founding editor of J1PP and as the editor who began the peer review process for JCCP. In addition, I will be credited for founding the Section on Child

Maltreatment in Division 37. Donald Routh, in his book on the history of clinical child psychology (1994), has already placed my name in a history book, crediting me for my editorial activities.

The lessons I've learned are to work hard, be creative and visionary in your thinking, and surround yourself with outstanding professionals. Be open to input from others and realize that there is more to life than just psychology. Use your skills and your knowledge to open doors for others, and take the time to help open those doors. Be involved in your professional organizations by membership, attendance at meetings, and contributing to task forces, business meetings, and through presentation of papers or symposia. However, be active locally in organizations that benefit people less fortunate, or start groups for disenfranchised people or people in need of psychology's assistance. Be unselfish by giving psychology away to others through group work or through donation of time to speak, consult, or advocate on behalf of the needs of others. Be civic-minded and politically active by attending precinct meetings, joining political organizations of your choice, informing policymakers about psychology and what it can do for others, and even testifying on legislation at the state or local level. It is as imperative to me that psychologists be good and interested citizens as they are psychologists. Life will be richer because of our involvement, and we can contribute more to others.

REFERENCES

Routh, D. K. (1994). *Clinical psychology since 1917: Science, practice, and organization.* New York: Plenum Press.

Tuma, J. (Ed.) (1985). *Proceedings of the Conference on Training Clinical Child Psychologists.* (Division 12, Section 1, American Psychological Association.) Baton Rouge, LA: Land & Land Printers.

U.S. Advisory Board on Child Abuse and Neglect. (1990). *Child abuse and neglect: Critical first steps in response to a national emergency.* Washington, DC: Department of Health and Human Services, Administration for Children and Families.

U.S. Advisory Board on Child Abuse and Neglect. (1991). *Creating caring communities: Blueprint for an effective Federal policy on child abuse and neglect* (Second Report). Washington, DC: Department of Health and Human Services, Administration for Children and Families.

U.S. Advisory Board on Child Abuse and Neglect. (1993). *Neighbors helping neighbors: A new national strategy for the protection of children* (Fourth Report). Washington, DC: Department of Health and Human Services, Administration for Children and Families.

Willis, D. J. (Ed.). (1976a). Abused and neglected children [Special issue]. *Journal of Pediatric Psychology, 1*(2).

Willis, D. J. (Ed.). (1976b). Child neuropsychology [Special issue]. *Journal of Pediatric Psychology, 1*(3).

Willis, D. J. (Guest Editor). (1991). Psychotherapy with victims [Special issue]. *Psychotherapy: Theory and Research, 28,* 1–191.
Willis, D. J. (Guest Editor). (1995). Psychological issues related to child maltreatment [Special issue]. *Journal of Clinical Child Psychology, 24*(Supplement).
Willis, D. J., Bagwell, W., & Campbell, M. (1991). *Child abuse: Abstracts of the psychological and behavioral literature, 1,* 1967–1985. Washington, DC: American Psychological Association.
Willis, D. J., Broyhill, G., & Campbell, M. (1991). *Child abuse: Abstracts of the psychological and behavioral literature, 2,* 1986–1990. Washington, DC: American Psychological Association.
Willis, D. J., Holden, W., & Rosenberg, M. (1992). Child abuse prevention: Introduction and historical review. In D.J. Willis, W. Holden, & M. Rosenberg, (Eds.). *Prevention of child maltreatment: A development and ecological perspective* (pp. 1–4). New York: Wiley.

REPRESENTATIVE PUBLICATIONS

Culbertson, J. L., & Willis, D. J. (Eds.). (1993). *Testing young children.* Austin, TX: Pro–Ed.
Culbertson, J. L., & Willis, D. J. (1993). Introduction to testing young children. In J. L. Culbertson & D. J. Willis (Eds.), *Testing young children* (pp. 1–10). Austin, TX: Pro–Ed.
Culbertson, J. L., & Willis, D. J. (1998). Interventions for young children who have been multiply abused. In B. Rossman & M. Rosenberg, (Eds.), *Multiple victimization of children* (pp. 207–232). New York: Hayworth Press.
Culbertson, J. L., & Willis, D. J. (1998). Interventions with young children who have been multiply abused. *Journal of Aggression, Maltreatment, and Trauma, 2,* 207–232.
DeLeon, P. H., Folen, R. A., Jennings, F. L., Willis, D. J., & Wright, R. H. (1991). The case for prescription privileges: A logical evolution of professional practice. *Journal of Clinical Child Psychology, 20,* 254–267.
Holden, E. W., & Willis, D. J. (1992). Preventing child maltreatment during the prenatal/perinatal period. In D. J. Willis, E. W. Holden, & M. Rosenberg (Eds.), *Prevention of child maltreatment: A developmental & ecological perspective* (pp. 17–46). New York: Wiley.
Roberts, M., Koocher, G., Routh, D, & Willis, D. J. (Eds). (1993). *Readings in pediatric psychology.* New York, NY: Plenum.
Silovsky, J. F., & Willis, D. J. (2000). Foster parenting. In F.W. Kaslow (Ed.), *Handbook of couple and family forensics* (pp. 62–81). New York: Wiley.
Sipes, D. & Willis, D. J. (1993). *Helping Indian parents discipline their children.* Chicago, IL: National Committee to Prevent Child Abuse.
Willis, D. J. (Guest Editor). (1991). Psychotherapy with victims [Special issue]. *Psychotherapy: Theory and Research, 28,* 1–191.
Willis, D. J. (1993). Professional issues and training. In M. Roberts, G. Koocher, D. Routh, & D. J. Willis (Eds.), *Readings in pediatric psychology* (pp. 281–293). New York: Plenum Press.

Willis, D. J. (1995). Psychological impact of child abuse and neglect. *Journal of Clinical Child Psychology, 24,* 2–4.

Willis, D. J. (1995). A selected listing of measures of depression for children. In E. Beckham & B. Leber (Eds.), *Handbook of depression: Treatment, assessment, and research* (2nd ed., pp. 600–605). New York: Guilford.

Willis, D. J. (1996). Psychotherapy in the real world. *Psychotherapy: Research and Practice, 33,* 131–134.

Willis, D. J., Bagwell, W., & Campbell, M. (1991). *Child abuse: Abstracts of the psychological and behavioral literature, 1,* 1967–1985. Washington, DC: American Psychological Association.

Willis, D. J., Coyle, T., & Leber, W. (1998) Clinical interviewing. In C. Reynolds (Ed.), *Comprehensive clinical psychology: Assessment* (pp. 81–97). Oxford: Elsevier Science Publishers.

Willis, D. J., Dobrec, A., & Sipes, D. S. B. (1992). Treating American Indian victims of abuse and neglect. In L. A. Vargas & J. D. Koss-Chioino (Eds.), *Working with culture: Psychotherapeutic interventions with ethnic minority children and adolescents* (pp. 276–299). San Francisco: Jossey-Bass.

Willis, D. J., & Holden, E. W. (1990). Etiological factors contributing to deviant development. In J. Johnson & G. Goldman (Eds.), *Developmental assessment in clinical child psychology. A handbook* (pp. 38–57). New York: Pergamon.

Willis, D. J., Holden, W., & Rosenberg, M. (1992). Child abuse prevention: Introduction and historical review. In D. J. Willis, W. Holden, & M. Rosenberg (Eds.), *Prevention of child maltreatment: A development and ecological perspective* (pp. 1–14). New York: Wiley.

Willis, D. J., & Silovsky, J. F. (1998). Prevention of violence at the societal level. In P. K. Trickett & C. Schellenbach (Eds.), *Violence against children in the family and community* (pp. 401–416). Washington, DC: APA Publications.

Willis, D. J., & Vargas, L. (Guest Editors). (1994). New directions in the treatment and assessment of ethnic minority children and adolescents [Special issue]. *Journal of Clinical Child Psychology, 23.*

CHAPTER 10

Elaine Hatfield

Photographer: Richard L. Rapson.

Elaine Hatfield

FAMILY BACKGROUND

Charles Hatfield was my father, and his family arrived in America long before the American Revolution. They were the Hatfields of Hatfield and McCoy fame. They were mostly English, but there was a sprinkling of Irish, Scottish, French, and Native American thrown in. My grandfather, Hally Hatfield, was a hardshell Baptist minister but when the Baptists failed to be "fire-and-brimstone" enough to suit him, he started his own religion—named, modestly enough, "The Hatfields."

My father was very good at any number of things. After he left school in the 10th grade (in the midst of the Great Depression of the 1930s), he worked at more than 35 jobs. He finally became a Detroit policeman.

Eileen Kalahar Hatfield is my mother. Her parents were immigrants too—they traveled from Ireland to Canada, and then to the United States. She was an Irish-Catholic and a housewife. Ideologically, the Church's views on women, birth control, mixed marriages, and so on were not congenial to her. Had she the courage, she would have been a critic of the Church, but she grudgingly followed its dictates.

I was born in Detroit, Michigan on October 22, 1937 and I have two younger sisters—Patricia Rich, a social worker, and Mary Hatfield, a psychologist. She has also held a number of jobs ranging from advertising executive to stockbroker.

I grew up during World War II in a then racially segregated, low-income housing project (Herman Gardens), in a segregated city, Detroit.

Detroit has long been marred by ethnic and racial conflict. Soon after my father joined the police force, a fight between Black and White teenagers exploded into a full-scale race-riot in June of l943. Portions of downtown Detroit went up in flames and 34 people were killed. Finally, the Detroit police and Federal troops restored order. A few weeks before my father's retirement in July of 1967, rioting broke out when an after-hours speakeasy was raided in a Black section of Detroit. Rioters looted 1,700 stores and set fire to 1,383 buildings. This time, 43 people were killed. After more than a week, Detroit police officers, state police, national guardsmen, and Federal troops were finally able to contain the riot.

In spite of the fact that my family was caught up in the midst of social change, none of us ever thought seriously about issues of gender, social class, race, or ethnicity. We never talked about much of anything. We simply existed.

EDUCATION

College and graduate school were wonderful, liberating experiences for me. I entered a world I hadn't known existed! I felt truly at home. I attended the University of Michigan from 1955 to 1959 and graduated with highest honors in English literature and psychology. They remain the two main interests of my life, although I have also long been intrigued by cultural anthropology, history, world literature, and film as well.

In 1959, I entered the PhD program at Stanford University. By then, I had become intellectually interested in passionate love and sexual desire. I was, of course, aware that it was "taboo" to theorize about such topics. Passionate love was considered to be a trivial phenomenon; it wasn't a respectable topic of study; it wasn't amenable to scientific investigation. There wasn't any hope of finding out very much about it in my lifetime. It wasn't "hot." The hot topic in the 1960s was mathematical modeling.

Math modeling and rat runways. If we ignored the first and last thirds of the runway in rat experiments (too much variability in rat behavior there) and concentrated on the middle third (where rat behavior generally settled down), we had a real chance of making intellectual breakthroughs and importantly contributing to the field of psychology. Thus, the conventional wisdom.

At the same time, late in the evenings at Stanford University after our work was done, we confided endlessly to one another about our personal problems. There our concerns went beyond the perambulations of rodents. For most people, the rigors of graduate school were taking a toll on their romances. At one time, all the members of our group were having terrible trouble in their close relationships. Some of us couldn't find anyone to date, others were trapped in unhappy romantic relationships or getting divorces. One night, several in the corridor lamented that things were so horrific that they sometimes thought about committing suicide. One set of topics was interesting in the day; another, a source of near-obsession in our evening chats. Because of the bravery and generosity of my mentor, Leon Festinger, I was permitted to start rigorous investigations of love as part of my graduate work, but the road was never easy.

CAREER DEVELOPMENTS

The first signs of trouble appeared when I tried to find a faculty position. I came on the job market during the "Sputnik era." America was in a race, fueled by misinformation and terror, with the USSR and huge amounts of money were being poured into education. Anyone could get a job, or so I thought. My advisor, Leon Festinger, kindly told me that I was the best graduate student he'd ever had—probably he told *everyone* that—and, in a burst of hubris, promised that he could get me a job anywhere I wanted. I wanted the best, which at that time meant Harvard, Yale, or Bell Labs. We soon discovered that it was not to be as easy as we thought. Chairs were frank about saying that a woman would not fit in at their universities. They assured us that they were personally in favor of hiring women, but lamented that their colleagues or their students would not accept such an appointment. I finally found and accepted a job at the University of Minnesota, at the Student Activities Bureau, arranging dances, and embarked on a program of scientific research on close relationships in dating situations. I volunteered to teach two social psychology courses and to supervise graduate students. So, in the next year, apparently not having offended anyone, I was offered a position in the University of Minnesota Psychology Department with tenure.

I had a wonderful time. The Minnesota social psychology laboratory was wonderful then. I worked with Ellen Berscheid (then a student, now the winner of an APA Distinguished Scientist Award), Elliot Aronson (also an APA winner, both for his teaching and his research), Dana Bramel, and Ben Willerman. Stanley Schachter was a frequent visitor.

A few years later, in 1967, I moved to the University of Wisconsin (the Department of Sociology—the UW Psychology Department was not yet considering the appointment of woman to faculty positions), where I had a chance to work with another collection of social psychology luminaries, including Jerry Marwell, Jane Piliavin, John DeLamater, and Shalom Schwartz, among others.

My prime interests then were equity theory, research on physical attraction, and close relationships, focusing primarily on passionate love (crushes, obsession, infatuation, and the like) and sexual desire.

The most damaging blow to my research program came in 1975. Wisconsin's U.S. Senator, William Proxmire, discovered that the National Science Foundation had granted Dr. Ellen Berscheid, one of my research partners, and me $84,000 to expand our work on passionate and companionate love. He awarded us his first "Golden Fleece Award," Proxmire's famous public relations effort to "save" taxpayers from funding "unneeded" scientific research.

He launched his well-publicized publicity campaign by firing off a press release:

> I object to this not only because no one—not even the National Science Foundation—can argue that falling in love is a science; not only because I'm sure that even if they spend $84 million or $84 billion they wouldn't get an answer that anyone would believe. I'm also against it because I don't want the answer.
>
> I believe that 200 million other Americans want to leave some things in life a mystery, and right on top of the things we don't want to know is why a man falls in love with a woman and vice versa.
>
> So National Science Foundation—get out of the love racket. Leave that to Elizabeth Barrett Browning and Irving Berlin. Here if anywhere Alexander Pope was right when he observed, "If ignorance is bliss, tis folly to be wise." (cited in Hatfield & Walster, 1978, p. viii).

In subsequent weeks, Senator Proxmire and his supporters issued a series of *reductio ad absurdum* press releases. I received bags of mail, mostly critical. A Chicago tabloid, *The Chicago Tribune*, ran a contest. People could call in and vote: Who was right—Proxmire or me? Three University of Chicago Nobel Prize winners wrote in to say "Hooray for research on love!" but massive numbers of readers (and even a few friends!) wrote in to say I was naïve to think love and sex could be studied scientifically. They also argued, "If she can't even manage her own love life (they must have been foretelling marital problems I didn't yet see) how can she advise other people what to do?" and then presented their academic or clinical views. I lost the election, Proxmire 87.5%, me 12.5%.

Even my mother's bishop got into the act. He issued a message to the Detroit parishes denouncing the National Science Foundation for awarding scientists $84,000 to unravel the "most sacred mysteries of love and life."

"Who granted these 'scientists' the ability to see into men's minds and hearts?" he asked. Were our findings going to eliminate pride, selfishness, jealously, suffering, and war? "Jesus Christ has taught us all that we need to know about love and life," he insisted. "His word waits there, in *The Holy Bible*, for us. He has been waiting for us for almost 2,000 years. It is *His* commands we must follow, not the childish 'advice' of some arrogant, secular scientist, who presumes to know more than Our Lord."

Senator Barry Goldwater came to my defense. So did columnist James Reston. In his column in *The New York Times,* Reston (1978) wryly agreed that love will always be a mystery. "But if the sociologists and psychologists can get even a suggestion of the answer to our pattern of romantic love, marriage, disillusions, divorce—and the children left behind—it would be the best investment of federal money since Jefferson made the Louisiana purchase."

How did I cope? Not very well, I'm afraid. Though some of my friends think I must look back at this time as one of personal and scholarly triumph, given the centrality of love research in psychology today, it was actually very hard for me. I am essentially a shy person, not on the lookout for conflict. I just like to pursue my intellectual interests. So the *L'Affaire Proxmire* was actually painful to me and when I remember it, I do so mostly with embarrassment, despite the eventual positive outcome.

I was blessed in this instance, however, by coming from a family and a community that cared not a bit about academic pursuits. It comes as no surprise to me that most of the world thinks my interests, in books, foreign films, and scholarly pursuits, are a bit absurd. In my working class family, I was not expected to succeed brilliantly at anything, just to do my best. So, when things are terrible, I tend to be shell-shocked for a few hours, then, reeling, begin plodding doggedly along. Sooner or later, the tide changes.

In 1978, I wrote a little book, *A New Look at Love*, in an attempt to review what social psychologists knew about passionate and companionate love and to explain why the study of love is important. In 1979 the book won the American Psychological Foundation's National Media Award. Even so, not everyone welcomed such a book.

I have hung around long enough to see things change. Eventually it became clear to politicians, scholars, and the general public that even "irrational" emotions such as passionate love can be studied scientifically. In 25 years, the field of social psychology has become much smarter about the nature of relationships. In 1969, when Ellen Berscheid and I wrote the first text that considered passionate love, *Interpersonal Attraction*, we had difficulty finding much material on the topic. The 1980s and 1990s have seen a tremendous surge in interest in love and intimacy.

In the 1980s, Steve Duck and Robin Gilmour (1981a, 1981b, 1981c; Duck, 1982) inaugurated a series of books on the initiation, maintenance, and dissolution of relationships. Scientists banded together to form four international, interdisciplinary organizations designed to foster research on close relationships: the International Society for the Study of Personal Relationships (ISSPR), the International Network on Personal Relations (INPR), the International Society for Research on Emotions, the International Academy of Sex Research, and the Society for the Scientific Study of Sex. In 1984, Steve Duck and his colleagues at INPR founded the *Journal of Social and Personal Relationships* which is devoted entirely to research on close relationships. Later, in 1994, Patricia Noller and her colleagues at ISSPR inaugurated a second journal, *Personal Relationships*, dedicated to publishing research on the same topics. Since then, thousands of studies concerning love, sex, and intimacy have been published in these and various other journals.

THE HAWAII FACTOR

In 1981, I moved to the University of Hawaii to be Chair of the Psychology Department. I met my current husband, Richard L. Rapson, a year later, in 1982. At that time, he was deeply committed to a program called "Semester at Sea." The S.S. Universe is a college afloat that spends 100 days each year traveling around the globe. Dick wanted to know if I would be interested in sailing on the next voyage. I was, but because I had agreed to serve as Chair at UH for 3 years, I could not. Since then, of course, we have spent all our summers traveling around the world.

For both Dick and me, our move to Hawaii assumed critical importance in increasing our fascination with, and a realization of the importance of cultural and ethnic variety in shaping psychological behavior. Hawaii is a multicultural society—European-American (28%), Japanese-American (26%), part-Hawaiian (16%), Filipino-American (12%), Chinese-American (6%), and sizable numbers of African Americans, Samoans, Korean-Americans, Tongans, southeast Asians, and so forth. Everyone is a member of a minority and so everyone must adapt to unexpected conditions for which few are prepared. Hawaii forms an extraordinary spectacle that, although far from perfect and universally harmonious, functions rather well, probably as well as any multicultural society in the world.

One remarkable dimension to life in Hawaii is that more than 60% of the marriages performed in the past 15 years have been interracial marriages. Since more than 99% of ethnic Hawaiians are already products of intermarriage, these statistics count all marriages involving part-Hawaiian as already mixed. No matter how it's counted, the roughly 60% may be compared with less than 4% on the American mainland! Families are often so mixed in their ethnic expectations that the younger generation has a great deal of trouble answering questions regarding their ethnic identity. In Hawaii, one often notices the striking combinations of the cosmopolitan names routinely heard: Farouk Wang, Tennyson Yamasaki, Kenji Klein, and so on. Each individual may represent a brief truce among surprisingly juxtaposed cultures, peoples who would never have crossed paths in previous ages. Now they are joined in the pedigrees of living persons.

When asked to identify their ethnic heritage they often and proudly say Portuguese, Chinese, Swedish, Hawaiian, and Irish. When asked to check one on a demographic questionnaire, they can be at a total loss. Soon, survey researchers in Hawaii learn to repeat the mantra: "If you don't know what to check, just check the ethnic group with which you identify the most." If people were to check "Other," almost everyone would fall into that category. As a consequence, it is not unusual for one child in a family to claim to be European-American whereas his brother checks off Chinese-American.

When I first came to Hawaii, one of my colleagues, Jerold Shapiro, asked if I would fill in at his psychotherapy practice at King Kalakaua Clinic while he was on sabbatical. My first step was to secure a Hawaii license. At that time, in Hawaii, licensing was much more informal than it is now. In 1981, I was merely required to take the American Psychological Association national examination, a Hawaii examination to make sure I was *au courant* with Hawaii laws, and submit to an interview with a Hawaii licensing board. By chance, in the course of my career I had taken all the clinical psychology courses Hawaii required. I had completed two internships as well. In Wisconsin, I had worked with Drs. Morton Perlmutter and Constance Arons at the Wisconsin Family Practice Institute and Dr. and Mrs. Carl Whitaker in the Wisconsin Psychiatry Department as a volunteer therapist. At that time, family therapy and husband and wife teams were much in vogue.

I accepted Dr. Shapiro's offer and liked dealing with a wide spectrum of Hawaiian society so much, I decided to stay on. Dick Rapson soon agreed to share co-therapy duties with me. At that time, co-therapists were allowed to participate in therapy sessions, given that they were volunteers (i.e., they did not charge), and that a note was filed with the state of Hawaii outlining their function in the therapy session.

As co-psychotherapists in a wide-ranging practice, my husband and I have gotten to know clients from a variety of cultural and ethnic groups. We have seen three generations of Japanese, Chinese, and Pacific Islanders; adherents of every religious group ... or none; couples who had arranged marriages and who had married for love; and couples who formed a single, nuclear family or who congregated in large extended families.

In most of the United States and in most of the nations of the world, such casualness about ethnicity is not the norm. In most societies, unlike Hawaii, there is a definite majority—and minority members are often made to feel it. With the breakup of communism in Eastern Europe and the renewed rise of tensions in the Balkans, we have seen a resurgence of malignant ethnic, national, and religious identity. Like Rip Van Winkle, hatreds and passions that were asleep for decades have awakened among peoples with names that had been mistakenly consigned to the dustbin of history: Estonians, Serbs, Croats, Bosnians, Uzbeks, Georgians, Slovaks, Lithuanians, Latvians, Ukrainians, Armenians, Azeris, Kosovars, Albanians, Macedonians, and on and on.

There are currents that flow in the opposite direction from ethnic, national, and religious division. Besides the intermarriage rate in Hawaii, the growth of the World Wide Web, increased trade and travel, and the communications revolution, there is the epochal movement toward European unity called the *European Union* that seeks to stem the tide of fragmentation in favor of the larger human community. Nobody can predict if disintegration or integration will define the future. But we can safely predict that sensitivity to other cultures will be required by individuals and nations in that future. We personally have found such sensitivity and knowledge to be an enlarging dimension to life.

MAJOR CONTRIBUTIONS

It is extremely difficult to decide what one's own contributions to psychology might be. Thus, I asked my husband, co-author, and co-therapist Dick, an American historian at the University of Hawaii whose business it is to look at the "big picture," to address what *he* considered to be my major contributions to psychology. Our combined wisdom follows.

At a time when the study of passionate love and sexual desire was considered to be "unscientific, trivial, or impossible to study," my colleagues and I pioneered the rigorous scientific study of these "taboo" topics. We focused on the passionate beginnings of relationships: How people meet, mate, fall in love, and make love. But this led us also to the study of later events in the cycle that befall many: falling out of love, only to risk it all over again. Sometimes, this happens over and over again.

Soon, this led us to investigate issues of equity in relationships, an attempt to find patterns for what works and what doesn't work when it comes to love. After that, in a series of tightly conceived laboratory experiments, my colleagues and I began the study of emotional contagion—the process by which people coordinate their facial expressions, vocal expressions, and postures with those of others and thereby gain the ability to "intuit" what others are feeling. We have explored the factors that make people good senders versus good receivers of emotion, and we have tried to assess the advantages and costs of being sensitive or insensitive to others emotional states.

Most recently, we have tried to broaden the range and reach of psychological research itself, first by trying to help move scholarship beyond Western perspectives. This we have done through our cross-cultural studies of love and sex. Second, we have integrated a generation of historical studies of marriage, love, sex, and emotions over the past 500 years to provide richer perspective to the contemporary scene and even attempt some informed speculation about future possibilities.

Although our research topics have varied and our interests continue to evolve and grow, the common thread appears to be the effort to move psychology into territories that have been previously unexplored or under-explored, investigating areas that were once regarded as marginal or even thought to be taboo. We have not been afraid.

I have certainly been more highly acclaimed for these efforts than I deserve and I am grateful for all the honors that have been bestowed on me. In 1999, I was president of the Society for the Scientific Study of Sex (SSSS) and have been a professor of psychology at the University of Hawaii since 1981. I am probably best known as the scholar who pioneered the scientific study of passionate love and sexual desire. In 1993, I won my university's award for Excellence in Research. In 1994, Ellen Berscheid and I became the first two women to receive the Distinguished Scientist Award of the Society of Experimental Social Psychology. In 1995, I earned the Distinguished Scientist Award from the Society for the Scientific Study of Sex (preceded among women only by Mary Calderone and, decades later, Virginia Johnson). In 1998, I won the Alfred Kinsey Award from the Western Region of SSSS. For the past two decades, I have been ranked in citation reviews as the most frequently quoted social psychologist in the world. I have written many books on my research, among them two books which both won the American Psychological Foundation's National Media Award: *A New Look at Love* (1978) and *Mirror, Mirror: The Importance of Looks in Everyday Life* (1986).

My husband and I have collaborated on three recent books. *Love, Sex, and Intimacy: Their Psychology, Biology, and History* (1993) and *Love and Sex: Cross-Cultural Perspectives* (1996). The first book was consciously multi-disciplinary, whereas the second reached into the area of cultural comparisons. Cambridge University Press published our third book, *Emotional Contagion*, in 1994, completing the trilogy.

In my "old age" I have returned to an interest of my youth—creative writing. My first novel, *Rosie* (Hatfield & Rapson, 2000) was published in 2000. I have also published more than 30 poems and short stories in American, Canadian, Australian, and Indian literary magazines such as *Aim, Aura Literary/Arts Review, fourW, Green's, Nite-Writer's Literary Arts Journal, Manushi, Phoebe, Pleiades, Studio,* and *Tucumcari Literary Review.*

REFERENCES

Berscheid, E. & Hatfield, E. (1969). *Interpersonal attraction.* New York: Addison-Wesley.

Duck, S. (1982). *Personal relationships: Vol. 4: Dissolving personal relationships* (pp. 1–30). New York: Academic Press.

Duck, S., & Gilmour, R. (Eds.). (1981a). *Personal relationships: Vol. 1: Studying personal relationships.* New York: Academic Press.

Duck, S. & Gilmour, R. (Eds.). (1981b). *Personal relationships: Vol. 2: Developing personal relationships.* New York: Academic Press.

Duck, S., & Gilmour, R. (Eds.). (1981c). *Personal relationships: Vol. 3: Personal relationships in disorder.* New York: Academic Press.

Hatfield, E., Cacioppo, J., & Rapson, R. L. (1994). *Emotional contagion.* New York: Cambridge University Press.

Hatfield, E., & Rapson, R. L. (1993). *Love, sex, and intimacy: Their psychology, biology, and history.* New York: HarperCollins.

Hatfield, E., & Rapson, R. (1996). *Love and sex: Cross-cultural perspectives.* New York: Allyn & Bacon.

Hatfield, E., & Rapson, R. L. (2000). *Rosie.* Pittsburgh, PA: Sterling House.

Hatfield, E., & Sprecher, S. (1986). *Mirror, mirror: The importance of looks in everyday life.* New York: SUNY Press.

Hatfield, E., & Walster, G. W. (1978). *A new look at love.* Lanham, MD: University Press of America.

REPRESENTATIVE PUBLICATIONS

Carlson, J. G., & Hatfield, E. (1992). *Psychology of emotion.* New York: Harcourt, Brace, Jovanovich.

Griffitt, W., & Hatfield, E. (1984). *Human sexual behavior.* Glenview, IL: Scott, Foresman & Co.

Hatfield, E. (1995). Self-esteem and passionate love relationships. In G. G. Brannigan & M. R. Merrens (Eds.), *The social psychologists: Research and adventures* (pp. 129–144). New York: McGraw-Hill.

Hatfield, E. (1997). Teaching Tips: Cultural and gender in teaching close relationships. *ISSPR Bulletin: Culture, race, and diversity in close relationships, 14,* 22.

Hatfield, E., Berscheid, E., Abrahams, D., & Aronson, V. (1967). Effectiveness of debriefing following deception experiments. *Journal of Personality and Social Psychology, 6,* 371–380.

Hatfield, E., Cleary, T. A., & Clifford, M. M. (1970). The effect of race and sex on college admission. *Sociology of Education, 44,* 237–244.

Hatfield, E., & Rapson, R. (1987). Passionate love/sexual desire: Can the same paradigm explain both? *The Archives of Sexual Behavior, 16,* 259–278.

Hatfield, E., & Rapson, R. L. (1996). Stress and passionate love. In C. D. Spielberger & I. G. Sarason (Eds.), *Stress and emotion: Anxiety, anger, and curiousity, 16,* 29–50.

Hatfield, E., & Rapson, R. L. (2000, January). The future. *Popular Mechanics.*

Hatfield, E., Sprecher, S., & Traupmann, J. (1978). Men and women's reaction to sexually explicit films: A serendipitous finding. *Archives of Sexual Behavior, 7,* 573–592.

Hatfield, E., Walster, G. W., & Berscheid, E. (1978). *Equity: Theory and research.* Boston: Allyn and Bacon.

CHAPTER 11

Phyllis A. Katz

Photographer: David Schlatter.

Phyllis A. Katz

FAMILY BACKGROUND

I was born on April 9, 1938 in Brooklyn, New York to Alice Weiner and Martin Alberts. Place of birth may often be incidental, but I have often suspected that growing up Jewish in Brooklyn may have been formative in overcoming later barriers. The subculture I grew up in instilled a pervasive belief that obstacles were inevitable, but could be overcome if one applied sufficient effort.

Both of my parents were immigrants. My mother came from Russia as an infant and never finished high school. My father also emigrated from Russia when he was 10-years old. He only completed the 6th grade in school because he had to work to help support his family. He was a foreman in a leather goods factory. My mother was the prototypical housewife of that era. She did not work outside the home, never expected to, and was unprepared to do so. This was a particular hardship for her when my father died of cancer at 46 years-old, and she had to find a job.

Despite my father's lack of education, he was a very intelligent man, and recognized this educational lack as a deprivation for him. He read avidly, was self-taught in many areas, and always extolled the value of education. He valued my intellectual accomplishments, and always preached the importance of excellence. He counseled me never to do anything unless I did my best at it, and insisted that people could always expand their horizons if they wished to. Thus, I never felt limited by my gender or background.

I had no brothers or sisters. I believe that this was also an important factor for me, because I was probably given more encouragement to continue my education than I would have if I had had a brother, given the prevalent degree of sex role stereotyping. (Later in my life, I would do research in this area, cf., Katz & Boswell, 1984, that substantiated this speculation.)

Being an only child seemed to preclude my focusing very much on gender. Perhaps I was simply too insensitive to be negatively influenced by stereotypes, at least with regard to what I was not supposed to do. I had no female role models for academic excellence or professional accomplishment. If I had stopped to ponder this, it might have thwarted my early ambitions, but I didn't. Since I had no male role models for this either, the issue of gender discrimination never came up when I was a child. The previously cited work on only children and two-child families (Katz & Boswell, 1984) suggests that I was not alone. Females in single-child families were the most androgynous.

A love of learning is often an inherent part of Jewish culture, and my home was no exception. Being a good student earned a lot of points in my family, particularly from my father. Although both of my parents enacted very traditional gender roles, I always retained the possibility that I did not have to follow them, but could do whatever I wanted in life. Nevertheless, there was always some conflict between all the redundant information conveyed that girls were supposed to grow up to be housewives and mothers, and messages about intellectual achievement. I seemed to absorb both messages. Unlike the generation of women that succeeded my own, mine never questioned that marriage and children would be central to our lives. But somehow, I always believed that this could be combined with a career. The specifics of how to accomplish this was never an issue for me until I was pregnant with my first child and had to find some solutions.

Besides my family and friends, I had two loves as a child—school and music. School was a wonderful experience for me. Because I did well, teachers took a great deal of interest in me, and I was often given extra things to do because I finished the required work very quickly. One experience I remember was being asked to help tutor a class for retarded children when I was in the second or third grade. I thought this was terrific, and decided I wanted to be a teacher. Soon, however, my aspirations changed, and I wanted to be a pianist and composer. I spent hours every day practicing the piano, and scoured the library for biographies of the famous composers. I did not focus on the fact that they were all men. Perhaps more bothersome was the fact that so many of them were impoverished and died at an early age. Nevertheless, this choice seemed terribly romantic, and my main desire was to play Chopin's *Polonaise* in A Flat Major as Cornell Wilde played it in the movie biography.

When I entered Lincoln High School in Brooklyn, some of the zeal for practicing piano faded as social activities became more prominent. Nevertheless, I did attend the preparatory school at the Juilliard School of Music during high school, which entailed traveling 4 hours on the subway on Friday afternoons and Saturdays.

As seems to be true today as well, the adolescent period had particular conflicts for girls. Being a good student counted for very little, except to my teachers and my father. My peers were much more impressed when I became a cheerleader or dated a cute football player. Academic expectations were pretty low for girls at that time—even from some of the teachers. My high school counselor, for example, strongly suggested that I take stenography instead of physics because she thought it would be more useful to me. In the short run, she was right since it enabled me to earn money as a secretary in the summers. Despite this, however, new worlds became open to me during this time. My uncle was in graduate school studying to become a clinical psychologist, and I was intrigued by all the tests he gave to all my friends. Even more exciting was reading about anthropology. Margaret Mead's *Coming of Age in Samoa* (1961) and the concepts of cultural differences and relativism were wonderful discoveries that I still recall vividly.

EDUCATION

Going on to college from the milieu in which I was brought up was unexpected and unusual. Most of my friends married right after high school graduation and did not attend college. The few that did commuted by subway to Brooklyn College, which was free. Although I never knew anyone who had gone to college away from home, movies enlarged my horizons. My father agreed that I could go out of town to college if I won a scholarship, and I did receive a New York State scholarship that would cover my tuition if I went to a college within the state.

When this happened, all of my father's brothers and sisters called to say how crazy it was for my father to spend his hard-earned money on a girl. Why, they argued, should money be spent on an education for someone who was only to wash diapers? To his credit, my father withstood this pressure, and noted that even if I was going to wash diapers, I still had to think. So thank goodness for my father's incipient feminism. (And I never did wash diapers.)

It took 6 hours to drive from Brooklyn to Syracuse University in September of 1954 and my mother cried the whole way there. Once in college, I became interested in many things. My mother, who was the one with musical talent in the family, wanted me to become a pianist; my father, on the other hand, wanted me to be a lawyer. Since I did not wish to show favoritism toward either of them, I decided to compromise by majoring in psychology, with minors in mathematics and philosophy. At this time, I intended to go to medical school.

I was fortunate to get a part-time research assistant job with Professor Wallace MacAllister, an experimental psychologist trained at Iowa. This enabled me to have a number of perks. I helped run studies in eyelid conditioning, had a cubicle in the graduate student office, and could sit in on graduate courses.

Sadly, my father died of cancer at the end of my sophomore year, and I realized that I did not have the financial resources to attend medical school. I decided to attend summer school and graduated college in 3 years (in 1957), in part to reduce expenses. Graduate school seemed like a good alternative since financial support was much more probable there than in medical school. I wanted to become a clinical psychologist, but was also very interested in doing research. My counseling was less sexist in college than it was in high school. My mentor suggested that I apply to a number of schools that I never would have on my own. They included Yale, Columbia, New York University, and Radcliffe. At that time, if you were female and wanted to go to Harvard, you had to apply by way of Radcliffe. I was accepted at both Yale and Harvard with financial aid (a traineeship from NIMH) and chose Yale on the basis of Dr. MacAllister's advice and the fact that it was closer to New York where my mother still lived.

My entering class in the Psychology Department at Yale had 17 students, and five were women. The undergraduate college was all male at that time, but the graduate and professional schools had been coeducational for quite some time. I recall an early lecture given to the entering class by an illustrious developmental psychologist decrying the presence of women. He said that the only reason we were admitted was that we had better records than the other male applicants, and he admonished us not to waste the very expensive graduate school education by leaving the program to get married. Interestingly, there was a lack of sensitivity to women's issues on the part of the five women in my class. Although it did feel peculiar to be addressed this way, we never discussed it. This was typical of the 1950s. Interestingly, surveys of graduate student alumni conducted several years later revealed no gender differences in productivity. Nevertheless, the beliefs remained.

Discrimination against women was very openly expressed at that time. I recall my first summer at graduate school where my stenography came in handy. I worked as a secretary to Professor Neal Miller. For several days that summer, I was asked to take notes at a Social Sciences Research Council meeting where a president was being selected.

There were three candidates, one of whom was female. The Council members chose to have lunch at Mory's, an all-male establishment that did not permit women. Part of my job, therefore, was to have lunch with the female candidate (who did not get the presidency) at a nearby luncheonette. I felt sorry for her, but she gave me good advice which I followed: Never tell anyone I was a good typist.

Intellectually, the Yale psychology program was a very exciting place to be. There were so many bright faculty members whose research was on the cutting edge. Stanley Milgram was conducting his famous obedience studies, Larry Kohlberg was formulating his theory of moral development, and behaviorism and cognitive dissonance theory were in full bloom. The fact that there were no female faculty at Yale did not seem strange at that time. Their relatively small number today, however, does seem peculiar. Initially, I did not fit in very well because I was much younger than anyone else (I was 19), and was unfamiliar with the protocol of the Ivy League. In retrospect, the somewhat negative reactions I experienced in my first year were probably more attributable to my New York outspokenness than to my gender.

My interests always focused on children, but they never fit neatly into any of the programs. As a first year student, I worked with Neal Miller, and was the only one doing research with children rather than rats. I was a clinical psychology student with strong research interests. This was encouraged at Yale, as long as they were deemed to be "basic" rather than applied science.

While at Yale, I was fortunate to have had the opportunity to learn from a number of illustrious psychologists, including Neil Miller, John Dollard, Carl Hovland, Irving Janis, Robert Abelson, and Edward Zigler. My internship was done at the West Haven Veterans Administration Hospital. My doctoral dissertation was conducted with Ed Zigler as my advisor. I was Zigler's first doctoral student, and he was a demanding but excellent mentor. My thesis topic was "The Effects of Language on Children's Perception," and was influenced by the writings of Benjamin Whorf, the anthropologist. Whorf noted that different languages had varying numbers of descriptive words for particular domains, and believed that linguistic differentiation (or lack of it) influenced the way the speakers of different languages saw the world. My doctoral research tested this in an experimental manner with children and ambiguous, very similar forms. There were three groups in the research design: one group received a different name for each of four forms; one received two names for the four forms (i.e. same name for two forms); and the third was a control, no-name group. Subsequently, they were asked to judge the degree of similarity of pairs of the forms. As predicted, the distinctive label group saw the forms as least similar, whereas the common label group saw the two forms that had been associated with the same label as most similar. The control group fell between the other two in similarity judgments. I was very pleased by the confirmation of these predictions since this enabled me to receive my degree in four years (in 1961) at the age of 23. This seemed old to me at the time, and I wanted to get on with my career and my raising a family.

CAREER DEVELOPMENT

Graduate school was eventful in many respects since I married my present husband, Aron Katz, just prior to receiving my PhD. He had completed Yale Law School the year before and was working as a lawyer in New York. Thus, my initial job search was restricted to the New York area. It never occurred to either of us to consider moving elsewhere on the basis of my job possibilities. This early career limitation was, therefore, gender-based. Fortunately, New York offered a number of interesting possibilities.

Although I wanted to teach, the first job I held was with the Institute for Developmental Studies, a research institute headed by Martin Deutsch. I was intrigued with what was then the very novel work of the institute—designing preschool intervention programs for poor children. This antedated Headstart programs, and the idea that one could prevent later educational failure by working with three year-olds was then ground breaking. I worked there for a year on a number of interesting projects and continued to consult with them. My desire to teach, however, led to my becoming an instructor of psychology at Queens College the following year. I taught five courses there, including statistics, and had little time for research other than the work I had done at the Institute the previous year.

My first publication (Katz, 1963) brought an unexpected bonus. The write-up of my dissertation was accepted by the *Journal of Experimental Psychology*, and the editor, Dr. Howard Kendler, asked me if I would be interested in an Assistant Professor position at the uptown campus of New York University. The psychology faculty at the uptown campus was very actively devoted to research, and the teaching load was much smaller (only four courses) so I took the job, in part because of the urging of Phil Zimbardo, a friend from graduate school, and a member of the faculty. NYU also had the advantage of working with graduate students who attended the campus at Washington Square.

The 6 years that I spent at New York University were extremely productive for me, both professionally and personally. In the research area, I decided to test the possibility that the theory I tested in my dissertation might have some important application to real-life problems.

The first problem I chose to investigate was how labels affected children's racial attitudes. I received two grants to study this, and developed an active research program. On the personal side, I gave birth to my son and daughter during this period. Amazingly, both were timed to accord with the academic year. My first child, Martin, was born during intersession in 1965; my daughter, Margaret, was born at the end of May, 1968, and I read my final exams in the hospital right after her birth so I could have the grades in on time. Although there was no such thing as maternity leave in those years, I did get a reduced teaching schedule after the birth of my first child. Since I was teaching courses in child psychology, I used my children in my classes. They became very familiar with an academic environment during their first few years of life, as my students witnessed a variety of their behaviors, such as walking, talking, and problem-solving.

My first pregnancy became a time of problem-solving for me as well, both in terms of feelings and in terms of logistics. I did not want to give up my career, even briefly. Someone had to care for the baby, however. This was not something that could be shared with my husband, who was working about 80 hours a week as a beginning lawyer. There were no day care centers for infants anywhere near where I lived or worked. Moreover, at that time, children were not permitted to attend nursery school if they were not toilet-trained. Apart from the logistics of child care, however, I did initially question whether I was doing the right thing. As was the case earlier in my career, there were no available female role models that combined a career with a family. There were very few female faculty members on the NYU campus, and they were all unmarried. In my husband's law firm (where almost all of the lawyers were men), the wives with children did not work outside the home.

Some of my peers were guilt-inducing about my plan to continue working, but my husband was very supportive. There was no research at the time on the effects of working mothers on their children, and most people I knew thought it would be detrimental. I reasoned, however, that since children loved their fathers as much as their mothers, working out of the home could not possibly matter that much. I am happy to note that most of the subsequent research supported my beliefs, and that my children turned out to be terrific. I believe that my willingness to trust my own instincts in this area was a very important factor that shaped both my career and my subsequent contributions to psychology. It took me a while, however, to see that my problem was scarcely a unique one. I did manage to work out decent child-care arrangements as well (which took most of my salary). Having financial support from a spouse or family was necessary then—and certainly makes things easier today as well.

After 5 seemingly idyllic years of teaching at NYU, I discovered that gender discrimination existed and was affecting me. I discovered, accidentally, that my cohorts in the department (all male) were teaching fewer courses than I was, and were making more money, even though I had more publications and more grant money than most of them did. I decided to confront the Chair of my department about this state of affairs. He responded that I was not being discriminated against because of my gender; men were getting treated better, he argued, because they had more geographical mobility than I did—I could not leave New York as readily. This was an eye-opening experience. I told him that there were other positions in New York, and proceeded to obtain one as Associate Professor at the Graduate Center of The City University of New York (CUNY). Until that time, I had not even considered looking for another position, so it was good to discover that I was salable, particularly with a large research grant to study how to modify racial prejudice in children.

My new position paid considerably more, had less teaching, better research facilities, and more interested graduate students to work with. Many of the students were older women who had returned to school. Although I continued my research on race, I also became interested in gender development and women's issues during my tenure at CUNY. The Zeitgeist of the early 1970s was a heady one, as feminism became salient for psychologists. There were many more female faculty members at CUNY (but still very few in my department), and the discussions became more and more interesting as we shared notes, experiences, complaints, and consciousness-raising. It was during this time that it became very evident as to just how political the personal aspects of our lives were. It was particularly refreshing to consider these issues with other women faculty and graduate students after being in so many essentially all-male environments. This was also a time for activism since so much needed to be done. We organized a day care center at the Graduate Center; we organized for more equitable job treatment; and, for the first time any of us could remember, we wanted our gender requirements to be considered. It was during this period (1975) that I decided to found the journal *Sex Roles: A Journal of Research* because there was great concern that a publication outlet was needed that focused on this newly burgeoning area of research.

The formation and editing of this journal took a lot of time and energy, but it was also interesting and exciting. It put me in touch with a lot of women in different fields (it was interdisciplinary) who were very smart, and were all dealing with the same issues. It was the first time I had ever encountered a women's network in the intellectual realm. Every day brought new developments as more research came in. Moreover, I could relate on a personal level to many of these findings, again a very novel experience at that time. The women's movement, therefore, was a major influence on me, both professionally and personally. I think this was true for most of my peers as well, since we all had the feeling that we were living in a very important historical time. Creativity of every kind was on the increase.

Although my experience was primarily positive, I still had to do a great deal of juggling of many roles: teaching, research, writing, editing and childrearing. I recall feeling quite fragmented, but unwilling to give up any of the things I was doing.

Living in New York was becoming more stressful for my family in 1974, when I took my first sabbatical leave. My husband decided to leave the law firm where he was a partner, and we moved to Boulder, Colorado where the quality of life seemed better for raising a family. I commuted to New York for the year after my sabbatical, but this turned out to be impossible to continue. Thus, I decided, in 1976, to found the Institute for Research on Social Problems, a nonprofit organization devoted to research on children and social issues.

This was not something that had ever been a part of my career plans, and was somewhat frightening since it was the first time since I was 5 years-old that I was not in school. This was also not something I would have done if I had not encountered a great deal of sexism in Boulder. I was associated with another research institute as a consultant at that time, and wrote a grant that was to be submitted through them. The director, however, seemed upset that I had more publications than he did, and seemed to think that if the grant came through, I might wield more power in his institute than he wanted. Since the grant was subsequently funded, he clearly made a mistake in asking me to leave.

The sexism I encountered in Colorado (and this includes the university) was somewhat different than what I experienced previously. By the time I moved to Colorado, I was a Full Professor at CUNY, had been chair of the department, and was well-known because of my research and the journal I edited. My accomplishments, however, seemed to be the problem. The male academics that I met were not happy about dealing with a women who was equal to them in terms of their achievements.

Although the Institute was dependent on grant funds, the absence of faculty and committee meetings did give me more time for research and writing. I wrote many of my chapters summarizing empirical studies, and edited a book about race and one about health issues in minority adolescents during this time (Kagawa-Singer, Katz, Taylor, & Vanderryn, 1996; Katz & Taylor, 1988). I also had more time for professional and community activities that I was not able to engage in when I was a full-time academic. I even learned to play Chopin's *Polonaise* in A Flat Major. Founding the Institute was a non-traditional way of fulfilling my career goals.

On a professional level, I became more active in APA affairs. I served as a representative to the APA Council for both Divisions 9 (Society for the Psychological Study of Social Issues) and 35 (Psychology of Women). Additionally, I served in many capacities for both divisions, including the presidencies. My own research agenda was concerned with gender and race stereotype formation in children, and there was a good match between my research interests, my values, and the organizations I was involved with. I also became active in a number of community organizations as well, including the Women's Foundation of Colorado, and the Colorado Music Festival.

My major research activity of the past few years involved a longitudinal study of children during the first 6 years of their lives. The focus of this investigation was to investigate the developmental forerunners of later race and gender attitudes. This has been a mammoth project, involving 220 White and African American families over an 8 year period, where the children have been assessed 11 times, and the parents 3 times.

The results suggest that the precursors of attitudes toward those in other groups begin very early, and that there are many cognitive and social predictors of whether or not a child will show race and/or gender bias by the time they enter school. For example, the more racially heterogeneous the child's early social environment, and the more willing the parents are to talk about race, the less biased their children are. Findings regarding the first part of our study are contained in a chapter written for a commemorative book by the students of Professor Zigler (Katz & Kofkin, 1997). Findings regarding the predictors of racial attitudes at 6 years of age were presented at an APA Convention (Katz & Watson-Acosta, 1999), and my colleagues and I are preparing a book that describes our findings. We believe that these findings will be very useful to other scholars, as well as to parents and teachers.

I have always been interested in both the scholarship aspects of social issues and the policy issues related to them. Consequently, my career path has involved several interesting and unanticipated detours since moving to Colorado. The first detour involved opening a non-sexist toy store called Play Fair, together with a mail-order catalogue. I did this because research findings suggested that stereotyped sex roles were learned very early in life, and toy choices played an important role in this process since toys were typically channeled either to boys or girls. Consequently, the store contained only toys that would be bought for both sexes. I have since sold the store, but parents liked the concept very much (to my knowledge, it is still the only toy store in the country espousing this philosophy), and it seems to be quite successful financially as well.

The second detour that took several years to complete was the writing of a trade book, together with my journalist daughter Margaret Cann, called *The Feminist Dollar* (Katz & Katz, 1997). The purpose of this book was a call to action to female consumers. It gives information about the corporations that treated women either well or poorly, and suggests enlightened shopping on the basis of these ratings of those products and services offered by female-friendly companies.

MAJOR CONTRIBUTIONS AND ACHIEVEMENTS

My major intellectual accomplishments lie within the areas of social issues and social development. Since childhood, I have had a long-standing concern for the inequitable treatment that people experience because of their membership in a group accorded low status by society. Most of my research has been directed toward trying to understand the developmental origins of these phenomena.

I have worked and made scholarly contributions in basically five different areas, again with a few detours. My research career began with a more theoretical, basic science orientation than is evident in my later work. This is undoubtedly due to my graduate school training which viewed socially relevant research as inferior. The first area I worked in focused on whether and how language and perceptual processes interact with one another. The studies I have conducted, often with colleagues, have demonstrated the importance of language cues in an individual's perception of their world. These studies were among the earliest to demonstrate the significance of this interaction, and the types of variables that affected it.

A second issue of research interest has been what variables influence children's educational achievement. As part of my first job, I studied the determinants of reading achievement in young disadvantaged children, with a particular emphasis on perceptual components. Later work I engaged in, in this area, was done in collaboration with colleagues at the University of Colorado, and focused more on motivational factors. These included whether the source of achievement motivation was intrinsic or extrinsic, and on how learning challenges affected subsequent performance. One of our most interesting findings in this vein was that success and failure experiences affect boys and girls quite differently. Because teachers tend to be more protective of girls, failure experiences cause greater decrements in girls' academic performance than in boys'. These differing gender patterns suggest that teachers need to take gender into account in their teaching styles.

A third and less prolific area of research has focused on self concept in children and adolescence. An early collaboration with my former mentor (Katz & Zigler, 1967) produced a paper that has been widely cited. It is a developmental study of self image disparity that found that high self image disparity is associated with higher cognitive-developmental levels, and is not necessarily an ominous sign of psychopathology, as had been previously believed.

A fourth area, and perhaps the one most frequently associated with me, has concentrated on how children are socialized with regard to race. This interest derived in part from the first research area described above, dealing with the effects of labels on perceptions, and represented an attempt to apply basic theory to socially relevant problems. My early studies in this area demonstrated a number of important principles with regard to how children develop racial attitudes: (a) There are important perceptual underpinnings to racial attitudes (Katz, 1973a; Katz, 1973b); (b) Perceptions of people and groups are very much affected by the nature of the labels that are used (Katz & Seavy, 1973); and (c) It is possible to change these perceptual mechanisms in ways that reduce racial bias in children (Katz, Sohn & Zalk, 1975; Katz & Zalk, 1978).

These studies are widely cited in accounts of children's racial attitude development. Other major publications in this area have included two books that I edited on racism (Katz, 1976; Katz & Taylor, 1988), that have also been widely cited, a number of chapters for other books, and a great variety of journal articles based on the research I conducted with students and colleagues. More recently, we expect that the longitudinal study of race and gender learning previously described should make an important contribution to our knowledge base in this area, particularly in regards to the very early determinants of racial attitudes.

The last area of research I have been extensively involved in has to do with gender roles and their socialization. My interest in this area began in the 1970s when I founded the journal *Sex Roles*, an accomplishment that I believe has had an important influence for many feminist researchers. My own early work was largely theoretical in nature, dealing with the development of female identity (Katz, 1979) and the similarities and differences in how children develop race and gender attitudes (Katz, 1983).

An important construct that emerged from our studies in the 1980s was that of sex-role flexibility with regard to children's behavior. The research literature during this time devoted a lot of attention to the concept of androgyny, and the varying definitions of it put forth by Sandra Bem and Janet Spence (Bem, 1974; Spence, 1985). Formulations about androgyny, however, were basically applicable only to adults, since they focused on self-described personality traits that were unfamiliar to young children. Since we (and others) were discovering that not all children exhibited stereotypic behaviors, we conceptualized sex role flexibility as an inclusive, multidimensional construct that combined information about the child's preferences for play, activities, and peers with their attitudes and beliefs regarding gender roles and stereotypes (Katz & Boswell, 1986). Moreover, sex-role flexibility was hypothesized to change over the course of development in a curvilinear fashion, for example, from not very flexible in early childhood, to quite flexible in the prepubertal phase, to more traditional in later adolescence (Katz, 1980).

These various articles and chapters were significant because they were among the first to focus on girls and women in a positive way, and to consider how gender-role flexibility might develop as a positive attribute in children. This was in sharp contrast to the then current theoretical positions that took the male as the norm, and viewed departure from sex-role traditionality as psychologically troublesome. Influenced both by my feminist orientation and studies which have shown that excessive gender-role stereotyping may be harmful to children (e.g., Silvern & Katz, 1986), I have also devoted considerable research attention to the issue of how we can raise less sex-typed children.

I was particularly gratified to have this body of work recognized by being awarded the Carolyn Wood Sherif Award of the APA Division on the Psychology of Women, and also by being chosen for inclusion in this volume of eminent women. Other awards I have received included a Leadership Citation from the Committee of Women in Psychology of the American Psychological Association, a media award from Division 46 for co-authoring a book (Huston et al., 1992) entitled *Big World, Small Screen: The Role of Television in American Society* (another detour), and an Outstanding Service Award from the Society for the Psychological Study of Social Issues.

CONCLUDING THOUGHTS

It is clear that I was limited, to some extent, in my original career choices, at least geographically. Hopefully, this will not be as true for today's graduate students, but it would appear that they often have to be willing to maintain a long distance relationship if they wish to be in academia. It was also clear that I was subject to gender discrimination. Interestingly, it took me quite a while to become aware of it, particularly at the beginning of my career. Whether this is typical of women, as Faye Crosby's work suggests (Crosby, 1984), or whether these issues had not yet fully entered into women's consciousness is not entirely clear. Once awareness had occurred, however, it was easier to confront sexism, even if not always successfully.

Integrating my professional and personal lives was difficult, but I had a great deal of help from a non-sexist father, a very supportive husband, and two children who were very tolerant of my professional involvement. It is disheartening to note how little progress has been made on this front. Certainly, many more women are striving to combine working and raising families than was true when I began my career; it is estimated that two thirds of women with children are now in the workforce. Despite this, however, we still lack the sensible, inexpensive system of child care that most other industrialized countries have. I still hope that I will see the day when good fortune is not the major prerequisite for women to fully develop their capabilities.

On the basis of my early experiences, I would urge female readers to follow their own paths, and try to ignore the well-intended, but too cautious types of socialization we are all subjected to. As one of our early heroines, Amelia Earhart, once remarked: "Courage is the price that life exacts for granting peace." I wish you all the courage of your convictions.

REFERENCES

Bem, S. L. (1974). The measurement of psychological androgyny. *Journal of Consulting and Clinical Psychology, 42,* 155–162.

Crosby, F. (1984). The denial of personal discrimination. *American Behavior Scientist, 27,* 371–386.

Huston, A. C., Donnerstein, E., Fairchild, H., Feshbach, N. D., Katz, P. A., Murray, J. P., Rubinstein, E. A., Wilcox, B. L., & Zuckerman, D. (1992). *Big world, small screen: The role of television in American society.* University of Nebraska Press: Lincoln & London.

Kagawa-Singer, M., Katz, P. A., Taylor, D. A., & Vanderryn, J. H. M. (Eds.). (1996). *Health issues for minority adolescents.* University of Nebraska Press: Lincoln & London.

Katz, P. A. (1963). The effects of labels on children's perception and discrimination learning. *Journal of Experimental Psychology, 66,* 423–428.

Katz, P. A. (1973a). Perception of racial cues in preschool children: A new look. *Developmental Psychology, 8,* 295–299.

Katz, P. A. (1973b). Stimulus predifferentiation and modification of children's racial attitudes. *Child Development, 44,* 232–237.

Katz, P. A. (Ed.). (1976). *Towards the elimination of racism.* New York: Pergamon Press

Katz, P. A. (1979). The development of female identity. In C. Kopp & M. Kirkpatrick (Eds.), *Becoming female: Perspectives on development* (pp. 3–28). New York: Plenum.

Katz, P. A. (1980). *Correlates of sex-role flexibility in children: Detailed findings.* National Institutes for Mental Health, Grant no. 29417 (ERIC Document Reproduction Service No. ED 191 584).

Katz, P. A. (1983). Developmental foundations of gender and racial attitudes. In R. L. Leahy (Ed.), *The child's construction of social inequality* (pp. 41–78). New York: Academic.

Katz, P. A., & Boswell, S. L. (1986). Flexibility and traditionality in children's gender roles. *Genetic, Social and General Psychology Monographs, 112,* 103–147.

Katz, P. A., & Katz (Cann), M. (1997). *The feminist dollar: The wise woman's buying guide.* New York: Plenum.

Katz, P. A., & Kofkin, J. A. (1997). Race, gender and young children. In S. S. Luthar, J. A. Burack, D. Cicchetti, & J. Weisz (Eds.), *Developmental psychopathology: Perspectives on adjustment, risk, and disorder* (pp. 51–74). New York: Cambridge University Press.

Katz, P. A., & Seavy, C. (1973). Labels and children's perception of faces. *Child Development, 44,* 770–775.

Katz, P. A., Sohn, L., & Zalk, S. R. (1975). Perceptual concomitants of racial attitudes in urban grade school children. *Developmental Psychology, 11,* 135–144.

Katz, P. A., & Taylor, D. A. (Eds.). (1988). *Eliminating racism: Profiles in controversy.* New York: Plenum.

Katz, P. A., & Watson-Acosta, D. (1999, August). *Factors influencing the development of race bias in children.* Poster session presented at the annual meeting of the American Psychological Association, Boston.

Katz, P. A., & Zalk, S. R. (1978). Modification of children's racial attitudes. *Developmental Psychology, 14,* 447–461.

Katz, P. A., & Zigler, E. (1967). Self image disparity: A developmental approach. *Journal of Personality and Social Psychology, 5,* 186–195.

Mead, M. (1961). *Coming of age in Samoa.* New York: Morrow Quill.

Silvern, L. E., & Katz, P. A. (1986). Gender roles and adjustment in elementary school children: A multidimensional approach. *Sex Roles, 14,* 181–202.

Spence, J. T. (1985). Gender identity and its implications for the concepts of masculinity and femininity. In R. Dienstbeir & T. Sonderegger (Eds.), *Psychology and gender: Nebraska Symposium on motivation, 1984* (pp. 59–95). Lincoln, NE: University of Nebraska Press.

REPRESENTATIVE PUBLICATIONS

Boggiano, A. K., & Katz, P. A. (1991). Maladaptive achievement patterns in students: The role of teachers' controlling strategies. *Journal of Social Issues, 47,* 35–51.

Kagawa-Singer, M., Katz, P. A., Taylor, D., & Vanderryn, J. (Eds.). (1996). *Health issues for minority adolescents.* Lincoln, NE: University of Nebraska Press.

Katz, P. A. (1963). The effects of labels on children's perception and discrimination learning. *Journal of Experimental Psychology, 66,* 423–428.

Katz, P. A. (1967). Verbal discrimination performance in disadvantaged children: Stimulus and subject variables. *Child Development, 34,* 233–242.

Katz, P. A. (1973). Perception of racial cues in preschool children: A new look. *Developmental Psychology, 8,* 295–299.

Katz, P. A. (1973). Stimulus predifferentiation and modification of children's racial attitudes. *Child Development, 44,* 232–237.

Katz, P. A. (1976). The acquisition of racial attitudes in children. In P. A. Katz (Ed.), *Towards the elimination of racism* (pp. 125–154). New York: Pergamon Press.

Katz, P. A. (1976). Attitude change in children: Can the twig be straightened? In P. A. Katz (Ed.), *Towards the elimination of racism* (pp. 213–241). New York: Pergamon Press.

Katz, P. A. (1976). Racism and social science: Towards a new commitment. In P. A. Katz (Ed.), *Towards the elimination of racism* (pp. 3–18). New York: Pergamon Press.

Katz, P. A. (Ed.). (1976). *Towards the elimination of racism*. New York: Pergamon Press.

Katz, P. A. (1979). The development of female identity. In C. Kopp & M. Kirkpatrick (Eds.), *Becoming female: Perspectives on development* (pp. 3–28). New York: Plenum.

Katz, P. A. (1982). A review of current research in children's racial attitude acquisition. In L. Katz (Ed.), *Current topics in early childhood education* (pp. 17–54). Norwood, NJ: Ablex.

Katz, P. A. (1983). Developmental foundations of gender and racial attitudes. In R. L. Leahy (Eds), *The child's construction of social inequality* (pp. 41–78). New York: Academic.

Katz, P. A. (1986). Modification of children's gender-stereotyped behavior: General issues and research considerations. *Sex Roles, 14*, 591–602.

Katz, P. A. (1986). Gender identity: Development and consequences. In R. D. Ashmore & F. K. Del Boca (Eds.), *The social psychology of female-male relations: A critical analysis of central concepts* (pp. 21–67). Orlando, FL: Academic.

Katz, P. A. (1987). Family constellation: Effects on gender schemata. In L. S. Liben & M. Signorella (Eds.), *Children's gender concepts: New directions in child development* (pp. 39–56). San Francisco: Jossey-Bass.

Katz, P. A., Albert, J., & Atkins, M. (1971). Mediation and perceptual transfer in children. *Developmental Psychology, 4*, 268–276.

Katz, P. A., Boggiano, A. K., & Silvern, L. (1993). Theories of female personality. In F. Denmark & M. Paludi (Eds.), *Handbook of the psychology of women* (pp. 247–280). Westport, CT: Greenwood.

Katz, P. A., & Boswell, S. L. (1984). Sex-role development and the one-child family. In T. Falbo (Ed.), *The single-child family* (pp. 63–116). New York: Guilford.

Katz, P. A., & Boswell, S. L. (1986). Flexibility and traditionality in children's gender roles. *Genetic, Social and General Psychology Monographs, 112*, 103–147.

Katz, P. A., & Deutsch, M. (1967). The relationship of auditory and visual functioning to reading achievement in disadvantaged children. In M. Deutsch & Associates (Eds.), *The disadvantaged child* (pp. 238–258). New York: Basic Books.

Katz, P. A., & Kofkin, J. A. (1997). Race, gender and young children. In S. S. Luthar, J. A. Burack, D. Cicchetti, & J. Weisz (Eds.), *Developmental psychopathology: Perspectives on adjustment, risk, and disorder* (pp. 51–74). New York: Cambridge University Press.

Katz, P. A., & Ksansnak, K. R. (1993). Developmental aspects of gender-role behavior in childhood and adolescence. *Developmental Psychology, 30*, 272–282.

Katz, P. A., & Seavey, C. (1973). Labels and children's perception of faces. *Child Development, 44*, 770–775.

Katz, P. A., Sohn, L., & Zalk, S. R. (1975). Perceptual concomitants of racial attitudes in urban grade school children. *Development Psychology, 11,* 135–144.

Katz, P. A., & Taylor, D. A. (Eds.). (1988). *Eliminating racism: Profiles in controversy.* New York: Plenum.

Katz, P. A., & Taylor, D. A. (1988). Introduction. In P. A. Katz & D. A. Taylor (Eds.), *Eliminating racism: Profiles in controversy* (pp. 1–16). New York: Plenum.

Katz, P. A., & Walsh, P. V. (1991). Modification of children's gender-stereotyped behavior. *Child Development, 62,* 338–351.

Katz, P. A., & Zalk, S. R. (1978). Modification of children's racial attitudes. *Developmental Psychology, 14,* 447–461.

Katz, P. A., & Zigler, E. (1969). The effects of labels on perception: Stimulus and developmental factors. *Journal of Experimental Psychology, 80,* 73–77.

Katz, P. A., & Zigler, E. (1967). Self-image disparity: A developmental approach. *Journal of Personality and Social Psychology, 5,* 186–195.

Katz, P. A., Zigler, E., & Zalk, S. R. (1975). Children's self-image disparity: The effects of age, maladjustment and action-thought orientation. *Developmental Psychology, 11,* 546–550.

Seavey, C. A., Katz, P. A., & Zalk, S. R. (1975). Baby X: The effect of gender labels on adult responses to infants. *Sex Roles, 1,* 103–109.

Taylor, D. A., & Katz, P. A. (1988). Conclusion. In P. A. Katz & D. A. Taylor (Eds.), *Eliminating racism: Profiles in controversy* (pp. 359–369). New York: Plenum.

Taylor, D. A., & Katz, P. A. (1996). Health and related services available to black adolescents. In M. Kagawa-Singer, P. A. Katz, D. Taylor, & J. Vanderryn (Eds.), *Health issues for minority adolescents* (pp. 36–79). Lincoln, NE: University of Nebraska Press.

CHAPTER 12

Linda M. Bartoshuk

Photographer: Michael Marsland.

Linda M. Bartoshuk

I was raised in a small town—Aberdeen, South Dakota. My father, Hubert Lee Buswell, joined the army at the beginning of World War I. Given his farm background, he was assigned to care for horses, the Great War's motor pool. A gifted mechanic, he returned to become the foreman of a maintenance shop owned by Socony-Vacuum (now Mobil Oil). My mother, Edna May Sherwood, traces her ancestry back to the Mayflower, and her family kept newspaper clippings and letters, so I grew up with stories about the accomplishments of women in our family (Louisa May Alcott was my first cousin eight times removed). My brother, Gordon, was 9 years older, and left home for the army when he was young, making me, essentially, an only child for most of my youth.

I saw myself as an ordinary kid but my desire to be an astronomer seemed a bit peculiar to my teachers. For career day in junior high, each of us named the profession we hoped to enter and the school arranged interviews with the relevant professionals. I chose astronomy, hoping the school would at least find me a scientist, but I was assigned to interview a secretary. Nights in a vacant lot with a flashlight and a star map taught me the constellations; I read science fiction and dreamed of learning about other worlds. My mother says I always got good grades, but I only remember the shock of discovering that my percentile scores on junior high achievement tests were in the high 90s. In the culture of my teens, academic accomplishment was not socially rewarded.

In high school, I wanted to take math and science courses because I liked them. The school counselor (with, I am sure, the best of intentions) told me that these were not practical choices. We struck a deal: I agreed to take typing and bookkeeping in return for being allowed to take algebra, trigonometry, chemistry and physics. I didn't fit into the world of my senior high school class I graduated in 1956, the year teenagers in the movie *Grease* were freshmen: Patty Simcox, that was me. I couldn't dance, I was bad at sports, and I wasn't engaged. Thank goodness for college. I visited the South Dakota School of Mines and Technology because I was intrigued by the idea of being an engineer—only to discover that the vast majority of the students were men. Carleton College in Northfield, Minnesota, not only had more women but also an observatory and an astronomy major. It was very expensive, and I didn't know if my family could afford to let me attend for 4 years, but I enrolled anyway.

At one of the receptions for freshmen, we got to meet Carleton's President, Lawrence Gould. He was second in command on Byrd's 1928 to 1930 expedition to the Antarctic and a larger-than-life hero to us. As I went by in the receiving line, he whispered that I had just been awarded a National Merit Scholarship. My father died of lung cancer in my junior year, and the scholarship let me stay in school.

I had been warned that because I came from a small town high school, Carleton College would be difficult for me, but I did very well academically. However, in my sophomore year, I was summoned to the Office of the Dean of Women. The Dean noted that my grades were fine but said that I was not living up to the standards expected of Carleton women. In particular, I had failed to attend some class social event. She went on to tell me that Carleton women married important men and needed to be well-rounded. I explained that I was a scholarship student, that even with this assistance my family was making sacrifices to let me attend college, and I felt it was my responsibility to study hard. I remember being very polite; in retrospect, I don't see why.

I signed up as an astronomy major, took the required mathematics and science courses, and the ideas changed my world. Psychophysics played a role in the first measurements of the size of the universe (see Glanz, 1999 for a modern view of these measurements). The brightness of a star as seen from earth is a function of its distance and absolute brightness (i.e., energy production). Once the absolute brightness of some stars was known due, in part, to the pioneering work of the astronomer Henrietta Swan Leavitt, the distances could be determined from the psychophysical observations of brightness (the first scale used dated back to earlier than 100 B.C.). My enthusiasm dimmed when I was told that although a few women were able to work as astronomers, the field did not welcome them.

The Psychology Department was willing to give me credit for the mathematics and science I had already taken so I signed up for the introductory course. It was taught by John Bare and it was wonderful. When we got to psychophysics, I was enthralled. The scale devised to measure the perceived brightness of stars was just the beginning. A philosophy course introduced me to epistemology and I realized that what appealed to me was how we know what we know. If you like epistemology, sensory psychophysics is a deeply satisfying field. Bare had done his PhD at Brown with Carl Pfaffmann, a pioneer in the sense of taste. When my father contracted lung cancer, one of his most distressing symptoms was a change in the taste of food. In retrospect, I wonder if this influenced my early fascination with taste. When it came time to decide what to do after graduation, I followed Bare's lead and applied to Brown.

My trip to Brown was my first trip east of Chicago. I remember going into a deli and ordering a corned beef sandwich on white bread with mayonnaise and the counterman refused to give it to me. I was a rube with a lot to learn. In 1960, the Psychology Department at Brown viewed women as something of a risk because they might marry and leave the field. I was told that this was why each entering class was limited to no more than one-third women. It was harder for me to understand why I did not get the same stipend added to my National Science Foundation Fellowship that was given to my male classmates. But these were minor issues compared to Pfaffmann's rejection. He told me that he did not want women in his lab. His male students thought that this was unfair. While Pfaffmann was away for a few days, one of them taught me how to record from a taste nerve. When Pfaffmann returned, he found me in the lab and relented but gave me a difficult problem that I did not like. I worked hard on it, made no progress, and finally told him I thought it was impossible. Shortly thereafter, he told me he had checked my grades and found that I was a good student. He said that I could choose my own problem. I was stunned but I knew what I wanted to study: the taste of water.

Strange as it sounds, the taste of water is important theoretically. Pfaffmann did his PhD with Lord Adrian at Cambridge University. Pfaffmann (1941) made the startling discovery that the cat's taste neurons are not specific to the four basic tastes: sweet, salty, sour and bitter. This led him to propose that the brain could only determine quality by making use of the pattern of activation across a population of neurons (*pattern theory*). Water was simply a solvent in this view, but Yngve Zotterman, a Swedish pioneer in sensory studies who had also worked with Adrian, later found neurons that responded to water (Cohen, Hagiwara, & Zotterman, 1955). Pfaffmann and Zotterman were friends but competitors as well. Pfaffmann told me to go prove the water responses were an artifact.

The early 1960s felt like a golden era to those of us in Pfaffmann's lab. My classmate Don McBurney had the office across the hall from mine. He was doing psychophysical studies and we collaborated to show that adaptation could make water take on a taste: Water after NaCl tasted bitter/sour (Bartoshuk, McBurney, & Pfaffmann, 1964). This helped me understand Zotterman's water fibers (Bartoshuk, Harned, & Parks, 1971). They were neither what they had seemed nor an artifact. They were dependent on adaptation just as the water taste in humans was. Why did it take so long to find such a simple explanation? I believe this is an example of the danger of theories. The pattern theory made us suspicious of simple explanations. As more species were studied, it became clear that the cat was something of an anomaly. Pfaffmann ultimately recanted the pattern theory and embraced labeled lines (Pfaffmann, 1974).

In my second year of graduate school, I married a young faculty member, Alexander Bartoshuk. The marriage was not to last but it introduced me to the dubious pleasures of life as a faculty wife. When Pfaffmann left Brown in 1965 for Rockefeller University, he offered to take me with him. Though my marriage was ending and I was free to go, I felt it was time to cut the cord. I told him that I could never be devoted to science with a capital S as he was, that I liked solving puzzles and the day I got bored would be the day I found something else to do. He told me I had just described a real scientist. That remark was the most wonderful gift he gave me. I still did not go with him; I wanted to grow up and I found it almost impossible to disagree with him.

My first job was with Harry Jacobs at the Natick Army Labs. This was an interesting place for a young woman with a slightly radical political bent during the Vietnam War. With my long hair and granny glasses, I evoked enough suspicion to be summoned to the director's office to explain a package addressed to me being held at the Natick post office. I had ordered Gymnema sylvestre leaves from India and they had been shipped in large fabric pouches. When I explained that a tea made from the leaves could inhibit sweetness (and that I was not planning to smoke the leaves), the director called the post office and I got the packages.

While I was at Natick, I fell in love with a theoretical physicist at Yale, Charles Sommerfield. We married in 1969 and Charles spent a sabbatical year at MIT to let me finish up studies that were underway. I knew that I had picked the right man after a discussion about ethics. He told me of a time he felt he had been scooped after giving a lecture on a new theory. I reacted with horror, suggesting he should keep his work secret until it was published; Charles disagreed. He asked me what kind of person I would rather be: The kind that shares work and occasionally suffers for it, or the kind that guards intellectual property with such vigilance that there is no open discussion. Chastened, I replied that of course we should be the generous types who share but occasionally suffer for it. Charles then smiled and said, "Besides, the theory was wrong." My husband has a wonderful sense of humor and a good set of values. After that I never hesitated to talk publicly about work in progress.

In New Haven, I joined Joe Stevens's group of sensory psychophysicists at the John B. Pierce Foundation; a year later I was appointed an Assistant Professor at Yale. Natick had provided a wonderful environment for women in science. We were protected from discrimination by civil service regulations. At Brown there was bias, but, except for my initial difficulties getting into Pfaffmann's lab, I never felt meanness—not so at the Pierce Foundation. Sexism started at the top and trickled down.

My son, Daniel, was born in 1971. When I was visibly pregnant, the director, James Hardy (an expert in thermoregulation), stopped me in the hall and told me he would be sorry to see me go. Genuinely puzzled, I told him that I was not going anywhere. He told me that he expected me to resign to take care of my child. When I told him that I planned to keep working, he said, "Women like you are going to destroy Western civilization." He subsequently refused to sign a grant application I had planned to submit to the National Institutes of Health (NIH). I went to see Pfaffmann and discovered an unexpected side to him. He listened carefully, leaned back in his chair and told me that he did not like Hardy and feared if he attempted to intervene for me, Hardy would be even more abusive. But he said he thought he could help me nonetheless. He then told me some delicious, high-level gossip that I would normally never have gotten to hear. He was right. It did help. I never used any of it but it was armor, and Hardy's verbal jabs didn't touch me after that.

The gossip improved my daily life but my prospects at the Pierce Foundation were decidedly dim. I went to see the Deputy Provost for the Sciences at Yale to see what opportunities might be available, but I did not tell him about Hardy's behavior. Hardy found out about the visit, concluded that I had "turned him in" and decided to fire me. When I learned about this, I told Hardy that I had not talked about my grievances (which I surely had the right to do) and asked him to call immediately to verify this. Smelling disaster, Hardy backed down. I reported the entire episode to the Deputy Provost who, though blameless, apologized profusely. I was promoted, given a raise (making my salary equal to some junior colleagues) and, when Hardy was out of town, the Associate Director signed my grant proposal. I got the grant. The Associate Director asked me to tell Hardy that I was not planning to sue (the possibility was apparently disturbing him) and I did so. Years later, Hardy saw me Xeroxing a very old book on taste and asked me about it. My interest in the history of my field touched a responsive chord and we had our first and only cordial conversation.

I learned two lessons at the Pierce Foundation. One was the importance of support. I was not the only woman there who felt the oppression of the environment. We exchanged "war stories" and helped each other survive. The other was the importance of family. My daughter, Elizabeth, was born in 1974. Having two wonderful children and an extremely supportive husband made my life very happy in spite of the work situation. I am in awe of women who have survived sexism in the workplace without a safety net.

Child care was a continuing worry. I was initially active in a group of Yale women who founded a child-care program. We had input from experts but they seemed to have negative views of working mothers. My mother made the trip east to look after our children but missed her life in South Dakota. A series of devoted baby-sitters came to our aid. These included the wife of a student from Taiwan who defected, with her husband, to mainland China during their stay in New Haven (our children were read stories about Chairman Mao). Our subsequent options included a winner: the Foote School. Teachers were creative and parents involved (my husband got a van license so he could drive kids to special activities).

These were exciting years to be in taste. Max Mozell, with the support of advocates at the National Science Foundation, led the effort to form a chemical senses society in the United States (Mozell, 1998). Every 3 years, there was a Gordon Conference for Olfaction and Taste, and, at the 1978 conference, which I chaired, Mozell led the discussion that resulted in the first meeting of the Association for Chemoreception Sciences (held in Sarasota, Florida, in April, 1979). Mozell was the first Executive Chair of AChemS; I was the second.

I worked on a number of problems while at Pierce. For example, Bathsheva Rifkin, one of my PhD students, and I worked on synergism in taste (Rifkin and Bartoshuk, 1980). But genetic variation proved to be an area that would involve me for years. About 25% of Americans (called nontasters) cannot taste a group of compounds (containing the $N-C=S$ group) that the other 75% taste as bitter. Two geneticists (apparently oblivious to the pioneering work of Fechner in 1860) invented a threshold technique that became the gold standard (Harris & Kalmus, 1949). The dependence on thresholds was fortunate for me. In 1975, the way was clear to apply S.S. Stevens' revolutionary scaling methods to genetic variation in taste (Hall, Bartoshuk, Cain, & Stevens, 1975). However, Stevens' methods were designed to study differences across stimuli (using within subject comparisons). They did not permit comparisons across subjects. I reasoned that if we could assume that one stimulus was the same, *on average*, to nontasters and tasters, we could express tastes relative to that standard, thus giving us absolute comparisons between nontasters and tasters. Our first standard was NaCl, but later advances in psychophysics let us switch to tones (e.g., Marks, et al., 1988).

As data accumulated, it was clear that some tasters experienced much more intense tastes than others. We started calling them supertasters and the name stuck (Bartoshuk, 1991). Interestingly, women are more likely than men to be supertasters. We suspect that supertasters carry two copies of the dominant allele; the recent discovery of the location of the gene for tasting (Reed et al., 1999) may help us determine whether or not this is true.

Inglis Miller, a leading taste anatomist, suggested the genetic variation might have an anatomical basis, and he was right. The differences between nontasters and supertasters were amazing (Bartoshuk, Duffy, & Miller, 1994). Near the tip of the tongue in a 6-millimeter circle (the size of the hole in a reinforcement for notebook paper), a nontaster can have fewer than 10 and a supertaster can have as many as 50 fungiform papillae.

Fungiform papillae contain neurons mediating pain and touch as well as taste. Thus it is not surprising that supertasters perceive more intense oral burn from irritants like chili peppers and more intense touch sensations (oily, viscous, etc.) from fats in foods (see Bartoshuk et al., 1999 for a review). Valerie Duffy and her students are pursuing the implications of this sensory variation for food preferences and body weight (see Peterson, Bartoshuk, & Duffy, 1999).

Three postdoctoral students played important roles in the discoveries involving supertasters. Susan Marino's interest in feminist issues led her to become Director of The Program for Women in the Institute of Technology at the University of Minnesota. Duffy and Laurie Lucchina earned their doctorates in human nutrition and were among the first to analyze food behavior in terms of the sensations evoked by foods as well as their nutritional content. Duffy joined the faculty of the University of Connecticut, and its proximity to Yale has let us continue to collaborate. Lucchina joined the Research and Development Laboratories of Unilever International and is using psychophysics to solve a range of problems going far beyond those she initially solved in taste. The work on supertasters also owes much to a series of undergraduates, particularly three (Katie Fast, Derek Snyder, and Jordan Prutkin) who served as research assistants while preparing for medical and graduate school.

As with most U.S. medical researchers, my funding comes from the NIH. The need to write applications for continued funding is always a source of anxiety. I was fortunate to receive a Pepper Award in 1984 that provided 7 years of funding instead of the usual 3 to 5. The toxic environment at the Pierce Foundation finally convinced me that there had to be a better life, and the Pepper Award gave me time to consider options. Happily, the Dean of the Medical School at Yale made it possible for me to move into the Department of Surgery. In 1989, when I became a Professor in Dr. Clarence Sasaki's section of Otolaryngology, I got the job of my dreams. However, I discovered that a male colleague, several years behind me on the academic ladder, received a higher salary. A request that this be at least evaluated raised my salary equal to his. Salary equity is still not a reality in academia.

I did not fully realize the toll that survival at the Pierce Foundation had taken until after I was safely ensconced in Otolaryngology. A trivial experience finally put things in perspective. I was doing the *New York Times* crossword puzzle and commented to my husband that the *Times* must have a new editor because the puzzles had gotten much easier. He said, gently, that the editor had not changed. This was a time of transition for my children as well. Daniel graduated from Stanford (he also got a master's degree there) and Elizabeth graduated from Yale. Both now have successful careers in the computer industry.

The move to Otolaryngology came as I was serving a term as President (1988–1989) of Division 6 of the American Psychological Association (then called "Physiological and Comparative Psychology" and now "Behavioral Neuroscience and Comparative Psychology"). Shortly after that, I served as President of the Eastern Psychological Association (1990–1991). Medical schools offer important opportunities for experimental psychologists. I gained access to talented medical students, residents and clinical colleagues as well as fascinating patients (see Schwartz, Janjua, Kveton, Green, & Bartoshuk, 1998). Frank Catalanotto, a pediatric dentist now Dean of the School of Dentistry at the University of Florida, and I had set out to study patients who had suffered extensive damage to their taste systems but experienced no change in their taste worlds.

One of my new colleagues, Dr. John Kveton, a leading otological surgeon, gave us the tool we needed to continue this work. Kveton explained that a small amount of lidocaine injected under the skin near the eardrum would move into the middle ear, contact the chorda tympani taste nerve, and anesthetize it for up to an hour. Connie Lehman, an MD/PhD student, showed that unilateral anesthesia of the chorda tympani nerve (anterior tongue) intensified taste (especially bitter) mediated by the glossopharyngeal nerve (posterior tongue) (Lehman, Bartoshuk, Catalanotto, Kveton, & Lowlicht, 1995). Ken Yanagisawa, a resident, showed that about 50% of the subjects so anesthetized experienced a taste phantom

(Yanagisawa, Bartoshuk, Catalanotto, Karrer, & Kveton, 1998). We concluded that input via the chorda tympani normally inhibits input via the glossopharyngeal nerve (this occurs in the brain). Damage to the chorda tympani releases that inhibition compensating for the injury. But for some, there is a cost: taste phantoms, a serious clinical problem.

Our emerging understanding of inhibition in the taste system got a boost when Pfaffmann became my patient; a virus had damaged taste on his left side. For 3 years, I tested him each month. In the beginning, he could not taste on the left but tastes on the right were very intense. As taste returned on the left, it diminished on the right, reflecting the reestablishment of inhibition (Pfaffmann & Bartoshuk, 1989, 1990). The time with Pfaffmann was precious because he suffered a stroke that ultimately took his life in 1994 (Bartoshuk, 1995).

My brother also became one of my patients. Prior to his death from cancer in 1984, he, like our father, experienced altered taste sensations. By then I understood the symptoms; I was able to evaluate him and explain what had happened but to my intense frustration there was nothing I could do. We still cannot repair the ravages of cancer and/or its treatments on taste.

In the past decade, my students and I have worked on oral pain as well as taste. Our first studies focused on capsaicin, the compound in chilis that burns. Paradoxically, capsaicin desensitizes pain receptors. Tracy Karrer, a PhD student, did the basic psychophysics (Karrer & Bartoshuk, 1991) and Wolffe Nadoolman, a medical student, suggested putting capsaicin in candies. This proved an effective oral analgesic for cancer patients (Berger et al., 1995).

Work on interactions between taste and oral pain led to one of the most satisfying "aha" experiences of my scientific life. Burning mouth syndrome consists of intense oral pain, often located on the anterior tongue; it occurs primarily in postmenopausal women. Sadly, because there is no visible pathology, sufferers are often further burdened by being told the pain is "all in their heads." Discovering that the disorder is a phantom sensation in the central nervous system produced by damage to the chorda tympani nerve gave me great pleasure (Bartoshuk et al., 1999). The disorder occurs in supertasters, presumably because of their superabundance of taste and oral pain innervation. It occurs predominantly in postmenopausal women because women are more likely than men to be supertasters and because menopause takes a toll on taste, thus acting like damage to the chorda tympani. Studies of interactions between the taste and trigeminal nerves need expertise in both systems. The work on burning mouth syndrome owes much to Miriam Grushka, a pioneer in the treatment of this disorder (Grushka, Epstein, & Mott, 1998). Work on neural interactions has been made possible by collaborations with Barry Green, an expert in oral touch, pain, and thermal sensations.

In 1995, I was elected to the American Academy of Arts and Sciences and to the Society of Experimental Psychologists (SEP). SEP represents continuity in psychology back to 1904 (Boring, 1938). I was particularly curious to see SEP in action because I was briefly a member of the Psychological Round Table (PRT), the "youth-fired rebellion" founded in 1936 that originally called itself the Society of Experimen*ting* Psychologists to pique the more august group (Stevens, 1974; Benjamin, 1977). Both groups originally excluded women. SEP admitted two women in 1929 but admitted no more until Eleanor Gibson in 1958 (Furumoto, 1988). PRT first admitted women in the 1970s.

In 1998, I received the first AChemS Award for Outstanding Achievement in the Chemical Senses. Psychophysics provided the tools that made this work on taste possible. Now taste can make a contribution to psychophysics. We know that perceived taste intensities are proportional to the number of fungiform papillae. Thus we can know something about a person's taste experience by looking at that person's tongue. This allows us to test the ability of psychophysical scales to capture differences across subjects. The scales that produce the best correlations between taste intensity and number of fungiform papillae are those most able to compare intensity experiences across subjects. Taste has taken us closer than we have ever been to conquering the epistemological gap that separates us. We can measure our distance from the stars; we can measure the differences among ourselves.

When I look back, my life seems to be a series of lucky accidents. I was born late enough to be able to enter science, but early enough to get to work on problems that seemed to be waiting just for me. Best of all, I had the good fortune to be a psychologist. The difficulties of studying behavior have made us sophisticated about experimental design and statistical analysis. We can study the big picture, but we know how to look beneath the surface to explore underlying mechanisms. The results of our work have impact on the lives of real people (Blakeslee, 1997; Goode, 1999). We have low tolerance for nonsense. To me, it doesn't get any better than this.

REFERENCES

Bartoshuk, L. M. (1991). Sweetness: History, preference, and genetic variability. *Food Technology, 45,* 108–113.
Bartoshuk, L. M. (1995). Carl Pfaffmann (1913–1994). *American Psychologist, 50,* 879–880.
Bartoshuk, L. M., Cunningham, K. E., Dabrila, G. M., Duffy, V. B., Etter, L., Fast, K. R., Lucchina, L. A., Prutkin, J. M., & Synder, D. J. (1999). From

sweets to hot peppers: Genetic variation in taste, oral pain, and oral touch. In G. A. Bell & A. J. Watson (Eds.), *Taste and aromas. The chemical senses in science and industry* (pp.12–22). Sydney: UNSW Press.

Bartoshuk, L. M., Duffy, V. B., & Miller, I. J. (1994). PTC/PROP tasting: Anatomy, psychophysics, and sex effects. *Physiology and Behavior, 56,* 1165–1171.

Bartoshuk, L. M., Grushka, M., Duffy, V. B., Fast, K., Lucchina, L., Prutkin, J., & Snyder, D. (1999). Burning mouth syndrome: Damage to CN VII and pain phantoms in CN V (abstract). *Chemical Senses, 24,* 609.

Bartoshuk, L. M., Harned, M. A., & Parks, L. H. (1971). Taste of water in the cat: Effects on sucrose preference. *Science, 171,* 699–701.

Bartoshuk, L. M., McBurney, D. H., & Pfaffmann, C. (1964). Taste of sodium chloride solutions after adapatation to sodium chloride: Implications for the "water taste." *Science, 143,* 967–968.

Benjamin, L. T. (1977). The Psychological Round Table revolution of 1936. *American Psychologist, 32,* 542–549.

Berger, A., Henderson, M., Nadoolman, W., Duffy, V., Cooper, D., Saberski, L., & Bartoshuk, L. (1995). Oral capsaicin provides temporary relief for oral mucositis pain secondary to chemotherapy/radiation therapy. *Journal of Pain and Symptom Management, 10,* 243–248.

Blakeslee, S. (1997, February 18). Chocolate lover or broccoli hater: Answer's on the tip of your tongue. *The New York Times,* p. C2.

Boring, E. G. (1938). The society of experimental psychologists: 1904–1938. *The American Journal of Psychology, 51,* 410–423.

Cohen, M. G., Hagiwara, S., & Zotterman, Y. (1955). The response spectrum of taste fibres in the cat: A single fibre analysis. *Acta Physiologica Scandinavica, 33,* 316–332.

Fechner, G. T. (1860). *Elemente der Psychophysik.* Leipzig: Breitkopf and Härterl.

Furumoto, L. (1988). Shared knowledge: The experimentalists, 1904–1929. In J. G. Morawski (Ed.), *The rise of experimentation in American psychology* (pp. 94–113). New Haven, CT: Yale Press.

Glanz, J. (1999). The first step to heaven. *Science, 285,* 1658–1661.

Goode, E. (1999, April 13). If things taste bad, 'phantoms' may be at work. *The New York Times,* p. F1.

Grushka, M., Epstein, J., & Mott, A. (1998). An open-label, dose escalation pilot study of the effect of clonazepam in burning mouth syndrome. *Oral Surg Oral Med Oral Pathol Oral Radiol Endod, 86,* 557–561.

Hall, M. J., Bartoshuk, L. M., Cain, W. S., & Stevens, J. C. (1975). PTC taste blindness and the taste of caffeine. *Nature, 253,* 442–443.

Harris, H., & Kalmus, H. (1949). The measurement of taste sensitivity to phenylthiourea (P.T.C.). *Annals of Eugenics, 15,* 24–31.

Karrer, T., & Bartoshuk, L. (1991). Capsaicin desensitization and recovery on the human tongue. *Physiology and Behavior, 49,* 757–764.

Lehman, C. D., Bartoshuk, L. M., Catalanotto, F. C., Kveton, J. F., & Lowlicht, R. A. (1995). The effect of anesthesia of the chorda tympani nerve on taste perception in humans. *Physiology and Behavior, 57,* 943–951.

Marks, L. E., Stevens, J. C., Bartoshuk, L. M., Gent, J. G., Rifkin, B., & Stone, V. K. (1988). Magnitude matching: The measurement of taste and smell. *Chemical Senses, 13,* 63–87.

Mozell, M. M. (1998). AChemS: The beginning. *Chemical Senses, 23,* 721–733.
Peterson, J., Bartoshuk, L. M., & Duffy, V. B. (1999). Intensity and preference for sweetness is influenced by genetic taste variation. *Journal of the American Dietetic Association, 99*(Suppl.), A-28.
Pfaffmann, C. (1941). Gustatory afferent impulses. *Journal of Cellular and Comparative Physiology, 17,* 243–258.
Pfaffmann, C. (1974). The sensory coding of taste quality. *Chemical Senses and Flavor, 1,* 61–67.
Pfaffmann, C., & Bartoshuk, L. M. (1989). Psychophysical mapping of a human case of left unilateral ageusia (abstract). *Chemical Senses, 14,* p. 738.
Pfaffmann, C., & Bartoshuk, L. M. (1990). Taste loss due to herpes zoster oticus: An update after 19 months (abstract). *Chemical Senses, 15,* 657–658.
Reed, D. R., Nanthakumar, E., North, M., Bell, C., Bartoshuk, L. M., and Price, R. A. (1999). Localization of a gene for bitter taste perception to human chromosome 5p15. *American Journal of Human Genetics, 64,* 1478–1480.
Rifkin, B., & Bartoshuk, L. M. (1980). Taste synergism between monosodium glutamate and disodium 5'-guanylate. *Physiology & Behavior, 24,* 1169–1172.
Schwartz, S. R., Janjua, T., Kveton, J., Green, B. G., & Bartoshuk, L. M. (1998). Alteration in lingual somatosensation as a result of tran section of the chorda tympani nerve (VII) (abstract). *Chemical Senses, 23,* 560.
Stevens, S. S. (1974). S. S. Stevens. In G. Lindzey (Ed.), *A history of psychology in autobiography* (Vol. VI, pp. 393–420). Englewood Cliffs, NJ: Prentice-Hall, Inc.
Yanagisawa, K., Bartoshuk, L. M., Catalanotto, F. A., Karrer, T. A., & Kveton, J. F. (1998). Anesthesia of the chorda tympani nerve and taste phantoms. *Physiology and Behavior, 63,* 329–335.

REPRESENTATIVE PUBLICATIONS

Anliker, J. A., Bartoshuk, L. M., Ferris, A. M., & Hooks, L. D. (1991). Children's food preferences and genetic sensitivity to the bitter taste of PROP. *American Journal of Clinical Nutrition, 54,* 316–320.
Bartoshuk, L. M. (1971). Taste. In K. J. & L. Riggs (Eds.), *Woodworth and Schlosberg's experimental psychology* (pp. 169–191). New York: Holt, Rinehart and Winston.
Bartoshuk, L. M. (1975). Taste mixtures: Is mixture suppression related to compression? *Physiology and Behavior, 14,* 643–649.
Bartoshuk, L. M. (1979). Bitter taste of saccharin: Related to the genetic ability to taste the bitter substance 6-n-propylthiouracil (PROP). *Science, 205,* 934–935.
Bartoshuk, L. M. (1988). Taste. In R. C. Atkinson, R. J. Herrnstein, G. Lindzey, & R. D. Luce (Eds.), *Stevens' handbook of experimental psychology* (pp. 461–499). New York: Wiley.
Bartoshuk, L. M. (in press). Comparing sensory experiences across individuals: Recent psychophysical advances illuminate genetic variation in taste perception. *Chemical Senses.*

Bartoshuk, L. M., Dateo, G. P., Vandenbelt, D. J., Buttrick, R. D., & Long, L. (1969). Effects of *Gymnema sylvestre* and *Synsepalum dulcificum* on taste in men. In C. Pfaffmann (Ed.), *Olfaction and taste* (Vol. III, pp. 436–444). New York: Rockefeller University Press.

Bartoshuk, L. M., & Duffy, V. B. (1995). Taste and smell. In E. J. Masoro (Ed.), *Handbook of physiology, Section 11: Aging* (pp. 363–375). New York: Oxford University Press.

Bartoshuk, L. M., Duffy, V. B., Etter, L., Fast, K., Garvin, V., Lucchina, L. A., Rodin, J., Snyder, D. J., Striegel-Moore, R., & Wolf, H. (1997). Variability in taste, oral pain, and taste anatomy: Evidence for menstrual control over oral perception (abstract). *Appetite, 29,* 388.

Bartoshuk, L. M., Duffy, V. B., Reed, D., & Williams, A. (1996). Supertasting, earaches, and head injury: Genetics and pathology alter our taste worlds. *Neuroscience and Biobehavioral Reviews, 20,* 79–87.

Bartoshuk, L. M., Harned, M. A., & Parks, L. H. (1971). Taste of water in the cat: Effects on sucrose preference. *Science, 171,* 699–701.

Bartoshuk, L. M., Lee, C. H., & Scarpellino, R. (1972). Sweet taste of water induced by artichoke (Cynara scolymus). *Science, 178,* 988–990.

Bartoshuk, L. M., Rifkin, B., Marks, L. E., & Bars, P. (1986). Taste and aging. *Journal of Gerontology, 41,* 51–57.

Bartoshuk, L. M., Rifkin, B., Marks, L. E., & Hooper, J. E. (1988). Bitterness of KCl and benzoate: Related to genetic status for sensitivity to PTC/PROP. *Chemical Senses, 13,* 517–528.

Duffy, V. B., & Bartoshuk, L. M. (1996). Genetic taste perception and food preferences (abstract). *Food Quality and Preference, 7,* 309.

Duffy, V. B., & Bartoshuk, L. M., Striegel-Moore, R., & Rodin, J. (1998a). Taste changes across pregnancy. In C. Murphy (Ed.), *International symposium on olfaction and taste XIX* (Vol. 855, pp. 805–809). New York: New York Academy of Sciences.

Duffy, V. B., Lucchina, L. A., Fast, K., & Bartoshuk, L. M. (1998b). Taste and cancer. In A. Berger, M. H. Levy, R. K. Portnoy, & D. E. Weissman (Eds.), *Principles and practice of supportive oncology* (pp. 141–151). Philadephia: J. B. Lippincott Co.

Kveton, J. F., & Bartoshuk, L. M. (1994). The effect of unilateral chorda tympani damage on taste. *Laryngoscope, 104,* 25–29.

Miller, I. J., & Bartoshuk, L. M. (1991). Taste perception, taste bud distribution, and spatial relationships. In T. V. Getchell, R. L. Doty, L. M. Bartoshuk, & J. B. Snow (Eds.), *Smell and taste in health and disease* (pp. 205–233). New York: Raven Press.

Rodin, J., Bartoshuk, L., Peterson, C., & Schank, D. (1990). Bulimia and taste: Possible interactions. *Journal of Abnormal Psychology, 99,* 32–39.

Todrank, J., & Bartoshuk, L. M. (1991). A taste illusion: Taste sensation localized by touch. *Physiology and Behavior, 50,* 1027–1031.

CHAPTER 13

Patricia Keith-Spiegel

Photographer: unavailable.

Patricia Keith-Spiegel

Much of what I have accomplished is what people had tried to lead me to believe I could never do. And, what I have cherished would never show up on a resume. Rather, they were the more quiet, behind-the-scenes activities that brought a special kind of personal satisfaction, a kind of warm glittery feeling that accompanies self-satisfaction as opposed to impressing others.

THE EARLY YEARS

My first memories from childhood in Los Angeles are painted in bleak tones. I even recall food as gray. The occasional splash of color was from a rare meat dish or a piece of fruit. The meat was almost always Spam and the fruit was usually an orange. (I still eat oranges, but I would not go anywhere near Spam.) A minuscule two-room apartment over a garage on my grandmother's property housed my mother, little sister, and me. The only sanctuary where I could be completely alone was inside my own head.

Being a child of a single mother in the early 1940s was not an enviable status. My father took off well before I was able to record any memories of him. Family whispers gave a faint but clear message that this was not an individual I would want to know, and his name remains unspoken in the family to this day.

World War II was raging. The adults seemed nervous, but I could not quite figure out why. My questions received puzzling, condescending answers like, "The outside of our window blinds had to be painted black because the city likes it when our windows look alike." Then, one day as I watched in terror, three men drove up in a squatty, steel truck and took away the gardener who worked for my grandmother. The gardener, Johnny Nakamura was a friend of mine. Suddenly, the world outside of me made no sense at all. Books did. I asked anyone who would listen to teach me some words. Words from any printed material would do.

Life perked up considerably with my entry into kindergarten. School was so exciting that I could hardly contain myself every weekday morning. I wasn't anywhere near as thrilled as my peers when the last bell rang on Friday afternoons. My mother encouraged inquisitiveness and exploration. I realized early on that having few resources but considerable encouragement and positive attention for making something from little or nothing—like bits of paper or junk—appeared to be rich breeding soil for creativity. For example, an oblong cardboard box, a worn-out feather pillow, and some heavy yarn pieces looked like the making of a great pair of wings to me. I spent most of a day pasting the pillow feathers, one at a time, onto the cardboard flaps that I then affixed to my back. That I couldn't get off the ground was very discouraging, but another project was just around the corner. I always believed in combating disappointment by trying something else.

My mother also forced her own kind of early lesson so repeatedly that it became my mantra well before puberty. Her message was, "If you don't get an education, you may end up like me, alone with two kids." Motivated, then, by an amalgam of fear and passion, I never considered dropping out of school, and still haven't. I take continuing education courses regularly.

I describe the dynamics of my early life because I do consider the formative years, for better and for worse, to be the most critical determinants of what people later become. I became a staunch believer in the powerful effects of early experience, especially after working for 4 years as an informal post-doc alongside Charlotte Buhler, the Viennese psychologist who is often referred to as the "mother of child experimental psychology." I loved her stories about how much she disliked Sigmund Freud and would cross the street to avoid speaking to him. But, I also embraced her theoretical views of the life span and the importance of early childhood in determining the quality and meaning of life's course.

EDUCATION

I attended Occidental College in Los Angeles without a clue as to what I wanted to do. High school had been mostly a disaster. In those days, girls were not encouraged to take exacting courses and were even barred from taking physics. I took an "F" (for female) career aptitude battery—consisting of hands-on tests of clerical skills—and failed miserably. The career counselor solemnly informed me that I might not be employable. I told her that I liked the idea of teaching high school or college and maybe writing books. She smiled in that sympathetic but smirky and confident way, and broke her truth to me gently. "Neither is likely to happen," she almost whispered. She didn't know about my stubborn determination and sincerity. I decided not to listen to her.

I was hooked on psychology about halfway through the introductory course during my first year of college. The subject seemed to encompass everything that made life involving and exciting. Four years at Occidental was a time of great growth, despite the virtual absence of female role models. But, fortunately, the men in the psychology department were excellent mentors and did not seem to care that some of us were young women. They encouraged every promising student, and I wanted to be just like these men—college teachers who cared about encouraging the next generation of students.

I wasn't quite ready to leave home, so I went to what is now Claremont Graduate University about 30 miles away. I received a PhD in general experimental psychology in 1968. Money remained a family problem (although I had gained a wonderful stepfather at age 10), but even though I was one of only two women in the entering class of about 18, I was offered full financial support. I had some wonderful teachers at Claremont: F. Theodore Perkins, Stuart Oscamp, Gene Sackett—again, all men. The sole exception was Margaret Faust at Scripps College who taught the developmental psychology courses for the graduate school. She was a fabulous teacher and fun to be around. It was exciting to finally see a woman doing what I wanted to do. The downside was that her title was something like Visiting Instructor, even though she had been at Scripps for many years. I surmised that it was possible for a woman to be a college teacher, but you had to take what you could get, and what you could get might not be much.

Claremont gave me a great many tools. Its labs were poorly endowed, and I found that my early childhood "scraps and junk" experiences came in especially handy. We built most of the equipment ourselves out of whatever we could find. My first authorship credit was for an article published in *Science* (1963) using equipment made from three 5-gallon tin cans and little bits of wood. Another early published project involved the use of plastic pieces that some local business tossed in the trash bin.

General experimental psychology allows a person who loves it all to flourish. However, the Claremont faculty (like most doctoral programs) wanted its graduates to find their ways into tenure track positions in research universities. I was attracted, however, more to comprehensive universities that promoted research but not at the expense of teaching and caring about students. Talking to friends who were recent research university hires revealed what, to me, was a disturbing insight: Teaching undergraduates was often described as an inconvenience, something to get out of the way so that you could get back to the laboratory and your graduate students. It was from my professors at Occidental that I received encouragement to embrace the teacher–scholar model as my career goal.

I will never regret this decision. Working with students at the beginning of their college training, especially those who are excited about their education and eager for mentoring, is extremely rewarding. Watching waves of them grow and mature across a span of 3 to 4 years, and taking part in those transformations, keeps the passion for my own work strong.

If someone had told me when I first started my career that my primary path would be professional ethics rather than in experimental child psychology, I would have thought them quite silly. Although we were taught proper research methodology in graduate school, ethics and standards of professional conduct were never mentioned that I recall. Besides, although I never considered myself an immoral person, that topic seemed far more uptight than anything with which I would want my name associated. Worst of all, no other topic that I could think of sounded more boring. However, around 1970, two events occurred that were seemingly unrelated or significant enough to redirect a person's career. Together they set me off on a life long path in a totally unexpected direction.

In 1971, my infant son went into convulsions. A wild ride to the emergency hospital with an unconscious baby put me into a state of intense anxiety. While I stood tense vigil, a physician entered the room and told me that his team would like to monitor my son for several years to ensure that this episode had not rendered him permanently brain damaged.

When we arrived a few days later for the EEG test, the neurologist who appeared to be in a great hurry said, "Well, let's get on with it." He pushed a piece of paper in front of me to sign. I started to do so, while also taking a quick glance up the page expecting to see a procedure release form. But, it was the language of a research consent form. I stopped at about the sixth letter of my name and queried the physician about the purpose of the form. He said, in a most annoyed tone, "Well, yes, this is a research project. Please finish signing because the technician is waiting." I pressed for more detail, which emerged slowly and with much prodding. In short, had I signed the form, I would have consigned my son to serve 7 years in a "no treatment control" group. If he ever convulsed again, he would be given aspirin only. I suppose he was somewhat fortunate because another control group of babies was to be being given daily doses of Phenobarbital for 7 years! The lucky control group was to receive the best-known treatment of the day while the experimental group would be treated with something new—I never found out what. What got to me at a deep button-pushing level was that I, who was already conducting research on human beings on a daily basis, learned the true meaning of "voluntary and informed consent" the hard way.

As is my pattern, the accomplishments that mean the most to me are not necessarily on my vita. After the incident with my son, I decided to learn more about research ethics with children. I was disappointed to find almost nothing, including little in the way of any clear policy that would prevent investigators from doing even more invasive research on children without meaningful parental permission. It would not be until 1982 (my son was, by then, 12) that the U.S. government issued a reasonably coherent policy regarding research with minors. But, I was writing letters to the human protection research agencies raising my serious concerns from a few days after I refused to sign the form. I am not sure if my efforts had impact, but drafts of a policy regarding minors started emerging in 1972, and my most passionate and personally favored writings are on research ethics with children. It was in these regards that I was to meet and link up with Gerald P. Koocher at Harvard University, a professional friendship that remains active to this day. Together, we have written three books and several book chapters.

I started my career as a full-time research assistant at Brentwood Veterans Administration Neuropsychiatric Hospital while finishing my doctoral dissertation. This was a facility tightly dominated by the medical model, and hidden behind the arrogance of the medical staff was an astounding lack of research sophistication. Compared to my classmates at Claremont, I was only a modestly talented statistician. But, at Brentwood I was seen as the goose that could lay golden eggs. I did literature reviews, helped formulate the research designs, ran thousands of subjects, computed the statistics, explained what the findings meant, and was lucky to get a footnote recognition.

Later I was offered junior authorships by the psychologists. But, other higher status professional staff members would often insist on authorship credits, even though they may have done nothing on the project itself or even taken a quick peek at the final manuscript. They had the power to make that practice policy, which seemed to me both an abuse of position and fraudulent. This spurred in me an interest in authorship credit assignment practices. The results of a national survey on this topic that Donald Spiegel and I conducted was published in the *American Psychologist* (1970). With that event came a flood of correspondence and hundreds of requests for reprints that has never been exceeded by any other work I have done since.

Publications are the currency with which advancement and notoriety in academia and other professional settings are bought, and we had publicly raised the "counterfeit" issue. Mail from graduate students, post docs, and junior faculty presented horror tales of exploitation. This work has since been replicated by many others in different fields.

The authorship credit work is how the APA ethics office learned about my existence. In 1974, I received a call asking if I would stand in nomination for the Ethics Committee. I agreed, and over the next 6 years (I served two terms) I became hooked on ethics.

I have found professional ethics and standards to be quite the opposite of boredom. This territory is the dark, dangerous underbelly of our profession where ignorance, psychopathology, incompetence, greed, and exploitation flourish. It is also a place where many people of decency and fitness stumble, sometimes without realization, in an instant of poor judgment. It is an exciting and sometimes heart-wrenching beat.

Another accomplishment that means a great deal to me, one that does not show up on any vita, occurred during my first term on the APA Ethics Committee. The Committee created a major revision of the ethics code (1977). This was an intensive 2 years of work, and an awesome responsibility. Included for the first time in an APA's ethics code was an explicit prohibition against sexual intimacies with psychotherapy clients. Now, you would think that this would have been a breeze to pass. But it wasn't back then. We had a bit of a battle on our hands. Where was the research evidence that sex with therapists is so harmful that there should be an all out ban on it? (It is interesting how the demand for research-based proof varies according to whose ox is being gored.) Since when do ethics committees interfere in consensual activity between two adults? After all, there is therapy and there is sex. When a client and a therapist are having sex, they are obviously not doing psychotherapy, so it is none of our business.

We finally prevailed (without benefit of the mountain of work that has since revealed the harm that accompanies the sexualization of therapy) in codifying a prohibition against engaging in sex with psychotherapy clients. Then the fun began. How would we say it? After all, intercourse is only one form of sexual expression. But, if we listed every conceivable forbidden act or gesture, the ethics code would be pages longer and possibly considered pornographic. After considerable discussion, we settled on the phrase, "Sexual intimacies with clients are unethical." Though somewhat vague, "sexual intimacies" allows for a consideration of an activity in its context. For example, hugging can be erotic or not, as when a client and therapist who have already established a trusting relationship embrace with hearty pats on the back on the client's announcement that the bar exam was passed, or when a reassuring arm encircles a client stooped in deep sorrow.

MY FAVORITE WORKS

Perhaps the most influential work in my career is the ethics textbook, first published in the mid-1980s with Gerald Koocher (Keith-Spiegel and Koocher, 1985), and recently revised (Koocher & Keith-Spiegel, 1998). To be honest, I cannot recall exactly when and how Gerry and I decided to write an ethics textbook. I do know that we wanted to create a scholarly and rigorous work that was also interesting and enjoyable to read. Others thought we were quite mad, insisting that "fascinating ethics" was an oxymoron. But, when that first review described our ethics textbook as a "page turner" that the reviewer could not put down, we were thrilled. The spice, we think, comes from the cases we present, all real, even though some people cannot believe that. Both of us had collected them over time and from many different sources. Our writing styles are quite similar as are our political ideologies and senses of humor, the latter of which leans toward quirky. But, I don't think Gerry and I realized at the time that we would be training generations of psychologists in ethics. What an awesome responsibility!

The book I wrote on getting into graduate school, first published in 1991 (Keith-Spiegel, 1991) and revised with my young colleague (Keith-Spiegel & Wiederman, 2000) is very special to me. This book was a labor of love with an unexpected afterglow. I, myself, was quite perplexed when trying to figure out how to apply to graduate school. How do I choose a school? How can I maximize my chances of getting in? I fantasized at the time that there was someone friendly and knowledgeable with whom I could talk. I didn't want anyone to tell me what to do, but I did want someone who knew a lot about the process and could answer my questions.

When I began to teach, I set myself up as the unofficial graduate school advisor. My little volunteer service began to grow beyond my ability to handle students individually, especially when students from UCLA, USC, and other campuses started knocking on my office door. So, I wrote a series of informal pamphlets to give to students who came by or called. I also decided to collect a great deal of survey data on program directors and others who made decisions or knew how they were made. (I am a vocal critic of advice books that are not developed from an empirical base.) Wanting to retain my old desire of having someone to talk to, the book became a conversation between the reader and me. Lawrence Erlbaum Associates agreed to sell the 500-page book at a reasonable price so that students could afford it. The most rewarding impact is, without a doubt, the scores of letters from grateful students I have never met. These letters and e-mail messages are among my most cherished recognitions.

At age 25, and still not quite finished with my dissertation, the call to teach became louder. My husband's career was firmly rooted, which kept me stuck in southern California. I was delighted to learn that San Fernando Valley State College (now California State University, Northridge) was looking for an assistant professor. I was invited for an interview, found the large psychology faculty very much to my liking, and was offered the job later that same day. I was to stay there for 25 years.

I have many fond memories of Cal State Northridge. (I was gone before much of it toppled over in a 1994 earthquake, and cried like a baby when I visited the site and saw the devastation.) I loved teaching there. Despite high teaching loads and little support for anything else, working with undergraduate students on projects using whatever resources we could put together (again, thank God for those early, deprived years that fostered creative alternatives to a high budget) was very rewarding. What was also wonderful about this university was that the psychology department had so many splendid women: Michelle Wittig, Barbara Tabachnick, Brennis Lucero-Waggoner, Linda Fidell, Dee Shepherd, Joyce Brodsky, Karla Butler, Nora Weckler, Susan Cochran, Helen Giedt, to name but some. The men were great also, but just being around so many women colleagues provided considerable camaraderie. I never felt a "chilly climate" at Cal State Northridge. But, I did choose to leave.

THE MOVE TO THE GREAT UNKNOWN

There was a big problem that had been brewing for years in all of southern California. Along with the glitzy excitement, the marvelous diversity, and the good weather was danger, smog, and a rapidly declining economy. I decided to try to escape, but at age 50 I was advised that my chances were next to none. I was too old and too expensive.

There it was again. "You can't do that." I nevertheless diligently scrutinized every issue of the *APA Monitor*, the *Chronicle of Higher Education*, and the *APS Observer*. I had to admit that unless I wanted an administrative position, which I did not, my prospects looked pretty bleak. Post docs, time-limited instructor positions, and tenure track assistant professors dominated the ads.

Alas, that process I believe in—a determination to meet fate halfway—popped out looking like a red rose in a gravel pit during my third month of searching. Ball State University was looking for a very particular sort of person to fill a newly-created endowed distinguished professorship. Along with the usual publications and other credentials needed to qualify for a senior position, the successful candidate had to be intensely interested and involved in teaching, especially undergraduate teaching. Could this be for real? I sent in my credentials, received a call a week later for an interview, and was informed that I would be recommended for the job at the end of a grueling two-day interview period.

Ball State University is the Midwest's best kept secret. We all have time for research, partially because release time is easily granted for it and research support is extensive, but also because there are rewards in many forms for creativity and scholarship. Comprehensive universities like Ball State have the potential to make very exciting contributions to society by fostering in their faculty that wonderful teacher–scholar model. The problem is that too many comprehensive universities want to mimic research universities—a sure path to futility, frustration, and perpetual feelings of being second-class. I love working in a comprehensive university that, for the most part, recognizes its special niche and potential.

AWARDS AND PROFESSIONAL RECOGNITION

The professional recognition that means the most to me is for my teaching. First came the California State University system's Trustee's Award for Outstanding Teaching in 1989. This competition was across all disciplines on all 19 campuses. I didn't interpret this award to mean that I was the very best teacher from among the 15,000 of us. But, what did give me great satisfaction was that so many of my students and colleagues initiated the awesome and labor-intensive nomination process. This award served as outside validation of my choice to do what I really wanted to be doing and that I was doing it in a way that meant something to those with whom I worked. The second, in 1994, was the American Psychological Foundation's Distinguished Teaching Award given by APA. Although this award uses more traditional criteria (e.g., publications), I again felt honored and validated about making a decision to put teaching first so many years ago. If I had been told that I could choose from among any of the awards that APA bestows, I would have chosen the one I got.

At the beginning of my career, I saw a great potential for psychologists to be major players in alleviating the world's social ills. That is, except for natural disasters, everything that goes wrong seems to be based on how people behave toward one another and how they interact with the environment. I have served on many social action committees of professional organizations and although the gains have not matched the idealism of my youth, I believe in psychologists' potential to create a better world. I enjoyed serving on APA's Council of Representatives, and as President of the Western Psychological Association, President of APA's Division 2 (The Society for the Teaching of Psychology), and National Vice President of Psi Chi. I enjoyed even more the completed committee tasks that made me feel that we accomplished a little something that made the profession more responsive to society's needs.

CAREER AND A FAMILY

I always wanted a child, but early gynecological difficulties drew me toward adoption. A mixed-race 9 week-old boy came into our lives in 1970. That little baby had feet so huge that the pediatrician laughed out loud when he saw him for the first time, putting us on notice that he would have to grow into those "colossal foundations." Our son, now at 6'4", is an attorney. He is my life's greatest delight.

I do have to admit that juggling an active career, a partner, and motherhood was never easy. I often felt that I was letting my family take a back seat to the demands of my career. My pace was sometimes so frantic that I sometimes felt lost inside myself. I have always been grateful to have a partner who understands my diverse goals and also assures that many of the tasks of daily living are quietly completed. But, it can be done. I was lucky to have a husband and a child who were actually interested in my work and enjoyed traveling with me to various meetings. These "almost vacations" aren't quite the same as the real thing, but we almost always enjoyed ourselves and saw much of this country and some others in the process.

I have come to realize that I could have done better at setting priorities. I should have listened to that little voice inside that often said, "You don't have to say 'yes' just because someone asked you to do something" or that whispered, "This doesn't feel quite right for you, so don't get involved with it." I could have made more time for my family. However, it is never too late. I have taken my own advice in recent years and very much enjoy the results.

THE PRESENT AND MOVING TOWARD INTEGRATION

The remainder of my professional time and energy will be spent integrating what has interested me most over almost 4 decades. Until recently, I have made separations among teaching developmental psychology and ethics classes, writing and research, social action activities, and other side interests that I enjoy but have not had much time to express. These include cartooning, graphic design, making dolls, and teaching technology development. However, they can all merge in the form of multimedia programs to teach children and young people values. I created The Center for the Teaching of Integrity at Ball State in

1997 and serve as its director. Most of the Center projects are created in a multimedia format. Other projects include teaching cross-cultural research ethics through role-playing using a science fiction motif, and how to present academic dishonesty matters in the course syllabus.

It is said that multimedia design is extremely difficult, very specialized, and has a steep learning curve. Not the kind of trick that us "old dogs" could possibly learn. Women are still rarities in this business dominated by very young males who are as comfortable with computers as they are with pulling on their socks. Again, I am so glad that I paid this stereotype no mind. With a large grant from the Fund for Improvement in Postsecondary Education (United States Department of Education), I created an interactive educational program on CD-ROM for first offenders of academic honesty codes. Lisa Gray-Shellberg served as the Companion Site Director at California State University, Dominguez Hills. The program has similarities to assignment by a judge to traffic school for the first speeding ticket. For example, the "F" remains on the plagiarized term paper (as is the fine paid for going 80 in a 35 mph zone). However, something proactive and educational is also offered as an option instead of pressing formal charges (cheating) or reporting a speeding ticket to the insurance company (traffic violation). Everything I love doing was given to this project, including intense collaboration with scores of undergraduate students.

A current parallel project that will extend into my retirement years is a system for teaching very young children values, again using a multimedia, nonlinear paradigm. Fanciful characters symbolize moral principles, temptations, and conflicts. This project is joyful, fun, and very fulfilling. Rag toy figures are involved, which means I have pulled out my old sewing machine that thankfully still works and those scraps of cloth, buttons, feathers, paints, sequins, and other decorative paraphernalia that have been piling up for years because one never knows when such items might come in handy. Watch for a quirky moral fable storyteller named Granny Grit!

REFERENCES

American Psychological Association (1977). *Ethical principles of psychologists.* Washington, DC: Author.

Keith-Spiegel, P., & Koocher, G. P. (1985). *Ethics in psychology.* New York: Random House.

Keith-Spiegel, P (1991). *The complete guide to graduate school admissions: Psychology and related fields.* Hillsdale, N.J.: Lawrence Erlbaum Associates.

Keith-Spiegel, P., & Wiederman, M. (2000). *The complete guide to graduate school admissions: Psychology and related fields* (2nd ed.) Mahwah, N.J.: Lawrence Erlbaum Associates.

Koocher, G. P., & Keith-Spiegel, P. (1998). *Ethics in psychology* (2nd edition). New York: Oxford University Press.
Sackett, G. P., Keith-Spiegel, P., & Treat, R. (1963). Food versus perceptual complexity as rewards for rats previously subjected to sensory deprivation. *Science, 141*, 518–520.
Spiegel, D., & Keith-Spiegel, P. (1970). Assignment of publication credits: Ethics and practices of psychologists. *American Psychologist, 8*, 738–747.

REPRESENTATIVE PUBLICATIONS

Buhler, C., Keith-Spiegel, P., & Thomas, K. (1972). Developmental psychology. In B. Wolman (Ed.), *Handbook of psychology* (pp. 861–917). Englewood Cliffs, NJ: Prentice Hall.
Keith-Spiegel, P. (1976). Children's rights as participants in research. In G. Koocher (Ed.), *Children's rights and the mental health profession* (pp. 5381). New York: Wiley.
Keith-Spiegel, P. (1977). Violation of ethical principles due to ignorance or poor professional judgment vs. willful disregard. *Professional Psychology, 8*, 288–296.
Keith-Spiegel, P. (1994, September). Ethically risky situations between students and professors outside the classroom. *The American Psychological Society Observer, 24–25*, 29.
Keith-Spiegel, P. (1994). A mid-life academic career change. In P. Keller (Ed.), *Academic paths* (pp. 81–94). Hillsdale, NJ: Lawrence Erlbaum Associates.
Keith-Spiegel, P. (1994). Teaching psychologists and the new ethics code: Do we fit in? *Professional Psychology: Research, Theory and Practice., 25*, 362–368.
Keith-Spiegel, P., & Cole, D. (1979). Resistance to changing undergraduate career training in psychology. In P. J. Woods (Ed.), *The psychology major* (pp. 275–281). Washington, DC: American Psychological Association.
Keith-Spiegel, P., Tabachnick, B. G., & Allen, M. (1993). Students' perceptions of the ethicality of professors' actions. *Ethics and Behavior, 3*, 149–162.
Keith-Spiegel, P., Tabachnick, B., & Spiegel, G. (1994) When demand exceeds supply: Second order criteria in graduate school selection criteria. *Teaching of Psychology , 21*, 7985.
Keith-Spiegel, P., Wittig, A., Perkins, D., Balogh, D., & Whitley, B. (1993, revised 2000). *Ethical issues in teaching and academic life: A casebook*. Muncie, IN: Ball State University Publication Services.
Keith-Spiegel, P. Wittig, A. Perkins, D., Balogh, D., & Whitley, B. (1996). Confronting unethical colleagues. In L. Fisch (Ed.), *Ethical issues in teaching* (pp. 75–78). San Francisco: Jossey-Bass.
Koocher, G. P., & Keith-Spiegel, P. (1990). *Ethical and legal issues in children's mental health services*. Lincoln: University of Nebraska Press.
Koocher, G., & Keith-Spiegel, P. (1993). Scientific issues in psychological and educational research with children. In M. Grodin and L. Glantz (Eds.), *Research ethics with children* (pp. 47–81). New York: Oxford University Press.
Pope, K., Keith-Spiegel, P., & Tabachnick, B. (1987). Sexual attraction to clients: The human therapist and the (sometimes) inhuman training system. *American Psychologist, 41*, 993–1006.

Pope, K., Tabachnick, B., & Keith-Spiegel, P. (1987). Ethics of practice: The beliefs and behaviors of psychologists as therapists. *American Psychologist, 42*, 993–1006.

Pope, K., Tabachnick, B., & Keith-Spiegel, P. (1989). Good and poor practices in psychotherapy: A national survey. *Professional Psychology, 19*, 547–552.

Sanders, J., & Keith-Spiegel, P. (1980). Formal and informal adjudication of ethics complaints against psychologists. *American Psychologist, 35*, 1096–1105.

Spiegel, D., & Keith-Spiegel, P. (Eds.). (1973). *Outsiders U.S.A.: Original essays on 24 outgroups in American society.* New York: Holt, Rinehart & Winston.

Tabachnick, B., Keith-Spiegel, P., & Pope, K. (1991). The ethics of teaching: Attitudes and behaviors of psychologists who teach. *American Psychologist, 46*, 506–515.

CHAPTER 14

Kay Deaux

Photographer: unavailable.

Kay Deaux

EARLY YEARS

As my passport now states, I was born in Ohio on November 4, 1941, the first and only child of Jack and Mildred Kujala. At that time of my life, however, I had no need for a passport. After an early move from Warren, Ohio, where I was born, to Lakewood (a suburb of Cleveland), I spent the next 17 years of my life in Ohio, only once crossing the state line. My mother, whose education went no further than high school, worked as a secretary until she married my father when she was in her early 30s. My father had 1 year of college, beginning an engineering curriculum. He then worked as a surveyor and later as what he described as an analyst at the American Steel and Wire Company in Cleveland, Ohio. Money was never in abundance, but we lived comfortably, and college education was always a goal that my parents held for me and saved their money to achieve.

The early influences on my goals of college and career that seem in retrospect most important, however, were two other relatives: on my mother's side, my grandfather Scott Murphy; and on my father's side, my uncle Matt Kujala. Despite the fact that my grandfather, over the course of his 95-year life, never lived anywhere but the mid-Ohio farmhouse in which he was born, the horizons of his interests were much more extensive. He made a number of trips, including to the World's Fair in St. Louis and to Alaska, though by the time I came to know him the trips were memories on postcards rather than current adventures.

He was always curious and interested in the world around him, and would avidly question me about my own activities as I went to college and later graduate school.

The second influence was my uncle, whose college degree, career as an architect, and collection of books showed me a world that I wanted to experience firsthand. Matt and his wife, Sarah, had no children, and I was a pleasant occasional diversion in their otherwise all-adult, work-focused life. When I was a child my uncle gave me Erector sets and pedal cars for birthdays and holidays, presents that my mother deplored but that I adored. Tours of my uncle's architectural sites were major events in my childhood; I loved to tag along with him as he toured his buildings in progress and introduced me to his crew of workers. His faith in my abilities seemed unquestioning, and though I did not join in an architectural partnership with him, as he more than once suggested I do, his confidence in me was an important support and incentive.

Perhaps the other significant aspect of my childhood was the development of self-reliance. With no siblings and low-activity parents, I learned early to set my own agenda if I wanted to have any fun. Being alone has never been a problem for me; at the same time, the desire to create positive climates around me has always been important.

EDUCATION

My choice of Northwestern University for undergraduate education represented a melding of several factors: my mother's mandate that I not go more than 350 miles from Cleveland, my father's antipathy to all-women schools (at a time when the Ivy League schools were still single-sex), and my own desire to be at a large university, and preferably one near a city that would constitute new territory (feeling quite certain that there was more for me to learn and experience, perhaps as a result of my grandfather's tales). Northwestern University in Evanston, Illinois—350 miles from Cleveland, coed, and located only a few miles from downtown Chicago—filled the bill.

I began studies at Northwestern with little idea of what I might want to do when I completed college. Because I had enjoyed math in high school, that seemed as good a place as any to start. One quarter later, however, the abstraction of math proved less appealing, and I shifted to French. I persisted longer there, but by my sophomore year, I knew that I still had not found the right field. During the final quarter of that second year, I took my first psychology course, a stimulating one taught by Steven Glickman who is now at the University of California, Berkeley. Although the physiological work that Glickman stressed was far different from what I had imagined psychology to be, the range of problems and the human relevance captured me. From then on, my goal was clear.

Several experiences during the next 2 years influenced my actions. Participation in the senior honors seminar with Carl Duncan introduced me to the pleasures of concentrated, independent work. A small project on attitudes and cognitive dissonance with Barry Collins, then a graduate student in the department, gave me an inkling of what it was to do social psychological research. So, too, did a class project for Raymond Mack, a charismatic professor of sociology, in which I observed racial segregation in seating patterns at O'Hare airport. Two years of work with Benton Underwood and Geoffrey Keppel, employing the now-archaic memory drum apparatus to study verbal learning, gave me extensive training in scientific method and the experience of working on a research team. At the same time, the tedium and artificiality of memory drum research led me to question many of the assumptions of psychological research and wonder how relevant it was to human concerns. Finally, work with Donald Campbell, Eugene Webb and others on the classic *Unobtrusive Measures* (Webb, Campbell, Schwartz, & Sechrest, 1966), a job that continued for the summer after my graduation, gave me a glimpse of creative thinking and an appreciation for the multiple paths that a scientific approach might take.

As graduation approached, I knew that I wanted to continue in an academic setting, although whether I really understood what an academic career might mean is unclear to me now. In some inchoate way, I defined myself as a social psychologist, but I was not at all certain how to pursue that course. This being 1963, the expectations for women in graduate school were very slight, and in fact, some professors in the department openly said that they would oppose accepting women for graduate work. Donald Campbell was curiously absent from my decision-making process—a circumstance that I later learned was associated with a period of severe depression for him (Campbell, 1981).

The outcome of this pondering was a decision to go to a social work program—not to become a practicing social worker, but to get a PhD doing research on human social issues. Had I been a man, I suspect my professors would have dissuaded me from this "off-track" choice, but at the time, clinical practice was seen as far more appropriate for an ambitious woman than was a research career. So off I went to Columbia University School of Social Work, probably the best social work program in the country at the time, and one that was attempting to upgrade its academic standards to match the quality of the clinical curriculum. The benefits of a special honors program notwithstanding, it was quickly apparent to me that social work was not the right choice and that, if I wanted to do research on social psychological phenomena, I should go to a graduate program in psychology. Although the social work program at Columbia was not what I wanted, the experience of living in New York City was immensely satisfying, creating a life long enthusiasm for New York. Consequently, I decided to enroll at Brooklyn College to stay in the city another year.

While at Brooklyn on a research assistantship with James Bieri, I had the opportunity to take courses with Hal Proshansky who, many years later, turned out to be the president of the City University of New York Graduate Center when I moved there. From Jim, I acquired more research skills and gained my first published authorship (Bieri, Deaux, & Atkins, 1966); from Hal, I learned to question the status quo of academic social psychology and to take seriously Kurt Lewin's advocated symbiosis of theory and practice.

After a year, I moved to the University of Texas, on the suggestion of James Bieri who was moving there to head the clinical program. Having just been awarded a predoctoral fellowship from the National Institute of Mental Health, I had numerous options available. Texas at that time was in a growth period, having recently hired Gardner Lindzey as Chair and several other highly visible psychologists. Perhaps it was the grandfather-inspired curiosity to see another part of the country that led me there; or perhaps it was Donald Campbell's belief, conveyed in a phone call in which I sought his advice, that I might get more faculty time at this newly-energized department than I would at a more established venue. Whatever the motivations, now somewhat dim with time, I headed off to yet another academic setting.

My time at Texas was short. In 2 years I completed the requirements and received a PhD in the summer of 1967. Looking back now, from the current realities of more extensive requirements in most graduate programs and certainly a much larger knowledge base to master, it is difficult to see how I managed to get through so quickly. I took qualifying exams, did research, and published. At the same time, I enjoyed the excitement and energy of Austin, Texas in the mid-1960s, including beer and country music, encounters with the then-unknown Janis Joplin, frequent motorcycle trips to Mexico, and the counterculture that was beginning to challenge the country's political and social policies. During that time I also married Edward Deaux, a fellow graduate student in psychology who was working with Kenneth Spence.

It is worth noting that during my education, both at Northwestern and at Texas, not a single woman was on the psychology faculty. At Northwestern, however, the aura of Janet Taylor Spence was there. She had left Northwestern only a few years before I became a psychology major, and people still talked admiringly about her. At Texas, the image became a reality. Janet was then a faculty member in the Educational Psychology Department, having recently moved from Iowa with her husband Kenneth and prevented by nepotism policies from being in the same department with her husband (Spence, 1988). Although I never took a course with Janet, I did get to know her while I was at Texas, and I can't help but think that the awareness of her existence as an active research psychologist and professor, helped to create a link for me between concepts of woman and scholar, previously known only through very occasional text references.

ACADEMIC APPOINTMENTS

My first academic job was at Wright State University, then a newly-established branch campus in the Ohio State system. That job, and one at Antioch College for Edward Deaux, was the only opportunity we had to resolve dual career needs at a time when (a) dual careers were still rare; (b) jobs were not advertised but were passed through the old boy network; and (c) neither one of us seemed to have any old boys working very hard for us. Furthermore, beyond the issue of dual careers, many departments discriminated against women in their hiring.

Although we were able to get two jobs in the same geographic area, discrimination was still at work, as I learned some months later. At the time we were hired, the chairmen of the two psychology departments conferred and decided that it would not be proper for me to have a much higher salary than my husband, even though the pay scale at Wright State was considerably above that at Antioch. Accordingly, my salary was adjusted downward by a few thousand dollars—not a negligible amount when starting salaries hovered around $10,000 on the average!. As it turned out, both that job and the marriage were short-lived, and I moved on my own to Purdue University in 1970.

Rural Indiana was never high on my list of places to live, and I anticipated a stay of perhaps 3 or 4 years, allowing me time to establish a research program, develop a creditable vita, and then look for non-green, non-pastured environments in which to continue my career. As it turned out, I remained there for 17 years, an outcome that owes a great deal to Jim Naylor, who chaired the department during most of my time at Purdue, and to a strong and predominantly supportive group of colleagues. (A long-term relationship with Jim O'Connor, a stage director and professor of theater at Purdue, contributed to my inertia as well.) My work on gender issues began in earnest at Purdue, and Jim Naylor was unwavering in his support, despite the somewhat unusual course that I was pursuing. Although at least one colleague warned me that a focus on gender research would be professional suicide, the only issues for Jim were the quality of research and the successful communication of that research in the professional arena.

At Purdue, I also worked with Irene Diamond, a political scientist, to found a women's studies program. As was true at many campuses in the 1970s, these efforts were not always enthusiastically received and rarely attracted high levels of resources. Furthermore, although we were successful in our efforts to establish a program, Irene's promotion to associate professor was turned down, a clear case, I believe, of unfair evaluations of her work and contributions.

The years at Purdue University, 1970 to 1987, represent a significant portion of my academic career, as I moved through the ranks from assistant professor to full professor, and from novice researcher to established professional. The department was large (between 40 and 50 faculty, as I recall) and, thanks to Naylor's leadership, became a very strong academic department during the time I was there. In addition, it had a reasonably large number of women for its time and place. Three of us were full professors: Betty Capaldi (who in my last years there served superbly as chair of the department, and later became Provost at the University of Florida), Alice Eagly (a well-known feminist social psychologist), and me. Several other women were at the assistant and associate level during my time there, making the department the most gender-integrated psychology environment I had ever experienced. While in the Psychology Department at Purdue, I always felt on a par with my departmental colleagues (and inequitable salary decisions were never again the issue for me that they had been at Wright State University). The financial resources of the department were strong, and support for research was readily available. In fact, given the level of support and the type of research that I was doing, I was slow to engage in the grant-getting game, finding sufficient support for my work without the extra funds.

The departmental atmosphere supported my growth as a scientist; the culture of rural Indiana, in a more oblique way, influenced my professional reputation. My continuing interest in travel and in more urban exposure led me to readily accept invitations to give colloquia, participate in conferences, and serve on boards and committees that met in Washington and elsewhere. This exposure and involvement opened many doors for me, and gave me the opportunity to participate in a variety of professional activities. These included membership on the Board and then the Presidency of the Midwestern Psychological Association, membership and chair of the APA Publications and Communications Board, President of the Society of Personality and Social Psychology (Division 8 of APA), and Chair of the Executive Committee of the Society of Experimental Social Psychology. In addition, I began a collaborative relationship with Larry Wrightsman in the continuing development of what was and continued to be a leading textbook in social psychology for nearly 2 decades (Wrightsman & Deaux, 1981; Deaux & Wrightsman, 1984, 1988; Deaux, Dane, & Wrightsman, 1993). During these years, I was also fortunate to spend 2 separate years at the Center for Advanced Study in the Behavioral Sciences in Stanford, splendid sabbatical years that allowed me to expand my thinking and set off in new research directions, as well as to be engaged with wonderful thinkers from a wide range of the social and behavioral sciences.

THE WORK ON GENDER

As a graduate student, my concerns with gender were incipient but unarticulated. For example, I rather clumsily used masculinity and femininity in a study of person perception (Deaux & Bieri, 1967), and I used attitudes toward women being drafted as the topic of an otherwise traditional study of attitude change in my dissertation work (Deaux, 1968). My choice was in fact questioned by one of my committee members, who thought the topic of women in the military would not be sufficiently involving—this during a period when men were being drafted for military service in Vietnam! Although these projects involved gender, they were not consciously feminist in their conceptualization.

My first attempt to address issues of gender and position directly was a replication and extension of a study by Aronson, Willerman, and Floyd (1966), motivated by a sense that the reported findings did not ring true. This study considered how we evaluate people who make minor blunders, such as spilling a cup of coffee during an interview. Aronson et al. (1966) reported that highly competent people appeared to benefit from evidence of minor flaws, being rated more favorably when they spilled the coffee than when they did not. In contrast, a pratfall did not help people who were low in initial competence. The problem, however, was that like many studies of the time, all the players were men—the evaluators, the target person, and even the experimenters. Guided more by hunch than by theory, I simply constructed the other three cells of a design, wherein both evaluators and targets of the evaluation could be either male or female. Sure enough, the previously reported results held only in the male–male condition. Women targets, for example, received no praise for making a blunder, in the eyes of either men or women, nor did women judges show any preference for the competent male who blundered (Deaux, 1972).

As the women's movement grew in the 1970s, my feminist consciousness grew as well, and I tried to think how I might address issues of gender discrimination from the perspective of social psychological theory and methodology. I relied heavily on attribution theory in these early years, exploring the ways in which prior assumptions about the capabilities of women and men influence the causal attributions that people make about performance. My best-known study from that period (Deaux & Emswiller, 1974) showed that given the same information about successful performance, people are more likely to attribute the woman's success to luck while invoking ability to explain male success. It is interesting to recall that this particular study, now a part of the research canon, was not immediately accepted by the journal editor. Despite a positive review (and in those days, a single review was typical), the editor himself claimed to see little value in the findings and he rejected the piece. Unwilling to accept that verdict, I wrote back to the editor and was able to persuade him to reverse his decision—paving the way for hundreds of citations and dozens of replications of these findings.

During the 1970s, I also wrote *The Behavior of Women and Men* (1976), perhaps the first research-based social psychological analysis of gender. Feeling much like an anthropologist digging in long-buried sites, I combed footnotes and paragraphs embedded deep in discussion sections to get my material. Never before had a project been such fun for me. Even the photographs that began each chapter and that appeared on the cover were part of the adventure, planned in conjunction with Cathy De Lattre, a photographer and friend in Lafayette. The impact of the book was positive and sustained. Especially gratifying to me was the fact that interest in the book spanned a wide range, from use as a supplement in introductory psychology and social psychology courses to a reference text that was cited frequently in technical journal reports and reviews. Also rewarding is the fact that many of the conclusions and speculations I offered have, in the wake of considerable subsequent research and sophisticated meta-analyses, continued to be valid interpretations of gender-related patterns of behavior.

A persistent theme in my research has been the impact of social categories—to demonstrate how judgments are biased by categorical information and to show how it is often the interpretation of behavior, rather than the behavior itself, that sustains beliefs in sex differences. The early work within the framework of attribution and equity theories showed the consequences of these beliefs. Subsequent work explored in more depth the nature of gender stereotypes, charting the various components and their interconnections (e.g., Deaux & Lewis, 1984). Through this work we have shown that gender stereotypes are broadly defined, including not just traits but also role expectations, assumptions about occupational position, and implications about physical characteristics. The latter set of beliefs are particularly important, in that their immediacy triggers stereotypic thinking before more individuating and potentially counterstereotypical information can be supplied. In addition, we showed that beyond the broad general stereotypes of women and men, there exists a set of subtypes with distinctive associated traits, physical characteristics and the like (Deaux, Winton, Crowley, & Lewis, 1985). Particularly with regard to women, these subtypes are strongly endorsed and distinct from one another: The homemaker, the business woman, and the sexy woman, as three examples.

The influence of categorical thinking, with its related beliefs and expectations, is further elaborated in the theoretical framework that Brenda Major and I offered for analyzing gender-related behavior more generally (Deaux & Major, 1987). Here we proposed an alternative to the more dominant view of static sex differences, arguing that the enactment of gender is a dynamic process, influenced by goals of the actors, expectations of others, and contextual factors. The scope of "context," defined primarily by experimental manipulations in Deaux and Major, was broadened by Marianne LaFrance and me in a subsequent chapter (Deaux & LaFrance, 1998). Our perspective is fundamentally social psychological, emphasizing the possibilities of variation and change in contrast to the more common essentialist positions of difference. It is also a position that I believe offers the most possibilities for the development of policies and practices that can alter the constraints that women and men experience in their currently defined roles.

The practical operation of gender beliefs was quite apparent to me in the research that I did in the steel industry in the late 1970s and early 1980s (Deaux & Ullman, 1983). Our goal in this project was to assess the impact of affirmative action policies that had mandated an increase in the numbers of women being hired into blue-collar positions in the basic steel industry. Through interviews with the women themselves, their male peers, and managers in two selected plants, we came to see how beliefs could channel behavior and how observed behavior could alter stereotypic beliefs. On the positive side, we found that women were able to perform their assigned jobs well. Furthermore, the more closely men worked with the women, the more likely they were to be favorable toward them. On the negative side, the influence of stereotypic thinking was much in evidence as well, perhaps most dramatically illustrated by the shunting of women, and particularly women of color, into dead-end janitorial jobs. Unfortunately for us, the potential of our findings to have any real impact on the ongoing operation was cut short by a sharp downfall in steel industry employment, causing many of the most recently hired workers, that is, most of the women, to be laid off.

These findings, however, in conjunction with many of the basic laboratory studies of gender stereotyping, have had an impact in other employment settings. Indeed, one of the most rewarding experiences for me has been the utility of our research for women fighting employment discrimination, as the research findings become the basis of testimony and supporting briefs in the legal arena. In the watershed case of Price

Waterhouse v. Hopkins, Susan Fiske first brought social psychological evidence to bear in Ann Hopkins' appeal. Subsequently, in an amicus brief prepared by the American Psychological Association for the Supreme Court case, Susan and I, together with Eugene Borgida, Madeline Heilman, and Donald Bersoff (Fiske et al., 1991), compiled the scientific case to show how stereotypes operate to discriminate against women at work. I have continued to make use of this extensive and persuasive database, created by social scientists, in cases in which I have served as an expert witness. These cases are rarely easy, and not all judges and juries are fully persuaded by our knowledge base. Yet in many cases, including that of Hopkins, the data have made a difference.

LIFE TRANSITIONS

The year 1987 marked an important transition point in both my professional and my personal life. After spending the previous year at the Center for Advanced Studies (CASBS), I took two giant steps: I accepted a new position as Professor of Psychology at the Graduate School and University Center of the City University of New York, and I married Sam Glucksberg, a cognitive psychologist at Princeton. Sam and I had met a few years earlier when we both were on the APA Publications and Communications Board, and we spent the year together at the Center to see if the challenges of dual careers were worth the effort. Fortunately for our dual career arrangements (and happily for the NYC-loving part of me!), I was able to get a job in New York and Sam could remain in the Princeton department in which he was so grounded.

As an academic environment, the Graduate Center is a special place. Less than 100 faculty, spread across the disciplines, are full-time appointments at the Graduate Center where their primary responsibilities are to teach graduate students and to do research. For graduate training at CUNY, these 100 are only part of nearly 1,500 faculty in the CUNY system who have doctoral appointments and are actively involved in a unique consortial system of graduate education. For people like me who value interdisciplinary contact, the Graduate Center is a wonderful place to be, as links across disciplines are made almost as easily as intradisciplinary ones. Furthermore, the Social-Personality program that has evolved creates an environment that is both supportive and exciting, with energetic and committed colleagues and a talented and diverse group of graduate students. At the same time, the continuing and accelerating political storms that surround public education in New York keep one constantly attuned to the interplay between scholarship and society.

New York City also provides enormous opportunity for me to enjoy many of my non-academic interests. Sam and I are regular theatre and concert-goers, and the jazz clubs that are scattered throughout our Greenwich Village neighborhood are another source of pleasure. As a collector of contemporary prints (and with a certificate but not a practice in art appraisal), I find the art galleries and museums of New York a constant source of delight. The restaurants of the city surely add to the overall enjoyment of city living as well. We are fortunate to have both an apartment in the Village and a house in Princeton, and the coordination of two careers in two locations now seems quite routine. In addition, my passport is now well used, as both professional and pleasure trips abroad have become a regular part of our life.

THE WORK ON SOCIAL IDENTITY

As I have become immersed in the culture of CUNY and the context of New York City, my research focus has shifted as well. In fact, the seeds were already sown during the preceding year that I spent at CASBS, when I participated in a project group discussing issues of self, affect, and society with three other psychologists (Robbie Case, Tory Higgins, and Dan Olweus) and three sociologists (George Bohrnstedt, the late Roberta Simmons, and Sheldon Stryker). In ongoing discussions throughout the year, we explored and debated the boundaries and links between individual self and social system. The trajectory of my thinking about gender had already prepared me for these extensions. When Brenda Major and I developed our *Psychological Review* (1987) piece, we realized that gender is embedded in a matrix of identities, and that these other identities will assert priority over gender on some occasions and/or combine with gender in complex and not well-understood ways.

Thus, when I arrived in the diverse-on-every-dimension culture of New York City, I was prepared to expand my research horizons. In my first year at the Graduate Center, I offered a seminar on self and identity. At that time, it was somewhat of a challenge to find readings for a course that had not been established in the psychology curriculum, and I sampled broadly from the social sciences, as well as using autobiographical accounts. Since then, the challenge is to make selections from what has become an enormous cross-disciplinary literature covering gender, ethnicity, sexual orientation, immigration, religious and political identities, and many other topics of interest to me and the students who enroll in what is now a regularly-offered course and who participate in our ongoing research group on identity.

Theoretically, my work on social identity is influenced by a number of perspectives, including the tradition of symbolic interaction, originating with George Herbert Mead and transmitted to me most directly in the work of Sheldon Stryker and of Tajfel's social identity theory, enriched for me in a sabbatical spent at the University of Kent in Canterbury, England, with Rupert Brown, Steve Hinkle, and Dominic Abrams. With these perspectives as a backdrop, my work focuses on two key issues in social identification. The first of these concerns the definition and meaning of a social identity. Rather than consider social identities as equivalent categories whose content is relatively unimportant, we have sought to articulate and differentiate forms of social identity (Deaux, Reid, Mizrahi, & Ethier, 1995). Furthermore, we have tried to learn more about the functions that identification serves for people, both at an individual and a collective level (Deaux & Reid, 2000; Deaux, Reid, Mizrahi, & Cotting, 1999; Reid & Deaux, 1996). Even more broadly, we have begun to think about how social representations of categories, defined at the level of society or culture, interplay with individual constructions of identity (Deaux & Philogene, in press). Addressing these questions of meaning and motive forces us to think much more carefully about the "stubborn particulars" (a phrase I borrow from Fran Cherry, 1995) of social identities as they play out in people's lives.

The second key issue that guides my recent work is the negotiation of social identity. Rather than consider social identities to be static categories that define the person, we assume that identity is an actively negotiated process. We explore, for example, how people manage their identities when they enter a new environment, a process that we have termed "remooring" (Ethier & Deaux, 1994; Deaux & Ethier, 1998). Other questions in this domain concern how identities are added to the repertoire and how meanings of identities change over time. In collaboration with Claude Steele, Mary Waters, Jennifer Eberhardt and Ewart Thomas, we will consider how the negotiation of ethnic identity by West Indian immigrants makes them more or less vulnerable to stereotype threat and decrements in academic performance. In each case, we are attempting to chart the active identity work people engage in throughout their lives.

LOOKING BACK AND GOING FORWARD

I continue to be involved in professional activities related to the infrastructure of psychology, even though I am no longer motivated by urban deprivation. Much of my recent activity has been with the American Psychological Society, first as a Board member and then as President (from 1996 to 1999, including terms as President-Elect and Past President). In addition, my involvement with the Human Capital Initiative and the Summit Steering committee, both efforts to broaden the base of funding in behavioral and social science and increase the contributions of psychology to public policy, gives me the chance to continue my long-standing habit of trying to make the climate that surrounds me more positive. I believe that psychology has much to offer, and I feel obligated to work on projects that seem likely to make a difference.

Over the years, I have been fortunate to work with many wonderful students, at the undergraduate and more often in recent years at the graduate level. At Purdue, the graduate students included Nyla Branscombe, Frances Cherry, Elizabeth Farris, Mary Kite, Laurie Lewis, James Martin, Brenda Major, Arie Nadler, and Janet Taynor. Since coming to the Graduate Center, Yael Bat-Chava, Kathleen Ethier, Barton Poulson, and Anne Reid have earned their degrees with me, and many, many other students have been part of my intellectual life. At the Graduate Center, in particular, the interchange between faculty and students is constant, and a community of scholars takes on real meaning in our day-to-day life.

I've also had the benefit, in more than 30 years as a professor in the field, of seeing some exciting changes in the discipline of psychology. Psychology has grown from a fledgling and tentative discipline to a major contributor of knowledge. For social psychology in particular, the beginning of the 21st century is a period of increased breadth and greater sophistication. What was in the 1960s a rather narrow field, both in methodological preference and in domain of applicability, has now become a discipline more willing to recognize complexity and diversity and more ready and able to use a variety of methodological tools to analyze the issues. For me, social psychology's unique contribution to knowledge is its ability to link the individual to the social context and the broader realm of social representations that shape our understanding. We are now, I believe, closer than ever to meeting the challenge of that goal.

As for lessons that I have learned, I offer only one guideline with absolute certainty: the importance of addressing questions that are meaningful and important to you, whether or not they are intellectually fashionable at the time. It is difficult at best to predict the course of scientific discovery. Rather than attempt to predict where others will go, I have found it far more rewarding to carve out my own path—and often, quite happily, to find others going the same way on a shared intellectual journey.

REFERENCES

Aronson, E., Willerman, B., & Floyd, J. (1966). The effect of a pratfall on increasing interpersonal attractiveness. *Psychonomic Science, 4*, 227–228.

Bieri, J., Deaux, K. K., & Atkins, A. L. (1966). Stimulus saliency and anchoring: Temporal and end stimulus effects. *Psychonomic Science, 6,* 47–54.
Campbell, D. T. (1981). Comment: Another perspective on a scholarly career. In M. B. Brewer & B. E. Collins (Eds.), *Scientific inquiry and the social sciences* (pp. 454–486). San Francisco: Jossey-Bass.
Cherry, F. (1995). *The 'stubborn particulars' of social psychology: Essays on the research process.* London and New York: Routledge.
Deaux, K. (1972). To err is humanizing: But sex makes a difference. *Representative Research in Social Psychology, 3,* 20–28.
Deaux, K. (1976). *The behavior of women and men.* Monterey, CA: Brooks/Cole.
Deaux, K. (1968). Variations in warning, information preference and anticipatory attitude change. *Journal of Personality and Social Psychology, 9,* 157–161.
Deaux, K. K., & Bieri, J. (1967). Latitude of acceptance in judgments of masculinity–femininity. *Journal of Personality, 35,* 109–117.
Deaux, K., Dane, F. C., & Wrightsman, L. S. (1993). *Social psychology in the 90s* (6th ed.). Monterey, CA: Brooks/Cole.
Deaux, K., & Emswiller, T. (1974). Explanations of successful performance in sex-linked tasks: What is skill for the male is luck for the female. *Journal of Personality and Social Psychology, 29,* 80–85.
Deaux, K., & Ethier, K. A. (1998). Negotiating social identity. In J. K. Swim & C. Stangor (Eds.), *Prejudice: The target's perspective* (pp. 301–323). San Diego: Academic Press.
Deaux, K., & LaFrance, M. (1998). Gender. In D. Gilbert, S. T. Fiske, & G. Lindzey (Eds.), *Handbook of social psychology* (4th ed., pp. 788–827). New York: McGraw-Hill.
Deaux, K., & Lewis, L. L. (1984). The structure of gender stereotypes: Interrelationships among components and gender label. *Journal of Personality and Social Psychology, 46,* 991–1004.
Deaux, K., & Major, B. (1987). Putting gender into context: An interactive model of gender-related behavior. *Psychological Review, 94,* 369–389.
Deaux, K., & Philogene, G. (Eds.) (in press). *Representations of the social: Bridging theoretical traditions.* Oxford, England: Blackwell.
Deaux, K., & Reid, A. (2000). Contemplating collectivism. In S. Stryker, T. J. Owens, & R. S. White (Eds.), *Self, identity, and social movements.* Minneapolis: University of Minnesota Press.
Deaux, K., Reid, A., Mizrahi, K., & Cotting, D. (1999). Connecting the person to the social: The functions of social identification. In T. R. Tyler, R. Kramer, & O. John (Eds.), *The psychology of the social self* (pp. 91–113). Mahwah, NJ: Lawrence Erlbaum Associates.
Deaux, K., Reid, A., Mizrahi, K., & Ethier, K. A. (1995). Parameters of social identity. *Journal of Personality and Social Psychology, 68,* 280–291.
Deaux, K., & Ullman, J. C. (1983). *Women of steel: Female blue-collar workers in the basic steel industry.* New York: Praeger.
Deaux, K., Winton, W., Crowley, M., & Lewis, L. L. (1985). Level of categorization and content of gender stereotypes. *Social Cognition, 3,* 145–167.
Deaux, K., & Wrightsman, L. S. (1984). *Social psychology in the 80s* (4th ed.). Monterey, CA: Brooks/Cole.

Deaux, K., & Wrightsman, L. S. (1988). *Social psychology* (5th ed.). Monterey, CA: Brooks/Cole.
Ethier, K. A., & Deaux, K. (1994). Negotiating social identity in a changing context: Maintaining identification and responding to threat. *Journal of Personality and Social Psychology, 67,* 243–251.
Fiske, St. T., Bersoff, D. N., Borgida, E., Deaux, K., & Heilman, M. E. (1991). Social science research on trial. The use of sex stereotyping research in Price Waterhouse v. Hopkins. *American Psychologist, 46,* 1049–1060.
Reid, A., & Deaux, K. (1996). The relationship between social and personal identities: Segregation or integration? *Journal of Personality and Social Psychology, 71,* 1084–1091.
Spence, J. T. (1988). [Autobiography]. In A. N. O'Connell & N. F. Russo (Eds.), *Models of achievement: Reflections of eminent women in psychology,* Vol. 2 (pp. 191–203). Hillsdale, NJ: Lawrence Erlbaum Associates.
Webb, E. J., Campbell, D. T., Schwartz, R. D., & Sechrest, L. (1966). *Unobtrusive measures: Nonreactive research in the social sciences.* Chicago: Rand McNally.
Wrightsman, L. S., & Deaux, K. (1981). *Social psychology in the 80s* (3rd ed.). Monterey, CA: Brooks/Cole.

REPRESENTATIVE PUBLICATIONS

Branscombe, N. R., & Deaux, K. (1991). Feminist attitude accessibility and intended behavior. *Psychology of Women Quarterly, 15,* 411–418.
Cherry, F., & Deaux, K. (1978). Fear of success vs. fear of gender-inappropriate behavior. *Sex Roles, 4,* 97–101.
Deaux, K. (1968). Graduate education: Final rehearsal for a career. In S. Lundstedt (Ed.), *Higher education in social psychology* (pp. 210–217). Cleveland: The Press of Case Western Reserve University.
Deaux, K. (1972). Anticipatory attitude change: A direct test of the self-esteem hypothesis. *Journal of Experimental Social Psychology, 8,* 143–155.
Deaux, K., & Farris, E. (1975). Complexity, extremity, and affect in male and female judgments. *Journal of Personality, 43,* 379–389.
Deaux, K., & Farris, E. (1977). Attributing causes for one's own performance: The effects of sex, norms and outcome. *Journal of Research in Personality, 11,* 59–72.
Deaux, K. (1976). Sex: A perspective on the attribution process. In J. Harvey, W. J. Ickes, & R. F. Kidd (Eds.), *New directions in attribution research* (Vol. 1, pp. 335–352). Hillsdale, NJ: Lawrence Erlbaum Associates.
Deaux, K. (1984). From individual differences to social categories: Analysis of a decade's research on gender. *American Psychologist, 39,* 105–116.
Deaux, K. (1985). Sex and gender. In M. R. Rosenzweig & L. W. Porter (Eds.), *Annual review of psychology* (Vol. 36, pp. 49–81). Palo Alto, CA: Annual Reviews.
Deaux, K. (1991). Social identities: Thoughts on structure and change. In R. C. Curtis (Ed.), *The relational self: Theoretical convergences in psychoanalysis and social psychology* (pp. 77–93). New York: Guilford.
Deaux, K. (1992). Personalizing identity and socializing self. In G. Breakwell (Ed.), *Social psychology of identity and the self-concept.* London: Academic Press.

Deaux, K. (1993). Reconstructing social identity. *Personality and Social Psychology Bulletin, 19,* 4–12.

Deaux, K. (1995). How basic can you be? The evolution of research on stereotypes. *Journal of Social Issues, 51,* 11–20.

Deaux, K. (1996). Social identification. In E. T. Higgins & A. W. Kruglanski (Eds.), *Social psychology: Handbook of basic principles* (pp. 777–798). New York: Guilford.

Deaux, K. (1999). An overview of research on gender: Four themes from three decades. In W. B. Swann, Jr., J. H. Langlois, & L. A. Gilbert (Eds.), *Sexism and stereotypes in modern society: The gender science of Janet Taylor Spence* (pp. 11–33). Washington, DC: American Psychological Association.

Deaux, K. (in press). Emotion and the social psychology of gender. In A. Fischer (Ed.), *Gender and emotion: Social psychological perspectives.* Cambridge, England: Cambridge University Press.

Deaux, K., & Kite, M. E. (1993). Gender stereotypes. In F. Denmark & M. Paludi (Eds.), *Handbook on the psychology of women* (pp. 107–139). Westport, CT: Greenwood Press.

Deaux, K., & Perkins, T. (in preparation). The kaleidoscopic self. In C. Sedikides & M. B. Brewer (Eds.), *Individual self, relational self, and collective self: Partners, opponents, or strangers?* Philadelphia: Taylor & Francis.

Deaux, K., & Stewart, A. (in press). Framing gender identity. In R. Unger (Ed.), *Handbook of the psychology of women and gender.* New York: Wiley.

Deaux, K., White, L., & Farris, E. (1975). Skill vs. luck: Field and laboratory studies of male and female preferences. *Journal of Personality and Social Psychology, 32,* 629–636.

Kite, M. E., & Deaux, K. (1987). Gender belief systems: Homosexuality and implicit inversion theory. *Psychology of Women Quarterly, 11,* 83–96.

Lorenzi-Cioldi, F., & Deaux, K. (1998). Group homogeneity as a function of relative social status and information processing goals. *Swiss Journal of Psychology, 57,* 255–273.

Major, B., & Deaux, K. (1982). Individual differences in justice behavior. In J. Greenberg & R. L. Cohen (Eds.), *Equity and justice in social behavior* (pp. 43–76). New York: Academic Press.

Spence, J. T., Deaux, K., & Helmreich, R. L. (1985). Sex roles in contemporary American society. In G. Lindzey & E. Aronson (Eds.), *Handbook of social psychology* (3rd ed., pp. 149–178). New York: Random House.

Taynor, J., & Deaux, K. (1973). When women are more deserving than men: Equity, attribution, and perceived sex differences. *Journal of Personality and Social Psychology, 28,* 360–367.

Taynor, J., & Deaux, K. (1975). Equity and perceived sex differences: Role behavior as defined by the task, the mode and the actor. *Journal of Personality and Social Psychology, 32,* 381–390.

CHAPTER 15

Judith E. N. Albino

Photographer: unavailable.

Judith E. N. Albino

For as long as I can remember, I have had a boundless curiosity about other people, their lives, their cultures, and most of all, their work. Although a shy child, I seemed to have an insatiable hankering to explore the unfamiliar, move outside prescribed boundaries. That tendency has made for a somewhat unconventional career in psychology, with a number of detours into other fields and disciplines. But a need to understand behavior has always been with me. A second theme that has influenced my career enormously has been the search to find a comfortable place as an achieving woman in a man's world. That theme has involved the realization that obstacles exist, and then, a journey of learning to overcome those obstacles.

I was born on June 2, 1943, in Jackson, West Tennessee, into a family of preachers and teachers on my mother's side, and farmers and merchants on my father's side. My father died when I was 12 years old. Over the next few years, my mother struggled; first, to keep my father's small grocery business going, and then to complete the college education she had abandoned for marriage. We were a family of four, including Bill, a brother who was 2 years older than me, and Camille, a sister 5 years younger.

Succeeding against overwhelming obstacles, my mother inspired me and instilled in me a determination to pursue my education and my chosen work. I had an ever-changing series of dreams. Most were literary, so I wrote poems and stories, and directed plays when I could round up enough willing actors. My mother repeatedly assured me that I could be anything I wanted until I declared, at the age of 10, my intention to become President of the United States. At that point, my mother doled out the conventional wisdom of the time. "Women aren't allowed to be President; it's in the Constitution," she said. I was disappointed, but I also knew that this was wrong, and that some day it would change. After all, when I asked why water fountains and rest rooms were labeled "Colored" and "White" and why some children didn't go to our school, my Methodist minister grandfather had told me, "That will change when everybody realizes that all God's children are just the same."

In high school, I was a very good—but not great—student, mostly because I was too busy trying to sort out whether I wanted to be "smart" or not. Boys didn't like girls who were too smart, we were told, and that seemed to be important. But I couldn't quite toe the line. I was angry when I learned that an exciting summer science program was for boys only. I objected to having to study home economics and put it off until my senior year. That summer, I was accepted as an American Field Service exchange student to France, and I gleefully clarified with my high school principal that I would not need to meet the usual requirements for graduation. In that way, I became the first woman to graduate from my high school without taking home economics—many years before the requirement was actually dropped. After 6 months in Roubaix, France, I returned to my hometown high school to fight another battle for women's rights—although no one thought to call it that at the time.

I had been chosen to compete, along with two other women and three men, in a speech competition sponsored by the Daughters of the American Revolution. I was thrilled, until I learned that I would have to wear a long white formal gown. It wasn't fair, I declared, that "the boys" could wear suits, while we had to go up on the stage half naked, stumbling on our crinolines, as dictated by the strapless and bouffant-skirted style of the time. But the DAR wouldn't budge, and I decided that it was more important to win than to be comfortable—and I did!

After high school, my family moved to Florida, and I enrolled at Florida Southern University, majoring in French and German. My year there was a good one academically, with some excellent faculty, in particular, Dr. Raymond Lott, an English professor who especially encouraged my writing. But I had heard about co-operative education and I was fascinated by the possibility of beginning a career while still in school, so I transferred to Antioch College in Yellow Springs, Ohio, to begin exploring political science and philosophy.

My first co-op job was in New York, as an editorial assistant at *Parents'* magazine. I spent the evenings dashing around that city and learning what the 1960s were all about. During the following quarters back in Ohio, however, a major depressive episode led to my eventually leaving college. It was a dark time, and it seemed to come from nowhere, although there was no denying that I had been the victim of some serious mood swings over the past few years.

I moved home, which was then Fort Worth, Texas, with my mother and her new husband. My subsequent struggles with depression, as well as the reactions of family and friends, were critical to the development of my interests, although not yet to my studies. I read Sigmund Freud, Carl Jung, and Alfred Adler, and I began working (always my best therapy) in a library. I also enrolled in literature courses at Texas Christian University. Within a year I transferred to the University of Texas at Austin, where I majored in journalism, with minors in English and political science. I loved that enormous campus, with its unlimited opportunities.

DISCOVERING PSYCHOLOGY

Before graduation, I interned at *Forbes* magazine in New York and was offered a job there as a reporter—the first time a woman had been made such an offer. I was intimidated, as well as flattered, and opted to return to Austin, where I became editor of a weekly trade paper for bus and trucking company owners. I wrote and edited the paper, and even sold advertising. I also learned about state politics and lobbying, and soon gravitated back to the University of Texas, where I began taking graduate courses in journalism on a part-time basis.

My interests soon turned to issues of behavior. In the course of a study about how people use the media to obtain information, I took psychology courses in research methods and in personality theory. When I attempted to enroll in a course in the Educational Psychology Department, however, I was told that I couldn't take graduate courses as a non-degree candidate. "Well, then, what degree should I sign up for?" I asked. "I would recommend the PhD," Dr. Beeman Phillips told me, and I was admitted to the program in very short order. Because of the casual nature of that process, I have often referred to myself as an "accidental psychologist."

I gave up my editorial position for what obviously was going to be an exciting journey. I began to use psychology to understand myself, to see a pattern emerging in my life, in the choices I had made, and in the directions I had taken in my education and career. I'd gone to Antioch because of its experimental approach in combining work experiences with study. Even in childhood, I'd made forays into uncharted territory to see what new knowledge could be found there. I did not care for cultivating a narrow focus on just one field, and I wanted to apply ideas, as well as talk about them. I realized, too, that these interests would take me out of the mainstream, but for the first time, I began to see this as an opportunity, rather than a problem.

These revelations had a profound impact on the direction my graduate work would take. I gravitated toward the study of human motivation in learning, always with a strong emphasis on measurement and evaluation. My first research assistantship was with the Research and Development Center for Teacher Education at the University of Texas; later I worked with Dr. Paul Kelley at the university's Measurement and Evaluation Center. While there, I wrote and presented papers on the nature and measurement of perceptions of teaching quality. I had also begun to study the measurement of achievement motivation, and both my qualifying paper for candidacy and my dissertation incorporated this construct. I was particularly struck by the work of Dr. Matina Horner, who had conceptualized the motive to *avoid* success in women—something I felt I had grappled with and observed in other young women of my generation.

I based my dissertation on an application of Horner's work to the real-life decisions of 1,300 students who had left the University of Texas, analyzing student exit interviews to see if a motive to avoid success was at work for women students. The research (Albino, 1973) made a small ripple in a body of literature confirming that social expectations can derail the ambitions and success of women at a number of critical points. The work also earned me a guest spot on the *Phil Donahue Show*, a national television talk show. Pleased that my work was being regarded as important by lay audiences, I remember fearing that this popularizing of my work might cause me to be seen as less than serious in the academic world. This was critically important to me as an assistant professor and the only woman faculty member in my department.

INTEGRATING PSYCHOLOGY WITH DENTAL MEDICINE

Leaving the University of Texas in 1972 with an unfinished dissertation, completed the following year, and a new husband, I was immediately juggling a personal life and an academic career. My husband, Sal Albino, often said that we spent our honeymoon at the computing center. In those days, most academic projects required use of the mainframe computer, which meant carrying boxes of punch cards to the center and waiting, usually hours, for analyses to be completed. Since I wanted to leave Austin with my dissertation data analyzed, I felt we really didn't have time for a trip following our wedding in August of 1972.

Fortunately, I had several job offers in the region my husband was being transferred to, and I took the one that placed me in a research university, the State University of New York at Buffalo. The fact that the position was in a School of Dental Medicine did not daunt me, for I viewed it as another opportunity to explore a new field. My husband and I thought we would be in Buffalo for only a few years; we actually stayed for 18. Our two sons, Austin and Adrian, were born there in 1975 and 1977, while I was an assistant professor. Neither birth required me to miss so much as one class, largely because my husband took on a major share of child-care responsibilities.

My work at this time was energizing and engaging. I taught dental students a little psychology, developed a research program in behavioral aspects of preventive dentistry and the psychological impact of dental-facial disfigurement, and also served as a sort of research mentor for clinical faculty in dentistry who were feeling the pressure to publish.

My research program progressed and was supported by major grants from the National Institute of Dental and Craniofacial Research. I also worked with my clinical colleagues to explore a number of topics important to specialists within dentistry, such as examiner reliability in assessing malocclusion (Lewis, Albino, Cunat, & Tedesco, 1982), shared concerns in orthodontics and prosthodontics (Albino, Tedesco, & Conny, 1984), expectations of denture patients (Davis, Albino, Tedesco, Portenoy, & Ortman, 1986), and so on. A number of dental students became interested in the behavioral aspects of dentistry and completed master's theses under my guidance. I also worked with students in clinical psychology, counseling psychology, and educational psychology.

Outside my university-based work, I developed an interest in incarcerated populations and, while pregnant with my first child, worked at the maximum security prison in Attica, providing achievement motivation workshops for inmates. I also consulted with a county probation department, developing and directing a program for training personnel to work with migrant and ethnic minority clients.

DENTAL HEALTH BEHAVIORAL SCIENCES

My career in dentistry developed along with a new field that we now know as health psychology. For the first time, medical professionals and psychologists were beginning to work together in universities, hospitals, and clinics around the nation, and I was excited to be one of the few involved in this ground breaking work in dentistry. Even here, I was a bit out of the mainstream, since most health psychologists were working in such areas as cancer and cardio-vascular disease—areas decidedly more glamorous than dentistry. But dentistry is a superb field for piloting behavioral change strategies that might be transferred to other health settings. Not only does it offer a low-risk set of health behaviors to deal with (most dental disease is not life threatening), but it also gives us a conservative test of our strategies. I often commented, "If you can persuade adolescents to floss their teeth, you can get people to do anything."

Nevertheless, psychologists working in dentistry (there were probably 150 to 200 by the late 1970s) often found it difficult to publish in major health psychology journals or to get research proposals approved by behavioral medicine study sections. Reviewers often labeled dental problems as unimportant. We did prevail from time to time, of course, and spent a lot of time talking to one another, particularly within the Behavioral Sciences Group of the American and International Associations for Dental Research, a group I served as president in 1983 to 1984.

The early 1980s were my most prolific period for research, as the longitudinal data from preventive dental studies and my own work on the psychosocial impact of malocclusion became available. Several colleagues from outside my department became major collaborators and contributors to my work. They included Drs. Malcolm Slakter and David Farr, superb methodologists who helped to shape most of our measurement studies. Dr. Lisa Tedesco, now Vice President at the University of Michigan, began working with me while still a graduate student and quickly became a full partner in the work. She subsequently took a faculty position in dentistry and was my closest colleague during our remaining years at SUNY. We have continued to work together on projects related to dentistry and, later, academic leadership.

My research program covered a range of issues and made contributions to the literature on perceptions of appearance as well as dentistry (Albino & Tedesco, 1988). The work on dental-facial disfigurement demonstrated that the psychological impact of dental-facial appearance is more specific to an individual's perceptions of facial appearance than to overall self-perception or self-esteem (Albino, Lawrence, & Tedesco, 1994; Albino & Tedesco, 1991).

We also showed that adolescent cooperation with orthodontic treatment correlates with different variables, depending on whether we look at it early or late in the course of treatment (Albino, Lawrence, Lopes, Nash, & Tedesco, 1991). Early cooperation is strongly influenced by parental attitudes and perceptions. Later in treatment, adolescent patients' own cognitions are the most salient predictors of cooperation. "Locus of control" is important in that adolescents who attribute responsibility for outcomes to chance or to their orthodontists' efforts are less likely to cooperate adequately over the long run than those who perceive themselves as influencing outcomes (Tedesco, Albino, & Cunat, 1985).

My research in behavioral aspects of dentistry had few precedents on which to build, but Dr. Grant Phipps, my department chairman and one of the first dentists to obtain a doctoral degree in psychology, was a significant source of early encouragement. The eminent oral biologist, Dr. James English, also offered encouragement, as did Drs. Robert Genco and Michael Levine. Dr. Lois Cohen, a sociologist at the National Institute of Dental and Craniofacial Research, was an important source of advice and support. Even so, I did not have the experience of working under the mentorship and tutelage of experienced psychologists—there simply weren't any in my specific field.

We were on the cutting edge of those working within a cross-disciplinary model. While specialization certainly leads to new knowledge, it can also blind us to insights that come only from utilizing different perspectives in our work. This approach also can be seen in some of my writing on community health and women's health issues (Albino & Tedesco, 1984, 1987; Albino, Tedesco, & Shenkle, 1990).

I am equally proud of my accomplishments in dental education and on the teaching and training of dental professionals (Albino, 1980, 1984; Albino et al., 1981; Albino & Lawrence, 1993; Albino & Ogle, 1977; Albino, Tedesco, & Phipps, 1982). Perhaps as a result of this work, I soon found myself chairing the School Curriculum Committee and playing a key role in preparation for accreditation. It was Dr. Bill Feagans, then the Dean, who pushed me to pursue other opportunities in academic administration, including an American Council on Education (ACE) Fellowship in Higher Education Administration.

MOVING INTO ACADEMIC ADMINISTRATION

The timing of my ACE Fellowship seemed perfect, since I had received feedback suggesting that my latest grant proposal might not be renewed. However, within days of beginning my fellowship in the office of SUNY-Buffalo President Steven B. Sample (now president of the University of Southern California), I received notice of my largest research award yet. I was traumatized, at least momentarily, by this abundance of opportunities. I had looked forward to focusing my energies on learning about administration, but I couldn't bear the thought of not pursuing my research program. I decided there was no alternative but to do both.

Those years working as part of Dr. Steve Sample's presidency at the University of Buffalo were exciting ones, since he, more than anyone else I know, has made a science of academic leadership. Along with Provost Bill Greiner (now President at UB), he offered me innumerable opportunities to learn about and practice administration. When my fellowship year was over, Bill invited me to stay on as Associate Provost. What that meant, of course, was that I now had two full-time jobs—one in administration and one in dental behavioral sciences research.

By this time, my husband and I had realized that my career was going to be more demanding than his. Although he continued to pursue his own work, he was truly the primary caregiver for our two children during this period, and this made my career possible. He made important contributions to gender equity in the process, too. He was the first male "room mother" (of course, they later changed the term to "room parent") in our children's school and was awarded a lifetime membership in the PTA. He also coached one son's soccer team and spent long weekends breathing chlorinated air at swim meets all over New York State.

My research program thrived because of the contributions of a superb group of clinical faculty, graduate students, post-doctoral residents, and staff. More surprisingly, my administrative career also flourished. I became responsible for most faculty personnel issues and much of the academic program work in the Provost's Office. Bill continually pushed me to take on new and risky ventures; for example, he assigned to me administrative oversight for our intercollegiate athletics program, which we were upgrading from Division III to Division IA status. Just when I was feeling spread too thin and thinking of taking at least a year to concentrate on research, I was offered another irresistible opportunity—the interim deanship of the School of Architecture and Environmental Design. I quickly accepted.

The great surprise for me was how much design is related to psychology. The school's former Dean, Harold Cohen, was among the first to show me how the use of space and the solution of design problems are fundamentally human problems. The students, too, talked about architectural design in terms of its effects on comfort, mood, and other terms that I translated as "psychological well-being."

With the assistance of a wonderful Associate Dean by the name of John Bis, we engaged in some major reorganization and also launched the school's first fundraising campaign. At some point during that year and a half, the faculty asked whether I would consider taking the Dean's position on a permanent basis. I have rarely been more pleased, but declined nonetheless, believing the school needed someone closer to their own discipline.

My next assignment was as Dean of the Graduate School, an administrative role that challenges the incumbent's persuasive talents at many institutions. The Dean of the Graduate School often is seen as not much more than a keeper of rules and records, with few resources for stimulating and rewarding change. Yet there are many compelling issues in graduate education that require leadership beyond a narrow, disciplinary perspective. I immersed myself in working with faculty across the university to address such questions as time-to-degree, training of teaching assistants, and enhancing interdisciplinary opportunities—until Colorado beckoned.

THE UNIVERSITY OF COLORADO YEARS

I accepted the position of Vice President for Academic Affairs and Dean of the Systemwide Graduate School at the University of Colorado against the advice of some trusted mentors. Colorado's higher education system, they warned, is plagued by an intrusive state legislature and an elected and partisan Board of Regents that politicizes educational decision-making. Board members, I was told, use their positions to gain visibility to run for higher office. At the time I thought, "How bad can it be?" I had never encountered an academic setting where I could not connect with faculty and students to develop a sense of shared mission. I thought those pursuits surely would be more important than politics.

Colorado University President Gordon Gee, who now is President of Brown University, was the person most influential in recruiting me to Colorado. He possesses amazing leadership talents, and I was eager to work with him. I believed that my strong foundation in academic work, program leadership, and planning could provide an ideal complement to his strengths. But he left Colorado just as I arrived. Dr. Bill Baughn, a trusted Dean Emeritus who had served CU once before as interim president, was a wonderful mentor in my first months there, and I was finding the systemwide challenges of academic leaderhip familiar, since again, this was a role where persuasion and relationship-building were critical.

Six months into the search for a new president, I was asked by the Search Committee to be a candidate, but I believed that it would have been inappropriate to come to Colorado to assume one position and then seek another so soon. The Board of Regents, however, ended up with four candidates upon whom they could not agree. They called me, interviewed me, and offered me the position that same day—at a salary considerably less than I was making as vice president! The Board, it turned out, had never seen nor approved the salaries paid to any of the vice presidents, even though approval was required by Regents' rules. That was when I began to learn that everything at the University of Colorado was not exactly regular. The local newspapers quickly picked up the story, referring to the difference between reported and actual salaries as "secret bonuses." Needless to say, this was not an auspicious beginning.

My appointment set off a tirade of public, and often televised, complaints, some from insiders who had been candidates for what was now my job, and who would now report to me. Perhaps I wanted this opportunity too much to see the situation clearly. I know that I believed that I could overcome the obstacles and bring people together as a team. With the wisdom of hindsight, I now believe that I should have told the Board of Regents I would serve as president only for 1 or 2 years while they conducted another search; certainly that was my last opportunity to leave the position gracefully.

What followed were nearly 5 years of 16-hour days, during which I never received the full support of the Board. This situation resulted not only from my inability to resolve partisan differences on the Board and to win over the administrative "insiders" who resented my position, but also because I was a strong advocate for students of color and other underrepresented groups. In addition, I vigorously attacked the internal "spoils" system, where financial rewards and even promotions often appeared to be a function of personal relationships rather than of merit. Those actions on my part were not well-received by many who stood to lose if I succeeded.

Nevertheless, there were many successes on behalf of the university. I developed a vision focused on maintaining the university's strength as a major research institution while making our research expertise and resources available to a broader community, particularly our undergraduates. My administration saw unprecedented increases in sponsored program support that rose toward $300 million annually. We completed the university's first capital campaign, raising $271 million. I launched a major effort to improve undergraduate education, providing more than 60% of our first-year students with access to small group academic programs. We worked with faculty to restructure and strengthen faculty governance. We also improved the institution's planning and strategic processes through a Business Process Transformation Initiative, enhancing efficiency by reducing proportionate administrative costs to the lowest of all public higher education institutions in Colorado.

During all this, the level of scrutiny and criticism I received was unparalleled, and it had a decidedly sexist bent. From the beginning, there were editorials suggesting that I was not qualified for the position, although both my academic and administrative experience exceeded that of most of the earlier candidates for the presidency. My appearance and dress were described in reports of my activities, something I have never seen occur for a male university president. My salary, modest by the standards of other AAU universities, was deemed too much by the newspapers, and I was criticized for serving on a corporate board, although my predecessor had held such seats, as did other administrators. The Board of Regents required my husband to leave university employment although he did not report to me and his position violated no nepotism rules. In fact, my predecessor's spouse received a university salary and a spousal functions allowance for supporting the presidency. The newspapers seemed to treat me as a curiosity rather than a public figure, and occasionally printed blatant untruths. When challenged on one such incident, a Denver reporter told me, "If two people say it, I can print it."

In efforts to improve communication and advocacy for the university, I kept up a grueling schedule of statewide travel, offered legislative testimony, made presentations and speeches, and hosted more than 6,000 individuals at presidentially sponsored events each year.

Even so, I was constantly caught between warring factions of the Board, and although the majority of the Board insisted that I stay in my role for the good of the university, I did not always bear up gracefully under the pressure of personal attacks on my administration. Instead, the more the criticism grew, the harder I worked. Finally, I was subjected to a televised "kangaroo court," open to the public, where members of the Board, as well as faculty and staff who opposed my administration, were invited to present their views, while I was denied the opportunity to ask others to speak on my behalf. Even so, the opposing Regents could not muster the votes to terminate my contract.

Life has many lessons. Mistakes often teach us far more than successes. This experience taught me that there are some controversies that shouldn't be engaged, not just because they can't be settled, but because they cannot be discussed within a context of truth, or outside of narrow personal interests. After 4½ years, the toll these events were taking on my family and me simply was not worth it, no matter how much good I hoped that I was doing for the university. I negotiated my resignation from the presidency and took up my professorship in the Department of Psychiatry with a sense of going home to what I knew and loved best.

There were wonderful friends and supporters during the hard times, many of them the faculty and students of color whose causes I had championed. At one point, I had been harshly criticized for meeting with striking students, and at another time my life was threatened because I had agreed to open a conference on gay and lesbian scholarship. During those Colorado years, I had often cringed when described as combative, or just too forceful in stating my position. I recall, however, as one of my proudest moments, the day in 1994 that I was honored by the Colorado Women's Political Caucus as recipient of their Susan B. Anthony Award. The plaque they gave me carried the words of that leader of the women's suffrage movement:

> Cautious, careful people, always casting about to preserve their reputation and social standing, never can bring about a reform. Those who are

really in earnest must be willing to be anything or nothing in the world's estimation, and publicly and privately in season and out, avow their sympathies with despised and persecuted ideas and their advocates, and bear the consequences.

After resigning as president, I was granted the title of President Emerita and entered a wonderful period of work as a senior scholar and advisor to a number of groups. I joined Colorado's superb Department of Psychiatry, and was welcomed by an interdisciplinary group led by Dr. James Shore, now Chancellor of the Colorado Health Sciences Center. I became again actively involved with the American Psychological Association, which I had served as Treasurer from 1990 to 1995, this time serving on the Board of Educational Affairs. I chaired a controversial National Technical Assessment Conference on temporomandibular disorders at the National Institutes of Health. The National Collegiate Athletics Association asked me to continue as Chair of the Presidents Commission (I was the first woman elected to that position), as we completed an historic restructuring of the NCAA, bringing major reforms to college athletics.

THE CALIFORNIA SCHOOL OF PROFESSIONAL PSYCHOLOGY

A year later, I was contacted about the Presidency of the California School of Professional Psychology. At first reluctant, I agreed to visit and soon became excited about the opportunity to assist this institution in shaping its future. Founded in 1969 by the eminent psychologist, Dr. Nick Cummings, CSPP was the first freestanding professional institution to train psychologists, and it is still the largest. Originally created to meet needs for mental health resources that were not being met by California's public higher education institutions, CSPP was now facing unprecedented challenges.

By 1997, the singular focus on clinical psychology was becoming problematic. Changes in the profession of clinical psychology, many of them wrought by the ascendance of managed health care, made it essential that we find ways of impacting CSPP's institutional economy so that we could continue to offer excellent psychology programs at a reasonable cost. It was clear to me that CSPP's mission of providing socially-relevant educational and service programs with a special emphasis on multicultural perspectives had to be preserved. The Board of Trustees had developed an excellent strategic plan that called for the growth of programs in new areas, such as organizational and forensic psychology, to stabilize and support the institutional base. Now they needed new leadership committed to that goal.

My first years at CSPP were exciting times, of getting to know many outstanding psychologists and the staff who supported them as we developed an action plan for the future. We decided to become a broader-based institution that would expand the knowledge base of psychology in such fields as management, legal studies, teacher education, community development and policy studies, and other human resource fields. To accomplish this, we launched a new university, called Alliant University, and made CSPP (now the California School of Professional Psychology at Alliant University) one of several distinct schools within the larger institution. We now anticipate developing an undergraduate college that will offer BA completion programs in applied psychology. At Alliant/CSPP, the academic community is committed to change in ways that larger, more traditional institutions cannot. We like to say that our tradition is breaking the mold.

LOOKING BACK AT LEADERSHIP ISSUES

Although the institution I now lead is less than one tenth the size of the previous one, the need for change and the difficulty of leading change are no less pressing. Yet at CSPP, the experience has been different. In this setting, my roots in community psychology and feminism, and my belief in a leadership that embodies these values, are more widely understood. I can work with faculty and other educational leaders who recognize that we share a responsibility for insuring that the resources of this institution are allocated in service of the greater good. I also continue to believe that psychology's "methods and values, its understanding of complex and intersecting spheres of influence, and its focus on problem-solving" are assets for leadership within an institution undergoing rapid change (Albino, 1999, p. 39).

Paradoxically, there are also ways in which having one's roots in psychology can be a hindrance. I have had to learn to recognize when my background and experience as a research psychologist is beneficial, and when it is not. Psychologists tend to care a lot about individuals. Leaders often need to take a system-level view of things. These tendencies can come into conflict. A leader must make institutional outcomes more important than individual ones. This means that we need to step back from the psychologist's role, which seeks to maximize individual potential. In these situations, as I asserted in the aforementioned article, it helps to be guided by a strategic plan based on a solid vision and a mission rooted in fundamental values.

As a woman often working in settings where other women were scarce, I maintained my interest in gender issues and began to consider how managerial styles are affected by gender. I think of myself as a feminist leader and as a champion of leadership styles often associated with women, but that are in reality often used by effective leaders of either gender. As a woman who brought the legacy of her own socialization to her eventual leadership style, I feel strongly about the need for appreciating diverse ways of working. In an article written for the *Educational Record* (Albino, 1992), I pointed out that although men and women—and by extrapolation, people of varying ethnic backgrounds—differ as to their levels of comfort with various professional behaviors, research had shown that these differences are not necessarily relevant in terms of overall *performance*.

As I look back on what is becoming a long and winding career in psychology, I am proud of my successes, but I am just as proud of what some would call failures. I say this because I have never regretted the goals that prompted my choices and actions, and because I have learned from my failures how better to achieve those goals. I believe the real key to success is to pay attention to larger, more enduring values and insure that we have personal mission statements tied to those values. For psychologists, that comes with the territory, for we have always viewed psychology itself as rooted in a fundamental belief in the value of human beings, and in their capacity to grow and to change. For my part, I hope to be helping others to do just that, grow and to change through higher education, for a long, long time.

REFERENCES

Albino, J. E. (1973). Sex differences on factor dimensions related to withdrawing from college. *Research in Education* (ERIC Document Reproduction Service No. ED 080 926).

Albino, J. E. (1980). Motivating underserved groups to use community dental services. In S. L. Silberman & A. F. Tryon (Eds.), *Community dentistry: A problem-oriented approach* (pp. 135–154). Littleton, MA: PSG Publishing Co.

Albino, J. E. (1984). Scholarship and dental education: New perspectives for clinical faculty. *Journal of Dental Education, 48*, 509–513.

Albino, J. E. (1992). Strategy: The dirty word that women must learn. *Educational Record, 73*(2), 47–51.

Albino, J. E. (1999). Leading and following in higher education. *The Psychologist–Manager Journal, (3)*1, 27–40.

Albino, J. E., Cunat, J. J., Fox, R. N., Lewis, E. A., Slakter, M. J., & Tedesco, L.A. (1981). Variable discriminating individuals who seek orthodontic treatment. *Journal of Dental Research, 60*, 1661–1667.

Albino, J. E., & Lawrence, S. D. (1993). Promoting oral health in adolescents. In S. G. Millstein, A. C. Petersen, & E. O. Nightingale, (Eds.), *Promoting the health of adolescents: New directions for the twenty-first century* (pp. 249–259). New York: Oxford University Press.

Albino, J. E., Lawrence, S. D., Lopes, C. E., Nash, L. B., & Tedesco, L. A. (1991). Co-operation of adolescents in orthodontic treatment. *Journal of Behavioral Medicine, 14*(1), 53–70.

Albino, J. E., Lawrence, S. D., & Tedesco, L. A. (1994). Psychological and social effects of orthodontic treatment. *Journal of Behavioral Medicine, 17* (1), 81–98.

Albino, J. E., & Ogle, R. E. (1977). Involving dental students in community dental health education. *New York State Dental Journal, 43,* 275–277.

Albino J. E., & Tedesco, L.A. (1984). Women's health issues. In A. U. Rickel, M. Gerrard, & I. Iscoe (Eds.), *Women and society: A community psychology perspective* (pp. 157–172). New York: McGraw-Hill/Hemisphere Publications.

Albino J. E., & Tedesco, L.A. (1987). Public health and community wellness. In L. Jason, R. Hess, R. Felner, & J. Moritsugu (Eds.), *Prevention: Toward a multi-disciplinary approach* (pp. 207–239). New York: The Haworth Press.

Albino J. E., & Tedesco, L. A. (1988). The role of perception in treatment of impaired facial appearance. In T. R. Alley (Ed.), *Social and applied aspects of perceiving faces* (pp. 217–237). Hillsdale, NJ: Lawrence Erlbaum Associates.

Albino J. E., & Tedesco, L.A. (1991). Esthetic need for orthodontic treatment. In B. Melsen (Ed.), *Current controversies in orthodontics* (pp. 11–24). Chicago: Quintessence.

Albino, J. E., Tedesco, L. A., & Conny, D. J. (1984). Patient perceptions of dental–facial esthetics: Shared concerns in orthodontics and prosthodontics. *Journal of Prosthetic Dentistry, 52,* 9–13.

Albino, J. E., Tedesco, L. A., & Phipps, G. T. (1982). Social and psychological problems of adolescence and their relevance to dental care. *International Dental Journal, 32,* 184–193.

Albino, J. E., Tedesco, L. A., & Shenkle, C. L. (1990). Images of women: Reflections from the medical care system. In M. Paludi & G. A. Steyernagel (Eds.), *Foundations for a feminist restructuring of the academic disciplines* (pp. 225–253). NY: Harrington Park Press.

Davis, E. L., Albino, J. E., Tedesco, L. A., Portenoy, B. S., & Ortman, L.F. (1986). Expectations and satisfaction of denture patients in a university clinic. *Journal of Prosthetic Dentistry, 54,* 59–65.

Lewis, E. A., Albino, J. E., Cunat, J. J., & Tedesco, L. A. (1982). Reliability and validity of clinical assessments of malocclusion. *American Journal of Orthodontics, 81,* 473–477.

Tedesco, L. A., Albino, J. E., Cunat, J. J. (1985). Reliability and validity of the Orthodontic Locus of Control Scale. *American Journal of Orthodontics, 88,* 396–401.

REPRESENTATIVE PUBLICATIONS

Albino, J. E. (1978). Evaluation of three approaches to changing dental hygiene behaviors. *Journal of Preventive Dentistry, 5,* 4–10.

Albino, J. E. (1983). Health psychology and primary prevention: Natural allies. In R. D. Felner, L. A. Jason, J. Moritsugu, & S. S. Farber (Eds.), *Preventive psychology: Theory, research, and practice in community interventions* (pp. 221–233). Elmsford, NY: Pergamon.

Albino, J. E. (1983). Psychological aspects of oral conditions and treatments. *Clinical Preventive Dentistry, 5,* 21–28.

Albino, J. E. (1984). Prevention by acquiring health enhancing habits. In M. C. Roberts & L. Peterson (Eds.), *Prevention of problems in childhood: Psychological research and applications* (pp. 200–231). New York: Wiley.

Albino, J. E. (1984). Psychosocial aspects of malocclusion. In J. D. Matarazzo, N. E. Miller, S. M. Weiss, & J. A. Herd (Eds.), *Behavioral health: A handbook of health enhancement and disease prevention* (pp. 918–929). New York: Wiley.

Albino, J. E. (1984). Psychosocial factors in orthodontic treatment. *New York State Dental Journal, 50,* 486–489..

Albino, J. E. (1999). Who will lead dental education in the future? In N. K. Haden & L. A. Tedesco (Eds.), *Leadership for the future: The dental school in the university* (pp. 14–22). American Association of Dental Schools 75th Anniversary Summit Conference discussion papers and proceedings, October 12–13, 1998. Washington, DC: AADS.

Albino, J. E. (2000). Factors influencing adolescent cooperation in orthodontic treatment. In P. Lionel Sadowsky (Ed.), *Seminars in orthodontics.* Philadelphia: W. B. Saunders Company.

Albino, J. E., Alley, T. R., Tedesco, L. A., Tobiasen, J. A., Kiyak, H. A., & Lawrence, S. D. (1990). Esthetic issues in behavioral dentistry. *Annals of Behavioral Medicine, 12,* 148–155.

Albino, J. E., Gale, N. E., Lewis, E. A., & Slakter, M. J. (1980). Self and family perceptions of children's malocclusion. *Journal of Dental Research, 59,* 216.

Albino, J. E., Juliano, D. B., & Slakter, M. J. (1977). Effects of an instructional-motivational program on plaque and gingivitis in adolescents, *Journal of Public Health Dentistry, 37,* 281–289.

Albino, J. E., Schwartz, B. H., Goldberg, H. J. V., & Stern, M. E. (1979). Effects of an oral hygiene program for severely retarded children. *The Journal of Dentistry for Children, 46,* 25–28.

Albino, J. E., & Tedesco, L. A. (1987). Public health and community wellness. In L. A. Jason, R. D. Felner, R. Hess, & J. N. Moritsugu (Eds.), *Prevention in Human Services, 5*(2/3), 206–237.

Albino, J. E., & Tedesco, L. A. (1988). The role of perception in treatment of impaired facial appearance. In T. R. Alley (Ed.), *Social and applied aspects of perceiving faces* (pp. 217–237). Hillsdale, NJ: Lawrence Erlbaum Associates.

Albino, J. E., & Tedesco, L. A. (1991). Esthetic need for orthodontic treatment. In B. Melson (Ed.), *Current controversies within orthodontics* (pp. 11–24). Berlin: Quintessenz Verlags-Gmbh.

Albino, J. E., Tedesco, L. A., & Lee, C. Z. (1980). Peer leadership and health status: Factors moderating responses to a children's dental health program. *Clinical Preventive Dentistry, 2,* 18–21.

Albino, J. E., Tedesco, L. A., & Phipps, G. T. (1982). Social and psychological problems of adolescence and their relevance to dental care. *International Dental Journal, 32,* 184–193.

Albino, J. E., Tedesco, L. A., & Shenkle, C. L. (1990). Images of women: Reflections from the medical care system. In M. Paludi & G. A. Steuernagel (Eds.), *Foundations for a feminist restructuring of the academic disciplines* (pp. 225–253). New York: Harrington Park Press.

Schwartz, B. H., Albino, J. E., & Tedesco, L. A. (1983). The effects of psychological preparation on children hospitalized for dental operations. *Journal of Pediatrics, 102,* 634–638.

Slakter, M. J., Albino, J. E., Fox, R. N., & Lewis, E. A. (1980). Reliability and stability of a measure of orthodontic patient cooperation. *American Journal of Orthodontics, 78,* 559–563.

Tedesco, L. A., Albino, J. E., Cunat, J. J., Green, L. J., Lewis, E. A., & Slakter, M. J. (1983). A dental–facial attractiveness scale: Part I, reliability and validity. *American Journal of Orthodontics, 83,* 38–43.

Tedesco, L. A., Albino, J. E., Cunat, J. J., Slakter, M. J., & Waltz, K. J. (1983). A dental–facial attractiveness scale: Part II, consistency of perception. *American Journal of Orthodontics, 83,* 44–46.

CHAPTER 16

Margaret W. Matlin

Photographer: Linda M. Kuehn.

Margaret W. Matlin

FAMILY OF ORIGIN

Often when we reflect on our lives, we focus on the barriers that hindered our professional development. Although I experienced some modest barriers, I have been fortunate because I grew up in a family that valued education and because important people in my life have been encouraging and helpful.

For example, I grew up in a family that provided a wonderful setting for a young woman growing up during the 1950s and 1960s. I am the oldest of three sisters. My father, Donald E. White, is a geologist who worked with the U.S. Geological Survey. He is a member of the National Academy of Science and has received international recognition for his theories and research on the origin of mineral deposits. My dad provided a model of intrinsic motivation; it has always been clear to me that he is absolutely fascinated by his work. He has also been incredibly productive, and he taught me the very useful phrase "terminal velocity," about always finishing the projects you start.

My mother, Helen Severance White, taught fifth and seventh grade for about 10 years, primarily to finance the education of three daughters. One important message I received from my mother was the joy and value of writing clearly. She also emphasized the pleasure of reading. (In fact, I'm still very firmly attached to the 19th century British novels she taught me to love.) My family did not emphasize material possessions. Instead, for both of my parents, intellectual achievement was one of the highest possible values.

Also, I never received the message from my parents that my future had to be limited because I was female. I've recently asked my parents how they managed to have such an enlightened viewpoint about their aspirations for me and my two younger sisters. (After all, I was in high school during the late 1950s and early 1960s.) They emphasize that this perspective seemed only fair—why should children's horizons be limited simply because they are female?

My mother has also mentioned that she was probably thinking that her daughters could develop professional opportunities of the kind she had been discouraged from pursuing after college. She had competed, at the national level, on debate teams during high school, and she graduated from Stanford University in 3 years with Phi Beta Kappa standing. She had thought about pursuing law school, but she had received the very clear message from many people that "girls don't go to law school." My mother would have been a superb lawyer, with a logical mind and superb verbal skills. This kind of discouraging experience in her own life undoubtedly shaped the kinds of positive messages she provided with respect to my own achievement and professional possibilities.

My family lived in Menlo Park, California, for most of my childhood, though we moved to Washington, DC, for 2 years when I was in high school. My parents often figured out interesting ways for us to broaden our horizons. For example, during those years in Washington, we frequently visited museums, historic sites, and interesting cities throughout the east. One of my favorite memories was a trip our family took to Europe prior to my senior year in high school. My father had been invited to work with some geologists in Italy, so my parents decided to make it a family adventure. We spent about 2 months there camping most of the time and cooking many of our own meals to save money. This experience helped me appreciate other cultures, and it certainly kindled a life long interest in traveling.

My parents both came from politically conservative backgrounds. However, both of them developed a more liberal perspective. This perspective may have been encouraged by the fact that they lived in Mexico for 2 years before I was born. My father was a consultant for Mexican geologists at the time, and they lived in remote mining villages where people spoke only Spanish and indigenous languages. My mother has often commented about what this experience had taught her: Many people in the world live in poverty, even though they work hard and try their best; life is not equally fair to all people.

EDUCATION

I have often reflected on the three mentors who personally guided me through high school, college, and graduate school. It's interesting that all three were male. However, not one was a White Anglo Saxon Protestant.

My high school biology teacher in California, Harry K. Wong, was extremely proud of his Chinese heritage, and he emphasized his cultural identity in his lectures and personal interactions. Mr. Wong encouraged me to apply for a small grant for a science fair project—this was my first taste of the joy of doing research. Mr. Wong also created an organization for aspiring high school science students. It had the very lofty title of "The Menlo Atherton Scientific Society." About 30 of us basically hung out together in the biology laboratory, and we had a place where it was acceptable to be a bright kid who liked to study. As I recall, we were chosen on the basis of our overall grade point average, and the group had slightly more males than females. However, I don't recall any overt sexism or chilly climate for the young women in the organization. With this cohort, I didn't have to hide the fact that I was smart, that I loved learning, and that I had high aspirations.

Mr. Wong also found out about a job opening in the Biobehavioral Division of Stanford Research Institute. I worked there for several summers in psychopharmacology research. Some of my research at S.R.I. led to my first publication as an undergraduate (Uyeno & White, 1967). Again, Mr. Wong never gave the slightest hint that my gender made me less competent. Incidentally, Mr. Wong later returned to school for his doctorate in education. He and his wife currently write a popular series of books for student teachers and for other educators who want to enhance their students' learning.

I was an undergraduate psychology major at Stanford University from 1962 to 1966. By far, the most influential professor for me at Stanford was Dr. Leonard Horowitz. He was an active researcher in what was then called *verbal learning*, though he shifted to clinical psychology several years after I left Stanford. He encouraged me to do research with him, and I was immediately captivated by his work with human memory. He treated me like a graduate student, and he also obtained a grant for me to conduct research during the summers after my junior and senior years of college. One of the most empowering things he did was to tell me about some of the interesting articles he was reading. Here I was, a mere undergraduate, and a professor was telling me about the most recent research in memory and asking for my thoughts about it! We also coauthored two journal articles on memory (Horowitz, Day, Light, & White, 1968; Horowitz, White, & Atwood, 1968).

Horowitz strongly urged me to pursue graduate school and helped me decide that the University of Michigan would be the best choice. Again, I need to emphasize that if any of the important people in my life had been sending me subtle gender-based messages, these messages were not loud enough to be heard!

I should also mention that I had only one female psychology professor during my years at both Stanford University and the University of Michigan, and that was Dr. Eleanor Maccoby. Maccoby, together with Carol Jacklin, wrote an influential book on gender comparisons in 1974 that helped shape the discipline of psychology of women. I did not know Dr. Maccoby personally, but she clearly provided a very positive professional role model. An interesting observation, in retrospect, is that I wasn't upset by the absence of women professors at Stanford. Why wasn't I more irate that I had been taught by only one woman professor? I also wonder whether my sense of professional identity would have developed more quickly if more of my professors had been female.

I entered the PhD program in experimental psychology at Michigan in September, 1966, and I completed my PhD in 1969. At Michigan, I worked with Dr. Robert Zajonc. Zajonc is a prominent social psychologist, now at Stanford, who has conducted research and developed theories on topics such as social facilitation, the mere exposure effect, and the relationship between affect and cognition. I really admired Zajonc for the way he did not confine his academic interests to just one narrow topic. This diversity provided a model for developing my own interests in an eclectic direction. Bob Zajonc also made it clear that he admired both my research and my writing.

My first research at Michigan focused on social facilitation. More specifically, the research examined how the presence of another individual can influence the speed with which someone supplies a word association, as well as the unusualness of that association (Matlin & Zajonc, 1968). My dissertation explored another area of social psychology, the mere exposure effect. This research attempted to explain why people prefer stimuli that they have seen frequently (Matlin, 1970; Matlin, 1971). My research as a graduate student focused on the interface between social psychology and cognitive psychology, an area that I still find fascinating.

As it happened, Bob Zajonc also introduced me to my husband, Arnold Matlin. Arnie had been an undergraduate at Michigan, and Zajonc had been his advisor. After graduating, Arnie enrolled in the PhD program in psychology at Yale, working with Neal Miller in learning-theory research. But then Arnie decided to switch disciplines and go to medical school at McGill University in Montreal. After completing his M.D., he returned to Ann Arbor for his internship and residency. Arnie asked Bob Zajonc if he had any female graduate students working with him, and Zajonc, not exactly the Cupid type, reluctantly gave Arnie my name. We were both at an ideal time for a serious relationship, and we quickly realized how much we enjoyed being together. We were married 8 months later!

At this point, I was a 22-year-old graduate student and Arnie was a 27-year-old intern in pediatrics. Here I need to emphasize another very important source of strength. Arnie has always been extremely confident about my professional ability—sometimes more confident than I was. He has often urged me to take some interesting risks. Furthermore, he has always been extremely proud and enthusiastic when the risks work out, and incredibly supportive when they don't.

We continued to live in Ann Arbor for a year after we were married. Then the Army imposed the Doctor Draft of the Vietnam War. However, we were very fortunate—Arnie was stationed in Fort Hamilton, in his home town of Brooklyn, New York, rather than in Vietnam. Still, this meant that I would have to complete my PhD *in absentia*. I was able to locate research participants at two colleges near where we lived, and I completed my dissertation in 1969. The following year, we moved to Rochester, New York, for Arnie's final year of pediatric residency. He then began his pediatric practice in Geneseo, a small town about 30 miles south of Rochester, and I was hired for a part-time position at SUNY-Geneseo.

CAREER DEVELOPMENT AND MAJOR ACHIEVEMENTS

Our oldest daughter, Beth, was born in 1970, the year after I received my PhD. Sally was born in 1972, after I had taught half-time at SUNY-Geneseo for 1 year. I taught half-time for another year after Sally was born before deciding to become a full-time faculty member there. When Beth and Sally were young, we arranged for babysitting on the days I was teaching in the homes of other young mothers in our neighborhood.

My early years of teaching taught me something that I try to share with my student advisees: Don't be too sure about what you can and can't do, about what you do and don't like. Specifically, when I first began teaching, I was reasonably terrified. I had not been a teaching assistant in graduate school, because I was only interested in research. My first experience of standing in front of a classroom was during my first year of teaching at Geneseo. I was truly afraid that the students would ask me a question I couldn't answer. I also operated according to the "banker model" of professorship; I'd simply pour as much information into students' heads as I possibly could during each class period.

Those first couple of years were not enjoyable, because I lacked self-confidence and because, with that teaching style, the students and I typically did not interact. It was several years before I realized that students were perfectly satisfied when I answered a difficult question by saying, "I don't know the answer, but I'll try to find out and get back to you." It was also several years before I realized how much more the students and I would enjoy the teaching experience if I encouraged discussion, provided examples and anecdotes, and invited them to apply the theories and research to their daily lives. During those years, my self confidence grew enormously. Now, I can't imagine any more enjoyable or rewarding profession than teaching college.

My experience in teaching taught me that life requires taking moderate risks. I learned to ask myself, when faced with a new challenge, "What is the worst thing that can possibly happen?" I also learned that I could transform an unpleasant situation into work that became increasingly appealing—and eventually quite wonderful. At any rate, I soon found that I loved teaching in a classroom.

Meanwhile, I had been doing some research that was an outgrowth of my PhD dissertation. At this point, another researcher in the same area wrote to ask if I would be interested in writing a book together on the topic (Matlin & Stang, 1978). As it happened, this was not a pleasant experience. I ended up doing most of the work, and we did not obtain a prestigious publisher for the book.

Again, however, I learned that an unpleasant experience can still provide some valuable information. I discovered that I loved writing. I also learned that it was wonderfully challenging to work on a large-scale project. At this point, I decided to take a major risk. I would try writing an undergraduate psychology textbook. After all, I enjoyed writing, and I enjoyed teaching. Specifically, I signed a contract to write a textbook called *Human Experimental Psychology* (Matlin, 1979). Now, this was risky because all the other experimental psychology textbooks had been written by men, and all these books were quite formal. I decided to write a textbook that included examples, anecdotes, and applications to students' daily lives. This approach seemed to engage my own students' attention, and they also retained the material more effectively with this more personal approach. However, the project wasn't a complete success, because the publisher and I had not done the appropriate market research. As a result, the structure of the textbook wasn't close enough to the normative course design. We had a number of enthusiastic adopters, but not enough to produce a second edition of this textbook.

By the end of the 1970s, I really began to have a strong sense of professional identity, both as a classroom teacher and a textbook author. In 1977, I had received a teaching award from SUNY, called the Chancellor's Award for Excellence in Teaching. By this time, I also had written two books (Matlin, 1979; Matlin & Stang, 1978), that I thought were good books, even though they had not produced much professional recognition. I now knew for certain that I loved writing books. I truly enjoyed taking a huge area of knowledge and organizing it. I loved planning a book, and I loved the actual writing. I would sometimes become frustrated when a study didn't seem to make sense, or when I couldn't figure out how to make it relevant to undergraduates. However, I'd feel tremendous satisfaction when everything came together. In short, for me, writing is certainly intrinsically motivating.

When I was a student, I would never have believed that I could write a textbook. Certainly, I liked to write, and I really enjoyed writing papers in my psychology courses. But that goal would have seemed far beyond my grasp. When my students ask for career advice, I urge them to notice what they enjoy doing and what other people praise them for doing. Within the profession of psychology, we have so many different routes our careers can take. It had never occurred to me when I was younger that I would write textbooks. I encourage my students to keep reflecting about their talents, asking what gives them pleasure. I also encourage them not to give up too early.

At any rate, I now knew that I wanted to write another book. What happened next was perhaps the biggest risk I had ever pursued. I wanted to write a textbook in cognitive psychology, and so I sent out a prospectus to three different companies. Holt, Rinehart, and Winston (which is now Harcourt College Publishers) sent me a contract within a few weeks. A second publisher, Allyn and Bacon, told me that they already had a cognition book. However, the editor thought I would be an ideal person to write a textbook in sensation and perception, and they would like to offer me a contract for an S&P book. So I had to decide if I should sign both contracts and write two textbooks simultaneously. Once again, Arnie had tremendous faith in my abilities, and he encouraged me to go ahead with both books, especially because I had a sabbatical for one semester.

I did sign two textbook contracts, and for the next 2 years, I would write a few chapters of one book, then switch to the other (Matlin, 1983a, 1983b). The two topics overlapped somewhat. I also used the same style, the same pedagogical devices, and the same voice for both books. Both of these, like the broader domain of experimental psychology, are topics considered stereotypically masculine. Once again, though, I wanted to humanize these areas, to make them student-oriented. I try to imagine my students reading each passage. I also use numerous examples from everyday life. Many are my own experiences or the experiences of friends. Others are examples that students supply in class (and I make certain that they are cited in the acknowledgment section of each book). My students report that they can hear me talking to them in these textbooks, and that's exactly what I hope to accomplish—an informal but informative conversation.

I do find that both cognitive psychology and sensation/perception are inherently interesting, though it's sometimes a challenge to make them both clear and interesting to students. In fact, one of the most satisfying writing experiences for me is taking a topic such as signal detection theory in sensation and perception, or parallel distributed processing in cognition, and trying to make these accessible to undergraduates. Professors who use my textbooks tell me that their students appreciate the clear writing style, the strong organization, and the numerous examples. I specifically try to avoid a condescending perspective, a pompous tone, or theoretical arguments that are really addressed to the professor rather than the student.

Throughout all my writing in these three textbooks from the experimental side of psychology, I use examples from the lives of women and girls. This policy often draws harsh remarks from reviewers. For example, when I had written my experimental psychology textbook, one of the reviewers had complained that I had mentioned the Girl Scout Law, rather than the Boy Scout Law. This reviewer also wrote, "Even her children are both girls!" Fortunately, the editor of this book immediately told me that the complaints were ridiculous and completely dismissed them. In general, too, editors have continued to be supportive of my approach. I also make a special attempt to discuss the work of women researchers. When we write textbooks, we have a choice about the story we want to tell about our discipline, and I want women to be an important part of that story.

So I wrote two textbooks simultaneously, and I learned that I could not only survive, but I could thrive. After finishing those books, I made myself wait a year before another project. This next project was obvious. I wanted to write a psychology of women textbook, especially because I had now taught the course for about 10 years and I felt passionate about it (Matlin, 1987). I had originally proposed the course during the mid-1970s, and I had seen how the psychology of women could make a difference in the lives of my students in the classroom. Now I wanted to reach beyond my own classroom.

Writing a psychology of women textbook presented its own challenges. The discipline doesn't have its own inherent organization of topics. In contrast, textbooks in cognition and in sensation and perception have a fairly standard order for textbook chapters. Psychology of women is also much more interdisciplinary than the other two areas. I'd often find myself pursuing resources in political science, medicine, sociology, economics, and so forth.

Now that each of my three upper-level books is in its fourth edition, I've discovered another major difference between psychology of women and the other two books: Even though the research on working memory or the research on the rods and cones moves forward each year, the actual human equipment we are examining stays the same. The rods and the cones are the same in 1999 as they were in 1983, when I published my first sensation and perception textbook. In contrast, the women and the social processes I wrote about in the early 1980s have changed substantially by the late 1990s. I could not trust the results of a survey from the 1980s on attitudes toward rape, when I was writing the fourth edition of my psychology of women textbook, published in July, 1999. So every revision of that book feels like writing a book that is almost entirely new! However, I have been a political person for more than 20 years now and I've always enjoyed writing a book whose central message addresses social justice.

My final textbook-writing adventure began in the late 1980s, when I decided to write an introductory psychology textbook (Matlin, 1992). I wrote a chapter on my motivations for writing this textbook and on what I hoped to accomplish in this book (Matlin, 1997). However, just briefly, I viewed this book as a way of reaching students who will not necessarily become psychology majors. I hope to present the science side of psychology in an engaging fashion and to encourage them to think more critically about psychological issues in the popular media. I also hope to inspire students to think about a wide variety of social-justice issues in the remainder of the book—not just gender, but issues such as ethnicity, sexual orientation, ageism, and international conflict.

In addition to classroom teaching and writing textbooks, I've enjoyed several other areas of professional commitment. The first was a series of Pre-Convention Workshops, begun in 1988 and sponsored by Division 35, that Mary Roth Walsh organized each August prior to the annual meeting of the American Psychological Association. Mary, Janet Hyde, and I were the primary facilitators at these workshops. We were joined in recent years by other psychologists such as Ruth Hall, Angela Ginorio, Katherine Quina, Jan Yoder, and Beverly Tatum. Through this yearly workshop, we helped hundreds of individuals teach more effectively in their courses on the psychology of women and gender. We facilitated some productive networking among the workshop attenders, and we also learned some innovative techniques from these individuals. Mary Roth Walsh died tragically in 1998. I miss her generous encouragement and friendship, and I miss working together on those workshops.

Another fulfilling domain for me has been my affiliation with The Society for the Teaching of Psychology (Division 2 of the American Psychological Association). I was on the editorial board for *Teaching of Psychology* for many years, and I attended the St. Mary's Conference on Undergraduate Psychology in 1991. I'm often struck by the genuine commitment to teaching that the Division 2 people show. It's really a pleasure to be among people who love to teach and who want to improve the discipline.

More recently, I've had the interesting experience of working on the Graduate Record Examination (GRE) Psychology Committee. Under the auspices of the Educational Testing Service, a six-person committee writes questions and reviews hundreds of additional questions submitted by other psychologists. We also meet once a year in Princeton to review the material and help make policy decisions. I currently chair the committee. Each year, about 12,000 psychology students take the GRE Psychology Examination as one of the criteria for admission to graduate school. I've enjoyed being part of this process, especially because the committee can provide input about the topics in psychology that we feel deserve particular emphasis.

My interest in professional activities concerned with teaching has helped me win several teaching awards. Within the SUNY system, I received the title of Distinguished Teaching Professor in 1987. In 1985, I received Division 2's Teaching of Psychology Award in the 4-year college and university category. In 1995, I received the American Psychological Foundation's Distinguished Teaching in Psychology Award (Matlin, 1995). Because this is one of the most prestigious teaching awards in psychology, it represented a real turning point in my professional development. Again, however, I need to emphasize that I initially disliked teaching, and I was not an effective teacher. I was certainly not a born teacher. However, I knew that the work was important, and I figured out how to do a better job. And as I became more effective, I grew to feel passionately committed to teaching.

INTEGRATING PERSONAL AND PROFESSIONAL LIFE

One aspect of my life that I've only briefly mentioned so far is a commitment to social justice. This emphasis began in 1969, when my husband Arnie and I began our opposition to the war in Vietnam. One of the motivating factors for me was the ethnocentric view that the United States seemed to have that our American lives, political views, and doctrines were somehow more valuable than those of people in another country. Although I had sympathized with the civil rights movement, it was the antiwar movement that transformed me into an activist. Arnie and I worked together with four other individuals to found a peace group in our rural area of upstate New York, Genesee Valley Citizens for Peace. We began in 1972 by focusing on the Vietnam War. More recently, we have focused on topics such as antimilitarism, violence on television, and U.S. intervention in Latin American politics.

Through this focus on Latin America, our family developed a commitment to Nicaragua. Nicaragua once had admirable social justice policies, but they are now the second poorest country in the Western hemisphere. Following the Sandinista Revolution of 1979, Nicaragua had emphasized goals such as literacy and universal health care. However, the U.S. backed Contra War helped to impoverish the country and to destroy their humanitarian accomplishments. At any rate, Arnie and I and our two daughters worked together to establish and finance a Head-Start type program for 30 malnourished preschoolers in El Sauce, a town in rural northwestern Nicaragua. The parents decided to call this center Servicio Infantil Rural "La Norita," in honor of Nora Astorga, one of the heroines of the 1979 Nicaraguan Revolution. The center has been thriving for more than 10 years now. It survived the 1998 devastation from Hurricane Mitch. So far, more than 200 children have participated in the program.

Obviously, my understanding of the injustice I learned to see in the antiwar movement helped me appreciate gender inequalities. It's interesting that people involved with the psychology of women are typically very sensitive about other kinds of inequalities within the United States. They frequently address issues such as racism, heterosexism, and classism. However, international issues and antimilitarism are typically a low priority, even though the power inequalities are perhaps even stronger than the gender inequalities here at home. Also, if we didn't spend so much of our national budget on military expenses and on trying to influence the politics of other countries, we could have the financial resources to address more injustices here at home. (Just think how many creative feminist projects could be funded with a portion of the $627 billion given to the U.S. military in the year 2000!)

Our daughters, Beth and Sally, have also become passionately committed to addressing injustices. Beth teaches kindergarten in Dorchester, one of the most economically impoverished communities in Boston. She has seen some of the poignant consequences of these inequities, because her school has so little in the way of supplies. For example, she typically spends part of her own salary to buy crayons and other necessities for the children. However, Beth has also come to admire the strength of the mothers and fathers who volunteer in her classroom. The children and parents also appreciate her multicultural classroom and the humanitarian values she conveys to the children.

Sally lived and worked in rural Nicaragua for 2 years after graduating from college. Through her work, she helped communities to develop safe-water projects, rotating-loan funds, and a variety of other grass-roots projects. She's now living in San Francisco, where she works as a case manager for the American Arbitration Association, and she continues her political activities in California.

Obviously, our daughters no longer live at home. However, when Beth and Sally were young, they offered another source of strength for my professional development. I could accomplish most of my writing when they were in school on the days I wasn't teaching. I learned to be very efficient about using every hour of this time to move ahead on my writing. However, I'd usually prepare lectures and grade papers when they were home. They were almost invariably understanding, they didn't make me feel guilty, and they were so very clearly proud of my accomplishments. Interestingly, just as parents teach their children, our children are now teaching us. I've learned so much from Beth's stories about the insights of students from other ethnic backgrounds in her classroom, and from Sally's stories about the warmth and generosity of people in remote Nicaraguan communities.

The major problem I now face is a familiar one: Not enough time. As of 1998, I had four textbooks, each of which had to be revised every 3 or 4 years. This responsibility was especially difficult because I teach full time, with three courses each semester. I often feel like a juggler, with too many oranges up in the air. The realities of the time pressure recently forced me to make a difficult decision—not to revise the sensation and perception textbook. The third and fourth editions of that textbook had been coauthored by Hugh J. Foley, a dedicated and enthusiastic professor at Skidmore College. However, Hugh was also experiencing a time crunch, so the decision seemed appropriate for both of us.

Even so, I often feel overwhelmed by the revision schedules for three books. I've been learning to say no to most other commitments, no matter how enjoyable they may seem. I try not to feel guilty about saying no, but I'm not especially successful at eliminating this guilt. Basically, I have to acknowledge my own responsibility for being overcommitted. However, each of my professional activities is inherently enjoyable, and they all seem worthwhile to me.

As it happens, Arnie leads an equally hectic life as a pediatrician in solo practice. In addition, he spends hundreds of hours each year working on election campaigns for liberal political candidates and organizing delegations for people in the Rochester area to travel down to Nicaragua. In fact, some people he knows from the Nicaraguan solidarity movement thought he was a full-time organizer; they were surprised to learn he was a pediatrician. But we do make time for purely pleasurable activities. For instance, we love foreign movies, folk music, travel, art museums, and interesting restaurants. Like many busy couples, we need to resist the temptation to devote all our time to work.

In the first decade of the millennium, I will be making decisions about retirement. At this point, I do not have a clear sense of how I will phase out my professional commitments to teaching and writing textbooks. I've addressed this issue more completely in a chapter in a book called *Wise Women: Reflections of Women at Mid-life* (Matlin, 2000). I envision perhaps teaching an occasional course, and still continuing to write one or two books. I do look forward to having more leisure time and more opportunities to travel. Still, I cannot imagine abruptly ending my professional activities, and I anticipate continuing to be interested in our discipline of psychology throughout my lifetime.

SUGGESTIONS FOR PROFESSIONALS

So, what important words of advice can I provide for readers and for the individuals whom they mentor? First, remember that you may not know at this point exactly where your professional life will lead you many years from now. Second, notice what you enjoy and where your very specific talents may lie, even if it's not clear at this point how you will use those talents. Third, don't be too hasty to reject a professional activity. Instead, figure out how to do the job more skillfully. Fourth, try to learn from experience, even from your unpleasant experiences. Fifth, give your self-confidence time to grow. Sixth, when possible, use your professional talents and financial resources to support the kinds of social-justice issues that matter to you. Seventh, and finally, take some modest chances. Specifically, pursue some risks that are interesting, ones that may lead you to explore some new professional pathways that will turn out to be both enjoyable and fulfilling.

REFERENCES

Horowitz, L. H., Day, R. S., Light, L. L., & White, M. A. (1968). Availability growth and latent verbal learning. *Journal of General Psychology, 78,* 65–83.

Horowitz, L. H., White, M. A., & Atwood, D. W. (1968). Word fragments as aids to recall: The organization of a word. *Journal of Experimental Psychology, 76,* 219–226.

Maccoby, E. E., & Jacklin, C. N. (1974). *The psychology of sex differences.* Stanford, CA: Stanford University Press.

Matlin, M. W. (1970). Response competition as a mediating factor in the frequency–affect relationship. *Journal of Personality and Social Psychology, 16,* 536–552.

Matlin, M. W. (1971). Response competition, recognition and affect. *Journal of Personality and Social Psychology, 19,* 295–300.

Matlin, M. W. (1979). *Human experimental psychology.* Monterey, CA: Brooks/Cole Publishing Company.

Matlin, M. W. (1983a). *Cognition.* New York: Holt, Rinehart & Winston.

Matlin, M. W. (1983b). *Sensation and perception.* Boston: Allyn & Bacon.

Matlin, M. W. (1987). *The psychology of women.* New York: Holt, Rinehart & Winston.
Matlin, M. W. (1992). *Psychology.* Fort Worth, TX: Harcourt Brace.
Matlin, M. W. (1995). Award for Distinguished Teaching in Psychology. *American Psychologist, 50,* 596–599.
Matlin, M. W. (1997). Distilling psychology into 700 pages: Some goals for writing an introductory psychology textbook. In R. J. Sternberg (Ed.), *Teaching introductory psychology.* Washington, DC: American Psychological Association.
Matlin, M. W. (2000). Re-viewing our professional lives: Talking (and listening) for a living. In P. R. Freeman & J. Z. Schmidt (Eds.), *Wise women: Reflections of women at mid-life.* New York: Routledge.
Matlin, M. W., & Stang, D. J. (1978). *The Pollyanna Principle: Selectivity in language, memory, and thought.* Cambridge, MA: Schenkman.
Matlin, M. W., & Zajonc, R. B. (1968). Social facilitation of word associations. *Journal of Personality and Social Psychology, 10,* 455–461.
Uyeno, E. T., & White, M. A. (1967). Social isolation and dominance behavior. *Journal of Comparative and Physiological Psychology, 63,* 157–159.

REPRESENTATIVE PUBLICATIONS

Matlin, M. W., Cutler, B. L., & Matlin, A. H. (1986). Pediatricians' attitudes toward maternal employment. *Clinical Pediatrics, 25,* 419.
Matlin, M. W. (1989). Teaching psychology of women: A survey of instructors. *Pscyhology of Women Quarterly, 13,* 245–261.
Matlin, M. W. (1991). The social cognition approach to stereotypes and its application to teaching. *Journal on Excellence in Teaching, 2,* 9–24.
Wallach, H. R., & Matlin, M. W. (1992). College women's expectations about pregnancy, childbirth, and infant care: A prospective study. *Birth: Issues in perinatal care, 19,* 202–207.
Matlin, M. W., & Foley, H. J. (1997). *Sensation and perception* (4th ed.). Boston: Allyn & Bacon.
Matlin, M. W. (1998). *Cognition* (4th ed.). Fort Worth, TX: Harcourt Brace.
Matlin, M. W. (1999). *Psychology* (3rd ed.). Fort Worth, TX: Harcourt Brace.
Matlin, M. W. (2000). *The psychology of women* (4th ed.). Fort Worth, TX: Harcourt College Publishers.

CHAPTER 17

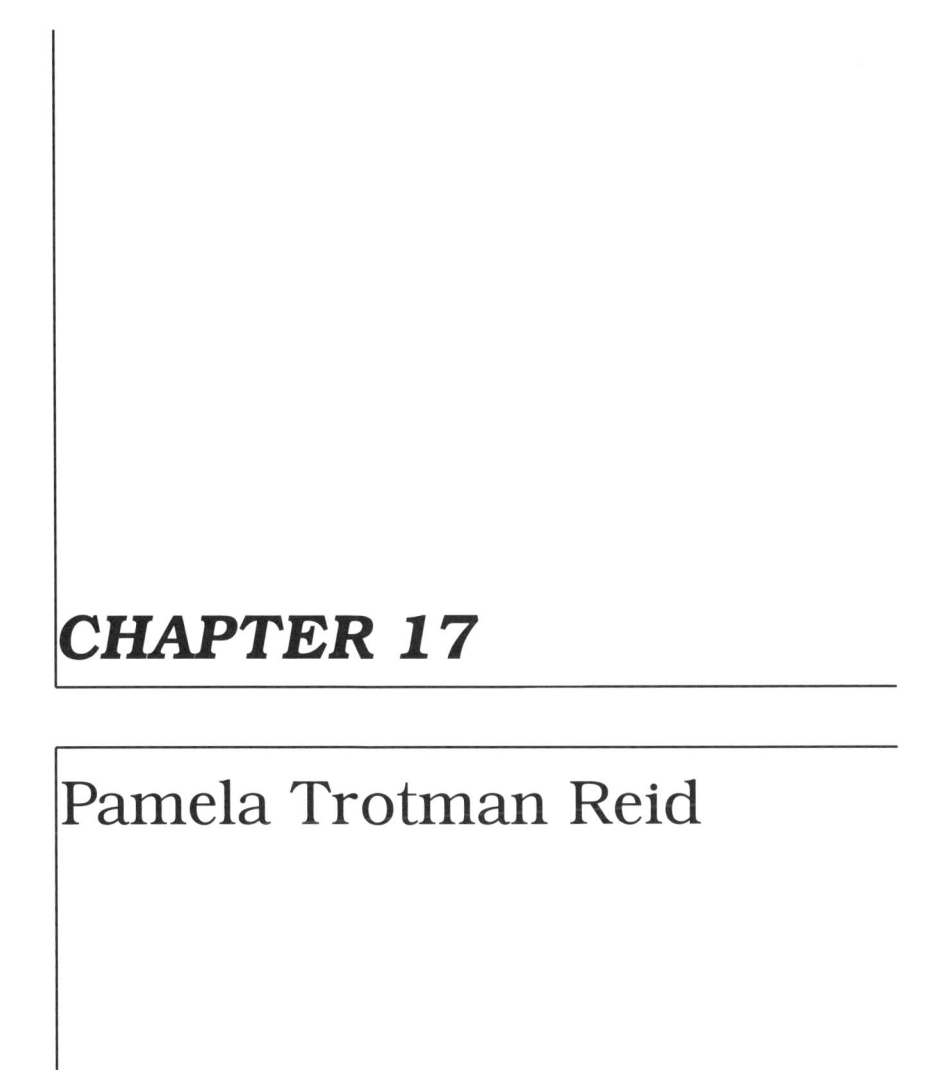

Pamela Trotman Reid

Photographer: Paul Jaronski.

Pamela Trotman Reid

FAMILY BACKGROUND AND EARLY EXPERIENCES

I enjoy introducing myself as a native New Yorker. My childhood in Brooklyn and Queens provided me with traveling skills and tolerance for large crowds that you cannot easily acquire living in smaller places. I even readily admit to having some of the "Big City" ethnocentrism, which I refuse to relinquish, even though I have lived more years outside of New York City than in it. I was born the oldest of three daughters to Gloria and Louis Trotman in the Bronx, New York on June 1, 1946. My father had just been discharged from the U.S. Navy shortly before my arrival. In fact, my mother claims I could have been born in California, except that she did take the long cross-country train ride (in a segregated car) back from the naval base to be with her family.

Having a child led my dad to give up his attempts to obtain training as an optician. Instead, he sought work as a machine operator and mechanic. My mother worked in a secretarial pool through my preschool years, but she stopped to stay at home with the birth of their second child, my sister, Deborah. She did not return to work until more than a decade later after my youngest sister, Candace, went to first grade.

My young parents were also native New Yorkers and high school graduates, but they did not have either the money or the encouragement to go on to college. Still, both sides of my family had middle-class aspirations, a strong sense of family identity, and high self-esteem that they passed along to me. My father, whose parents were immigrants from Trinidad, West Indies, worked two skilled labor jobs, and saved enough to buy the family our own brownstone in Brooklyn by the time I was 2 years old—and we had a television from the time I was 4. I was at the forefront of the baby boom.

There are three key experiences in my early life that I credit with the directions I have taken. They have also provided me with a perspective for my research efforts. These experiences are: being the oldest daughter, attending an all girls high school, and matriculating at an historically Black university. These set-up and confirmed my beliefs in the power of environmental influences, enabling me to see beyond stereotypes.

OLDEST DAUGHTER AND FIRSTBORN CHILD

Clearly, being firstborn set me on the path to achievement. Firstborn children typically get more attention and considerably more encouragement to excel. As the first child and the first grandchild of my paternal grandparents, I was well attended and applauded. On my father's side I was not only the oldest of three daughters, I was also the oldest of five granddaughters. So my attention and recognition extended to my grandparents. On my mother's side, there were several cousins older than I. Thus, I also had older children in my family to emulate, admire, tease me and join with in play.

Growing up through the 1950s and 1960s allowed me to see many social changes in this country. During those years, gender stereotypes were indelible and unequivocal on television and in school. The rules for girls were clearly defined. However, having no brothers and young parents who encouraged my ambitions and explorations, I did not have to fit the gender mold. Of course, I was given a doll every Christmas, but I never played with them. I preferred to act out my favorite television programs (The Lone Ranger and Superman), to build rocket ships in my backyard, play board games, such as Monopoly or Clue, or to join my friends in street games like hopscotch and stickball.

Being the oldest meant that I received consistent praise and admiration for my accomplishments at home and in school. Even as early as second grade, I remember that my mother encouraged high achievement aspirations. She would not say "If you go to college," she always said, "When you go to college." Reading and books were my greatest pleasure and my academic endeavors were proudly reported to all my family and friends.

Being the oldest meant that I did everything first and my sisters, who are much younger than I, were not even close as competitors for my place as the family achiever. Having no brothers meant that I escaped the obvious parental gender-based preferences, comparisons, and assignments. I got to do it all, wash the dishes *and* take out the garbage; sweep the walk *and* shovel the snow. At the time, of course, I did not always see this as an advantage.

I should mention that my dad also helped dispel gender myths. It was a family tradition for him to cook the family dinner on Saturday night. He also taught me about tools and gave me a comfort level with math when he enlisted me as an assistant in making home repairs or renovations. He played with my sisters and me whenever time permitted, taking us to see his workplace, getting up early on Saturday to take us ice skating, or playing paper dolls with my sister.

It was so alien to me that there might be certain male and female tasks, that as a young adolescent when I had the occasion to spend the weekend with a new friend who did have a brother, I couldn't help but comment. My friend was expected to clean up after every meal while he sat there and did not lift a finger to help. I was appalled when her mother explained that boys did not do dishes!

ALL-GIRLS IN HIGH SCHOOL

The second major influence in my development was attending an all-girls high school. This came about again due to my mother. Convinced of my academic abilities, she enrolled me in the closest thing to a private school that we could afford—the parochial (i.e., Catholic) school system. I began at the kindergarten level. I loved school, and borrowing books from the school library was a delight. I thrived in Catholic school and achieved admission to one of the best single-sex high schools, The Mary Louis Academy in Queens. Of course, that meant that I was one of only three African American girls, called "Negro" in those days, in a class of more than 350 ninth-graders!

Going to an all-girls school allowed me to see girls playing all the student roles: scholar and talented musician, president of class and editor of yearbook, athlete and cheerleader, as well as trouble maker and class clown. But as an insecure, not very outgoing adolescent, I was relegated to the margins of school activities. Being Black also meant that I lived in a different neighborhood and had different friends outside of school. Although I was a stellar student through ninth grade, in high school, my confidence and grades suffered. I was average at best, yet there were times when I realized that I could do more and could do better. This realization was not in response to what the teachers told me; in fact, sometimes it was in response to what they did *not* tell me.

I did have one or two teachers who inspired and encouraged me, but more ignored or overlooked what I did or could accomplish. There were even one or two who suggested that my options were limited. I was able to resist these suggestions, undoubtedly bolstered by the unlimited confidence that my mother always had in me. At her urging, I applied to Howard University and was accepted; this was the third major influence in my early development. I attended Howard University from September 1963 to June 1967, earning a bachelor of science degree in psychology.

ALL-BLACKS IN COLLEGE

Matriculating at an historically Black undergraduate school served to dispel ethnic stereotypes for me in the same way that an all-girls school reduced beliefs in gender stereotypic roles. There I saw African American students who were brilliant science majors, talented writers, and poised speakers. I had African American professors for the first time and the same group of friends in class and out.

My first year at Howard found me to be a very politically unaware and socially uninformed freshman. My *naïveté* did not last long. Two events of national importance occurred in my freshman year that raised my awareness about politics and helped me to put my experience within a broader context. They were the bombing of a Black church in Birmingham, Alabama, killing four little girls on September 15, 1963, and the assassination of John F. Kennedy on November 22, 1963. These events along with subsequent ones, such as, student sit-ins in North Carolina and freedom rides into other southern cities, prompted my participation in campus political activities.

I became involved in rent strikes and protest marches sponsored by the campus chapter of the Student Non-violent Coordinating Committee (SNCC, pronounced "snick"). I should mention that the chairperson of SNCC during that year was the late Kwame Toure, then known as Stokely Carmichael. Stokely, a senior at Howard, recruited me along with some other students to become voter registration workers in Mississippi. Our mission was to challenge the exclusionary policies of the southern Democrats. So I went to Mississippi in the summer after my freshman year, that summer of 1964, when three young civil rights workers were killed. I came back with experiences in politics and community organizing, as well as having had encounters with the Ku Klux Klan, the FBI, and the Mississippi police. I also returned with a heightened interest is studying society and social issues. I changed my major from chemistry to psychology and I served as a member of student government.

GRADUATE SCHOOL AND BEYOND

At the end of my junior year at Howard, I married Irvin Reid, a psychology graduate student. He had just completed his master's degree in psychology. After we married, he worked to support us while I completed my final year at Howard. We moved to Philadelphia, where I began working for the Board of Education. Initially I was a preschool teacher and later, I worked in the research department. Both assignments gave me firsthand training for my future research in child development. I still use examples gleaned from the experiences with my 3-year-old charges when I teach developmental psychology classes.

While my husband enrolled full time in a doctoral program, I matriculated part time at Temple University from 1967 to 1970, completing a master of arts degree in experimental psychology. I had intended to continue at Temple for a doctorate, but with the support of my advisor, Eileen Karsh, I went instead to the University of Pennsylvania. I entered the PhD program in Human Learning and Development in 1970 and completed my dissertation in December of 1975. During those years of graduate school my husband and I supported each other and our family grew. By the time we had both finished our dissertations, we had a daughter, Nicole and a son, Dexter, and we each were employed as assistant professors.

CAREER CHALLENGES, ACCOMPLISHMENTS AND STRATEGIES

I have laid out these personal and political contexts in which my life developed because all of them provided me with strengths, skills, supports and strategies that I would have to draw on as I met a variety of career challenges. During my career experiences, four major challenges stand out. These included finding mentors, managing a dual career relationship, dealing with racism and sexism at work, and meeting my personal career goals. As I managed the challenges, I was pleased that I was also able to manage some successes. As I relate these, I will try to indicate the strategies I used.

FINDING MENTORS AND ESTABLISHING NETWORKS

Finding mentors and establishing networks was the first challenge that I faced. Coming from Howard University before affirmative action or any institutional efforts to include African Americans or any minorities meant that I was frequently "the first one" or "the only one" in the class, in the department, and in professional meetings. Rarely did this result in direct confrontation or comment, but it did make me aware of the strategies used to silence and sideline women and men of color. I worked to develop a more outgoing style of interaction and to have confidence to assert my position and beliefs.

Sometimes I tell people that I did not have any mentors. But that is not entirely true. What I mean is that I did not have any senior professional who took me by the hand and gave me heart-to-heart advice, shared a research project with me, or seemed to feel responsible for my career development. But I did have help—no one can achieve success on her own. I would like to give credit to the many psychologists who helped me over the years.

During my studies, I had support from advisors both male and female. At Howard University, the psychology professors, Marvin Head, Lillian Blake, and Leslie Hicks, taught the psychology courses that gave me the confidence in my academic abilities. Their high expectations and demanding courses prepared me for graduate school. Eileen Karsh at Temple University was my master's level advisor and Joanna Williams at the University of Pennsylvania gave me my first and only research assistantship, which I had for one term before she left for Columbia University. Lafayette Powell, who is among the pioneers recognized in Guthrie's (1976) history of Blacks in psychology, was my boss at the Philadelphia Board of Education. He provided considerable support and the flexibility to pursue my degree while working in the department of psychological assessment.

Norman L. Thompson, Jr. was my advisor at the University of Pennsylvania. He offered encouragement as he guided my thinking about gender development, and he was patient in reading draft after draft of my dissertation. He also helped me in my employment search and ultimately set up my position at Howard University. Norm moved to Australia the year after my degree completion and I never heard from him again.

Through the rest of my professional career, the support and assistance of women in psychology was key. My first position as assistant professor in 1974 was at Trenton State College now called the College of New Jersey. I was hired by the female chairperson, Enid Campbell. I think I may have been the first Black faculty member in the department, I certainly was the only one at the time. When my husband and I moved back to Washington, DC, it was Martha Mednick, a well-known personality psychologist, who was an encouraging and supportive colleague. She connected me to a developmental psychologist, Phyllis Berman, who worked in the National Institute for Child Health and Human Development. It was through this connection that I became oriented to the federal agencies. Phyllis Berman's nominations to national review panels were invaluable.

Martha Mednick was also instrumental in my introduction to the American Psychological Association's (APA) Division of the Psychology of Women (Division 35), now called the Society for the Psychology of Women. She brought me into the division leadership along with two of her former students, Gwendolyn Keita and Sandra Rice Murray Nettles. Among the African American women colleagues I have had, Harriette McAdoo and Algea Harrison, developmental psychologists who have extensively studied Black children and families, stand out. At Howard University, they were part of a cohort of senior faculty who developed a network of Black psychologists. They helped connect me to other developmental psychologists, and they created a friendly space in the Society for Research in Child Development, a national organization of researchers interested in children, through their formation of the Black Caucus. They also provided mentorship and support through their conferences in Empirical Research in Black Psychology. Last but not least was Carolyn Payton, director of the Howard University Counseling Service. Her model of leadership and her mentoring smoothed the way for me to have a role in the American Psychological Association as a member in governance activities.

Most of these early supporters took it on themselves to aid in my development or career advancement. But, as I recognized the value of senior support and professional networks, I became more active in seeking these out for myself. My introduction to the Division of Women in Psychology was the beginning of my success in professional networking, and it led to numerous leadership opportunities. When I moved to Chattanooga, Tennessee, my division membership and participation as chair of the Committee for Black Women's Concerns gave me an opportunity for connection to a network of colleagues. What could have been an isolating experience in a new city far from friends and home was more palatable because of my national connections.

With support from the Division leaders, I was elected to the APA Committee of Women in Psychology. This position gave me a broader perspective of women's issues and problems. It particularly heightened my awareness of women's roles in academia and provided opportunities to move outside of the sphere of a single institution or environment. This led to other positions in the division, from newsletter co-editor to serving as the first African American woman on APA's Council of Representatives. I was elected to several other national groups within APA, such as, the Board on Social and Ethical Responsibility, and the Board on Education and Training.

I was the first African American woman to head APA's Office of Social and Ethical Responsibility in 1987. For me, a peak was reached when I was elected as the first woman of color to serve as president of the Division of Women in Psychology. During my term, we planned the division book series, launched the feminist therapy conference, and increased women of color in the division leadership by a significant amount. As president I named women of color not only to the traditional women of color committees, but also as program chair, continuing education chair, and liaison coordinator. Many of the women whom I appointed continued in active leadership positions for many years after my term expired.

MANAGING A DUAL CAREER

The second major challenge of my career has been managing it in a dual career relationship. While my husband and I have worked together to maintain a mutually supportive relationship, I have to underscore the fact that maintaining a dual career is indeed work and at various points has posed some obstacles. Children in the mix added even more. I struggled through the days when female graduate students were not often married and rarely had children. There was no child care for faculty, because the men had wives to care for their children. Department faculty meetings were scheduled for hours convenient for men, but not for a parent who wanted to be available for after school activities. The child care we were able to find was in homes of caring women, trusted neighbors who became friends, local preschool programs, and community centers.

I often point out in only partial jest that two people working on two dissertations with two babies have already been through a stress test. We survived it and sustained our relationship using strategies of communication, respect, and support. I feel that we have achieved success as parents. Our children are successful professionals. Our daughter, a lawyer, graduated from Penn and Chicago Law School and has been married for 3 years. Our son, a computer engineer, currently serves in the Peace Corps in Gambia, West Africa. But more than being successful professionals, they are good, ethical, and caring adults. I have celebrated more than 34 years of marriage and have a beautiful granddaughter. My family has been an important and rewarding part of my life, and my husband has been my primary advisor and a source of strength, both personally and professionally.

There are challenges that are sometimes overlooked in dual career relationships: career trajectories vary and wives may have more role conflict. With respect to career trajectories, women's are typically less steep than men's. This is true in my case. My husband's progress through faculty ranks and into administration was meteoric. He became President of Montclair State College (now Montclair State University) in 1989. I welcomed the opportunity to move back to the northeast, but it added a new role: university president's spouse, on top of the others, such as professor, mother, and community worker.

Negotiating the demands of an academic career, managing a family life, and sharing with a partner requires one to develop a clear sense of identity. I accomplished this with my partner through honest communication, mutual respect and support, and shared family responsibilities. It should be noted that it was necessary to practice and build on these qualities. I also found that for my identity and professional growth, I worked best in an institution separate from my husband's. When we actually were employed in the same institution, the University of Tennessee at Chattanooga, I found that in spite of the convenience, there were also major drawbacks. My husband was the Dean of the School of Business. Still, in spite of the fact that I was in a different college, it became obvious in meetings and discussions that our relationship could not be ignored by our colleagues. I found that being in a separate institution allowed me to establish my agenda without colleagues trying to connect it to the activities of my spouse. The separation also helped to avoid conflicts of interest, real or imagined. Based on anecdotal evidence, I think that this strategy of separate paths may be more necessary for women of color than for White women. There seems to be more suspicions and concern about career advancement of women of color. Connections to a spouse in the same institution may heighten them.

OVERCOMING RACISM AND SEXISM AT WORK

The challenges of networking and of a dual career relationship are in some ways very personal hurdles. How each relationship is managed will have to vary depending on specific factors. However, the challenges of dealing with racism and sexism are shared and held in common. My experiences of racism are not really unique. I know that most of my African American peers have had similar and even worse incidents in their careers. I will be surprised if my African American students and junior colleagues do not also have racist experiences at some point in their career. Dealing with racist reactions and situations is basically just part of being African American; it is something that is always there.

One example is an incident that I recall from my first job interview after completing my dissertation. It was with the Psychology Department at the University of Delaware. This was one my advisor recommended that I seek. I drove blithely down to Newark, Delaware, my Penn degree in hand. The interview was to begin with a collegial departmental reception at the department chair's house. It turned out that he was unprepared for me. In fact, he was so stunned to see a Black woman standing there on his doorstep that for a fleeting moment, he actually closed the door in my face. He quickly regrouped and cordially let me in, but there was no job offer forthcoming.

From 1976 to 1979 I taught in the Department of Psychology at Howard University, my undergraduate alma mater. It was a wonderful experience, and I greatly enjoyed the campus atmosphere and the fantastic students. It was also an interesting emotional experience to return to a setting from my youth. I greatly savored the pleasure of giving back the attention and support that I had received as an undergraduate.

My experience with my colleagues was not quite as joyful. In my first year, Martha Mednick, the only senior female faculty was on leave, and the men in the department were not always comfortable with me and the other two female assistant professors hired that year. I do, however, credit James Bayton for his generous help with my first journal publication (Reid, 1979). Jim was on the journal editorial board and I know that his thoughtful critique and sage advice for improving my manuscript were critical to its acceptance.

In 1979, I was recruited and hired as the first African American person hired by the Psychology Department at UT-Chattanooga (UTC). Since I had been already been an assistant professor for 3 years at Howard University, I was able to negotiate the rank of associate professor. I quickly learned that this caused quite a stir in the department. I was the first woman ever hired in the university above assistant professor rank—at the time there were only three female full professors in the entire institution, including one female administrator. Furthermore, the Psychology Department had no tenured women, and had previously denied two White women tenure. Later, a colleague told me that the department head was heard bragging at the regional meeting, "They can make us hire her, but they can't make us give her tenure." But I actually did receive tenure.

To make a long story short, when I first came up for tenure the department voted no unanimously and the department head concurred. The explanation I was given was that I did not have the necessary "commitment." I appealed and went through the university appeals process as well as to the Federal Equal Opportunity Commission. During the year of appeal, the tension surrounding me was palpable. People stopped speaking when I entered the room and graduate students were afraid to associate themselves with me. I sometimes had to sit for 5 to 10 minutes outside in my car gathering my strength to go into the office.

The amazing part, however, is not that they re-voted, gave me tenure, and then in 2 years, promoted me to full professor. The part of the story my friends particularly enjoy is that just 5 years later I became the department head. I was only the second woman in the College of Arts & Sciences to serve as department head and the first African American to do so.

I garnered other honors while at UTC. I was recognized by the student government association as an Outstanding Professor twice (I was the first woman and the first African American—my photograph still hangs among the others honored in the UTC student center). A newly-formed group of "adult students" voted me to receive their first faculty outstanding service award for my mentoring and advising. I was among the first to receive an award from the Dean for being an outstanding head of the department. I was also awarded a named professorship, and elected to the university's council of scholars.

That all of this happened at the same institution that attempted to eject me demonstrates that there are probably many other instances when judgments of me and of others have nothing to do with abilities or competence. It seems easy for people to say they are giving negative evaluations based on some standard that they have arbitrarily set, but I try to maintain my own set of standards and depend on friends and family for reality checks.

There are other major and minor experiences of racism I can recount. Some I have dealt with and some I have ignored. For me, and I suspect for many people of color, the experience of racism may most often be characterized as something that makes one weary. The fact is that in psychology, in academia, and in the United States, no matter what you do, or don't do, no matter who you are, where you are, or what you have accomplished, you are always made aware that you are Black and that is what is being judged. The strategies that work best for me are staying connected to family and friends, keeping grounded in values that I know to be true, and not allowing myself to get too seduced by the trappings of prestige or the appearance of power.

INTEGRATING CAREER GOALS

The final challenge I have dealt with is how I proceeded to develop a career that would allow me to integrate my goals of doing both research and advocacy. It may seem obvious that as an African American woman I would have an interest in exploring gender and ethnicity for my research topic. But now knowing some of my experiences, I hope it is clear that it is not that simple. I will not say that I have always known or had a plan for my research or administrative career, but I will say that many of the turns I have taken have been deliberate and thoughtful.

My epiphany about the neglect of gender and ethnicity in psychology occurred before I had thought about my dissertation topic. I was attending my first professional conference, a meeting of the Society for Research in Child Development (SRCD) in 1973, and among the program offerings was one with several eminent developmental scholars, Albert Bandura, Mary Ainsworth and others, presenting in a panel. I was among the 400-plus who swelled into the room. After Bandura presented his recent set of studies, one member of the audience asked the question, "Why is your research only on boys?" Bandura's reply totally surprised me. In so many words he explained that when he did his research on girls, the results did not turn out as expected. I began to look more closely and noticed that all the children's studies were really studies of boys.

My research led me to also recognize that whether they were boys or girls, the studies rarely included African American children. When African American children were studied, it was always specifically mentioned. The rule in developmental psychology appeared to be that everyone except White, middle-class children were ignored, excluded, or treated as special cases. This observation is still true more than 25 years later (Graham, 1992).

I determined that I would correct this inequity, starting about the same time that many White feminist researchers were also beginning to point out the biases based on gender in questions, in hypotheses, methods, analyses, and interpretation of data. I began to question how the contextual and cultural issues could be made part of the psychological research enterprise. My first publication was a conceptual paper challenging the widely held belief that African American boys were "feminized" because of female dominance in the African American community (Reid, 1976). However, my dissertation study examining the role of modeling in the gender-typed responses of African American girls was rejected by a journal editor (Reid, 1975). One reason given was that I did not have a White control group. In subsequent empirical research efforts successfully published, I examined racial stereotyping on television (Reid, 1979), the background and influences in the career development of African Americans who were successful (Reid, 1985), and gender role development in children (Reid & Trotter, 1993). All have the common theme that gender and ethnicity must be examined as intertwined, perhaps interacting, domains, not merely factors that can be statistically manipulated. I have argued for the importance of considering the interactions of ethnicity, social class, and gender, and not to assume that we can speak for the "other" perspectives.

As a feminist psychologist I worked for and espoused the feminist agenda. For example, I was a member of the Committee on Women in Psychology. I worked with the Committee to develop the first non-sexist guidelines for publication. Still, I also was painfully aware of the complicity of White feminists in excluding ethnicity in research. In 1984, I was among the first in psychology to write about the conflict that African American women felt in facing the choices of feminism versus minority group identity (Reid, 1984). Yet, 10 years later I could still review feminist journals and demonstrate that advances had been slim (Reid & Kelly, 1994). So although I understood well the need to do research, I felt that moving into academic administration was an opportunity to clear some hurdles and provide encouragement that would open the pipeline to others.

My administrative leadership has included several positions. My first was as the office director for the APA Office of Social and Ethical Responsibility in Psychology. I provided staff support and organizational leadership for one of APA's major boards (Board of Social and Ethical Responsibility in Psychology) and related committees (among them were the committees on gay and lesbian concerns, children youth and families, disabilities, conditions of academic employment, and some task forces). After APA I returned to UT-Chattanooga to Chair the Department of Psychology. The department offered masters level specialties in clinical, school and I/O. Under my leadership, my colleagues assisted in completing the department's first self-study and curriculum revision. I also secured the first major financial gift to the department. My next move was to the City University of New York Graduate School. There, I was granted tenure in the PhD Program in Developmental Psychology. In my second year, I was asked to head the PhD subprogram in developmental psychology and in the following year, the new president, Frances Horowitz (an eminent developmental psychologist), named me as the Associate Provost and Dean for Academic Affairs. This made me the third ranking academic officer and the only African American academic administrator at the Graduate School. I served in this position for 6 years, including a brief term as interim provost.

In addition to the pride that students and staff of color took in my role, I provided a model of a woman who was successfully negotiating career and marriage for the graduate students. As an administrator, one of my principal goals was to provide a supportive academic environment for both faculty and staff. In an economically-strained institution, this meant not only using our meager resources in creative ways, but also being aggressive in bringing in new resources. I was successful in bringing two major multi-year grants sponsored by the National Institute of Health to support students of color and facilitating several large private gifts to support undergraduate scholarships. I re-organized the minority student support office, but I also supported changes in the library, the computer center, and developed a support service and seminar series for students teaching undergraduate classes. I worked to improve the mentoring and departmental academic supports that served all of the students across the institution and provide a useful structure for faculty who sought to advance interdisciplinary studies. While conducting my administrative tasks, I continued to maintain my credentials as a professor and scholar. I taught seminars, supervised dissertation students, and supported students in an evaluation research project dealing with poor children and their mothers in Newark, New Jersey.

In the summer of 1998, I moved to join my spouse in the Midwest. He had moved the year earlier to accept the position as the first African

American President of Wayne State University. I decided to accept a professorship at the University of Michigan with a joint faculty appointment in the School of Education, the Department of Psychology, and a research post in the Institute for Research on Women and Gender. At the Institute, I head a program on Ethnicity, Class and Gender to explore the intersections of these status domains through discussions and research. Through this appointment, I have the opportunity to refine the perspectives of inclusion and complexity that I have been honing over the years. Still, I am not at the end of my academic journey and I expect that many academic opportunities and challenges lay ahead. Nevertheless, even while at this point, I feel that I have learned many lessons from my different roles.

LESSONS LEARNED AND ADVICE TO SHARE

As I prepared this autobiography, I had to think about my relationship to the field of psychology. I have focused on my structural relationships, but I have also tried to address the content of the field by examining issues of race, ethnicity, gender and social class (Reid, 1993; Reid & Kelly, 1994). My realization is that too often we look at the evolution of our theories and investigations as though we can separate our experiences from our interests. Psychologists and other scholars too often convey the sense that our intellectual pursuits are in no way related to the lives we live. This assumption that we are apart from, rather than a part of everything around us leads us not to recognize the pressures and influences that affect our theories and our research. I think that in psychology some oversights, and even errors, have evolved from the kind of abstracted and removed thinking that psychology encourages.

Instead of being reluctant to discuss our history, our differences, and our experiences, we should probably do it more so that we can learn from ourselves and each other about strengths and failings, promises kept, and disappointments overcome. As a child I loved hearing about the early life experiences of my parents and grandparents. The stories they told helped me to understand better who they are and who I am. I hope that hearing a bit about my life experiences and those of others will also be useful in some small way for other women and men struggling with their own challenges in life and career.

A major lesson I have learned is that who we are and what we believe can shape our science, so we should take steps to make explicit, at least for ourselves, our starting points and what our goals are. As a student and a teacher, I have learned that it may even be necessary to make some goals and assumptions explicit for our students. Even when we are clear in our own intentions, our words or actions can become distorted by virtue of having status and authority. I try to be aware of the power differential that exists in and out of the classroom. So I do my best to treat students and junior colleagues with care, concern and respect and I am attentive to providing support and mentoring.

As an academic leader, I have learned not to wait for others to make needed changes. Consultation is important, but I have tried to be ready to go first and modest enough to acknowledge the others who have assisted or smoothed the way. As a spouse, a daughter, a mother, and a friend, I have found that relationships, both familial and friendships, need as much work and attention as a career. We know what will happen if no attention is paid to a career—it can wither and stagnate. Relationships, too, will suffer from neglect. I do not plan to let such effects impact me; I intend to be an old woman who has family, friends, and memories—not just memories.

So, when asked for advice by my junior colleagues in psychology, I advise them to do careful and strategic research that will be meaningful and that they will be proud of now and in the future. But I also strongly suggest that people pay attention to all parts of their lives. I think it is particularly unwise to consider one's life as "on hold." So many people say they will pay attention to relationships once they get to graduate school, or once they graduate, or once they get a position and so on. But life does not stay on hold. It will go on whether it is fulfilling or not. So I suggest that one should regularly assess his or her goals and then look to see if his or her choices match priorities; and I try to do the same myself.

REFERENCES

Graham, S. (1992). "Most of the subjects were White and middle-class": Trends in published research on African Americans in selected APA journals, 1970–1989. *American Psychologist, 47*(5), 629–639.

Guthrie, R. V. (1976). *Even the rat was white: A historical view of psychology.* New York : Harper & Row.

Reid, P. T. (1975). *Reinforcement, modeling, maternal attitudes and sex-role preferences in preschool girls.* Unpublished manuscript, University of Pennsylvania.

Reid, P. T. (1976). Are black children feminized by maternal dominance? In R.C. Granger & J.C. Young (Eds.), *Demythologizing the inner city child* (pp. 125–130). Washington, DC: National Association for the Education of Young Children.

Reid, P. T. (1979). Racial stereotyping on television: A comparison of the behavior of both black and white television characters. *Journal of Applied Psychology, 64,* 465–471.

Reid, P. T. (1984). Feminism vs. minority group identity: Not for black women only. *Sex Roles, 10,* 247–255.

Reid, P. T. (1993). Poor women in psychological research: Shut up and shut out. *Psychology of Women Quarterly, 17,* 133–150.
Reid, P.T., & Kelly, E. (1994). Research on women of color: From ignorance to awareness. *Psychology of Women Quarterly, 18,* 477–486.
Reid, P. T., & Robinson, W.L. (1985). Professional black men and women: Attainment of terminal academic degrees. *Psychological Reports, 56,* 547–555.
Reid, P. T., & Trotter, K. H. (1993). Children's self-presentations with infants: Age, race and gender effects. *Sex Roles, 29,* 171–181.

REPRESENTATIVE PUBLICATIONS

Reid, P. T. (1982) Socialization of black female children. In P. Berman & E. Ramey (Eds.), *Women: A developmental perspective* (pp. 137–155). Washington, DC: Government Printing Office.
Reid, P. T. (1985). Sex–role socialization of black children: A review of theory, family, and media influences. *Academic Psychology Bulletin, 7,* 201–212.
Reid, P. T. (1987). Perceptions of sex discrimination among female university faculty and staff. *Psychology of Women Quarterly, 11,* 123–128.
Reid, P. T. (1988). Racism and sexism: Comparisons and conflicts. In P. A. Katz & D. Taylor (Eds.), *Eliminating racism* (pp. 203–221). New York: Plenum Press.
Reid, P. T. (1991). African American women in academe: Paradoxes and barriers. In Suzanne Lie & Virginia O'Leary (Eds.), *Storming the tower: Women in the academic world* (pp. 147–162). Kogan Page Ltd.
Reid, P. T. (1994). Identifying racism is necessary, but not sufficient for the future. A comment. *Medical Anthropology Quarterly.*
Reid, P. T. (1994). The real problem in the study of culture: A comment. *American Psychologist, 49*(6), 524–525.
Reid, P. T. (1997). The culture and politics of academia: Not for students only. In P. Alexander, I. Estrada, B. R. Heller, & P. T. Reid, *Before the class: A handbook for the novice college instructor* (pp. 233–242). New York: City University of New York Graduate School.
Reid, P. T., & Bing, V. M. (2000). Sexual roles of girls and women: An ethno-cultural lifespan perspective. In C. B. Travis & J. E. White (Eds.), *Sexuality, society, and feminism: Psychological perspectives on women* (pp. 141–166). Washington, DC: American Psychological Association.
Reid, P. T., & Clayton, S. (1992). Sexism and racism at work. *Social Justice Research, 5*(3), 249–268.
Reid, P. T., & Comas-Díaz, L. (1990). Gender and ethnicity: Dual perspectives. *Sex Roles, 7/8,* 396–408.
Reid, P. T., Haritos, C., Kelly, E., & Holland, N. (1995). Socialization of girls of color. In H. Landrine (Ed.), *Bringing cultural diversity to feminist psychology: Theory, research, and practice* (pp. 93–111). Washington, DC: American Psychological Association.
Reid, P. T., & Holland, N. E. (1997). Prejudice and discrimination: Old paradigms in new models for psychology. In D. F. Halpern & A. Voiskounsky (Eds.), *States of mind: American and post-Soviet perspectives on contemporary issues in psychology* (pp. 325–341). New York: Oxford University Press.

Reid, P. T., Kleiman, L.. & Travis, C. B. (1986). Sex discrimination in the employment interview. *Journal of Social Psychology, 126,* 205–212.

Reid, P. T., & Kliman, D. (1982). Measuring sex-role preferences in preschool girls: A replication and an expansion. *Replications in Social Psychology, 2*(1), 57–60.

Reid, P. T., & Paludi, M. (1993). Developmental psychology of women: Conception to adolescence. In F. L. Denmark & M. A. Paludi (Eds.), *Psychology of women: A handbook of issues and theories* (pp. 191–212). Westport, CT: Greenwood.

Reid, P. T., Roberts, C., & Ozbek, I. N. (1990). Occupational status and gender role orientation among university women. *Psychological Reports, 67,* 1064–1066.

Reid, P. T., & Smith, G. (1996). A structural methodology: Minority recruitment and retention at the doctoral level. *CGS Communicator, 29*(3), 1, 3–4.

Reid, P. T., & Stephens, D.S. (1985). The roots of future occupations in childhood: A review of the literature on girls and careers. *Youth and Society, 16*(3), 267–288.

Reid, P. T., Tate, C. S., & Berman, P. W. (1989). Young children's self-presentations in situations with infants: Effects of sex and race. *Child Development, 60,* 710–714.

Reid, P. T., & Wilson, L. (1993, July). How do you spell graduate success? N-e-t-w-o-r-k-s. *Black Issues in Higher Education, 15,* 100.

CHAPTER 18

Jeanne Brooks-Gunn

Photographer: A. Cabrera.

Jeanne Brooks-Gunn

In 1946, the year I was born, World War II was finished, men and women were returning to civilian life: marrying, starting families, building homes, and resuming interrupted education, careers, and relationships. America was ready for peace, prosperity, and parenthood. My parents were no exception to these demographic trends, with one interesting twist. My father was a Navy pilot who, after flying bombing missions over China (and receiving eight different medals for these efforts, a fact that he never mentioned to his children until 3 years ago) had become the lead pilot for the Secretary of the Navy. Unlike the more typical boy-meets-girl story after the war, my mother was also a naval officer, living in Washington, DC, decoding messages and having a grand time. While my parents met in Washington, DC, they shared the same hometown—Grand Rapids, Michigan. After a whirlwind romance, they married and started a family; I was the first child. Returning to Michigan, my father started a home-building business, responding to the pent-up demand for affordable housing in the 1950s. My mother became a homemaker and active volunteer. Three other children followed: Robert (1950), Lynne (1954) and Claire (1960).

CHILDHOOD AND ADOLESCENCE

In many respects, I had a quintessential Midwest upbringing living in a suburb, East Grand Rapids, which was adjacent to a small city. Today, my old neighborhood would be described as high in cohesion and collective efficacy. The fathers made a huge skating rink on one of the vacant lots each winter, complete with lights, music, and an old fashioned Zamboni (a garden hose). Parents and children would be found skating every night. The dads also set up a little park, raft, and dock on the lake in the neighborhood. We also had a revolving nursery for injured crows, skunks, and opossums. I started a club in fourth grade, called "The Quints," complete with a secret language and a camp outpost in our backyard and woods. Of course, we only accepted girls!

Schoolwork was always easy for me; several of us competed to see who could read the largest number of books in fifth grade (we probably should have counted pages and degree of difficulty, but I wasn't a social scientist yet). I was reading under the covers late into each night. In high school, my organizational skills (remember, I started a club in fourth grade) went into running school clubs and being editor of the yearbook. My love of water continued (swim team, water ballet, sailing). School studies were still a joy, but almost a separate aspect of life—one not to be discussed or entered into with enthusiasm, but one in which I was expected to do well, although perhaps not excel.

One event that had a tremendous influence on me was joining my church youth group. We were members of the only liberal church in our Dutch-reformed city. The minister, a University of Chicago theologian, opened intellectual doors as well as policy windows. We were active in the development of national parklands on Lake Michigan, literacy programs for poor mothers, and civil rights. I credit my passion for policy and equity to these high school experiences.

Going to a women's college in the east was a revelation. I had never known professional women, let alone those in academia. The intellectual atmosphere of a small liberal arts college in the late 1960s was heady. I had found a haven in Connecticut College, at that time a women's college, on the Thames River in New London. Psychology was appealing from the first course, and I don't remember ever thinking about another major after my freshman year. I still have a copy of my first developmental study that includes the raw data, now faded yellow mimeographed questionnaires on beliefs and feelings toward Hanukkah and Christmas holidays of conservative and reform Jewish children and Unitarian and Methodist Protestant children. My interests in developmental psychology coalesced when Eleanor Heider joined the faculty. She espoused a unique blend of cognitive and social psychology. After conducting a senior thesis in 1969, my mind was made up—I wanted to study developmental psychology in graduate school.

But what did I want to study, and with whom? And how was I going to make the decision and continue my deepening relationship with Bob

Gunn, who was a junior at Williams College? The answer was clear—my senior thesis was based on Kohlberg's work, so I applied to a master's program at the Harvard Graduate School of Education. Moving to Cambridge in the fall of 1969 was a jolt. All of a sudden, the academic nurturing so common in women's colleges at the time was replaced by big research university life, and the obvious discrepancy between how female and male graduate students were perceived and often treated. I joined a woman's group of Harvard graduate students almost immediately. I spent the year 1970 taking courses from professors whose work had become very familiar during my undergraduate years. During this year, Bob Gunn and I decided to get married. So the next phase of graduate studies had to be coordinated. We ended up at the University of Pennsylvania. I went into the Human Development program in the Graduate School of Education.

In terms of a career move, Penn was not optimal—Minnesota and Cornell were better matches. I was incredibly lucky, however, in that Sandra Scarr had moved to Penn and I became her research assistant studying twins in infancy. Given my nascent interest in social development, I also conducted a study on opposite-sex twins at Penn with my husband collecting data with me (Brooks & Lewis, 1974).

Michael Lewis was teaching an infancy course at Penn, and his research on young children and on social cognitive development fit my interests perfectly. He encouraged me to apply for a graduate student summer internship at his home institution, Educational Testing Service. I spent the summer of 1971 there and started a line of research with Lewis that would continue for a decade. After my husband completed his MBA, we moved to Princeton. We had worked out our first of many compromises vis-à-vis work—I had gone to Penn for my husband, and he moved to Princeton for me.

Lewis' laboratory was wonderful, lots of committed, inquisitive post-doctoral fellows and graduate students from around the country all focusing on social and cognitive development of infants and toddlers (Brooks-Gunn & Lewis, 1979). I studied the construction of social cognitive categories; this led to a question of how young children construct a sense of self, a dissertation topic, and a life long interest in how notions of self arise and are redefined over the life course. Lewis and I designed a series of studies to tap the ability of young children to recognize themselves and develop concepts of permanence and continuity, even in the face of changes in appearance or the contingency of their actions and images. Our book *Social Cognition and the Acquisition of Self* (Lewis & Brooks-Gunn, 1979) was followed by research focusing more on the contexts in which multiple conceptions of self develop and constraints on these processes (Brooks-Gunn & Lewis, 1981, 1982; Lewis, Brooks-Gunn & Jaskir, 1985).

The dissertation was completed in 1975, although it was just one event in my research life during the 1970s. The writing and publication of the book with Lewis and a book on sex-role identity with Wendy Matthews (Brooks-Gunn & Matthews, 1979) were more salient intrapsychic milestones. To my parents, however, the receipt of the PhD was more profound. My mother had spent a semester at the Merrill-Palmer Institute in Detroit in the 1940s; she was thrilled that I had become a developmental psychologist. My father was also proud, having always promoted doing well in school.

While at Penn, my concerns about women professionals (and the relative lack of them) continued. The women's studies program was initiated; being involved in its birth was extremely gratifying. I started teaching a Psychology of Women course at Penn in the mid-1970's—and was it fun! The undergraduates were always most vocal when discussing puberty and menstruation. We all found the descriptions of girls' and women's experiences to bear little resemblance to reality (at least our reality). The frameworks that I used in the study of social cognition and self had a lot to offer. How do females define and revise their sense of self as a result of reproductive events? What role did context play? Did social cognitive processes have any part in the interpretation of reproductive experiences? During my undergraduate years, I had done a diary study of mood and menstrual cycles, looking at whether menstrual symptom reports were influenced by the college stress of examination week. The Penn students were soon filling out similar diaries.

I had the extremely good fortune to meet Diane Ruble who was teaching a gender course at Princeton University and was interested in social expectancies. Our interests dovetailed nicely (social expectancies, social cognition, and the construction of self-identities during the life course). A wonderful friendship and collaboration grew, both of which have enriched my life. Talk led to a grant proposal and a series of studies on expectancies and experiences of menstrual-related symptoms in men and women (Ruble & Brooks-Gunn, 1979; Brooks-Gunn, 1985). Both of us became increasingly interested in menarche, since its sudden onset allowed for a study of girls' expectations, as well as their socialization around this reproductive event, before and after the event. Thank goodness National Institute of Mental Health (NIMH) funded this work, even in the face of some skepticism. Some colleagues worried that we would "ruin our careers" by following this line of reproductively-focused research. Our menarche results were relevant for social cognition and the self (Brooks-Gunn & Ruble, 1982; Ruble & Brooks-Gunn, 1982). This research led to an interest in the socialization experiences of girls around the time of puberty, as well as the context in which girls experience puberty.

Viewed from a historical perspective, the end of the 1970's found my research interests solidifying around central conceptual themes—social cognition and self, contextual features of key developmental transitions, and increasingly, the relationships that are central to re-definitions and adaptation.

Given the work on menarche, I initiated discussions at the Johnson and Johnson Company about pubertal health education, given that girls received most of their early information about puberty from the pamphlets and films produced by the feminine products industry. I had always cared about *how* developmental research could be used to promote well-being and equity. The result was an updating of their classic film on menarche, a conference on "Girls at Puberty," an edited volume (Brooks-Gunn & Petersen, 1983), and a life-long friendship with Anne Petersen.

At the end of the conference, I was determined to continue work on puberty, but with more of a focus on the intersection of pubertal changes, not just menarche, contextual influences, relationships, and biology. I was introduced to Michelle Warren, a reproductive endocrinologist at St. Luke's-Roosevelt Hospital in New York. Here was a highly respected physician who had been studying behavior as well as physical consequences of hormonal dysfunction and wanted to collaborate. We prepared a research agenda and spent 2 years trying to obtain funds to start it. When the W.T. Grant Foundation, with the encouragement of President Robert Haggarty and board member Betty Hamburg, funded us in the mid 1980s, the Adolescent Study Program was born. It continues with the generous continuing support of the National Institute of Child Health and Human Development.

We were interested in a variety of interlocking issues, including the biological (including hormonal) and environment contributions to adolescent girl's behavior; the antecedents and consequences of delayed puberty; the emergence of specific forms of developmental psychopathology during adolescence; the formation of gender identity and changes in self-definition; the meaning and salience of pubertal events; links between exercise, nutrition and bone growth; and the interaction of person and environmental characteristics using dancers and swimmers as case studies (Brooks-Gunn, 1984, 1990; Brooks-Gunn & Warren, 1985, 1988a, 1988b, 1989; Brooks-Gunn et al., 1989, 1994c; Gargiulo, Attie, Brooks-Gunn, & Warren, 1987). Our team of collaborators has included wonderful post-doctoral fellows, expanding into studies of risk and prevention of adolescent (physical and mental) health behaviors, always with a focus on context, self constructions, and relationships (Cox & Brooks-Gunn, 1999; Paikoff, Brooks-Gunn, & Warren, 1991; Petersen et al., 1993).

We also became curious about other transitional periods, first considering other reproductive events, specifically pregnancy, early parenthood (a natural for someone who had studied infants), and midlife (end of reproduction and usually, living with one's children). I co-edited a book entitled *Women in Midlife* that defined this period, as well as role changes and self-definitions (Baruch & Brooks-Gunn, 1984). These musings constituted my first foray into life-span developmental research.

Being invited to attend several meetings sponsored by the Social Science Research Council (SSRC) and the Aspen Institute altered my somewhat discipline-bound thinking. Paul Baltes, Orville Brim, Richard Lerner, Glen Elder, and Frank Furstenberg, among others, were thinking about development across time, as well as across psychology and sociology. At one meeting, Brim suggested to Furstenberg and me that we would be a perfect team for following up the Baltimore Study of Teenage Motherhood. Furstenberg had started the study as an evaluation of an early prenatal program for teenage girls in the late 1960s. The children of these mothers were now 16. Furstenberg was at Penn, and I was by then a Senior Research Scientist at the Educational Testing Service. As friends and colleagues we began designing a study which had, as a central feature, the intersection of life courses for the teenage mothers and their children, as well as an emphasis on the variability of outcomes for teenage mothers.

Our book, *Adolescent Mothers in Later Life*, was published in 1987 (Furstenberg, Brooks-Gunn, & Morgan, 1987). I was so proud when the book won an award from the American Sociological Association. Several wonderful younger scholars (Baydar, Paikoff, Chase-Lansdale, Harris, Guo, Hughes) started working with us on intergenerational issues, sexuality, and parenting (Baydar, Brooks-Gunn, & Furstenberg, 1993; Brooks-Gunn, Guo, & Furstenberg, 1993; Chase-Lansdale, Brooks-Gunn, & Paikoff, 1991; Furstenberg, Brooks-Gunn, & Chase-Lansdale, 1989; Furstenberg, Levine, & Brooks-Gunn, 1990).

The 1980s could be characterized as the enlargement of the adolescence agenda, a focus on pregnancy and early parenthood transitions (Ruble et al., 1990; Deutsch, Ruble, Fleming, Brooks-Gunn, & Stangor, 1988), and a move toward more life course concerns and more interdisciplinary work. My interest in young children also continued but took a turn toward the integration of research with practice and policy, unlike the childhood work of the 1970s, which had focused on social cognition and self (those themes moved into a study of puberty, pregnancy, early parenthood, and midlife). Lewis and I started the Institute for the Study of Exceptional Children, a joint venture between the Educational Testing Service and St. Luke's-Roosevelt Hospital. I began doing research on at-risk and delayed young children, many of whom were studied in the context of early childhood intervention programs, and became curious as to the efficacy of such programs even though the Institute was not in the business of evaluation.

Three such evaluation opportunities arose in the 1980s, the first having to do with examining the impact of Head Start on a large sample of poor children in three cities, (Lee, Brooks-Gunn, Schnur, & Liaw, 1990). The second was the opportunity to develop an outreach program at Harlem Hospital with Margaret Haegarty, Chair of Pediatrics and Marie McCormick (pediatrics at Harvard). We designed an intervention, helped implement it, and busily set about evaluating it. Meeting with the outreach workers several times a month in clinics throughout Harlem, I was provided a first-rate education on how difficult it is to implement an intervention, how top-down approaches to behavior change are not effective, and how beliefs and childrearing are contextually situated and therefore resistant to change by outside agents. This "education of Miss Brooke" altered my approach to research and to policy forever. It is also the only time that I have co-authored a paper with my husband (Brooks-Gunn, et al., 1989).

The third opportunity emerged through discussions with Ruby Hearn (at the Robert Wood Johnson Foundation) and Marie McCormick about the possible efficacy of early childhood intervention programs for biologically and environmentally at-risk children (Brooks-Gunn & Hearn, 1982). The Foundation initiated a large multi-site clinical trial in 1985, testing the efficacy of an early childhood intervention (home visits and center-based child care) from birth to age 3 on the health and development of low birth weight, premature children. I was extremely fortunate to "be at the table" during the design, site selection, implementation and analyses phase. The involvement in such a large program was heady. Again, I cannot imagine a better learning experience in yet another multidisciplinary setting. The program had very large positive effects on the children (IHDP, 1990; Brooks-Gunn et al., 1994a, 1994b). This work continued into the 1990s (Brooks-Gunn et al., 1993, 1994a; Liaw & Brooks-Gunn, 1993, 1994).

During the 1980s, my husband and I continued to live in Princeton. My research network expanded to include colleagues at Penn and at Columbia. I did adjunct teaching sequentially, not simultaneously, at Barnard, Princeton, and Penn, and I had an office at St. Luke's-Roosevelt Hospital in New York. My husband became a consultant, first in Princeton and then in New York City. We took a sabbatical before his New York City transition by taking several flying trips through the Caribbean, Central America, and Alaska in our 1947 single engine plane (I flew solo when I was 16, as my father continued to fly after the war; Bob began flying during college; we bought the airplane for $6,000 at the end of the 1970s). When we returned from the last sojourn, we took a very small apartment in New York City. We shuttled happily between Princeton and New York. The next sabbatical, in 1989, was taken in New York at the Russell Sage Foundation. We also built a little dream house on the top of a hill outside of Princeton. In the summers, we would fly to our beloved Lake Charlevoix in northern Michigan where we had gotten married, and later to Block Island and Sagaponick.

A major disappointment during these years was my inability to get pregnant, even with the help of the then new fertility procedures. We decided to adopt a child in the late 1980s. After several potential situations fell through, we were incredibly blessed with a private adoption situation through a lawyer in our extended family. Remy Quentin Gunn was born in February of 1990 and joined us when he was 3 days old. What a wonderful beginning to the decade!

Work life changed, of course. However, becoming a parent in the middle of my career rather than at the beginning had its advantages. I was working with a fabulous group of post-doctoral fellows. The large early childhood intervention program was finished, and post-doctoral fellows Fong-Ruey Liaw, Pamela Klebanov, April Benasich, and Lisa Berlin were working with me on numerous analyses. Cecelia McCarton and I took the lead in obtaining funding to follow up the children to see if the intervention program had sustained effects (Brooks-Gunn et al., 1994a, 1994b). Marie McCormick and I were analyzing data from another national sample of children born at varying birth weights (McCormick, Brooks-Gunn, Workman-Daniels, Turner, & Peckham, 1992; Klebanov, Brooks-Gunn & McCormick, 1994). The Adolescent Study Program was running smoothly, thanks to Julia Graber (Graber, Brooks-Gunn, Paikoff, & Warren, 1994; Graber, Brooks-Gunn, & Peterson, 1996). The Baltimore Study of Teenage Motherhood had added on a fascinating piece that involved observing the 2nd generation mothers with their toddlers and with *their* mothers (the grandmothers of the toddlers), that had been designed by Lindsay Chase-Lansdale and me (Chase-Lansdale, Brooks-Gunn, & Zamsky, 1994; Wakschlag, Chase-Lansdale & Brooks-Gunn, 1996).

I was learning about demographic approaches to mining national longitudinal data sets from Nazli Baydar (Baydar & Brooks-Gunn, 1991; Baydar, Greek & Brooks-Gunn, 1997). Remy was thriving, and I was loving motherhood. Life was good. My sleep deprivation from Remy's first year only resulted in one poorly written chapter.

Then, I was contacted about a position at Columbia University's Teachers College. A new center and chaired professorship had been endowed by Virginia and Leonard Marx. The goal was to integrate research, policy, and practice on children. While ETS had been a wonderful research home, the opportunity at Teachers College was too good to pass up. In January of 1992, we moved into a Columbia University apartment, found a fabulous preschool for our then toddler Remy on campus, and convinced our baby-sitter, Wendy Price Kopacz, to commute with us into New York during the week and back to Princeton on the weekends. She had come into our lives when Remy was 9 months old, and lived in a little apartment above our garage that is separate from our house. She has been a godsend, acting as Remy's second mother. She is now married and has a toddler, whom we all love.

Building the Center for Children and Families took a lot of time and much fund-raising. I am proud that each year we have seven post-doctoral research scientists, eight faculty affiliates, eight graduate fellows, and many masters' students. The Center runs a summer fellowship program in policy, and has trained more than 100 graduate students from across the country and from a variety of disciplines in the last 8 years.

My research became even more policy-oriented. I was asked to co-edit, with Chase-Lansdale, a special section of *Developmental Psychology* on studying lives through time as well as policy issues using national data sets (Brooks-Gunn, Phelps, & Elder, 1991; Chase-Lansdale, Mott, Brooks-Gunn, & Phillips, 1991). I also joined a SSRC committee on the urban underclass, a working group was formed to examine the effects of neighborhoods on children and families. This wonderful group provided a conceptual link between the sociological theories of neighborhoods with the more developmental psychological constructs. We conducted and published a series of complementary data and conceptual analyses of neighborhood effects (Brooks-Gunn, Duncan, & Aber, 1997a, 1997b).

Taking advantage of housing policy changes, Tama Leventhal and I have begun to explore, via experimental design, how moves out of public housing in high-poverty neighborhoods into less poor neighborhoods affect child, youth, and family well-being in two studies (Moving to Opportunity and the Yonkers Project). Additionally, I have become a Scientific Director of the Project on Human Development in Chicago Neighborhoods in which more than 6,000 children in seven age cohorts (age: 0, 3, 6, 9, 12, 15, and 18) were sampled from 80 randomly selected neighborhoods in Chicago and are being followed over time (other components of the study focus on evaluating neighborhood processes). Across these various studies, of particular importance is understanding the processes neighborhood effects might operate on child and family outcomes, such as family relationships, institutional resources, or collective efficacy (Brooks-Gunn et al., 2000; Leventhal & Brooks-Gunn, 2000).

Greg Duncan, an economist at Northwestern University, and I had met through the SSRC and began a wonderful collaboration and friendship on the effects of poverty and income on children and youth (Brooks-Gunn, Duncan, Klebanov, & Sealand, 1993; Brooks-Gunn, Klebanov, & Duncan, 1996). In the early 1990s, Chase-Lansdale and I organized and edited a book called *Escape from Poverty* (Chase-Lansdale & Brooks-Gunn, 1995) on welfare reform, children and families—in this case, the Family Support Act of 1988 and all of the state experiments on welfare. This line of research has expanded to consider effects of different policy regimes on children (early childhood education, child support, tax policy, welfare reform, and in-kind programs) as well as more basic research on the potential mediators and moderators of income poverty effects on children and families (Jackson, Brooks-Gunn, Huang, & Glassman, in press; Brooks-Gunn, Smith, Berlin, & Lee, in press).

More recently, I have become intrigued with the biological, social cognitive, relational, and environmental mechanisms underlying SES gradients in health and development that emerge in childhood and adolescence. This work has allowed me at last to merge my interests in equity, policy, social cognition, biobehavioral interactions, and relationships. Much of my research in the next decade will be devoted to tying these conceptual threads together, as well as looking at biological indicators of stress and discrimination in minority and non-minority children living in integrated neighborhoods.

The 1990s also meant more time spent in Washington, DC, as a result of my policy-oriented research. I served on three National Academy of Science/Institute of Medicine Committees: Measurement of Poverty (1992–1994), Child Abuse and Neglect (1992–1993), and Behavioral Aspects of HIV (1988–1989), and I am an advisory board member of the Institute for Research in Poverty (Wisconsin), the Joint Center for Research on Poverty (University of Chicago and Northwestern), and the Multidisciplinary Program in Inequality and Social Policy Institute (Harvard University). I am a member of several ongoing networks devoted to the promotion of policy and practice research on children and youth (the NICHD Research Network on Child and Family Well-Being, the NIMH Family Research Consortium, the MacArthur Network on Work and the Family, the Brookings Institute Roundtable on Children, the Canadian Institute for Advanced Research's Human Development Committee). All of these networks not only promote policy research, but also disseminate work to appropriate national, state and local policymakers. In 1999, Sheila Kamerman, Larry Aber, and I started the Columbia University Institute for Child and Family Policy, an exciting interdisciplinary, international endeavor.

I also served as President of the Society for Research in Adolescence in the mid-1990s, devoting my presidency to promoting policy research, enhancing coordination with the Society for Adolescent Medicine, and linking adolescent research with prevention efforts. I also was the Program Chair for the 1990 meeting, which occurred when Remy was 7 weeks old; Anne Petersen and Mavis Heatherton turned the Presidential Party into a baby shower! In 1996, I received the John P. Hill Award, for lifetime excellence in theory development and research on adolescence from the SRA.

I have been extremely fortunate to collaborate with a diverse and wonderful group of scholars and friends over the years. The opportunities afforded by these colleagues have influenced the course of my research and my development as a behavioral scientist. My husband wants to throw a party at the Society for Research on Child Development meetings, entitled "Celebrating Collaborations," with all of my writing collaborators invited. His support, love and co-parenting has been central to my research and my life.

I am fortunate to have a wonderful extended family with many children Remy's age and a little cottage on an island off the coast of Maine where there are no cars or telephones. Vacationing with my family there during the summer is a counterpart to the quick pace of research and policy life.

REFERENCES

Baruch, G., & Brooks-Gunn, J. (Eds.). (1984). *Women in midlife.* New York: Plenum Press.

Baydar, N., & Brooks-Gunn, J. (1991). Effects of maternal employment and child-care arrangements on preschoolers' cognitive and behavioral outcomes: Evidence from the children of the National Longitudinal Survey of Youth. *Developmental Psychology, 27*(6), 932–945.

Baydar, N., Brooks-Gunn, J., & Furstenberg, F. F., Jr. (1993). Early warning signs of functional illiteracy: Predictors in childhood and adolescence. *Child Development, 64*(3), 815–829.

Baydar, N., Greek, A., & Brooks-Gunn, J. (1997). A longitudinal study of the effects of the birth of a sibling during the first six years of life. *Journal of Marriage and the Family, 59*, 939–956.

Brooks, J., & Lewis, M. (1974). Attachment behavior in thirteen-month-old, opposite-sex twins. *Child Development, 45*, 243–247.

Brooks-Gunn, J. (1984). The psychological significance of different pubertal events to young girls. *Journal of Early Adolescence, 4*(4), 315–327.

Brooks-Gunn, J. (1985). The salience and timing of the menstrual flow. *Psychosomatic Medicine, 47*(4), 363–371.

Brooks-Gunn, J. (1990). Overcoming barriers to adolescent research on pubertal and reproductive development. *Journal of Youth and Adolescence, 19*(5), 425–440.

Brooks-Gunn, J., Berlin, L. J., Leventhal, T., & Fuligni, A. (2000). Depending on the kindness of strangers: Current national data initiatives and developmental research [Special issue]. *Child Development, 71*(1), 257–267.

Brooks-Gunn, J., Duncan, G., & Aber, J. L. (Eds.). (1997a). *Neighborhood poverty: Context and consequences for children, Vol. 1.* New York: Russell Sage Foundation Press.

Brooks-Gunn, J., Duncan, G., & Aber, J. L. (Eds.). (1997b). *Policy implications in studying neighborhoods, Vol. 2.* New York: Russell Sage Foundation Press.

Brooks-Gunn, J., Duncan, G. J., Klebanov, P. K., & Sealand, N. (1993). Do neighborhoods influence child and adolescent development? *American Journal of Sociology, 99*(2), 353–395.

Brooks-Gunn, J., Guo, G., & Furstenberg, F. F., Jr. (1993). Who drops out of and who continues beyond high school?: A 20-year follow-up of black urban youth. *Journal of Research on Adolescence, 3*(3), 271–294.

Brooks-Gunn, J., & Hearn, R. (1982). Early intervention and developmental dysfunction: Implications for pediatrics. *Advances in Pediatrics, 29,* 497–527.

Brooks-Gunn, J., Klebanov, P. K., & Duncan, G. J. (1996). Ethnic differences in children's intelligence test scores: Role of economic deprivation, home environment, and maternal characteristics. *Child Development, 67,* 396–408.

Brooks-Gunn, J., & Lewis, M. (1979). "Why mama and papa?": The development of social labels. *Child Development, 50,* 1203–1206.

Brooks-Gunn, J., & Lewis, M. (1981). Infant social perception: Responses to pictures of parents and strangers. *Developmental Psychology, 17*(5), 647–649.

Brooks-Gunn, J., & Lewis, M. (1982). The development of self-knowledge. In C. Kopp & N. Krokaw (Eds.), *The child: Development in social context* (pp. 332–389). Reading, MN: Addison-Wesley.

Brooks-Gunn, J. & Matthews, W. (1979). *He and she: How children develop their sex-role identity.* Englewood Cliffs, NJ: Prentice Hall.

Brooks-Gunn, J., McCarton, C., Casey, P., McCormick, M., Bauer, C., Bernbaum, J., Tyson, J., Swanson, M., Bennett, F., Scott, D., Tonascia, J., & Meinert, C. (1994a). Early intervention in low birth weight, premature infants: Results through age 5 years from the Infant Health and Development Program. *Journal of the American Medical Association, 272*(16), 1257–1262.

Brooks-Gunn, J., McCormick, M., Gunn, R.W., Shorter, T., Wallace, C.Y., Heagarty, M.C. (1989). Outreach as case findings: The process of locating low-income pregnant women. *Medical Care, 27*(2), 95–102.

Brooks-Gunn, J., McCormick, M., Shapiro, S., Benasich, A. A., & Black, G. (1994b). The effects of early education intervention on maternal employment, public assistance, and health insurance: The Infant Health and Development Program. *American Journal of Public Health, 84*(6), 924–931.

Brooks-Gunn, J., Newman, D., Holderness, C., & Warren, M. P. (1994c). The experience of breast development and girls: Stories about the purchase of a bra. *Journal of Youth and Adolescence, 23*(5), 539–565.

Brooks-Gunn, J., Phelps, E., & Elder, G. H. (1991). Studying lives through time: Secondary data analyses in developmental psychology. *Developmental Psychology, 27*(6), 899–910.

Brooks-Gunn, J., & Ruble, D. N. (1982). The development of menstrual-related beliefs and behaviors during early adolescence. *Child Development, 53*, 1567–1577.

Brooks-Gunn, J., Smith, J., Berlin, L., & Lee, K. (in press). Familywork: Welfare changes, parenting and young children. In G.K. Brookins (Ed.), *Exits from poverty*. New York: Cambridge University Press.

Brooks-Gunn, J., & Warren, M. P. (1985). The effects of delayed menarche in different contexts: Dance and nondance students. *Journal of Youth and Adolescence, 14*(4), 285–300.

Brooks-Gunn, J., & Warren, M. P. (1988a). Mother–daughter differences in menarcheal age in adolescent girls attending national dance company schools and non-dancers. *Annals of Human Biology, 15*(1), 35–43.

Brooks-Gunn, J., & Warren, M. P. (1988b). The psychological significance of secondary sexual characteristics in 9- to 11-year-old girls. *Child Development, 59*, 1061–1069.

Brooks-Gunn, J., & Warren, M. P. (1989). Biological contributions to affective expression in young adolescent girls. *Child Development, 60*, 372–385.

Chase-Lansdale, P. L., & Brooks-Gunn, J. (Eds.). (1995). *Escape from poverty: What makes a difference for children?* New York: Cambridge University Press.

Chase-Lansdale, P. L., Brooks-Gunn, J., & Paikoff, R. L. (1991). Research and programs for adolescent mothers: Missing links and future promises. *American Behavioral Scientist, 35*(3), 290–312.

Chase-Lansdale, P. L., Brooks-Gunn, J., & Zamsky, E. S. (1994). Young African American multigenerational families in poverty: Quality of mothering and grandmothering. *Child Development, 65*(2), 373–393.

Chase-Lansdale, P. L., Mott, F. L., Brooks-Gunn, J., & Phillips, D. (1991). Children of the NLSY: A unique research opportunity. *Developmental Psychology, 27*(6), 918–931.

Cox, M., & Brooks-Gunn J. (Eds.). (1999). *Conflict and cohesion in families: Causes and consequences.* Mahwah, NJ: Lawrence Erlbaum Associates.

Deutsch, F. M., Ruble, D. N., Fleming, A., Brooks-Gunn, J., & Stangor, C. (1988). Information-seeking and self-definition during the transition to motherhood. *Journal of Personality and Social Psychology, 55*(3), 420–431.

Furstenberg, F. F., Jr., Brooks-Gunn, J., & Chase-Lansdale, L. (1989). Adolescent fertility and public policy. *American Psychologist, 44*(2), 313–320.

Furstenberg, F. F. Jr., Brooks-Gunn, J., & Morgan, S.P. (1987). *Adolescent mothers in later life.* New York: Cambridge University Press.

Furstenberg, F. F., Jr., Levine, J. A., & Brooks-Gunn, J. (1990). The children of teenage mothers: Patterns of early childbearing in two generations. *Family Planning Perspectives, 22*(2), 54–61.

Gargiulo, J., Attic, I., Brooks-Gunn, J., & Warren, M. P. (1987). Girls' dating behavior as a function of social context and maturation. *Developmental Psychology, 23*(5), 730–737.

Graber, J. A., Brooks-Gunn, J., Paikoff, R. L., & Warren, M. P. (1994). Prediction of eating problems: An 8-year study of adolescent girls. *Developmental Psychology, 30*(6), 823–834.

Graber, J. A., Brooks-Gunn, J., & Petersen, A. C. (Eds.). (1996). *Transitions through adolescence: Interpersonal domains and context.* Mahwah, NJ: Lawrence Erlbaum Associates.

Jackson, A., Brooks-Gunn, J., Huang, C., & Glassman, M. (in press). Single mothers in low-wage jobs: Financial strain, parenting, and preschoolers' outcomes. *Child Development, 71*(5).

Klebanov, P. K., Brooks-Gunn, J., & McCormick, M. C. (1994). Classroom behavior of very low birth weight elementary school children. *Pediatrics, 94*(5), 700–708.

Lee, V., Brooks-Gunn, J., Schnur, E., & Liaw, T. (1990). Are Head Start effects sustained? A longitudinal follow-up comparison of disadvantaged children attending Head Start, no preschool, and other preschool programs. *Child Development, 61,* 495–507.

Leventhal, T., & Brooks-Gunn, J. (2000). The neighborhoods they live in: The effects of neighborhood residence upon child and adolescent outcomes. *Psychological Bulletin, 126*(2), 309–337..

Leventhal, T., Brooks-Gunn, J., McCormick, M. C., & McCarton, C. M. (2000). Patterns of service use in preschool children: Correlates, consequences, and the role of early intervention. *Child Development, 71*(3), 802–819.

Lewis, M., & Brooks-Gunn, J. (1979). *Social cognition and the acquisition of self.* New York: Plenum Press.

Lewis, M., Brooks-Gunn, J., & Jaskir, J. (1985). Individual differences in the expression of visual self-recognition. *Developmental Psychology, 21*(6), 1181–1187.

Liaw, F., & Brooks-Gunn, J. (1994). Cumulative familial risks and low birth weight children's cognitive and behavioral development. *Journal of Clinical Child Psychology, 23*(4), 360–372.

Liaw, F. R., & Brooks-Gunn, J. (1993). Patterns of low birth weight children's cognitive development and their determinants. *Developmental Psychology, 29*(6), 1024–1035.

McCormick, M. C., Brooks-Gunn, J., Workman-Daniels, K., Turner, J., & Peckham, G. (1992). The health and developmental status of very low birth weight children at school age. *Journal of the American Medical Association, 267*(16), 2204–2208.

Paikoff, R. L., Brooks-Gunn, J., & Warren, M. P. (1991). Effects of girls' hormonal status on depressive and aggressive symptoms over the course of one year. *Journal of Youth and Adolescence, 20*(2), 191–215.

Petersen, A. C., Compas, B., Brooks-Gunn, J., Stemmler, M., Ely, S., & Grant, K. (1993). Depression in adolescence. *American Psychologist, 48*(2), 155–168

Ruble, D. N., & Brooks-Gunn, J. (1979). Menstrual symptoms: A social cognitive analysis. *Journal of Behavioral Medicine, 2,* 171–194.

Ruble, D. N., & Brooks-Gunn, J. (1982). The experience of menarche. *Child Development, 53,* 1557–1566.

Ruble, D. N., Brooks-Gunn, J., Fleming, A. S., Fitzmaurice, G., Stangor, C., & Deutsch, F. (1990). Transition to motherhood and the self: Measurement, stability, and change. *Journal of Personality and Social Psychology, 58*(3), 450–463.

The Infant Health and Development Program Staff (Brooks-Gunn as member of Research Steering Committee). (1990). Enhancing the outcomes of low birthweight, premature infants: A multisite randomized trial. *Journal of the American Medical Association, 263*(22), 3035–3042.

Wakschlag, L.S., Chase-Lansdale, P.L., & Brooks-Gunn, J. (1996). Not just "Ghosts in the Nursery": Contemporaneous intergenerational relationships and parenting in young African American families. *Child Development, 67*(5), 2131–2147.

REPRESENTATIVE PUBLICATIONS

Attie, I., Brooks-Gunn, J., & Petersen, A. C. (1990). The emergence of eating problems: A developmental perspective. In M. Lewis & S. Miller (Eds.), *Handbook of developmental psychopathology* (pp. 409–420). New York: Plenum Press.

Baydar, N., & Brooks-Gunn, J. (1994). The dynamics of child support and its consequences for children. In I. Garfinkel, S. McLanahan, P. Robins (Eds.), *Child support and child well-being* (pp. 257–284). Washington, DC: Urban Institute Press.

Baydar, N., Hyle P., & Brooks-Gunn, J. (1997). A longitudinal study of the effects of the birth of a sibling during preschool and early grade school years. *Journal of Marriage and the Family, 59,* 957–967.

Benasich, A. A., & Brooks-Gunn, J. (1996). Maternal attitudes and knowledge of child-rearing: Associations with family and child outcomes. *Child Development, 67,* 1186–1205.

Brooks-Gunn, J., & Furstenberg, F. F., Jr. (1990). Coming of age in the era of AIDS: Sexual and contraceptive decisions. *Milbank Quarterly, 68,* 59–84.

Brooks-Gunn, J., Klebanov, P. K., Liaw, F., & Spiker, D. (1993). Enhancing the development of low birth weight, premature infants: Changes in cognition and behavior over the first three years. *Child Development, 64*(3), 736–753.

Brooks-Gunn, J., & Paikoff, R. L. (1993). "Sex is a gamble, kissing is a game": Adolescent sexuality and health promotion. In S. G. Millstein, A. C. Petersen, & E. O. Nightingale (Eds.), *Promoting the health of adolescents: New directions for the twenty-first century* (pp. 180–208). New York: Oxford University Press.

Brooks-Gunn, J., & Petersen, A. C. (Eds.). (1991). The emergence of depression and depressive symptoms during adolescence [Special issue]. *Journal of Youth and Adolescence, 20,* 1, 2.

Clewell, B. C., Brooks-Gunn, J., & Benasich, A. A. (1989). Evaluating child-related outcomes of teenage parenting programs. *Family Relations, 38,* 201–209.

Duncan, G., & Brooks-Gunn, J. (1998). Urban poverty, welfare reform, and child development. In F. R. Harris & L. A. Curtis (Eds.), *Locked in the poorhouse: Cities, race, and poverty in the United States* (pp. 21–32). Boulder, CO: Roman & Littlefield.

Lerner, R. M., Petersen, A. C., & Brooks-Gunn, J. (Eds.). (1991). *The encyclopedia of adolescence.* New York: Garland.

Linver, M., Brooks-Gunn, J., & Kohen, D. (1999). Parenting behavior and emotional health as mediators of family poverty effects upon young low-birthweight children's cognitive ability. *Annals of the New York Academy of Sciences, 896,* 376–378.

McCormick, M. C., Brooks-Gunn, J., Shorter, T., Wallace, C. Y., Holmes, J. H., & Heagarty, M. (1987). The planning of pregnancy among low-income women in central Harlem. *American Journal of Obstetrics and Gynecology, 156*(1), 145–149.

McCormick, M. C., Brooks-Gunn, J., Workman-Daniels, K., & Peckham, G. J. (1993). Maternal rating of child health at school age: Does the vulnerable child syndrome persist? *Pediatrics, 92*(3), 380–388.

Warren, M. P., & Brooks-Gunn, J. (1989). Mood and behavior at adolescence: Evidence for hormonal factors. *Journal of Clinical Endocrinology and Metabolism, 69*(1), 77–83.

Warren, M. P., Brooks-Gunn, J., Hamilton, L. H., Hamilton, W. G., & Warren, L. F. (1986). Scoliosis and fractures in young ballet dancers: Relationship to delayed menarcheal age and secondary amenorrhea. *New England Journal of Medicine, 314*(21), 1348–1353.

Warren, M. P. Holderness, C. C., Lesobre, V., Tzen, R. Vossoughian, F., & Brooks-Gunn, J. (1994). Hypothalamic amenorrhea and hidden nutritional insults. *Journal of Society for Gynecologic Investigation, 1*(1), 84–88.

Wilson, J. B., Ellwood, D. T., & Brooks-Gunn, J. (1995). Welfare to work through the eyes of children: The impact on parenting of movement from AFDC to employment. In P. L. Chase-Lansdale & J. Brooks-Gunn (Eds.), *Escape from poverty: What makes a difference for children?* (pp. 63–86). New York: Cambridge University Press.

CHAPTER 19

Diane F. Halpern

Photographer: unavailable.

Diane F. Halpern

Sometimes I think that the early psychologists who studied the way rats learn to run through mazes were on to something—the way rats traverse multiple alleys on the way to a goal can be a metaphor for understanding how we navigate through life's choice points. Of course, for the early learning theorists, rat-running wasn't a metaphor for conceptualizing the way humans find their way through a figurative maze of opportunities, obstacles, and blind alleys. They were interested in the rats' behavior as a way of generalizing cross-species laws of learning, motivation, and performance. When viewed from my current perspective, that of a cognitive psychologist in the zero-digit decade of the new millennium, the way rats run through mazes bears, at best, only surface similarity to human behavior. Unlike our rodent counterparts, the speed at which we run and the errors we commit along the way are far more complex than the size of the reward in the goal box. How can we understand the many variables that cause us to choose some paths and avoid others, and to bang our heads against some walls and walk right through others?

STARTING AT THE MIDDLE

In looking back at my own life choices, the logical starting point for explaining the roads both taken and not taken is the middle. Like many other women of my generation, I married my first husband, Sheldon, at a very young age—for me it was during the summer between my sophomore and junior years in college. He was only a year and a half older, and just about to begin the grueling ordeal of law school. Our early years of marriage were spent in an exhausting marathon of study and work. On the first day of law school, the Dean had warned my husband's class that "the law was a jealous mistress." I soon realized that the balance of two careers and a family life would not be easy.

For me, the decision to apply to doctoral programs in psychology was a watershed event that marked a change in the direction of my life. I had finished my bachelor's degree a few years earlier in 1969 and, at the time when I was seriously considering graduate school, I was in the second half of my 20s. By this time, my husband and I were lucky enough to have added two beautiful children, Evan and Joan (who later changed her name to Jaye) to our family. I stayed at home for several years when my children were babies and then toddlers. I am very glad that I had the option of being a stay-at-home mom for the first few years of my children's lives. As a young mother I probably didn't appreciate this luxury, which is not a real choice for many parents. I know that there appears to be superwomen who can do it all, care for infants, work at a demanding career, run several miles a day, and bake their own bread, but like all superhuman feats, doing it all has high costs.

As a married couple with two children, we may have looked like the prototypical American family, but we had already broken some of the traditional rules of society—we were among the first to adopt our children transracially (1971) and we were deeply in debt with college loans. Like many other people who came of age in the late 1960s and early 1970s, we recognized that the ideal of a traditional family, with its life long stay-at-home-mom and working dad, only existed in the fantasy world of television sitcoms and in the rhetoric of conservative politicians who longed for "good old days" that never were. The Cleavers and Ricardos and other fictional homes where "father always knew best," became America's surrogate families for my generation. The unspoken message was that if we tried hard enough, we could have lives like theirs. Later, we all came to learn that the televised versions of these happy homes also bore little resemblance to the real lives of the actors who played on them. It wasn't that I rejected the traditional model of an American family; I just never considered it. The grainy black and white images of ideal adult life that beamed into our home showed families that bore as much resemblance to my own life as that of aliens from outer space. My mother had died when I was 8 years old, after a horrendous battle with breast cancer, and I had been living on my own since I was 15. At times, home was rat-infested slum housing. Thankfully, a friend's mother opened her home to me so that I could complete high school. Like countless others, I saw higher education as the best way to gain entry into the middle-class. I was determined to find a way to go through that door.

As a child growing up, I was clearly given the message that education was not an appropriate priority for girls. My father often reminded me that "career women" were a detestable lot—hard, cold, and lonely, and that college was only for rich males. I realize now that he was as much a part of his own culture and historical background as I am of mine, so it makes no more sense to blame him for these attitudes than it makes to blame me for mine. Like many of today's young people, I was a first generation American who had to bridge the old world and the new one. School was one of the few places where I was successful, and several teachers throughout my years in Philadelphia's much maligned public schools encouraged me to study and keep the possibility of college in sight. They played an important part in shaping my thinking about who I am, a lesson that I try to remember every day in my interactions with my own students. I hope that I have changed the decisions that they will make about their lives. I realized at a young age that if I wanted a better life I would have to make it for myself, but what I didn't know was what sort of life did I really want? It's hard to know which path to take when you don't know where you want to go.

Through a combination of great luck and hard work, I received a full-tuition scholarship to the University of Pennsylvania. It was there that the world of academics opened to me. Although I was an engineering major my first year, I soon found that I was fascinated by psychology's big questions and that I loved academic life. I decided that, if I could, I would stay at a university my whole life. To this day, I am happiest teaching and learning, and reading and writing about contemporary topics in psychology. I also believed that if I could make a real contribution to this world, it would be in an academic area where I could study important issues and help others in their attempts to understand them. This recognition of who I am and who I wanted to be gave overall direction to subsequent life choices, although I didn't know it at the time.

Later, as a mother with two young children with large college loans, I considered the reasonable option of taking a job to pay off the debts, ideally one that would not be too demanding so that I would have ample time to be with my children. But that would be as logical as starting one's story at the beginning or telling it straight through in the order in which it occurred—options that don't fit with who I am or the story that I want to tell. Instead, I applied to graduate school. I didn't tell anyone that I had taken this momentous step, except for my husband, because I knew that this decision would be met with opposition. I had already sat through enough family discussions where all of the problems of contemporary society were blamed on working mothers and had attended dinner parties where mothers who stayed at home were introduced as women who loved their children. I felt a tremendous stigma about the decision to return to school when my children were so young. Working mothers still struggle with guilt, and there are many who view such decisions to return to work or school as tantamount to child abandonment. The opinion that mothers should be at home full time is hawked as though it were fact, despite the fact that every large scale study of child development (including multiple studies funded by the National Institute for Child Health and Development) has failed to find any negative effects for children of working mothers.

The decision to enter a doctoral program in psychology meant that I would have to find day care for my children and go even deeper into debt for the privilege of working long hours, taking stressful exams, and enjoying the "go-pher" (go-for) status of a lowly graduate student. I'm glad that I did. My husband was fully supportive of my decision, which is probably why we are both still working on our first spouse. At the time, I also applied to law school, not so much because I loved the law, but it seemed like a good alternative to graduate school because it would take fewer years to complete and promised higher salaries when I graduated. But, that's another path not taken among life's many choices. Without a control group, I'll never know if I made the best choices.

My two children are an important part of my identity and how I view the world. I never made a conscious decision to be a mother. I had always known that I would be a mother. I would no more have questioned that assumption than I would question the value of breathing or the laws of gravity. Although my children are young adults now, they are still an integral part of who I am. I cannot imagine a life without them. My experiences in a mixed-race family have colored my perception of the world and have influenced countless aspects of my work and my away-from-work life.

A "GOOD-ENOUGH" FEMINIST

There was another critical decision I made when I decided to return to graduate school and again at many other times throughout my life. This one was painful and personal. Throughout my adult life, I chose to go to school and then work at a location that was near my husband's employment. I decided that my marriage was more important than trying for the "really good" job or a top-rated graduate school, so I made choices that were near home, even when we moved to accommodate my husband's job changes. Real life means tough choices. Feminism is a term that conveys different meanings to different people. To me, feminism is about having choices to make and the freedom to make them.

We do not all have to think the same or make the same choices, as long as we are thinking for ourselves and making choices that are right for our own values and life styles.

KEEPING WORK FOCUSED AND BROAD AT THE SAME TIME

Ever since my first introductory course in psychology, when I was a young undergraduate at the University of Pennsylvania, I have been fascinated with individual differences in how people think, learn, and remember. Without knowing it then, I was a cognitive psychologist in the making. In fact, I don't think I ever heard the term "cognitive psychologist" until I started graduate school at the University of Cincinnati many years later. In the time between completing my undergraduate degree and starting graduate school, I worked briefly as a teacher in a seventh grade inner city school. Looking back, I don't think that I did a very good job because I was completely unprepared for the range of problems and vast differences among the children. With the benefit of hindsight, I think that this experience was influential in developing my interest in individual differences in cognition. With so many fascinating questions for psychologists to study, it was hard for me to pick an area in which I could specialize. What I eventually did was pick a broad area, cognitive psychology, and then roam within this broad framework to study critical thinking (applying the principles of cognitive psychology to help people improve their ability to think), sex differences in cognitive abilities (another controversial topic that some would prefer that we never study), and the assessment of cognitive abilities.

One problem for me is the interconnectedness of knowledge—how and what we think and remember is influenced by the joint actions of social and cultural influences, which create feedback loops for neural and hormonal events. I have a hard time compartmentalizing knowledge, yet I know that I have to have a focus to my work if I am to have any impact on the field. The tension created by this push and pull of generalization and specialization has been a good structure for studying human cognition in all of its complexities because I have zoomed in and out on many of the issues that require both a wide and narrowly focused lens for understanding.

I think that one of my greatest contributions to psychology is the emphasis I have placed on a psychobiosocial model of cognition, in which environmental and biological variables are conceptualized as being continuous and exerting reciprocal influences on each other. (Halpern, 1997, 2000) I believe that it will help to eliminate the dualism of nature–nurture controversies, which has created an artificial dichotomy of influential variables on cognition. I hope that by blurring the distinction between the biological and the environmental–social, we can call a cease fire on the nature–nurture wars and create a more holistic and integrative conceptualization of the forces that make us unique humans.

I also have been an active advocate for the internationalizing of psychology. We live in a big world, but you would not know it from our psychological literature. Most of our theories and data have been generated with Western (mostly United States) samples, and most of them have involved college students. In this endeavor, I co-edited, with a colleague from Russia, a comparative text on Western and post-Soviet issues in psychology, *States of Mind: American and Post-Soviet Perspectives on Contemporary Issues in Psychology* (Halpern & Voiskounsky, 1997). This project, supported by the Rockefeller Foundation, was an offshoot of a Fulbright Award in which I was the first American to teach my own classes at Moscow State University. I have also taught courses in universities in Canada, and Mexico in addition to Russia and the United States as one way of better understanding how one's sociopolitical and cultural background influences thinking, feeling, and acting. I urge present and future psychologists to become more international and cross-cultural when they seek to understand and define human psychology.

In the fall 1999 semester I was in Turkey, a country with a secular government that is 99% Muslim, where I taught a course on the Psychology of Sex and Gender (which may also be called Sex Differences and Similarities or the Psychology of Women and Men). I taught at Turkey's premiere university, and that was the first time that a course on this topic was offered. My experiences with this course in this and other countries have taught me that there are both some universal (transcultural) similarities and some culture-specific differences in the psychology of women and men. Like all complex questions, the only possible answer to the many questions about sex and gender is that "it all depends." It is our task as psychologists to find what "it" is that "it" depends on. There can be no simple answers to questions about sex and gender such as, "It all depends on mothers' attitudes" or "It all depends on hormone levels." If I am able to get this point across to future generations of psychologists and others, then I will consider my professional life a success.

EASY SECRETS

Complex problems in life cannot be solved with a handful of knowledge, but there are some secrets or tricks or "what-ever-you-want-to-call-its" that have helped me in my career as an academic psychologist who also wants a life outside of academia. Here are my reflections:

Lose the Anger. Anger is usually not a constructive response; anger is not a necessary antecedent for action, and it often interferes with clear thinking and good communication. I recall the struggle a colleague had during the tenure and review process that all professors undergo as they move from assistant to associate to full professor. Of course, not everyone who starts as an assistant professor makes it to the top rung. Some get stalled on the way, and others drop off and enter other professions. The tenure and review process is always arduous, but in this case, it was down right nasty.

There were the usual questions about the quality of the research the professor had completed and whether or not the work made a significant and original contribution to our scholarly knowledge. However, there were additional innuendoes about the topic she had chosen to study. The colleague's major field of research was a topic that is usually categorized as women's studies, and some of the members of the tenure and review committee hinted that no real scholar would choose such a field because there were no scholarly contributions possible. She was right to be angry, but the real test was how she handled the anger. The best approach would have been to document the scholarship she had accomplished and show the value of her work to our understanding of the way being female or male is important in many contexts. Instead, she lost her temper, cursed at the members of the committee, and stormed from the room. Ultimately, on appeal, she won the tenure and promotion that her work merited, but her display of anger was more damaging and the effects were more long-lasting. She had missed an opportunity to show the strength of her scholarship and to make some important points about the value of the area she had chosen to study—a sure winner in this case. Anger was detrimental to the desired outcome.

Be Persistent. If showing up is the most important determinant of success, then persistence is, at least, second best. Regardless of what goals you pursue, there will be setbacks and disappointments. In academics, there are many rejections that everyone will face—articles that are rejected by journals, jobs that are not offered, grants that are not funded, and promotions that are denied. Clinical psychologists will sometimes have clients who do not pay, are not appreciative of their hard work, and worse. Unfortunately, we rarely hear about other people's failures and setbacks; their successes are widely publicized, so we come to believe that failures are unique to us. The only people without failures are those who never attempt anything. It is important to learn from mistakes and then move on, but the moving on is the most important response to failure. Persistence is a critical attitude for success.

There is no substitute for hard work, so find work that you can love. The only way to meld a full family life and work life, or to be successful at either one, is through lots of hard work. Spontaneity sounds great, but in reality no one can have a responsible career and a committed family life without good planning and organizational skills. I make time for the people and activities in my life that are important to me, but that means that I have to work even harder to allow time for other activities. Fortunately, I found that being a professor is a work life that I can, and usually do, love. Work is an important part of life, so choose it with the same care that you choose a partner or make other important lifestyle decisions.

In academics, most of the rewards (i.e., salary increases, promotions, and tenure, which is a promise of lifetime employment) are based on research productivity. Students are often surprised to learn how little teaching counts toward the advancement of college faculty, especially when the students thought that teaching was most of what we do. Many of us, myself included, have a strong commitment to our students, to fostering their learning, and keeping them at the university until graduation. I was greatly honored and surprised when my dedication to teaching and learning was recognized with several awards, including the American Psychological Association Award for Lifetime Career Contributions to Education (1996), the American Psychological Foundation Award for Outstanding Teaching (1998), the California State University Award for Outstanding Professor (1986), and the Wang Family Excellence Award for Outstanding Faculty (1999).

Pick the right partner. When I teach courses in the psychology of women, I tell my students that I have the foolproof secret for a happy marriage (or other committed relationship)—select the right partner. If you want many children or no children at all, be sure that your life partner shares your views about these really major life choices. If your partner expects to assume only the helper role in child care or in the home, you plan for a career that requires long hours, and you both want a large family, you are not off to a good start. Children require huge commitments of time and energy, not to mention money and everything else. Even the best of relationships can be strained when you are faced with infant feedings throughout the night, a huge pile of diapers, sleep deprivation, and the demands of a career.

Have the Courage of Your Convictions. Psychologists conduct research on controversial questions, and sometimes we get results that are unexpected and unwanted. It is important that we stay true to what we have found, yet be flexible enough to change our beliefs when the data show that we may be wrong. Thus, it takes courage to stand one's ground when the naysayers are in the majority and to admit that you may be wrong, when additional data point to that conclusion. Courage offers many benefits both in academics and in our private lives.

Create a Supportive Environment. The women in my department, who arrived before I did, helped to make it a better department for those women who were hired later. I hope that I did the same for those who came after me. A work environment that fosters cooperative interactions, focuses on success for everyone, regardless of their job, and is flexible in response to family and other life demands, is a better place for everyone to work. Parents can form groups that share child care, work assignments can be rotated so that everyone can leave early on some days, and work schedules can be arranged in a way that accommodates the multiple demands from multiple roles that women and men face.

THE HEART OF ACADEMIC LIFE

A central focus in my work as an academic psychologist is the important role my students play in my life. They raise enough good questions about psychology to keep any research psychologist busy for several lifetimes. The original impetus for my decades of work in understanding sex differences in cognitive abilities came from the students in my classes on the psychology of women and cognitive psychology. The questions of similarities and differences in female and male cognitive abilities came up in both classes. I wanted to create a meaningful context for the study of social and physiological factors and their joint actions, while also understanding the political ramifications of studying such a controversial topic. I owe so much to the many superb students who have shared my passion for psychology with me. I hope that some will chose to join with me in a lifelong pursuit of psychological questions and answers.

REFERENCES

Halpern, D. F. (2000). *Sex differences in cognitive abilities* (3rd ed.). Mahwah, NJ: Lawrence Erlbaum, Associates.
Halpern, D. F. (1997). Sex differences in intelligence: Implications for education. *American Psychologist, 52,* 1091–1102.
Halpern, D. F., & Voiskounsky, A. (Eds.). (1997). *States of mind: American and post–Soviet perspectives on contemporary issues in psychology.* NY: Oxford University Press.

REPRESENTATIVE PUBLICATIONS

Halpern, D. F. (1994). A national assessment of critical thinking skills in adults: Taking steps toward the goal. In A. Greenwood (Ed.), *The national assessment of college student learning: Identification of the skills to be taught, learned, and assessed* (pp. 24–64). Washington, DC: U.S. Department of Education, National Center for Education Statistics.

Halpern, D. F. (Ed.). (1994). *Changing college classrooms: New teaching and learning strategies for an increasingly complex world.* San Francisco: Jossey-Bass.

Halpern, D. F. (1995). Cognitive gender differences: Why diversity is a critical research issue. In H. Landrine (Ed.), *Bringing cultural diversity to feminist psychology: Theory, research, practice* (pp. 77–92). Washington, DC: American Psychological Association. (Reprinted from *Questions of gender: Perspectives & paradoxes,* pp. 436–445, by D. L. Anselmi & A. L. Law, 1998, New York: McGraw-Hill.

Halpern, D. F. (Guest Ed.). (1995). Psychological and psychobiological perspectives on sex differences in cognition: I. Theory and Research [Special Issue]. *Learning and Individual Differences, 7.*

Halpern, D. F. (1995). The skewed logic of the Bell-Shaped Curve. [Special Issue]. Race & IQ. *Skeptic, 3,* 64–71.

Halpern, D. F. (Guest Ed.). (1996). Psychological and psychobiological perspectives on sex differences in cognition: II. Commentaries and Controversies [Special Issue]. *Learning and Individual Differences, 8.*

Halpern, D. F. (1996). Public policy implications of sex differences in cognitive abilities. *Psychology, Public Policy, and the Law, 2,* 561–574.

Halpern, D. F. (1996). Sex, brains, hands, and spatial cognition. *Developmental Review, 16,* 261–270.

Halpern, D. F. (1996). *Thinking critically about critical thinking: An exercise book to accompany thought and knowledge: An introduction to critical thinking* (3rd ed.). Mahwah, NJ: Lawrence Erlbaum Associates.

Halpern, D. F. (1996). *Thought and knowledge: An introduction to critical thinking* (3rd ed.). Mahwah, NJ: Lawrence Erlbaum Associates.

Halpern, D. F. (1997). *Critical thinking across the curriculum: A brief edition of thought and knowledge.* Mahwah, NJ: Lawrence Erlbaum Associates.

Halpern, D. F. (1997, March 14). The war of the worlds: When students' conceptual understanding clashes with their professors'. *Chronicle of Higher Education, XLII,* B4–B5.

Halpern, D. F. (1998). Recipe for a sexually dimorphic brain: Ingredients include ovarian and testicular hormones. *Behavioral and Brain Sciences, 21,* 330–331.

Halpern, D. F., Smothergill, D. W., Allen, M., Baker, S., Baum, C., Best, D., Ferrari, J., Geisinger, K. F., Gilden, E. R., Hester, M., Keith-Spiegel, P., Kierniesky, N. C., McGovern, T. V., McKeachie, W. J., Prokasy, W. F., Szuchman, L. T., Vesta, R., & Weaver, K. A. (1998). Scholarship in psychology: A paradigm for the 21st century. *American Psychologist, 53,* 1292–1297.

Halpern, D. F. (1998). Teaching critical thinking for transfer across domains: Dispositions, skills, structure training, and metacognitive monitoring. *American Psychologist, 53,* 449–455.

Halpern, D. F. (1999). How public policies support the skewed logic of the "Bell Curve." *Journal of American Ethnic History, 18,* 145–146.

Halpern, D. F. (2000, March). Creating cooperative learning environments. [Teaching Tips]. *APS Observer, 13,* 14–15, 29–31.

Halpern, D. F. (2000). Critical thinking applications. In W. Weiten, *Psychology: Themes and variations* (5th ed.). Pacific Grove, CA: Brooks/Cole.

Halpern, D. F. (2000). Mapping cognitive processes onto the brain: Mind the gap. *Brain and Cognition, 42,* 128–130.

Halpern, D. F. (in press). The "How" and "Why" of Critical Thinking Assessment. In D. Fasko (Ed.), *Critical thinking and reasoning: Current theories, research, and practice.* Cresskill, NJ: Hampton Press.

Halpern, D. F. (in press). Teaching for critical thinking: Helping college students develop the skills and dispositions of a critical thinker. In R. J. Menges & M. D. Svinicki (Eds.), *Teaching, learning, curriculum, and faculty development at the edge of the millennium: New directions for teaching and learning.* San Francisco: Jossey-Bass.

Halpern, D. F. (in press). Validity, fairness, and group differences: Tough questions for selection testing. *Psychology, Public Policy, and the Law.*

Halpern, D. F., Haviland, M. G., & Killian, C. D. (1998). Handedness and sex differences in intelligence: Evidence from the Medical College Admissions Test. *Brain and Cognition, 38,* 87–101.

Halpern, D. F., & Ikier, S. (in press). Causes, correlates, and caveats: Understanding the development of sex differences in cognition. In A. V. McGillicuddy-DeLisi & R. DeLisi (Eds.), *Biology, society, and behavior: The development of sex differences in cognition.* NY: Ablex.

Halpern, D. F., & LaMay, M. L. (2000). The smarter sex: A critical review of sex differences in intelligence. *Educational Psychology Review, 12,* 229–246.

Halpern, D. F., & Nummedal. S. G. (Guest Eds.). (1995). Psychologists teach critical thinking. [Special Issue]. *Teaching of Psychology, 22.*

Halpern, D. F., & Reich, J. (1999). Scholarship in psychology: Conversations about change and constancy. *American Psychologist, 54,* 347–349.

Loring-Meier, S., & Halpern, D. F. (1999). Sex differences in visual-spatial working memory: Components of cognitive processing. *Psychonomic Bulletin & Review, 6,* 464–471.

Neisser, U., Boodoo, G., Bouchard, Jr., T. J., Boykin, A. W., Brody, N., Ceci, S. J., Halpern, D. F., Loehlin, J. C., Perloff, R., Sternberg, R. J., & Urbina, S. (1996). Intelligence: Knowns and Unknowns. *American Psychologist, 51,* 77–101.

CHAPTER 20

Janet Shibley Hyde

Photographer: unavailable.

Janet Shibley Hyde

For someone who loves peace and concord, I find myself involved in some of the most controversial and contentious areas of psychology, feminist psychology, and human sexuality. Here I sit, writing this autobiography while I hold a faculty position at a major research university where the psychology department is one of the top 10 in the country. How did all this come about? Let me begin at the beginning.

CHILDHOOD AND ADOLESCENCE

I was an only child, born in 1948 at the height of the post-World War II baby boom, to Dorothy Reavy Shibley and Grant Shibley. My parents followed a pattern that was odd at the time, in that my mother was 35 when I was born and my father was 38. Their late childbearing probably had little to do with intending to set a new trend and much to do with a desire not to have a baby during a frightening war. My mother has made it clear that they were quite successful at practicing contraception.

For the first 7 years of my life, I grew up on a farm in central Ohio. I was a happy tomboy with two ponies that I rode with confidence and delight. My father farmed part time while he taught high school math and biology. When I was in second grade, he taught me algebra so that I could help grade his students' papers. Math was as comfortable to me as talking.

At the end of 2nd grade, we moved to Park Forest, Illinois, a southern suburb of Chicago. My parents' main motivation for the move was concern about the quality of the education I was receiving in the small farm town. In 2nd grade, the teacher had divided my class into two reading groups. She taught the high one and I taught the low one. My parents decided I needed a better school.

In Illinois, my father worked at his other favorite occupation, as a safety engineer for the National Safety Council in Chicago. My mother, an Oberlin Conservatory graduate, developed a good group of private piano students.

Then, just 2 years later, we moved back to Ohio, this time to Warren, where my father was safety director for a steel company. I doubt that there was a good reason for the move except for my father's restlessness. I was tested that summer and moved directly to fifth grade. I have clear memories in fifth grade of getting math assignments or tests and racing against twin boys in the class to see who would be the first to turn in the paper. I usually won. They usually made a lot of mistakes.

In sixth grade, an odd thing happened. My teacher thought I wasn't particularly good at math and gave me B's. My parents later told me that they were in pain about this issue the whole year. They knew the teacher was wrong, and not a very good teacher to boot, but as teachers themselves they didn't believe in discrediting a teacher to her student. So, they supported me quietly. I knew that the teacher was wrong about me, and my grades in math immediately bounced back in seventh grade. I have often wondered what would have happened to my later career if I or my parents had believed that teacher.

By seventh grade, the United States was in a recession and the steel company my father worked for was in decline. My father was laid off; a safety director was considered a luxury. He was forced to work a white-collar job on a night shift, which was very stressful to him, and his alcoholism came to the fore. By the end of ninth grade, we had moved back to Illinois where he worked as a safety engineer. All along the way, my mother started up new piano-teaching programs.

In the spirit of true confessions, I admit that I spent a year as a cheerleader. Actually, I wasn't on the real squad, I was on the reserve squad and ready to leap into the breech if someone on the real squad broke her leg. It was ninth or tenth grade. It's odd that I'm so fuzzy about it. Like all girls of that age, I was captured by the glamor of being a cheerleader. It epitomized female success. I played a pretty decent game of tennis, but there were no girls' sports teams and it didn't even occur to me that that was problematic. Perhaps most interesting about this cheerleading phase was my father's quite clear communication with me, on several occasions, that the future for me did not lie in cheerleading, but in chemistry—scarcely a typical father–daughter message in that era. He saw cheerleading as fluff. He thought science was a good, important career, and he wanted me to pursue it.

It should be clear by now that mine is not the story of a woman who lifted herself out of a working-class family who told her that her main goal in life should be to become a superb housewife. Both my parents were college graduates, although certainly my family lived simply and never had much money. All of us assumed that I would go to college. Perhaps more importantly, however, I learned no negative stereotypes about women in my family. My father wanted a career for me in science. My mother is highly intelligent and incredibly strong. A suggestion that women are not intelligent or are flighty or irresponsible simply would never have occurred in my family. My feminism, then, involves no rebellion against my family or the teachings of childhood. Instead, it is a logical extension. I just had to wait for the second wave of the feminist movement so that I could join up.

My mother has concluded, as have other members of my family, that her mother, my maternal grandmother Victoria Reavy, held a pretty clear view that girls and women were superior to men and boys. She would never have said such a thing directly, but she conveyed it in many ways. She insisted, for example, that my mother must attend college, even though it was the height of the depression and my grandfather thought it was a bad idea. There was a well-known family story about Victoria, who was 5 feet tall, getting out a huge metal frying pan and having a direct confrontation with her husband Louis, who was 6' 1" tall, on the college matter. No physical fighting occurred, but she prevailed.

My mother's strength became more apparent to me by the time I was in college. She truly held the family together as my father's alcoholism worsened. She kept a secret savings account of the money she made giving piano lessons, so that I would be sure to have money for college in case my father lost his job. She lived in constant fear of that possibility. The piano money wouldn't have begun to support her, much less a whole family. But the fact remains that I feel that I had a pretty normal, happy childhood, with occasional short periods of alcoholic excess on my father's part. My mother was the one who made it normal and happy. Finally, when I was a junior in college, she couldn't bear the situation any longer and left my father. To support herself, she became a housemother at a small college. I realize now that she stayed as long as she did to ensure his contributions to my college education. I come from a line of strong women.

Back to my time in high school. It was senior year and I needed to make a decision about what college to attend. Without even thinking hard, I chose Oberlin College, and applied for early decision. My mother had attended the school and I had visited many times as I was growing up. It had been rated as the number one small co-ed liberal arts college in the country by *The Chicago Tribune* that year, and I wanted the best. (It's worth noting that other co-ed colleges that exceed it in ranking today were all-male schools at the time—e.g., Amherst and Williams.) Oberlin accepted me and everything fell into place. I graduated from high school with a 3.98 GPA, deprived of a 4.0 by a chemistry teacher who insisted on giving me a B in advanced placement chemistry.

To summarize, I had received several messages from my family by the end of high school. Everyone, including girls, can do math well. Women are competent and intelligent. I should go to college. Science is definitely a reasonable major for a girl. I should not marry until after college because it might interfere with my education. Pregnancy was unthinkable; it would ruin my future. Independence is a good thing. I should be able to support myself. This last message was less explicit than the others, but my mother conveyed it, doubtless because of her experiences with an alcoholic husband who might not be able to be counted on for support, and her own inability to support herself giving piano lessons.

THE COLLEGE YEARS

I entered Oberlin College in September, 1965, and embarked on my chemistry major. By the end of sophomore year, when I had to declare a major, it was clear to me that chemistry was not for me. I did fine in the coursework, but I was a terrible klutz in the lab. I inadvertently swallowed acid while pipetting. To this day I have a scar on the calf of my right leg from a splash of sulfuric acid. I declared a math major. I was doing well in the courses and I didn't have to handle sulfuric acid. My expertise in mathematics has been a ticket to success at all stages of my career and I've never regretted that major.

I had been so busy with science courses and math that I hadn't yet taken a psychology course, but it sounded interesting and I took one at the beginning of my junior year. Within a month, I knew that I had found the field that I adored. Math was nice. Psychology was fantastic! I think it is no accident that it was the first real academic course I had in college taught by a woman, Celeste McCullough (of the McCullough effect in perception). She was incredibly brilliant, knowledgeable, and poised, and she taught a great introduction to psychology. By then it was too late to complete a psychology major, so I completed the math major while taking as many psychology courses as I could.

By the fall of my senior year, I was making plans for what I would do after college. I decided to apply for PhD programs in psychology. In all honesty, I have little recollection of my decision-making process. Oberlin students being who they are, the majority of my classmates were applying for PhD or professional programs. I think in part I was swept along with everyone else. I gave a bit of thought to going to work for IBM, based on my math major and a year's experience I had working as a student employee in the college computer center. It struck me as being an incredibly dull life. A career as a professor in psychology seemed exciting. I would be much richer today had I chosen IBM, but I wouldn't be nearly as happy. It is important to note, too, that I never experienced sexism from the faculty at Oberlin. They did nothing to undermine my self-confidence and everything to support it. I was accepted warmly as a math major and I think that probably 50% of the math majors were women. I had a wonderful mentor in math, Sam Goldberg, who taught probability and statistics. I also had a wonderful mentor in psychology, Norm Henderson, who got me started in mouse behavior genetics. More about that later.

Relationships, too, were influential in the process. In the fall of my first year I had, in sequence, two really lousy boyfriends. That led me to swear off boyfriends. It had become clear to me that being alone was preferable to being with a jerk, an experience that I believe all young women should have. Not a month later, I was playing bridge over the January break. We needed a fourth, and a young man named Clark Hyde popped up saying that he would love to play. He and I spent a lot of time talking and quickly found that we had a great match of interests. We began dating and never dated anyone else after that. We were married on our graduation day, June 2, 1969.

Therefore, as I was making decisions about graduate school in Fall of my senior year, my fiancé was a consideration. He was completely in agreement with my desires for graduate school and a career. His mother had been an elementary school teacher the entire time he was growing up. In fact, she had really been the one to support the family. To him, a wife with a career was perfectly normal. He also had enormous faith in my intellectual capacities. Our strategy was that we applied for pairs of graduate schools at about seven or eight places across the country. He was a political science major, so one of his possibilities was to get a PhD in political science and become a professor. The other possibility for him was to attend seminary and become an Episcopal priest. He opted for the latter, in part because the Vietnam War was in high gear and seminary was a draft deferment whereas PhD programs were not. Within a few months of entering seminary, he knew he had made the right decision.

It turned out that none of the top psychology graduate programs to which I had applied minded that I didn't have an undergraduate psychology major. They were delighted with the mathematics major (it was the era of great expectations for mathematical psychology) and the small number of psychology courses I had taken. I was accepted at Berkeley, Stanford, Michigan, and every other program to which I had applied. I didn't apply to Harvard or Yale because it didn't occur to me that I could get in. In retrospect, it was totally illogical that I thought I could get into Stanford and not Harvard. I suspect that I generalized from Harvard's all-male undergraduate program that I wouldn't be welcome at the graduate level.

It looked like the best match for us was for me to attend Berkeley and my husband to attend the seminary in Berkeley. In some ways I preferred Stanford at the time. Roger Shepard had asked me to work with him. But there was no seminary in Stanford and the commute would have been unreasonable. I have sometimes wondered what would have happened to me had I taken the Stanford option, particularly because Eleanor Maccoby was on the faculty there. Would she have trained me in developmental research on gender? Would I be a better researcher now?

THE GRADUATE SCHOOL YEARS

I entered Berkeley supported by the Institute for Human Learning, which was headed by Leo Postman and had a predoctoral training grant. They believed I would pursue research on mathematical models of learning. However, I found the research colloquia there incredibly dull and it didn't take me long to decide that I wouldn't follow that path. Meanwhile, I had to generate a first research project, rather like a masters thesis. I fell back on what was known and comfortable to me from my undergraduate days, mouse behavior–genetic research. I compared learning ability in three inbred strains. Unfortunately, two great behavior geneticists had left Berkeley before I arrived. Gerald McClearn had been wooed away to another university, and the great Edward Chase Tolman, of maze-bright and maze-dull rats, had, unfortunately, died. Remaining was Bill Meredith, who had worked with McClearn but whose real brilliance was in psychometrics. He was an unfailingly benevolent mentor.

By the middle of my first year, my penchant for planning ahead had led me to the realization that seminary took only 3 years, at which point my husband would be finished with his degree and would want to move to get a job. Four years was normative for PhD programs at the time. What was a woman to do? The answer was obvious: Finish her PhD in 3 years. I carefully analyzed the exact requirements. They were actually rather few in number: pass an exam on statistics, complete a first project, take a few seminars, pass prelims, and complete a dissertation. I passed the statistics exam in the first term, my statistics background from my undergraduate days giving me the edge I needed. I designed the research project, obtained the mice, wrote it up, and had it completed by the end of the first year. I took courses and passed prelims by the end of the second year. My major prelims topic was, as we termed it then, differential psychology, the study of individual differences. One dimension of individual differences was sex differences, so I read extensively in that literature—what there was of it in 1970—for my prelims. No one asked a question on it, but I still thought it was awfully interesting.

I designed the dissertation and ran it hard in my third year. It involved cross-breeding strains of mice and I could force it ahead only so fast because I had to get the mice to breed. Some of the cross-pairings did great but others were slackers. I tested over 1,000 mice for the project. As the Spring approached, time was tight. I wrote as much of the dissertation as I could and had all the data on computer punchcards except the last trickles, and had the statistical analysis programs written. We would move to Ohio in June. Two weeks before we had to move, all the data were collected. I spent all night at the computer center for 2 nights in a row (otherwise I had an absolute rule against all-nighters). I finished the draft of the dissertation and left it with my advisor before moving. Revision suggestions were mailed to me over the summer and I submitted the final version in August, 1972, just before my 24th birthday.

Over that last year in graduate school, Clark and I had to find jobs. It quickly became apparent that it was unlikely that we would both find good jobs simultaneously in the same location. So we adopted the decision rule that, whoever got the best job first, we would go there and the other person would find a job in that location. We never considered a commuter marriage, which became popular in those years. We were both highly committed to each other, and living at opposite ends of the country didn't sound like marriage to us. Both of us were willing to make some unknown sacrifice in our career to have the kind of marriage we wanted.

His job offer was to be the assistant at an Episcopal church in Eureka, CA. The area was lovely, but the pay was lousy (an apartment plus $5,000 a year, which wasn't much even in those days). In addition, the California State University there was experiencing cutbacks and it seemed unlikely that I would find a job at all, and it was hundreds of miles to the next possibility. I received an offer from Bowling Green State University—an absolutely perfect assistant professor position. We took my job, and my husband found a half-time job for the first year at a church in Toledo. After that he was offered a full-time job at the Episcopal church in Napoleon, Ohio.

THE FIRST FACULTY POSITION

I hit the ground running in the Fall of 1972 at Bowling Green. I offered a course in behavior genetics and set up a mouse behavior genetics lab, doing what I had been hired to do. In addition, I taught multivariate statistics. Yet, from that first year as a faculty member, another strain ran through my head and my heart. I must back up to explain where that melody came from.

During my middle year in graduate school, the university released a report on the status of women at the university, based on the work of a committee headed by the great psycholinguist, Susan Ervin-Tripp. I should note immediately that Ervin-Tripp was not a faculty member in the Psychology Department at Berkeley, but was in linguistics. The report deplored the absence of women on the faculty at Berkeley in general. The Psychology Department was singled out as one of the departments with the worst records. There were no women among the faculty of 45 men; moreover, the last time a woman had been hired was in 1927 (I imagine it was Nancy Bailey). Something snapped inside me when I heard the results of the report. I was upset that there were no women in my department and I was even more upset that I hadn't noticed it. I was outraged that the men faculty members, who were being so radical about the Vietnam War and injustices to Vietnamese peasants, were behaving so abominably to the women in their own backyard. It wasn't as if there weren't good women available—Jeanne Block was in the Institute for Human Development on soft money (i.e., she didn't have a secure salary from the University, but had to raise her own salary from grants), while her husband, Jack Block, was on the faculty. Ravenna Helson was on soft money at the Institute for Personality Assessment and Research while her husband was on the faculty in mathematics. It was 1970 to 1971, and I was an instant convert to feminism that, conveniently, was out there as an available ideology.

Therefore, when I began my first year on the faculty at Bowling Green, I had feminist political views and I had read two important works that summer: Kate Millett's *Sexual Politics* (1969) and Germaine Greer's *The Female Eunuch* (1970). I had studied the existing research on gender differences and, my last year in graduate school, Ravenna Helson offered an undergraduate course on psychology of women, which I audited.

I decided to offer a psychology of women course during the second quarter of the 1972 to 1973 academic year. There was one textbook available at the time, Judith Bardwick's *The Psychology of Women* (1971), which Ravenna Helson had used. I plowed into preparing lectures using the book and the very limited research that was available at the time. When I look back on it, I can't imagine how I filled up the entire course when so little research had been done at the time.

By the middle of the course, I had decided to write a psychology of women textbook. I thought Bardwick's was quirky and I thought I could do better—pretty audacious for a 24-year-old assistant professor. My self-confidence at the time amazes even me. I never really had a major academic failure and my parents and a lot of school successes had turned me into a seemingly unsinkable academic Molly Brown. At least as important was the fact that I had no children and thus had the time to accomplish everything I was undertaking.

A textbook needs a publisher, though, and no publisher would be interested in the work of a brand-new PhD. Ben Rosenberg was also on the faculty at Bowling Green and we had become friends. He had published some gender research and was a senior, established scholar. We agreed to be coauthors of the book. He snapped his fingers and DC Heath offered us a contract.

From the beginning, there were problems in our working relationship. He was psychodynamically trained and truly believed the Freudian party line, whereas I had developed a healthy feminist cynicism about it. I did all the work and he occasionally contributed a paragraph. Nonetheless, I was so happy to be working on a textbook that I didn't really mind. We (I) finished the book in 1975 and it was published in 1976.

The review of the book for *Contemporary Psychology* (1976) by Nancy Felipe Russo was scathing. I called Nancy and tried to talk to her about it, but she was dismissive. I had actually never heard of her before. I had really been a loner in developing my work on psychology of women; a number of clusters of important women graduate students had flourished around the same time as I was in graduate school, but they had not been at Berkeley. I had done my library work well, but I simply wasn't connected. I relate this episode so that younger readers will be clear that every academic has setbacks, sometimes harsh ones. The key to success is to develop "alligator skin," as I call it, from which slings and arrows are repelled while you march on. Today, Nancy Russo is a wonderful friend of many years whose work and opinions I respect greatly. Men learn these lessons so well in athletics. One day you are bitter enemies on opposing teams. Another day it's the next season and a new sport and you're on the same team, working together. The second edition of *Half the Human Experience* appeared in 1980 and I tried to fix the problems that had generated the criticisms.

When it was time to prepare the third edition, I sincerely did not want a coauthor any more. I had become too much of a feminist, and was too advanced in my career, to settle for doing all the work and splitting the credit and the royalties with another person. I stewed over what to do. Rosenberg had a fiery temper. I worried over what he might do: refuse to agree, prevent any more editions from being published, and on and on. By then I had moved to a different university. I finally decided that I cared so much about the issues, justice and equity, that I was willing to lose the book and never see a new edition rather than continue with the coauthor. A marvelous feeling of relief and power swept over me. Ironically, in letting go of what I cared most about, the book, I gained so much. I picked up the phone and dialed while feeling the jitters inside. He was angry and hurt, but he agreed not to continue as coauthor.

By the time the first edition had appeared in print, I had decided that I liked textbook writing. I had begun teaching an undergraduate human sexuality course for reasons detailed elsewhere (Hyde, 1997) and didn't like either of the two available textbooks. I decided to write an undergraduate, interdisciplinary textbook in human sexuality. Many things were different this time. As a published textbook author, I was pursued by the publishers and had a choice among them. And, of course, I had no coauthor. *Understanding Human Sexuality* appeared in 1979.

Meanwhile, I worked industriously in generating the empirical research that would earn tenure for me. Following my graduate school training, I conducted a behavior–genetic, selective breeding study for female aggressiveness in wild female mice. Clearly the feminist influence could be seen in the behavior I chose. The project was longitudinal and took several years that was, in some ways, not a wise choice when working toward tenure. Yet the results rolled in in plenty of time and the project was seen as substantial and worthwhile. I was granted tenure in my fourth year.

When I had begun as an assistant professor, I had set for myself the goal of earning tenure and having a baby by age 30. It sounds odd when expressed so plainly, but that is exactly what I had settled on. It was 1976 and I had tenure, so it was time to start working on the baby. Conception took longer than I expected but, by early 1978, I was very happily pregnant.

Dual-earner couple issues surfaced. Our deal on leaving graduate school had been that whoever got the best job first would take it and the other would follow, but then we would alternate. My husband was getting restless in the little Episcopal mission he had in Napoleon, Ohio. Arguably, it was his turn to find and take a position. Therefore, he searched and found the perfect position, as rector of the Episcopal church in Delaware, Ohio, a church nearly double the size of his previous one, in a college town (home of Ohio Wesleyan University) that provided us with a much richer intellectual and cultural life than we had in Napoleon. He took it, mindful of the fact that the area, the larger Columbus metropolitan area, had many colleges and therefore the potential for a job for me. Bowling Green was nearly a 2-hour drive away and, although I gave it much thought, simply not a feasible commute. We moved in January, 1978, and I pregnantly commuted for the remainder of the school year; I took a year leave-of-absence for 1978-79.

Margaret Hyde was born in June, 1978, by emergency cesarean following 24 hours of labor. The reason for the cesarean was cephalopelvic disproportion—the opening in my pelvis was too small for her head to pass through. I had lost a great deal of blood and I felt as though my body was wrecked. I was so weak that the doctor advised that I not even attempt to pick up the baby and carry her for at least a week, so when I returned from the hospital, my husband did all the diapering and brought her to me to nurse as I lay in bed. In terms of father–infant bonding, it was fantastic.

The event of that childbirth and the subsequent 2 years represented a major turning point for me psychologically. To that point, I had possessed a wonderful ability to control my life. My successes were many and my failures few and unimportant. Suddenly my eagerly anticipated Lamaze delivery was wildly out of control, and for several months, I wondered if I would ever feel in good health again. Viewed in a black mood, my career might be over because of the move. I generated creative schemes to make a commute to Bowling Green feasible. I would get a private pilot's license, buy a plane, and fly. The thought of flying a small plane was too petrifying to pursue. I applied for any faculty position I heard about in the area.

THE SECOND FACULTY POSITION

Then, in the Spring of 1979, I received a phone call from Chuck Morris, the chair of the psychology department at Denison University, a small liberal arts college in Granville, Ohio, just a 45-minute drive away. He had heard about me from another faculty member in his department, Jim Freeman, who had done his graduate work at Bowling Green when I was there, thought I was a fine teacher, knew I was in the area, and thought they should hire me. All they had was a 1-year sabbatical replacement, but I took it.

That first, and perhaps only, year at Denison was simultaneously wonderful and awful. It's tough to switch from being a tenured associate professor to being a 1-year temp. The Denison students were much more critical than the Bowling Green students and in the middle of the year, two students complained about my teaching. I experienced an anxiety attack as well as depression. I have pondered why that one event could precipitate such a severe reaction in someone who had never experienced real anxiety or depression before. I believe that several factors contributed. My life had gone so well to that point that I had little experience with failure and therefore had not developed the requisite coping skills. I was already feeling highly stressed because of the difficult childbirth, the loss of my secure job, and the insecurity of a 1-year position that I desperately needed to turn into a permanent position. I never stopped functioning though, and people close to me said that they didn't notice the depression. A couple of months later, the woman whom I was replacing resigned to take a different position. I was offered her tenured slot and quickly accepted it. All was well again.

Life settled down to expectable pleasantness. We had a second child, Luke, in 1981. I was promoted to full professor. One day in 1979, though, it struck me that I had accomplished the life goals I had set for myself—earning tenure and having a baby by age 30—and that I needed to set some new goals. Life was pretty good and it was hard to see a critical piece that was missing. I decided that my next goal was to produce a journal article that would become a classic, would make a strong contribution to the field, and be cited in many textbooks. I reflected for several months. I had read and been much influenced by Maccoby and Jacklin's *The Psychology of Sex Differences* (1974). I considered how to best forge ahead in that area, using my own strengths. My quantitative mind made me intensely curious about how large the gender differences were that Maccoby and Jacklin had documented. I began computing some Ω^2 values, knowing that measure of percent variance accounted for from my graduate school days. Maccoby and Jacklin had reported a few *d* values and I computed more. The results nearly knocked me over intellectually because the differences were so small. I wrote it all up as an article and submitted it to *Psychological Bulletin*. The reviews came back with an editorial decision of reject with invitation to revise and resubmit, but the revisions required extensive additional work that I estimated would take a year. I decided that I believed the article was excellent as it was, so I made more copies, put it in a new envelope, and sent it to the *American Psychologist*. It was immediately accepted pending minor revision, one of only two times in my career that I have received an acceptance on a first submission. The article appeared in 1981 (Hyde, 1981) and did, as hoped, become a minor classic, winning citations in many undergraduate textbooks. I am so glad that I had confidence in my work and was not discouraged by the critical reviews of the article that I received on the first submission.

In the process, I had independently discovered meta-analysis, albeit in a relatively crude form. While doing the research, I was unaware of the work of Glass, McGaw, and Smith (1981) and others. A colleague called it to my attention when I was preparing the article, so I added the term to my title!

THE THIRD FACULTY POSITION

It was January of 1985. My husband had been the priest at the Episcopal church in Delaware, Ohio, for 7 years and he was beginning to think about what he might do next. In our dual-earner approach to finding new jobs, it wasn't clear whose turn it was, since we had each taken a turn. I was settled and happy at Denison. My husband decided that his real desire was to teach in a seminary, but to land such a job he would need a PhD and he wanted to focus on the area of pastoral theology. He liked the program at Marquette University in Milwaukee. I asked what he thought I was going to do in Milwaukee. He paused, not having thought about that issue in his enthusiasm. He went to find a copy of the APA Monitor, opened it, and found a job advertisement for someone with a joint appointment between Psychology and Women's Studies at the University of Wisconsin-Madison. He pointed out that the perfect job was right there and it was obvious to me that he was right. I applied and, after some twists and turns in the process, was offered the job in late May.

Between January and May, though, some things had changed. The Provost at Denison decided to retire. The President called me into his office and told me about it. It dawned on me that he was going to ask me to chair the search committee for a new provost. People always seem to want me to chair committees. The President surprised me, though—he wanted me to be the interim provost for a year while they ran the search. I was taken aback. Although I had done a lot of committee work, I had no formal administrative experience, and I was expected to be a talented chameleon and turn into a provost? People had told me for some time that I would make a good administrator, but I hadn't really thought seriously about it. In the end, I agreed to do it. Therefore, when Wisconsin asked me to take their job, I had to request that they hold it for me for a year, to which they agreed.

I enjoyed the year as Provost, in large part because I had a wonderfully competent administrative assistant who had done the job for 10 years. She guided me through and people thought I did a fine job. Some people might find it difficult to understand how one could enjoy being a provost. I know that some people get their thrills from such high-level jobs because of the power, but wielding power is not my own turn-on. I do enjoy guiding a university through making good decisions. It's satisfying to run a smooth operation that gets notices of raises out on time and to be a mediator in disputes among faculty. I was asked whether I would want the permanent job, but I had already committed to Wisconsin.

We moved to Madison, Wisconsin, in 1986 and I began my job as Director of the Women's Studies Research Center and psychology professor. Being the director of a research institute at a major research university was both thrilling and frightening. The pressure to bring in grant dollars is enormous. In the summer before the move, I thought long and hard about what initiative I might launch for the Center. I happened to have a news program on one morning and saw an interview with Sylvia Hewlett, who was talking about the absence of a national policy on maternity leave in this country. I got a copy of her book, *A Lesser Life: The Myth of Women's Liberation in America*. From a feminist point of view, the book was problematic, but her argument was riveting, that the United States was the only industrialized nation in the world not to have a policy that guaranteed women a leave at the time of the birth of a baby. I decided that I wanted to be the one who collected empirical data on this policy issue and that it would be the perfect project for the Women's Studies Research Center.

About that time, Congresswoman Pat Schroeder introduced parental leave legislation into Congress and it was eventually passed, actually several times, but then-President George Bush, who claimed to be pro-family, vetoed it. As I read the expert testimony by psychologists, all of it focused on infants and their need to have a mother or other caregiver at home as a stable source of attachment for the first 4 to 6 months after birth. All that is wonderful, but as a feminist psychologist, I couldn't help but notice that the mothers were left out of consideration. After searching the literature, I concluded that no one had collected the relevant data on mothers. I decided to study mothers and their maternity leave experiences, especially as those experiences were related to their mental health. At Wisconsin, I hooked up with other colleagues with complementary areas of expertise, we wrote a grant proposal and, by 1989, we had a $1 million grant from National Institute of Mental Health (NIMH) to conduct the study, that by then had become elaborate. The result was the Wisconsin Maternity Leave and Health Project (Hyde, Klein, Essex, & Clark, 1995). We are still following the sample longitudinally and, as of this writing, the children are in third grade.

One of the advantages of the move to Wisconsin was that I now had graduate students—absolutely outstanding ones. Space limitations do not permit me to tell the stories of each of those collaborations, so I will say concisely that they resulted in interesting studies on moral reasoning about sexually transmitted diseases (Jadack, Hyde, & Moore, 1995), objectified body consciousness (McKinley & Hyde, 1996), a meta-analysis of gender differences in sexuality (Oliver & Hyde, 1993), and a meta-analysis of gender differences in self-esteem (Kling, Hyde, Showers, & Buswell, 1999). My thoughts today are very much about raising up the next generation of psychology of women researchers.

In my fourth year as Director of the Women's Studies Research Center, a new opportunity presented itself. Donna Shalala had become the Chancellor at the University of Wisconsin and it had become a very exciting place for women faculty. I could write several chapters about her, her brilliant leadership, and what a shot in the arm she was for women at the university. Under her benevolent watch, a task force on gender equity was formed, and I was a member. After more than a year of extensive research and writing, we issued a comprehensive report. As a committee we had come to realize that many fine reports were written at the university, but most ended up collecting dust on the shelf. We wanted to make sure that our recommendations were actually instituted and thought hard about how we might ensure that outcome. We finally decided to ask for a new position, an Associate Vice Chancellor whose portfolio was promoting gender equity for faculty and staff. Because the report was compelling and because Donna Shalala was Chancellor, the position was approved. Chancellor Shalala invited me to inaugurate the new position.

In the position as Associate Vice Chancellor, I served as ombudsperson for women faculty. I was able to engage in quiet negotiations on behalf of dozens of women who brought their difficulties to me—botched tenure decisions, chilly climates in the medical school and college of engineering—the standard but so important litany. We came to a remarkable number of satisfactory resolutions. I also initiated a gender equity study of faculty pay and, again with the leadership of Donna Shalala, who figured out how to allocate the needed funds, we were able to correct the salaries of more than 100 women.

Early in my term as Associate Vice Chancellor, my personal life was thrown into turmoil. My husband of nearly 20 years died of metastasized cancer, leaving me with a 7-year-old and a 10-year-old. I had lost my best friend and I was devastated. Being a single parent was exhausting. It seemed that every day I got up at 6 a.m. and worked straight through until 11 p.m., slept, and got up the next day to repeat the grind. Ironically, precisely because my husband had been so good about splitting household responsibilities, his loss was felt all the more keenly. I was a single mother for more than 4 years and I really cannot recommend it. It's sobering to think how difficult it was for me when, in some sense, I possessed great resources: a great job, financial security (I never appreciated tenure and its financial security so much), and education. It amazes me that women without those resources manage to hang together as single parents.

Two years into my term as Associate Vice Chancellor, the grind of being a single parent combined with the realization that I was neglecting my research in serious ways because of my administrative obligations, led me to the conclusion that I must give up that position and return to being a full-time faculty member, which I then did without administrative interruption for 6 years.

In my personal life, I had a relationship with one man, and concluded that he was totally unsatisfactory as a partner for me. A second relationship with another man led to the same conclusion. I decided that I wouldn't even think about marriage for years and wouldn't even date, at least until my children were out of the nest, because it seemed particularly rotten to put them through these unsatisfactory gentlemen friends.

Several months later I met John DeLamater at a meeting of the Society for the Scientific Study of Sexuality. I say met because he was a faculty member at Wisconsin, but he was in sociology and I was in psychology and, housed in separate buildings on a huge campus, we previously had done no more than bump into each other once a year. I had a favorable impression of him because he taught the undergraduate human sexuality course that was cross-listed between our two departments. If that weren't enough, he used my textbook even before I arrived at Wisconsin. At the meetings, we had long talks and realized that we were both unattached. We were (are) a perfect match in many ways and he is definitely one of a fine, elite group of men. We married in 1993.

In 1998, I was elected Chair of the Department of Psychology. The work is intense and meaningful and I enjoy it, but at the same time I detest the way in which it takes me away from teaching and research.

CLOSING REFLECTIONS

Two themes run through my career. The first is my commitment to balancing work and family and my willingness to make some career sacrifices to build a strong family. Fortunately, none of the sacrifices were devastating. The second is my strong commitment to gender equity and working on behalf of women, both in my teaching and my research.

I am deeply grateful because I have been lavishly recognized for the work I have done, something that might not have occurred because I work in two marginalized areas: feminist psychology and human sexuality. I have received the Kinsey Award from the Society for the Scientific Study of Sexuality for my contributions to sex research and the Heritage Award as well as the Sherif Award from APA's Division 35 for my contributions to psychology of women. I hold a named Chair at Wisconsin; the tradition here is that one can choose the name of the Chair so I chose Helen Thompson Woolley, a turn-of-the-century (1800s to 1900s, that is), pioneer woman psychologist. It is crucial that we keep alive organizations such as Division 35 of APA so that research in feminist psychology can be recognized and rewarded.

Although I certainly have encountered obstacles in my career and have passed through troubled waters, I feel that I am one of the lucky ones. I grew up in a wonderfully supportive family and have had not one, but two supportive husbands. My kids are great and I have not been distracted by having to bail them out of jail. I have never experienced sexual harassment at work. My feminist convictions flow not so much from horrors I have experienced, but rather from the injustices I have seen done to other women. I continue to be completely committed to working to eradicate those injustices. It is my particular talent and privilege to be able to do that through teaching, writing, and research, all of which have the potential to subvert systems of injustice.

REFERENCES

Bardwick, J. (1971). *Psychology of women: A study of biocultural conflicts.* New York: Harper & Row.
Glass, G. V., McGaw, B., & Smith, M.L. (1981). *Meta-analysis in social research.* Beverly Hills: Sage Publications.
Greer, G. (1970). *The female eunuch.* New York: McGraw-Hill.
Hewlett, S. A. (1986). *A lesser life: The myth of women's liberation in America.* New York: Morrow.
Hyde, J. S. (1979). *Understanding human sexuality.* New York: McGraw-Hill.
Hyde, J. S. (1981). How large are cognitive gender differences? A meta-analysis using Ω^2 and d. *American Psychologist, 36,* 892–901.
Hyde, J. S., Klein, M. H., Essex, M. J., & Clark, R. (1995). Maternity leave and women's mental health. *Psychology of Women Quarterly, 19,* 257–285.
Hyde, J. S., & Rosenberg, B. G. (1976). *Half the human experience: The psychology of women.* Lexington, MA: D. C. Heath.
Jadack, R. A., Hyde, J. S., & Moore, C. F. (1995). Moral reasoning about sexually transmitted diseases. *Child Development, 66,* 167–177.
Kling, K. C., Hyde, J. S., Showers, C. J., & Buswell, B. N. (1999). Gender differences in self-esteem: A meta-analysis. *Psychological Bulletin, 125,* 470–500.
Maccoby, E. E., & Jacklin, C. N. (1974). *The psychology of sex differences.* Stanford, CA: Stanford University Press.
McKinley, N. M., & Hyde, J. S. (1996). The Objectified Body Consciousness Scale: Development and validation. *Psychology of Women Quarterly, 20,* 181–216.
Millett, K. (1969). *Sexual politics.* Garden City, NY: Doubleday.
Oliver, M. B., & Hyde, J. S. (1993). Gender differences in sexuality: A meta-analysis. *Psychological Bulletin, 114,* 29–51.
Russo, N. F. (1976). On the psychology of women: The competition for the market begins. *Contemporary Psychology, 21,* 818–819.

REPRESENTATIVE PUBLICATIONS

Bargad, A., & Hyde, J. S. (1991). Women's studies: A study of feminist identity development in women. *Psychology of Women Quarterly, 15,* 181–201.
Carroll, J. L., Volk, K. D., & Hyde, J. S. (1985). Differences between males and females in motives for engaging in sexual intercourse. *Archives of Sexual Behavior, 14,* 131–139.
Clark, R., Hyde, J. S., Essex, M. J., & Klein, M. H. (1997). Length of maternity leave and quality of mother–infant interactions. *Child Development, 68,* 364–383.

Conley, T. D., Jadack, R. A., & Hyde, J. S. (1997). Moral dilemmas, moral reasoning, and genital herpes. *Journal of Sex Research, 34*, 256–266.

DeLamater, J. D., & Hyde, J. S. (1998). Essentialism vs. social constructionism in the study of human sexuality. *Journal of Sex Research, 35*, 10–18.

Ebert, P. D., & Hyde, J. S. (1976). Selection for agonistic behavior in wild female Mus musculus. *Behavior Genetics, 6*, 291–304.

Hyde, J. S. (1974). Inheritance of learning ability in mice: A diallel-environmental analysis. *Journal of Comparative and Physiological Psychology, 86*, 116–123.

Hyde, J. S. (1984). Children's understanding of sexist language. *Developmental Psychology, 20*, 697–706.

Hyde, J. S. (1984). How large are gender differences in aggression? A developmental meta-analysis. *Developmental Psychology, 20*, 722–736.

Hyde, J. S. (1990). Meta-analysis and the psychology of gender differences. *Signs: Journal of Women in Culture and Society, 16*, 55–73.

Hyde, J. S. (1994). Can meta-analysis make feminist transformations in psychology? *Psychology of Women Quarterly, 18*, 451–462.

Hyde, J. S. (1994). Should psychologists study gender differences? Yes, with some guidelines. *Feminism & Psychology, 4*, 507–512.

Hyde, J. S. (1995). Women and maternity leave: Empirical data and public policy. *Psychology of Women Quarterly, 19*, 299–313.

Hyde, J. S. (1997). Second generation. In B. Bullough, V. Bullough, M. Fithian, W. Hartman, & R. Klein (Eds.), *How I got into sex* (pp. 215–224). Amherst, NY: Prometheus.

Hyde, J. S., DeLamater, J. D., Plant, E. A., & Byrd, J. M. (1996). Sexuality during pregnancy and the year postpartum. *The Journal of Sex Research, 33*, 143–151.

Hyde, J. S., DeLamater, J. D., & Hewitt, E. (1998). Sexuality and the dual-earner couple. *Journal of Family Psychology, 12*, 354–368.

Hyde, J. S., Essex, M. J., Clark, R., Klein, M. H., & Byrd, J. E. (1996). Parental leave: Policy and research. *Journal of Social Issues, 52*(3), 91–109.

Hyde, J. S., Essex, M. J., & Horton, F. (1993). Fathers and parental leave: Attitudes and experiences. *Journal of Family Issues, 14*, 616–641.

Hyde, J. S., Fennema, E., & Lamon, S. (1990). Gender differences in mathematics performance: A meta-analysis. *Psychological Bulletin, 107*, 139–155.

Hyde, J. S., Fennema, E., Ryan, M., Frost, L. A., & Hopp, C. (1990). Gender comparisons of mathematics attitudes and affect: A meta-analysis. *Psychology of Women Quarterly, 14*, 299–324.

Hyde, J. S., & Frost, L. A. (1993). Meta-analysis and the psychology of women. In F. Denmark & M. Paludi (Eds.), *Handbook of the psychology of women* (pp. 67–103). Westport, CT: Greenwood Press.

Hyde, J. S., Geiringer, E. R., & Yen, W. (1975). On the empirical relation between sex differences in spatial ability and other aspects of cognitive performance. *Multivariate Behavioral Research, 10*, 289–310.

Hyde, J. S., Krajnik, M., & Skuldt-Niederberger, K. (1991). Androgyny across the life span: A replication and longitudinal follow-up. *Developmental Psychology, 27*, 516–519.

Hyde, J. S., & Linn, M. C. (1988). Gender differences in verbal ability: A meta-analysis. *Psychological Bulletin, 104*, 53–69.

Hyde, J. S., & McKinley, N. M. (1993). Beliefs about the consequences of maternal employment for children: Psychometric analyses. *Psychology of Women Quarterly, 17*, 177–192.

Hyde, J. S., & Phillis, D. E. (1979). Androgyny across the lifespan. *Developmental Psychology, 15*, 334–336.

Hyde, J. S., & Plant, E. A. (1995). Magnitude of psychological gender differences: Another side to the story. *American Psychologist, 50*, 159–161.

Hyde, J. S., Rosenberg, B. G., & Behrman, J. (1977). Tomboyism. *Psychology of Women Quarterly, 3*, 73–75.

Jadack, R. A., Keller, M. L., & Hyde, J. S. (1990). Genital herpes: Gender comparisons and the disease experience. *Psychology of Women Quarterly, 14*, 419–434.

Macdonald, N. E., & Hyde, J. S. (1980). Fear of success, need achievement, and fear of failure: A factor-analytic study. *Sex Roles, 6*, 695–712.

Madden, M. E., & Hyde, J. S. (1998). Integrating gender and ethnicity into psychology courses. *Psychology of Women Quarterly, 22*, 1–12.

O'Keefe, E. C., & Hyde, J. S. (1983). The development of occupational gender-role stereotypes: Effects of gender stability and age. *Sex Roles, 9*, 481–492.

Vandell, D. L., Hyde, J. S., Plant, E. A., & Essex, M. J. (1997). Fathers and "others" as infant care providers: Predictors of parents' well-being and marital satisfaction. *Merrill-Palmer Quarterly, 43*, 361–385.

Villemur, N. K., & Hyde, J. S. (1983). Effects of sex of defense attorney, sex of juror, and age and attractiveness of the victim on mock juror decision-making in a rape case. *Sex Roles, 9*, 879–889.

CHAPTER 21

Lillian Comas-Díaz

Photographer; Frederick M. Jacobsen.

Lillian Comas-Díaz

My life reflects a search for identity and connection. Like many working class Puerto Ricans, my parents arrived in the continental United States searching for the American dream with an empty stomach. Speaking broken English, my mother, María E. Díaz, a nurse, found work at a local hospital, while my father, Filiberto Comas, worked two factory shifts.

I was born in Chicago in 1950. I "journeyed back" to Puerto Rico in 1956. Leaving the frigid winter for the tropical Caribbean did not alleviate my adjustment crisis. I tasted culture shock at an early age, forcing me to integrate and dichotomize. Resistance, negotiation, and adaptation seasoned my identity development. Mediating the familiar with the strange, my need for belonging became intense.

My father, an only child, suffered early deprivation when his parents divorced before his birth. The combination of parental neglect, low socioeconomic status, and being a Black Puerto Rican prevented him from actualizing his enormous intelligence. Finding solace in anger and alcohol, he turned his frustration against himself and those he loved. My mother, the oldest of five, was the parental child in a family that constantly struggled with basic needs. A classic caretaker, her love and compassion could not nurse my father's condition. Never giving up hope, my parents retreated into the redemption of work. Growing up in this climate taught me significant lessons about survival, endurance, and flourishing.

I was forced to persevere. Born with a cleft palate, at age 4, I became a medical research subject at the University of Illinois Medical School as the first patient ever to undergo a radically new surgical repair. Although the operation was successful, I stammered until high school. Delving into literature for support and guidance, I found the story of Demosthenes, the Greek orator, who conquered his stammering by placing pebbles in his mouth while speaking. Consequently, I "developed" my own Caribbean speech therapy, placing small guavas in my mouth during practice, later rewarding myself by eating them after a good outcome.

My parents and my brother David, 4 years my junior, returned to Chicago shortly after our arrival in Borinquén (Puerto Rico's Taíno name). I remained with my maternal grandparents in the town of Yabucoa while my parents and brother returned to the Windy City. My father would have preferred his oldest child to be a son, but neither my brother nor I met his expectations of females and males—I was scholarly and David was artistic. Latino gender roles, although traditional, are plagued by paradoxes. For instance, my macho father, while preferring his son, encouraged my ambition. "You were born in Chicago, which means you can become president of the United States," he declared.

The pain of missing my nuclear family was overcome by the magic of being Alice in mangoland. Living with my maternal relatives soothed my wounds. Profoundly spiritual, my grandmother, Antonia Morales, was a self-directed, generous, and powerful woman. As a role model, she exuded strength, compassion and dignity. My grandfather, Juan R. Díaz, embodied the quiet power of love. Growing up with my extended family provided a sense of continuity found in an intimate community. Joining me in 1960, my nuclear family settled in a modest farm, a place where I learned to love nature.

Confined by the geography of a small island, I had to choose teachers inside as well as outside my environment. The public educational system in Puerto Rico afforded me a comprehensive humanist education, infused by Latin American, European, Caribbean, and North American influences. I voraciously read fiction and non-fiction, including history, theology, education, and political literature. Reading biographies of influential people, I adopted literary, historical, and political figures as my intellectual mentors. Looking for guidance in other people's stories gave me inspiration, courage and wisdom. Under the tutelage of female teachers, such as Luz M. Ramos, María Providencia Scott, Raquel Marrero and Laura Leticia Herrans, I was able to identify women's contributions neglected by "his-story."

At about age 6 or 7, I decided to become a psychologist. Classmates confided their problems in me and were appreciative of my "help." Being interested in humanities and science, I found in psychology a natural answer to my dilemma of whether to become a scientist or an artist.

From the late 1960s to the early 1970s, I attended the University of Puerto Rico aided by a full scholarship. During this epoch, *independentismo* (the political movement aspiring for the independence of Puerto Rico) had its unofficial headquarters at the University of Puerto Rico. Notwithstanding the university's progressive perspective, women's liberation and racial issues were relegated to the back of the bus. Puerto Rico's colonial status resulted in an identity crisis where internalized oppression—when inferiority feelings caused by oppression are accepted and projected toward peers—was rampant. One of its highest manifestations, *racismo*, branded me as a *jabá* (a pejorative racial term denoting a person with kinky hair and yellow skin). Adding insult to injury, zealous nationalists questioned individuals like me as not being Puerto Rican enough due to our continental birth. Rejected by my own, it took a very long time before I could sublimate my pain. Developing a historical and sociopolitical understanding of these dynamics helped me cope. Immersing myself in literature of people of color and reframing intra-racism as self-hate helped me integrate the contradictions caused by oppression.

Frustrated by colonial constraints, I migrated to *el norte*. Searching for the Golden Fleece in the form of a doctorate in psychology, I left my family behind. My partner, Gerald Giraud-Ríos, accompanied me in this pilgrimage in 1973. Jerry was born in New York and raised Puerto Rican. He trained as an engineer and became an artisan while rediscovering his ethnic roots on the island. I moved to Connecticut to direct a community mental health clinic for Latinos.

Armed with a master's degree in clinical psychology, I was unaware that I was entering battle. Coping with culture shock, lacking English proficiency, and deficient in racial socialization, I became an easy target for racism and sexism. As an unwilling warrior, I learned to dissociate. The biggest battle, however, took place in my heart. Ethnic, racial and gender discrimination claimed its toll. I pushed my self-esteem up the hill, but unlike Sisyphus, it was racism, and not its own weight, that caused it to fall back down.

Fortunately, I met other Puerto Rican psychologists, and founded the Puerto Rican Psychological Association of Connecticut. We became psychological guardian angels, taking a stand against discrimination through cultural awareness programs, antiracist workshops, and media presentations. As cultural warriors, we rescued our identity, cooking our grandmothers' recipes, singing Boricua ballads, and dancing salsa, while practicing Paulo Freire's (Freire, 1967, 1970) teaching on educating oppressed populations. We worked to change our mentality through awareness and critical analysis of oppression.

Because a woman of color's psychological work without a doctorate degree is invisible and silent, I enrolled at the University of Massachusetts-Amherst Clinical Psychology Department. I chose this program due to its reputation of being "student of color friendly," operationalized as recruiting and retaining a critical mass of students of color, tenuring its faculty of color, and providing financial aid to students. Another important requisite for my selection was an international presence. I desperately needed global air. Sensitive to linguistic differences, Castellano Turner, an African American professor, honored his name (Castilian Spanish) by supervising a Latino clinical team. A godsend, this group sustained our resilience and encouraged our productivity, becoming an extended family.

Like many female psychologists in that era, I was swimming in the sea of feminism. Interested in the relationship between gender and race, I explored the confluence of the Civil Rights movement and feminism. Today, I continue to be at home within feminism, albeit critically articulating its limitations with respect to women of color (Comas-Díaz, 1991).

Trying to survive psychology departmental politics, I asked Bonnie R. Strickland, an authority on depression and locus of control, to become my dissertation chairperson. Obtaining training in research and writing, I subsequently published my study on the applicability of cognitive-behavioral approaches to depressed Latinas (Comas-Díaz, 1981a) under Bonnie's direction. One of the few women presidents of the American Psychological Association, Bonnie Strickland continues to be a role model of female power, grace, and competence.

I returned to Connecticut to complete my clinical internship at Yale University. In this odyssey, I was fortunate to treasure African American psychologists: Robert Washington, Joan Duncan, and Juan Carlos Lovelace as teachers and mentors. After the internship, I secured a faculty position at the school of medicine, finding myself in the middle of a debate. A psychology faculty member objected to my appointment, labeling it *tokenism*. The assaults corroded my self-esteem. Fortunately, I had enough support from individuals in key positions and was confirmed in the job. This incident taught me important lessons about power inequality dynamics, sensitizing me to personality politics. I later discovered that the opposing professor was angry because I had dropped out of his seminar during my internship.

Plunging into my faculty position, perhaps to prove that I was not an "affirmative action baby," I delivered clinical services, conducted research, and trained psychology interns, social work students, and psychiatry residents. As the director of Yale's Hispanic Clinic, working in the areas of mental health, prevention and substance abuse rehabilitation, I was able to view my father's alcoholism through another prism.

Committed to the "personal is political" belief, I collaborated with the Puerto Rican and African American communities, facilitating women's groups, developing culturally relevant assertiveness training (Comas-Díaz & Duncan, 1985), and establishing cultural awareness programs for children of color. Based on this work, the Chi Omicron New Haven Chapter of the Omega Psi Phi Fraternity (an African American Fraternity) honored me with its Humanitarian Award in 1981.

My New Haven professional life chapter was exceptional. I was mentored by Boris Astrachan, an expert on mental health administration; Myrna Weissman, a renowned epidemiology researcher; Stephen Fleck, a superb clinician; Daniel Levinson, adult development expert; and Behnaz Jalali, an Iranian woman family therapist. Actively choosing diverse types of guides and mentors, including women and men, people of color and Whites, gays, lesbians, and heterosexuals, North Americans and other nationals, I found their world views enlightening.

My New Haven personal life chapter was devastating. I continuously struggled with racism and my personal attachments changed, including the end of my 10-year relationship with Jerry. Undergoing psychotherapy helped me to survive this period. Later on, I met and married Frederick M. Jacobsen, a union that became a full partnership both in personal and professional life. Fred, a White Anglo-Saxon Protestant psychiatrist specializing in neuropsychopharmacology, had lived in Brazil as an adolescent. Our experiences with translocation enabled us to build bridges, cementing a connection between our different cultures.

In 1984, the winds of change landed us in Washington, DC. As an interethnic couple, we felt more comfortable in a multicultural environment. While Fred completed a research fellowship at the National Institute of Mental Health, I directed the American Psychological Association Office of Ethnic Minority Affairs. Obtaining this position was a challenge. Excellent candidates made the application process highly competitive. When the selected applicant declined, I was offered the position after a long deliberation. I later learned that one of my interviewers felt that my Spanish accent was a hindrance—a perplexing reason, given that the job required an ethnic minority person. Moreover, this concern seemed ironic to me, given that the American Psychological Association's headquarters were situated in multi-accented, cosmopolitan, Washington, DC.

The APA expedition bathed me in the formidable rivers of organized psychology, sharpening my skills as a manager. In 1985, I joined a delegation investigating human right abuses and their mental health implications in Chile. Sponsored by both the American Psychological Association and the American Psychiatric Association, delegation members interviewed torture victims and their families (Padilla & Comas-Díaz, 1986), worked with clinicians attempting to repair the effects of repression (Comas-Díaz & Padilla, 1990), and emerged as transformed individuals.

Another journey resulted in full-time private practice and the founding of the Transcultural Mental Health Institute with Fred. After several years of administration, I had begun to miss clinical practice. Since 1986, we have offered clinical and consultative services to culturally diverse populations in the greater Washington, DC area. Additionally, we co-teach cross-cultural mental health within our responsibilities as clinical professors at the George Washington Department of Psychiatry and Behavioral Sciences. In 1995, I became the founding editor of an interdisciplinary journal, *Cultural Diversity and Mental Health*, which was later acquired by the APA Division 45, The Society for the Psychological Study of Ethnic Minority Issues. Division 45 named *Cultural Diversity and Ethnic Minority Psychology* its official journal, and I was asked to continue as editor-in-chief.

Having a strong work ethic, my professional efforts concentrate on scholarly, organizational, and social justice areas. Three themes organize my scholarship; namely, ethnic minority and cross-cultural mental health, women's issues and feminism, and social justice and international psychology. Integrating these topics, I gained new insights, regarding feminist therapy with women of color (Comas-Díaz, 1991, 1994) and women's resistance to violence in underdeveloped countries (Comas-Díaz & Jansen, 1995).

I am committed to delivering competent services to culturally diverse populations. In this vein, I have published articles on treatment for Latinos (Comas-Díaz, 1989, 1990), effective cross-cultural evaluations (Comas-Díaz, 1996; Comas-Díaz & Ramos Grenier, 1998), special populations, such as borderline clients (Comas-Díaz & Minrath, 1985), substance abusers (Comas-Díaz, 1986), victims of sexual abuse (Comas-Díaz, 1995), and professionals of color (Comas-Díaz, 1997; Comas-Díaz & Greene, 1994b). Additionally, I have examined the relationship between indigenous healing systems and traditional psychotherapies (Comas-Díaz, 1981b; 1991).

My work has promoted ethnocultural approaches to mental health by incorporating diversity variables into psychological interventions. Within this model, Fred and I (Comas-Díaz & Jacobsen, 1987) developed the Ethnocultural Assessment, a process-oriented clinical approach to explore factors that contribute to individuals' identity formation as they experience translocation. We also introduced the concept of "ethnocultural identification" to help the integration of identity (Comas-Díaz, & Jacobsen, 1987; Comas-Díaz & Griffith, 1988). Elaborating this concept, we extended it to ethnocultural transference and countertransference reactions between the client and the therapist (Comas-Díaz, & Jacobsen, 1991). By attending to ethnic, racial, and cultural factors among inter- and intra-ethnic dyads, we delineated their influence on the therapeutic process and outcome. We have also applied this model to the therapist of color and White client dyad (Comas-Díaz & Jacobsen, 1995a), and our ethnoculturally-based psychotherapy has been highlighted in an APA educational psychotherapy video, where I demonstrated this approach during a therapy session (APA, 1995).

Exploring the intersection of diverse variables in the lives of women of color, I published my work on *LatiNegra*, examining the unique realities of women who are both Latinas and African Americans (Comas-Díaz, 1994). Emphasizing the gender and race interaction has been fruitful. My award-winning edited book, *Women of Color: Integrating Ethnic and Gender Identities in Psychotherapy* (Comas-Díaz & Greene, 1994a) precipitated a paradigmatic shift in the field (Reid & Bing, 1996; Sanchez-Hucles, 1995; Tatum, 1995). The collaboration with Fred examined psychopharmacology for women of color (Comas-Díaz & Jacobsen, 1995b; Jacobsen & Comas-Díaz, 1999) stressing the biology, psychology, and culture connections. Disciplines other than psychology have recognized the integrative aspect of my work. The family therapy field published an interview discussing my views on feminist therapy, underscoring the relevance of cultural, historical, political, and societal domains (McGraw, 1998).

I found a nexus between psychology and political repression in the field of ethnopolitical psychology. Viewing colonization as a special type of oppression, I envisioned psychology as promoting empowerment, liberation, and healing (Comas-Díaz, 1994, Comas-Díaz & Griffith, 1988; Comas-Díaz, Lykes, & Alarcón, 1998). In addition to my human rights investigations, I have been a member of mental health delegations to the former Soviet Union, Eastern Europe (Comas-Díaz, 1993), South Africa, (Comas-Díaz & Jacobsen, 1996), India, and Nepal and have contributed to the American Psychological Association/Canadian Psychological Association Initiative on ethnopolitical warfare.

Involved in organized psychology, I have participated in numerous APA governmental groups, along with other mental health organization boards such as the American Orthopsychiatry Association and the American Society for Hispanic Psychiatrists. I am very fortunate that my work has been recognized through several awards. Some of these include the American Psychological Association Distinguished Contributions to Psychology in the Public Interest (Senior Career Award); the American Psychological Association Committee on Women Leadership Award; the American Association of Applied and Preventive Psychology Distinguished Humanitarian Award; the Frantz Fanon Award from the Postgraduate Center for Mental Health; the Association for

Women in Psychology Distinguished Publication Award; the American Family Therapy Academy Cultural and Economic Diversity Award; and the American Psychological Association Psychology of Women Heritage Award for services to the profession.

I know the burdens and gifts of the wounded healer. Although pain can be sublimated into healing, it can only be done after facing our demons. Searching for who I am while making sense out of dislocation, I have been fortunate to alchemize adversity into opportunity. As an illustration, my speech problems fostered a gift for storytelling, while socioeconomic barriers ignited my drive for achievement. When in my 20s in Puerto Rico, I was rejected for a fellowship that would have allowed me to complete graduate work in psychology on the mainland. I was shattered because I had no financial means to accomplish my goal. At first, emotionally devastated, I subsequently realized that merit had little to do with a selection process marked by classist favoritism. Eventually, I moved to the continent to work with inner city communities, an experience that significantly contributed to my efficacy as a psychologist of color.

Breaking hard shells to savor Caribbean coconuts taught me determination. The process of publishing my dissertation in a highly reputable journal, however, tested my perseverance. When my paper was accepted as a brief report, many congratulated my achievement. Nonetheless, after completing 13 revisions under Bonnie Strickland's relentless supervision, I felt that the study deserved to be published as a full article. I contacted the editor and requested reconsideration. The editor reversed his decision after listening to my reasons and published the study as a regular research article.

Like Jawaharlal Nehru, I see life as a game of cards where the hand you are dealt represents fate and the way you play it is free will. I temper hope with realism, achievement with stamina. Growing up in a developing country made me realize that as a woman, I can not have it all. Early on, I decided against having biological children. The trajectory of this decision, published in a book, *Pride and Joy: The Lives and Passions of Women without Children* (Cassey, 1998), highlights the broadening of my parenting through practice, teaching, and mentoring. The book offers inspiration to those struggling with the decision not to have children, by presenting biographies of women who feel self-realized with their choice.

Longing for connection I found conviviality; searching for identity, I uncovered meaning. I created my life with Fred around work and play, including books, music, art, films, and travel. As windows to other realities, these self-care activities restore and fulfill. Treasuring creative expression, we collect Hispanic, Native American and African art. For us, flow emerges in the continuation of the personal into the professional. Art reenergizes my clinical work, which nurtures my scholarship, and in turn, enhances my humanity.

Like Eleanor Roosevelt, I realize that somehow we need to learn who we really are and then live with that decision. Emphasizing journey over destination, I reach adult developmental ports accepting what I have accumulated. Cascading from personal, family, and ancestral narratives, my life is an installment of my mother's tale, while her story is a chapter in a collective Puerto Rican novella. As to my identity search, I resonate with Chita Rivera's words: "I am a reflection of everyone who has passed though my life." I hope my story touches your life in a reflection that pleases you.

REFERENCES

American Psychological Association Psychotherapy videotape series (1995). *Ethnocultural psychotherapy.* Washington, DC: APA.

Cassey, T. (1998). Joy and pride: *The lives and passions of women without children.* Hillsboro, Oregon: Beyond Words Publishers.

Comas-Díaz, L. (1981a). Effects of cognitive and behavioral group treatment in the depressive symptomatology of Puerto Rican women. *Journal of Consulting and Clinical Psychology, 49*(5), 627–632.

Comas-Díaz, L. (1981b). Puerto Rican *espiritismo* and psychotherapy. *American Journal of Orthopsychiatry, 51*(4), 636–645.

Comas-Díaz, L. (1986). Puerto Rican alcoholic women: Treatment considerations. *Alcoholism Treatment Quarterly, 3*(1), 47–57.

Comas-Díaz, L. (1989). Culturally relevant issues and treatment implications for Hispanics. In D. R. Koslow and E. Salett, (Eds.), *Crossing cultures in mental health* (pp. 31–48). Washington, DC: Society for International Education Training and Research (SIETAR).

Comas-Díaz, L. (1990). Hispanic/Latino communities: Psychological implications. *The Journal of Training & Practice in Professional Psychology, 4*(1), 14–35.

Comas-Díaz, L. (1991). Feminism and diversity in psychology: The case of women of color. *Psychology of Women Quarterly, 15,* 597–609.

Comas-Díaz, L. (1993). Eastern Europe begins to recognize women's mental health issues. *Psychology International, 4,* 5–8.

Comas-Díaz, L. (1994). LatiNegra: Mental health issues of African Latinas. *Journal of Feminist Family Therapy, 5,* 35–74.

Comas-Díaz, L. (1995). Puerto Ricans and sexual child abuse. In L. Fontes (Ed.) *Sexual abuse in nine North American cultures* (pp. 31–66). Thousand Oaks, CA: Sage.

Comas-Díaz, L. (1996). Cultural considerations in diagnosis. In F. Kaslow (Ed.), *Handbook of relational diagnosis and dysfunctional family patterns* (pp. 152–168). New York: Wiley.

Comas-Díaz, L. (1997). Mental health needs of Latinos with professional status. In J. García & M. C. Zea (Eds.) *Psychological interventions and research with Latino populations* (pp 142–165). New York: Allyn & Bacon.

Comas-Díaz, L., & Duncan, J.W. (1985). The cultural context: A factor in assertiveness training with mainland Puerto Rican women. *Psychology of Women Quarterly, 9*(4), 463–475.
Comas-Díaz, L., & Greene, B. (Eds.). (1994a). *Women of Color: Integrating ethnic and gender identities in psychotherapy.* New York: Guilford Press.
Comas-Díaz, L., & Greene, B. (1994b). Women of color with professional status. In L. Comas-Díaz & B. Greene (Eds.). *Women of color: Integrating ethnic and gender identities in psychotherapy* (pp. 347–388). New York: Guilford Press.
Comas-Díaz, L., & Griffith, E. H. E. (Eds.) (1988). *Clinical guidelines in cross cultural mental health.* New York: Wiley.
Comas-Díaz, L., & Jacobsen, F. M. (1987). Ethnocultural identification in psychotherapy. *Psychiatry, 50*(3), 232–241.
Comas-Díaz, L., & Jacobsen, F. M. (1991). Ethnocultural transference and countertransference in the therapeutic dyad. *American Journal of Orthopsychiatry, 61*(3), 392–402.
Comas-Díaz, L., & Jacobsen, F. (1995a). The therapist of color and the White patient dyad: Contradictions and recognitions. *Cultural Diversity and Mental Health, 1,* 93–106.
Comas-Díaz, L., & Jacobsen, F.M. (1995b). Women of color and psychopharmacology: An empowering perspective. *Women & Therapy, 16,* 85–112.
Comas-Díaz, L., & Jacobsen, F.M. (1996). Politics and South African mental health: Truth, hope and reconciliation. *Cultural Diversity and Mental Health, 2*(2), 133–138.
Comas-Díaz, L., & Jansen, M. A. (1995). Global conflict and violence against women. *Peace and Conflict: Journal of Peace Psychology. 1*(4), 315–331.
Comas-Díaz, L., Lykes, B. & Alarcón, R. (1998). Ethnic conflict and psychology of liberation in Guatemala, Perú and Puerto Rico. *American Psychologist, 53*(7), 778–792.
Comas-Díaz, L., & Minrath, M. (1985). Psychotherapy with ethnic minority borderline clients. *Psychotherapy: Theory, Research and Practice, 22*(2), 418–426.
Comas-Díaz, L., & Padilla, A. (1990). Countertransference in working with victims of political repression. *American Journal of Orthopsychiatry, 60*(1), 125–134.
Comas-Díaz, L., & Ramos-Grenier, J. (1998). Migration and acculturation. In J. Sandoval, C. L. Frisby, K. F. Geisinger, J. D. Scheuneman & J. Ramos-Grenier (Eds.), *Test interpretations and diversity: Achieving equity in assessment* (pp. 213–239) Washington, DC: American Psychological Association.
Cook, J. (Ed.). (1997). *The book of positive quotations.* Minneapolis: Fairview Press.
Freire, P. (1967). *Educação como prática da liberdade.* [Education as a practice of freedom]. Rio de Janeiro: Paz e Terra.
Freire, P. (1970). *Pedagogy of the oppressed.* New York: The Seabury Press.
Jacobsen, F. M., & Comas-Díaz, L. (1999). Psychopharmacologic treatment of Latinas. *Essential Psychopharmacology, 3*(1), 29–42.
McGraw, S. (1998). An interview with Lillian Comas-Díaz. *Journal of Feminist Family Therapy, 10,* 113–129

Padilla, A., & Comas-Díaz, L. (1986, November). A state of fear. *Psychology Today, 20*(11), 60–65.
Reid, P. T. & Bing, V. (1996). Women and the psychotherapeutic "color line". Review of Women of color: Integrating ethnic and gender identities in psychotherapies. *Contemporary Psychology, 41*(1), 19–20.
Sanchez-Hucles, J. (1995). Reweaving the tapestry: Embodying the lives of women of color. Book Review of Women of color: Integrating ethnic and gender identities in psychotherapy. *Psychology of Women Quarterly, 19*, 287–297.
Tantum, B. D. (1995). Review of Women of color: Integrating ethnic and gender identities in psychotherapy. *Women & Therapy, 12*(2), 111–112.

REPRESENTATIVE PUBLICATIONS

Comas-Díaz, L. (1982). Mental health needs of Puerto Rican women in the United States. In R. Zambrana (Ed.), *Latina women in transition* (pp. 1–10). New York: Hispanic Research Center, Fordham University.
Comas-Díaz, L. (1984). Content themes in group treatment with Puerto Rican women. *Social Work with Groups, 7*(3), 75–84.
Comas-Díaz, L. (1985). Cognitive and behavioral group therapy with Puerto Rican women: A comparison of content themes. *Hispanic Journal of Behavioral Sciences, 7*(3), 273-283.
Comas-Díaz, L. (1985, Winter). Puerto Rican women, sex roles, and mental health. *Intercambios Femeniles, 2*(4), 5–6.
Comas-Díaz, L. (1987). Feminist therapy with Hispanic/Latina women: Myth or reality? *Women & Therapy, 6*(4), 39–61.
Comas-Díaz, L. (1987). Feminist therapy with Puerto Rican women. *Psychology of Women Quarterly, 11*(4), 461–474.
Comas-Díaz, L (1988). Cross-cultural mental health treatment. In L. Comas-Díaz, & E. H. Griffith (Eds.), *Clinical guidelines in cross-cultural mental health* (pp. 337–361) New York: Wiley.
Comas-Díaz, L.(1988). Mainland Puerto Rican women: A sociocultural approach. *Journal of Community Psychology, 16*(1), 21–31.
Comas-Díaz, L. (1989). Puerto Rican women's cross-cultural transitions:
Developmental and clinical implications. In C. García Coll & M. Mattei (Eds), *The Puerto Rican woman: A psychosocial approach to lifespan developmental issues* (pp. 166–199). New York: Praeger Publishers.
Comas-Díaz, L. (1990). Ethnic minority mental health: Contributions and future directions of the American Psychological Association. In F. C. Serafica, A. I. Schwebel, R. K. Russel, P. D. Issac, & L. B. Myers (Eds.), *Mental health of ethnic minorities* (pp. 275–301). New York: Praeger.
Comas-Díaz, L. (1990). Independent practice and the delivery of services to ethnic minorities: An emerging trend. *The Independent Practitioner, 10*(3), 42–47.
Comas-Díaz, L. (1992). The future of psychotherapy with ethnic minorities. *Psychotherapy, 29*, 88–94.
Comas-Díaz, L. (1993). Diversifying clinical psychology. *The Clinical Psychologist, 46*, 5–9.

Comas-Díaz, L. (1994). An integrative approach. In L. Comas-Díaz & B. Greene (Eds.). *Women of color: Integrating ethnic and gender identities in psychotherapy* (pp. 287–318). New York: Guilford.

Comas-Díaz, L. (1994). Women of color in family therapy: Reconstructing their lives. *The Family Psychologist, 10*(2), 22, 27.

Comas-Díaz, L. (1998). Ethnic minority psychology: Identity, empowerment and transformation. *Cultural Diversity and Mental Health, 4*(3), 151–152.

Comas-Díaz, L. (1999). People of color as America's metaphor: On contact, rebirth, and evolution. *Cultural Diversity & Ethnic Minority Psychology, 5*(1), 3–5.

Comas-Díaz, L., Arroyo, A., & Lovelace, J. C. (1982). Enriching self-concept through a Puerto Rican cultural awareness program. *Personnel and Guidance Journal, 60*(5), 306–308.

Comas-Díaz, L., & Griffith, E. H. (Eds.). (1988). *Clinical guidelines in cross-cultural mental health.* New York: Wiley.

Comas-Díaz, L., & Padilla, A. M. (1992). The English-only movement: Implications for mental health. *American Journal of Orthopsychiatry, 62*(1), 6.

Comas-Díaz, L., & Stricker, G. (Eds.). (1993). Diversity in clinical psychology: Theory, research and practice [Special issue]. *The Clinical Psychologist, 46*(2).

Jacobsen, F. M., & Comas-Díaz, L. (1999). Donepezil for psychotropic-induced memory loss. *Journal of Clinical Psychiatry, 60,* 698–704.

Mays, V., & Comas-Díaz, L. (1988). Feminist therapies with ethnic minority populations: A closer look at Blacks and Hispanics. In M. A. Dutton-Douglas & L. E. Walker (Eds.), *Feminist psychotherapies: Integration of therapeutic and feminist systems* (pp. 228–251). NJ: Ablex Publishing Corp.

Padilla, A.M., & Comas-Díaz, L (1987). Miedo y represión en Chile [Fear and repression in Chile]. *Revista Latinoamericana de Psicologia, 19*(2), 135–146.

Ramos-McKay, J., Comas-Díaz, L., & Rivera, L. (1988). Puerto Ricans. In L. Comas-Díaz & E. H. Griffith (Eds), *Clinical guidelines in cross cultural mental health* (pp. 204–232). New York: Wiley.

Reid, P., & Comas-Díaz, L. (1990). Gender and ethnicity: Perspectives on dual status. *Sex Roles, 22*(7/8), 397–408.

PART IV

ACHIEVEMENT PATTERNS IN THE 20TH CENTURY

CHAPTER 22

Profiles and Patterns of Achievement

Profiles and Patterns of Achievement for 53 Eminent Women: Synthesis and Resynthesis 3

Agnes N. O'Connell

If knowledge is power, then the more knowledge we have about the "possessions" of eminent women, the more power we have available to us. With that equation in mind and in the search for insights, a multidimensional analytic strategy is essential. The structure of our knowledge about eminent women in psychology can be analyzed on several levels (O'Connell, 1983, 1988; Runyan, 1984): the universal level, for all women; the group level, for women in psychology; and the individual level, for particular individuals. In essence, to paraphrase Kluckhohn and Murray (1953), every woman is in certain respects like all other women, like some other women, and like no other woman (p. 53). These three levels of analysis are semi-independent (Runyan, 1981) and are found in this volume.

The autobiographies address the individual level of analysis presenting the complex reality of the varied demographics, experiences, and accomplishments of these distinguished women and the major influences on their lives. Chapter 2, "A Century of Contrasts," speaks of the historical and social contexts of the 20th century when these women were born, educated, and pursued a major part of their personal and professional lives. The present chapter delineates the group level of analyses, providing a synthesis of the similarities and differences in the personal and professional lives and achievements of these women. In addition, this chapter selectively analyzes and integrates parts of the earlier two volumes in a resynthesis of all three volumes to examine transhistoric and time-specific trends and patterns in the 20th century.

The eminent women were provided with the same detailed guidelines for writing their autobiographical chapters, yet each of the chapters is unique, revealing individual style, approach, and content. The database for these analyses and synthesis are: (a) the autobiographies; (b) the completed O'Connell Biographical Information Forms—Version E3; and (c) the authors' curriculum vitae. Through study of these sources, multiple variables and their interrelationships were identified. After several readings of the materials and the establishing of categories, content analyses were undertaken. The number of variables and analyses in this volume exceeds those in the first two volumes. Selective data from the earlier volumes are used in conjunction with the data in this volume to gain insights into trends and patterns for a total of 53 eminent women, the first study of the lives and careers of 53 eminent women.

These women are a sample of the many outstanding women in psychology whose accomplishments and achievements are truly remarkable. The contents of this volume and the analyses contained therein illuminate lives, experiences, and achievements from universal, group, and individual perspectives across the 20th century.

DEVELOPMENTAL INFLUENCES: FAMILIES OF ORIGIN

In the search for knowledge about the developmental context for these eminent women, we begin with their birth order and their families of origin. Eighteen of the 19 women in this book were born in a 19-year period beginning in 1932. Ten were born in the 1930s: Patricia M. Bricklin, Frances Degen Horowitz, Norine G. Johnson, Sandra Scarr, Dorothy W. Cantor, Diane J. Willis, Elaine Hatfield, Phyllis A. Katz,

Linda M. Bartoshuk, and Patricia Keith-Spiegel. Eight were born between 1941 and 1950: Kay Deaux, Judith E. N. Albino, Margaret W. Matlin, Pamela Trotman Reid, Jeanne Brooks-Gunn, Diane F. Halpern, Janet Shibley Hyde, and Lillian Comas-Díaz. Frances M. Culbertson was born in 1921. Sixteen of the 17 women in Volume 2 were born between 1906 and 1936; Lois Stolz was born in 1891. All 17 women in Volume 1 were born between 1897 and 1922. Thus, 50 of the 53 women were born in the first half of the 20th century; three were born in the last years of the 19th century, but were educated and pursued their careers in the 20th century.

The women in the present volume were born in various regions of the United States: the East, Northeast, Midwest, South, Southwest, and West; from New York City to Glendale, California; from Boston, Massachusetts to Jackson, Tennessee. Of the 53 women in the three volumes, 48 were born in the United States; five were born elsewhere (Canada, England, Germany, Russia, and South Africa).

These distinguished women have other commonalities with the women in the first two volumes of *Models of Achievement*. Firstborns are overrepresented. Fifteen (79%) of the 19 women in this volume are firstborns, including five only children. In addition, 3 (16%) (Frances Culbertson, Linda Bartoshuk, and Diane Halpern) were born after an interval of 5 or more years and therefore were likely to have benefited from the parenting and privileges generally reserved for firstborn children (Mellilo, 1983). Combining the women in all three volumes, 70% (37) of the 53 women are firstborn or only children. Another 13% (7) were born after a 5-year interval. The data clearly demonstrate a significant positive relationship between high achievement and birth order for these eminent women and support my earlier findings and that of other researchers on the importance of birth order for achieving eminence (O'Connell, 1983, 1988; Simonton, 1987).

Contrary to Hennig and Jardim's (1977) findings on executive corporate women, the collective experiences of these eminent psychologists do not support a relationship between achievement and lack of a male sibling. Although 5 had no siblings, 14 did (Table 22.1). Eight of the women with siblings had one or more brothers; of these three had no sisters. Ten had 1 or more sisters; of these, 6 had no brothers, 4 had both brothers and sisters, and 5 were only children. For the total of 53 models of achievement, 29 had one or more brothers, 29 had 1 or more sisters, 14 had both sisters and brothers, and 9 were only children. The mere presence or absence of a brother or a sister does not seem to have had a significant impact on achievement (O'Connell, 1988).

If the seeds of achievement "are sown within families of orientation" (Featherman, 1978, pp. 2-3), then the occupational choices of the siblings of these eminent women are noteworthy. The living siblings of the

TABLE 22.1
Demographic Variables of Eminent Women in Psychology

Families of Origin

Eminent Woman & Date of Birth	Place of Birth	Birth Order	Siblings[a]	Father's Occupation	Mother's Occupation
F. M. Culbertson January 31, 1921	Boston, MA	3	BBW	Tailor	Homemaker
P. M. Bricklin February 28, 1932	Las Animas, CO	1	W	U.S. Army officer Business	Caseworker
F. D. Horowitz May 5, 1932	Bronx, NY	1	W/S	Clothing manufacturer	Homemaker
N. G. Johnson	Indianapolis, IN	1	W/B	Dentist	Teacher
S. Scarr August 8, 1936	Washington, DC	1	WS	Physician	Teacher Homemaker
D. W. Cantor March 17, 1937	New York, NY	1	W	Lawyer	Teacher
D. J. Willis May 9, 1937	Tahlequah, OK	1	WSSBSBB	Teacher Merchant Real estate broker Oklahoma Legislator	Small business owner/clothing Homemaker
E. Hatfield October 22, 1937	Detroit, MI	1	W/SS	Policeman	Homemaker

P. A. Katz April 9, 1938	New York, NY	1	W	Factory foreman	Homemaker
L. M. Bartoshuk November 27, 1938	Aberdeen, SD	2	BW	Maintenance foreman	Homemaker
P. Keith-Spiegel March 16, 1939	Glendale, CA	1	WS	Unknown	Teacher
K. Deaux November 4, 1941	Warren, OH	1	W	White collar position	Homemaker
J. E. N. Albino June 2, 1943	Jackson, TN	2	BWS	Small business owner/grocer	Homemaker Teacher/Counselor
M. W. Matlin November 14, 1944	Washington, DC	1	WSS	Geologist	Teacher
P. T. Reid June 1, 1946	Bronx, NY	1	WSS	Insurance broker	Real estate broker
J. Brooks-Gunn December 9, 1946	Bethesda, MD	1	WBSS	Home builder/land developer	Teacher/Counselor

continued on next page

TABLE 22.1
(continued)

Eminent Woman & Date of Birth	Place of Birth	Birth Order	Siblings[a]	Father's Occupation	Mother's Occupation
D. F. Halpern May 31, 1947	Philadelphia, PA	4	BSSW	Sales	Homemaker
J. S. Hyde August 17, 1948	Akron, OH	1	W	Teacher Safety engineer	Piano teacher
L. Comaz-Díaz July 18, 1950	Chicago, IL	1	WB	Taxi driver	Nurse

[a]W = eminent woman, S = sister, B = brother

Note. N. G. Johnson's date of birth is omitted at her request.

350

women in this volume and in Volume 2 predominantly are in occupations that require advanced education; they are teachers, attorneys, engineers, professors, psychologists, social workers, company presidents, business managers, entrepreneurs, physicians, physicists, dentists, accountants, nurses, and academic counselors. These occupational choices may reflect parental values, support, and encouragement toward academic and career achievement.

Many women recall that they received much encouragement toward education and achievement in a nurturing environment. "Education was of prime importance in my family. And educating women was valued" (Norine G. Johnson). "I grew up in a family that valued education" (Margaret W. Matlin). "College education was always a goal that my parents held for me and saved their money to achieve" (Kay Deaux). "[My father] valued my intellectual accomplishments, and always preached the importance of excellence" (Phyllis A. Katz). "My father wanted a career for me in science" (Janet Shibley Hyde). "My mother inspired me and instilled in me a determination to pursue my education and my chosen work" and "My mother repeatedly assured me that I could be anything I wanted" (Judith E. N. Albino). "My mother encouraged high achievement aspirations; she would not say 'if you go to college,' she always said, 'when you go to college'" (Pamela Trotman Reid).

Some of the women came from problematic backgrounds that are difficult to identify in terms of parental occupation, education, attitudes, or financial situation as especially nurturant of high achievement. In fact, several write of the considerable difficulties they encountered in this regard. "And in my family, there was never any question upon graduation [from high school] I would go to work, even though my brothers were directed toward a college education" (Frances M. Culbertson). "My mother had died when I was eight, after a horrendous battle with breast cancer, and I had been living on my own since I was 15. At times, home was rat-infested slum housing. Thankfully, a friend's mother opened her home to me so that I could complete high school" (Diane F. Halpern). Some of the women received double messages, "'You can be whatever you choose' but also 'Be whatever the role for women prescribes'" (Patricia M. Bricklin) or clearly negative messages, "My father often reminded me that 'career women' were a detestable lot—hard, cold, and lonely, and that college was only for rich males" (Halpern) and "My mother was strongly against graduate degrees for women stating firmly that it would reduce my chances to marry by a significant degree" (Bricklin). The developmental environment created by the family of origin taught "significant lessons about survival, endurance, and flourishing" (Lillian Comas-Díaz).

Parental loss prior to chronological and functional adulthood was a factor in the lives of 26% of the 19 women. Exceptional achievement and creativity do not always emerge from the most nurturant environments. In some instances, exposure to diversifying and challenging experiences helps strengthen the ability to persevere in the face of obstacles (Simonton, 1994, 2000). Patricia Bricklin never knew her father who died of war injuries; Diane Halpern lost her mother at age 8; Judith Albino's father died when she was 12 years-old; Phyllis Katz lost her father as a sophomore in college; Linda Bartoshuk lost her father to lung cancer in her junior year of college.

In Anne Roe's (1952) study of eminent contemporary male scientists, 26% lost a parent by death before attaining adulthood. Coincidentally, that is the exact same percentage as in the present study of 19 eminent women psychologists. These proportions are well above the expected incidence in the general population (Simonton, 1987). Despite greater life expectancy as the 20th century progressed, the percentages for loss of a parent before chronological and functioning adulthood for eminent women increased with each volume. In Volumes 1 and 2, the percentages are 6% and 18%, respectively. It is possible that the loss of a parent before adulthood and the developmental consequences of this loss produce a coping mechanism that, under favorable circumstances, lead to strong achievement motivation and a high probability of distinction (Eisenstadt, 1978; Simonton, 1987) and that this distinction was facilitated by a more accepting environment for women and achievement as the century progressed.

Table 22.1 shows the occupations of the fathers and mothers of these eminent women. Eight (42%) of the fathers and 10 (53%) of the mothers can be identified as professionals. An additional 3 (16%) of the fathers and 1 (5%) of the mothers are engaged in business or entrepreneurial endeavors. For this group of women, there is a continuing decrease in percentage of fathers engaged in professional, business leadership, or entrepreneurial positions, 58% vs. 65% in Volume 2 and 88% in Volume 1. The percentage of mothers so engaged does not reveal a continuous pattern, 58% vs. 65% in Volume 2 and 47% in Volume 1. For the first time, an equal percentage of mothers and fathers could be identified as professionals or entrepreneurs, and for the first time, the percentage of mothers who graduated from college or professional school was greater than the percentage of fathers: 53% vs. 42% in contrast to 24% vs. 42% in Volume 2. In this volume, 63% of the women had one or more parents with college or professional education; 58% of the women had one or more parents with a high school education or less; 26% vs. 29% of the women in Volume 2 had one or more parents with education that ranged from none to some high school.

Regardless of occupational and educational attainments of parents, the eminent daughters surpassed their mothers' (and with four exceptions, their fathers') educational attainments by earning a doctorate. The exceptions were Cantor, Johnson, Matlin, and Scarr, whose fathers were an attorney, a dentist, a PhD geologist, and a physician. This finding on educational and occupational attainment is similar to the findings of the first two volumes in which one woman, Mary Henle, did not surpass her mother, and four women, Katharine Banham, Mamie Clark, Erika Fromm, and Margaret Ives, did not surpass their fathers, all five of whom were physicians.

The mothers of these eminent women had an average of 2.47 children, with a range from 1 to 7 children. Most (11, or 58%) of the mothers had 2 or 3 children each, 5 had one child each, 2 had 4 children, and one had seven children. Of their married eminent daughters, 83% became mothers including those through adoption. The comparable percentages for Volumes 1 and 2, 29% and 53% respectively, show a substantial increase in those who became mothers with each succeeding group of eminent women. These ascending percentages may reflect a more accepting social context for the integration of motherhood and career achievement as the century progressed.

LIFE-SPAN DEVELOPMENT: MARITAL PATTERNS

These 19 eminent women made several choices regarding marital pattern. One remained single; 3 married and remained childless; 15 married and became parents. Ninety-five percent of the women in this volume married at sometime during their lives (Table 22.2) in contrast to 88% in Volume 2, 76% in Volume 1, and 42% of 22 "first generation American women psychologists" born between 1847 and 1878 (Furumoto & Scarborough, 1986). The significant increase in married women in psychology over time in the 19th and 20th centuries clearly reflects the historical and social context. The greater acceptance of women as professionals is related to the increased occurrence of marriage for educated women. The married percentage (95%) found in the present group essentially replicates the percentage (94%) for women in the general population (SAUS, 1986).

For the present group, the age at first marriage averaged 23.6 years and ranged from 20 years (Cantor, Halpern, Hyde, Reid, and Scarr) to 33 years (Comas-Díaz); median age at first marriage was approximately 23 years. There was a continuing decrease in the median age at first marriage from the two earlier volumes, 27 years in Volume 1, 25 years in Volume 2. For women in the general population, the median age at first marriage was 23 years in 1985 (SAUS, 1986), the same as the median age in the present sample of eminent women. The vast ma-

TABLE 22.2
Demographic Variables of Eminent Women in Psychology

Marital Patterns

Eminent Women	Age at First Marriage	Marital Status	Husband's Occupation	Age at first child	Children
F. M. Culbertson	26	Married	Professor of Economics	30	1 son 3 daughters
P. M. Bricklin	25	Married	Clinical Psychologist	28	2 sons 2 daughters
F. D. Horowitz	21	Married	Professor of English (retired)	27	2 sons
S. Scarr	20	Divorced Divorced Divorced	Sociologist Psychologist Physician	26	1 son 3 daughters
D. W. Cantor	20	Married	Stockbroker	22	1 son 1 daughter
D. J. Willis		Single			None
E. Hatfield	25	Divorced Married	Statistician Historian		None
P. A. Katz	23	Married	Attorney/Business	26	1 son 1 daughter
L. M. Bartoshuk	23	Divorced Married	Psychologist Physicist	32	1 son 1 daughter
P. Keith-Spiegel	26	Divorced Married	Psychologist Businessman	32	1 son (adopted)

K. Deaux	24	Divorced Married	Psychologist Psychologist	None
J. E. N. Albino	29	Married	Army Officer/ Public administrator	2 sons
M. W. Matlin	22	Married	Physician/Pediatrician	32	2 daughters
P. T. Reid	20	Married	University Administrator/President	24	1 daughter 1 son
J. Brooks-Gunn	24	Married	President/Consultant	23	1 son (adopted)
D. F. Halpern	20	Married	Attorney	43	1 son 1 daughter (both adopted)
J. S. Hyde	20	Widowed Married	Episcopal priest Professor	24	1 daughter 1 son
L. Comas-Díaz	33	Married	Physician/ Neuropsycho-pharmacologist	29	None

Note. N. G. Johnson's data omitted at her request.

jority of women continued to marry in the last decade of the 20th century although at older ages—a median age approaching 25 years for women (U.S. Bureau of the Census, 1995). The postponement of first marriage in the general population can be related to increased societal acceptance of cohabitation. It can also be related to educated, career-minded lifestyles and societal acceptance of women as professionals tempering the extent of the delay (O'Connell, 1988).

Whether or not marriage is postponed, more eminent women, like others in the general population, married than remained single. Eighteen of the 19 women married, versus 13 of 17 and 15 of 17 women in Volumes 1 and 2. In the present volume, 11 who married are still married to their first husbands; 1 is divorced, 6 who were divorced are remarried, and 1 who was widowed is remarried. Of the 16 marriages before the doctorate, 5 ended in divorce, 1 in death. The one marriage after the doctorate continues. The mean length of marriage was 28.3 years with a range from 3 years to 53 years. Although these women were about as likely to marry, they were less likely to divorce and the mean duration of their marriages is much longer than the marriages of women in the general population. Both marriage and divorce can act as modifiers of career plans and goals, but there is little or no evidence that either was detrimental to long-range career achievement for these eminent women.

LIFE-SPAN CHOICES: MARITAL PARTNERS

The marital partners that the women chose as first husbands, like the husbands of the women in the first two volumes, were predominantly professionals. There were 4 psychologists, 2 physicians, 2 professors, 2 attorneys, 1 university president, 1 sociologist, 1 stockbroker, 1 president/consultant, 1 Episcopal priest, 1 businessman, 1 army officer/public administrator, and 1 statistician. These marriages to a large degree were marriages of professional couples that combined the multiple roles of career, marriage, and childrearing.

For the women who were married and childless or single (21%), there was greater flexibility in educational and career choices and in choosing a continuous career pattern. Educational and career patterns were affected by a great number of variables, including relocating with a spouse (Albino, Brooks-Gunn, Culbertson, Johnson, Horowitz, Katz, Matlin, Reid, and Scarr) or not relocating because of a spouse's career (Halpern). In some instances, husbands relocated with their wives for educational or career opportunities (Albino, Brooks-Gunn, and Hyde).

Husbands generally were very supportive, providing encouragement and new possibilities. Margaret Matlin writes, "Once again, Arnie

Agnes N. O'Connell

had tremendous faith in my abilities, and he encouraged me to go ahead with both books, especially because I had a one-semester sabbatical."

The person one marries clearly has a great influence on personal and professional lifestyle. Of the 46 eminent women who married, 33% married psychologists in a first or subsequent marriage; 67% married men from other fields. Being married to another psychologist brings with it the camaraderie, shared understanding, and informal learning that make such partnerships stimulating and rewarding. In productivity (number of articles published, papers presented at conventions, books published, or grants received), husbands of psychologists are the most productive of any group, but wives of psychologists surpass other women psychologists (Bryson, Bryson, Licht, & Licht, 1976). Being married to a psychologist brings entree into networks of psychologists, but being married to a professional in another or allied field can bring entree into other networks with varied perspectives.

LIFE-SPAN DEVELOPMENT: CHILDREN AND PARENTHOOD

Of the 18 married women in this volume, 83% had children including adopted children in contrast to 60% of the 15 married women in Volume 2 and 38% of the 13 married women in Volume 1. The average number of children, 2.3, for the women in this volume was higher than the average number of children, 1.8 and 2.1, in Volumes 1 and 2, respectively. In this volume, 9 women had 2 children each; 1 had 3 children; 3 had 4 children each; 2 had 1 child each. Average age at birth or adoption of first child was 28.2 years. The children were born or adopted after 2 to 19 years of marriage with an average of 5.1 years. The age at first child is indicative of current trends among educated women to delay parenting until they are established in their careers and financially stable.

Parenting was both stressful and rewarding, requiring juggling of multiple roles. Child care was facilitated by spouses, hired help, and a shifting of emphasis from career to family on a temporary basis. In some instances, parenting was a shared endeavor between wife and husband (Albino, Cantor, Hyde, and Reid), but in many instances the parent with primary responsibility for child care was the mother (Bartoshuk, Culbertson, Johnson, Halpern, Katz, Keith-Spicgel, and Matlin). For reasons of pregnancy or child care, these women took part-time employment (Matlin and Scarr) or a brief time-out (Cantor, Culbertson, Halpern, Hyde, and Johnson). Overall, marriage or children did not have a long-term effect on scientific production for these women, supporting and expanding the findings on women in science studied by Cole and Zuckerman (1987).

What about the children? What becomes of the children of psychologists? What becomes of the children of eminent "employed mothers?" For the most part, they become highly educated achievers (O'Connell, 1988). The 19 girls and 16 boys reared by the eminent women in this volume now include: 5 attorneys, 5 business managers, 3 psychologists, 3 scientists, 3 musicians, 2 doctoral candidates, 2 college students, 1 physician, 1 dentist, 1 arbitrator, 1 computer engineer, 1 banker, 1 consultant, 1 journalist, 1 marketing director, 1 professional chef, 1 social worker, 1 teacher, and 1 elementary school student. As in Volume 2, it appears that these women were role models of achievement for their own children and that the ambience of dual professional parents encouraged and supported achievement in education and occupation.

EDUCATIONAL DEVELOPMENT

There is considerable variety in the undergraduate majors chosen by these eminent women (Table 22.3). Many came to psychology from other fields. As undergraduates they chose 8 different majors or double majors. Although 11 chose psychology as their major and one (Elaine Hatfield) chose English and psychology as her double major, each of the following 7 majors was the choice of one woman: biology (Diane Willis), education (Dorothy Cantor), English (Patricia Bricklin), magazine journalism (Judith Albino), mathematics (Janet Hyde), philosophy (Frances Horowitz), and sociology (Sandra Scarr). At the masters level, Horowitz chose elementary education and Cantor chose reading. Eighteen earned doctorates in psychology, 1 in human learning and development. Of the 34 women in the earlier two volumes, 16 chose majors other than psychology. There was continuity in all three volumes in this pattern of varied undergraduate majors preceding psychology at the doctoral level.

The range in years from baccalaureate to completion of doctorate is 3 years (Janet Hyde and Margaret Matlin) to 19 years (Dorothy Cantor), with a mean of 7.7 years. For Volume 1, the range is 3 years (Margaret Rioch) to 18 years (Carolyn Wood Sherif) with a mean of 8.76 years; for Volume 2 the range was 2 years (Anne Anastasi) to 30 years (Lillian Troll) with a mean of 7.9 years. In the present volume, the age at doctorate ranges from 23 years (Phyllis Katz) to 39 years (Dorothy Cantor). The mean age at doctorate was 29.4 years; for Volume 1, the mean age at doctorate was 29.1 years; for Volume 2, the mean age at doctorate was 28.8 years, a variation of approximately half a year for all three volumes. In this volume, Phyllis Katz graduated from college at 19 years of age; Dorothy Cantor at 20 years. In Volume 2, Anne Anastasi graduated from college at 19 years and earned her doctorate at 21 years; Leona Tyler graduated from college at 19 years; Frances

TABLE 22.3
Education and Interests of Eminent Women in Psychology

Eminent woman	Bachelors	Masters	Doctorate	Graduate Support	Interests
F. M. Culbertson	1947 Psychology University of Michigan	1949 Psychology University of Michigan	1955 Social Psychology University of Michigan	1947–1948 Survey Research Center University of Michigan 1948–1950 Teaching Fellow University of Michigan	Clinical, clinical child Hypnotherapy (especially for aged) School Psychology International psychology
P. M. Bricklin	1948 English St. Joseph College	1954 Clinical Psychology Temple University	1963 Psychology Temple University	1955–1960 Graduate Assistantship Reading Center Temple University	Professional education/training Learning & emotional disorders Regulation, legal & ethical issues Media psychology Professional organizations & advocacy

TABLE 22.3
(continued)

Eminent woman	Bachelors	Masters	Doctorate	Graduate Support	Interests
F. D. Horowitz	1954 Philosophy Antioch College	1954 Elementary Education Goucher College	1959 Developmental Psychology University of Iowa	1953–1954 Ford Foundation Fellowship at Goucher College 1956–1959 Teaching and research assistantships University of Iowa	Developmental Infancy Theory of early childhood Assessment
N. G. Johnson	1957 Psychology Depauw University		1972 Clinical Psychology Wayne State University	1963–1967 NIMH Wayne State University 1967–1968 NIMH Training Stipend, University Hospital	Women's psychology Psychotherapeutic approaches Adolescent girls Children Assessment & training

S. Scarr	1958 Sociology Vassar College	1963 Psychology and Social Relations Harvard University	1965 Psychology and Social Relations Harvard University	1960–1964 NIMH Traineeship	Behavior genetics Intelligence Child development
D. W. Cantor	1957 Education City College of NY	1968 Reading Newark State (now Kean)	1976 School Psychology Graduate School of Applied and Professional Psychology Rutgers University	None	Women's issues Leadership Advocacy Practice
D. J. Willis	1960 Biology Northeastern State University	1965 Psychology George Peabody College	1970 Experimental Psychology University of Oklahoma	None	Clinical & pediatric developmental psychology Disabled, abused, disadvantaged, & American Indian children Assessment & training

TABLE 22.3
(continued)

Eminent Woman	Bachelors	Masters	Doctorate	Graduate Support	Interests
E. Hatfield	1959 English/Psychology University of Michigan		1963 Psychology Stanford University	1959–1960 Scholarship Danforth Foundation	Social psychology Passionate love & desire Emotional contagion Equity theory Emotion Physical attractiveness
P. A. Katz	1957 Psychology Syracuse University		1961 Clinical/Development Psychology Yale University	1957–1959 NIMH Traineeship Yale University 1960–1961 Boie Fellowship Yale University	Racial attitudes & gender concept development Effects of television on children Women's issues Social/Developmental psychology

L. M. Bartoshuk	1960 Psychology Carleton College	1963 Psychology Brown University	1965 Psychology Brown University	1960–1963 NSF Predoctoral Fellowship Brown University

1963–1964 PHS Predoctoral Fellowship Brown University | Experimental psychology Psychophysics of sense of taste Sensation & perception |
| P. Keith-Spiegel | 1961 Psychology Occidental College | 1964 Experimental Psychology Claremont Graduate University | 1968 Psychology Claremont Graduate University | 1961–1964 NDEA Predoctoral Fellowship Claremont Graduate University | Ethics Moral development Instructional design/technology Women's issues |
| K. Deaux | 1963 Psychology Northwestern University | | 1967 Social Psychology University of Texas at Austin | 1965–1967 NIMH Predoctoral Fellowship University of Texas at Austin | Gender-related behaviors Social psychology Stereotypes Social identity, constructions & representations |

TABLE 22.3
(continued)

Eminent Woman	Bachelors	Masters	Doctorate	Graduate Support	Interests
J. E. N. Albino	1967 Magazine journalism University of Texas at Austin		1973 General Psychology University of Texas at Austin	1970–1971 Texas Tuition Scholarships 1971–1972 U.S. Office of Education Research Traineeship	Health Psychology Psychology of women Sports psychology Dental behavior sciences Assessment & training
M. W. Matlin	1966 Psychology Stanford University	1967 Psychology University of Michigan	1969 Experimental Psychology University of Michigan	1966–1969 Public Health Service Traineeship University of Michigan	Cognitive Psychology Psychology of women Teaching of psychology Experimental psychology Sensation & perception

P. T. Reid	1967 Psychology Howard University	1970 Psychology Temple University	1975 Educational Psychology University of Pennsylvania	None	Gender socialization Gender/race ethnicity/class & their intersections African American women & children Women in higher education administration Role of university presidents' wives
J. Brooks-Gunn	1969 Psychology Connecticut College	1970 Human Learning and Development Harvard University	1975 Human Learning and Development University of Pennsylvania	1969–1970 Texaco Scholarship Harvard University 1971–1975 Research Funding Tuition Scholarship University of Pennsylvania	Policy-oriented research on development, education, health & intervention Children & youth development Transitions and life course Women's issues

TABLE 22.3
(continued)

Eminent Woman	Bachelors	Masters	Doctorate	Graduate Support	Interests
D. F. Halpern	1968 Psychology University of Pennsylvania	1973 Psychology Temple University 1977 University of Cincinnati	1979 Psychology University of Cincinnati	1977–1979 Graduate Assistantships University of Cincinnati	Cognitive psychology Applications to real world problems Gender differences Assessment
J. S. Hyde	1969 Mathematics Oberlin College		1972 Psychology University of California–Berkeley	1969–1972 NSF Fellowship University of California–Berkeley	Psychology of women Human sexuality Multivariate statistics Experimental psychology

| L. Comas-Díaz | 1970 Psychology University of Puerto Rico | 1973 Clinical Psychology University of Puerto Rico | 1979 Clinical Psychology University of Massachusetts | 1977–1978 NIMH Clinical Training Fellowship

1978–1979 NIMH Predoctoral Fellowship Internship Clinical psychology Yale University | Diversity (people of color) Women and SES Cultural and cross-cultural International issues Clinical psychology |

Graham graduated from college at 19 years and earned her doctorate at 23 years. Both Janet Hyde in the present volume and Patricia Cain Smith in Volume 2 earned their doctorates at 24 years of age. In comparison with others in the field of psychology, the average age at doctorate of the women in all three volumes is lower, and the average time lapsed from bachelors degree to doctorate is shorter (SAUS, 1985). This finding on 53 eminent women differs from Simonton's (1992) sample of leaders of American psychology (1879–1967). In his study, the 66 men earned their doctorates at about age 28 but the 3 women earned their doctorates at age 34; he attributed this age difference, not to his small sample of women, but to the difficulties women generally encounter in academe.

The majority of these 19 eminent women earned their doctorates in the 1960s and 1970s; two were earned in the 1950s (Frances Culbertson and Frances Horowitz). In contrast, 12 of the 17 doctorates in Volume 1 were earned in the 1930s; 13 of the 17 doctorates in Volume 2 were earned between 1940 and 1967. For the 53 women studied in all three volumes, doctorates were earned from 1925 to 1979, the 54-year period that spanned the middle of the 20th century.

Sixteen of the 19 women in this volume received financial graduate support through fellowships, assistantships, traineeships, and scholarships as did 29 of the 34 women in Volumes 1 and 2. For these women, graduate training did not necessarily predict the wide range of interests and innovations in the many subdisciplines in psychology. Interests changed as opportunities arose and curiosity and challenge motivated new directions, goals, and innovations.

INNOVATIONS AND 'FIRSTS'

Although this group of women is younger than the groups previously studied, they nonetheless have achieved eminence as pioneers, groundbreakers, and innovators. They have made major breakthroughs in academe and industry; in professional organizations, social action, research, training, and psychological testing. These women developed theories, policies, and assessments, did research, taught, consulted, led, and generally advanced the field of psychology.

The American Psychological Association (APA), founded in 1892, has had 9 women serve as president. To be elected president, the highest elected office of the national organization, is to be recognized and endorsed by colleagues as a leader in psychology. The first two women to serve were Mary Calkins in 1905 and Margaret Washburn in 1921 (their biographies are in O'Connell & Russo, 1980, 1990). After a gap of more than 50 years, Anne Anastasi served as president in 1972, followed by Leona E. Tyler (1973),

Florence L. Denmark (1980), Janet Taylor Spence (1984), Bonnie R. Strickland (1987), Dorothy Cantor (1996) and Norine G. Johnson (2001). The lives and accomplishments of the next 5 women who served as president are preserved in their own words in Volume 2, and the last 2 are preserved in the present volume. The American Psychological Society (APS), established in 1988, has had 6 women among its first 11 presidents: Janet Spence (1988–1989), Marilynn Brewer (1993–1995), Sandra Scarr (1996–1997), Kay Deaux (1997–1998), Elizabeth Loftus (1998–1999) and Elizabeth Capaldi (1999–2000) (American Psychological Society, 1999). The autobiography of Spence is in Volume 2; the autobiographies of Scarr and Deaux are in the present volume.

In academe, women presidents were a rarity in the 20th century; two of them, Judith Albino, the first woman to serve as president of the four–campus University of Colorado System and now President of the California School of Professional Psychology at Alliant University, and Francis Horowitz, President of the City University of New York Graduate School and University Center, have autobiographies in this volume.

In addition to the very notable distinction of being members of an elite group, these presidential leaders have made major contributions in a variety of areas (Table 22.4). They have advanced understanding of leadership, adolescence, and patients' rights (Dorothy Cantor) as well as feminist practice, adolescence, and therapeutic approaches for families of impaired children (Norine Johnson). They have done landmark research on behavior genetics, intelligence, and child development (Sandra Scarr) and the social psychology of gender and the pervasiveness and persistence of gender beliefs and biases (Kay Deaux). They are innovators in health psychology and dental behavioral sciences (Judith Albino) and in developmental psychology, the conceptualization of a structural/behavioral model, and research on infant attention and assessment (Frances Horowitz).

A commonality among the eminent women in this volume and in fact, the eminent women in the earlier volumes as well, is that they were often first to lead, to innovate, and to achieve. Table 22.4 contains "firsts" as well as major innovations for the 19 in this volume, several of whom were founding editors of professional journals: Phyllis Katz, *Sex Roles: A Journal Research*; Lillian Comas-Díaz, *Cultural Diversity and Mental Health/Cultural Diversity and Ethnic Minority Psychology*; and Diane Willis, the *Journal of Pediatric Psychology*. Sandra Scarr was co-founding editor of *Current Directions in Psychological Science*. Some were founders of institutes or entrepreneurs (Patricia Bricklin, Jeanne Brooks-Gunn, Dorothy Cantor, Lillian Comas-Díaz, Norine Johnson, and Phyllis Katz) or the first to receive

TABLE 22.4
Major Innovations and "Firsts" of Eminent Women in Psychology

Eminent Woman	Innovations and 'Firsts'
F.M. Culbertson	Pioneering leader, contributor, researcher, and mentor in International Psychology and leader at state and national levels. Mentor in school psychology and women's health research. Hypnotherapy research and practice in developing resilience behaviors in aging women. Research in developmental psychology, on children's issues in international contexts, physical and sexual abuse; and gifted children.
P. Bricklin	Pioneer in media psychology, in bringing psychology to the public through the media and popular press. Innovator in clinical and school psychology, in learning and related emotional disorders in children, adolescents, and young adults. Innovator in regulation of psychology, legal and ethical issues in professional psychology education and training, and in role of professional organizations as advocates for both the profession and the public. Co-founder, Bricklin Associates.
F. D. Horowitz	Among the first women to serve as university president. Prolific author and editor. Innovator in developmental psychology and assessment, particularly in the conceptualization of developmental structural/behavioral model of organismic (or constitutional) and experiential factors, and in research on infant attention and the Neonatal Behavioral Assessment Scale.
N. G. Johnson	Ninth woman to serve as President of APA. Pioneer in clinical and developmental psychology and the psychology of women, in development, education, and training of feminist practice, in approaches that value diversity and strengths in adolescent girls, and in therapeutic approaches for families of children with developmental, neurological, and/or traumatic conditions. Entrepreneur, founder or co-founder, and principal of four psychological consulting companies.
S. Scarr	Co-founder and editor of *Current Directions in Psychological Science*. Landmark research on behavior genetics, intelligence, and child development. Published more than 200 articles and wrote four books on intelligence, child care, and family issues. Won National Book Award of the American Psychological Association for her book, *Mother Care/Other Care*. Served as Chief Executive Officer and Chair of the Board of Directors of KinderCare Learning Centers, Inc., the largest child care company in the United States.

TABLE 22.4
(continued)

Eminent Woman	Innovations and 'Firsts'
D. W. Cantor	Eighth woman to serve as President of APA. Advanced clinical and developmental psychology in understanding of leadership, adolescence, and patients' rights. Delineated a model of women's leadership in her book, *Women in Power*. Co-founder of the Leadership Equation Institute. Leader in APA Task Force on adolescent girls. Founded the political action committee, "Women in Psychology for Legislative Action." Advocate instrumental in development (with eight other national associations of mental health professionals) of *Your Mental Health Rights: Framing the Advocacy for Our Patients*.
D. J. Willis	Founder and first editor of *Journal of Pediatric Psychology*. Instrumental in establishing the APA Division of Child, Youth, and Family Services, a forum for applying psychology to development of policies that improve the well-being of children, youth, and families. Pioneer in clinical and developmental psychology, and in two specialties: pediatric psychology and clinical child psychology. Pioneer in study of American Indian children.
E. Hatfield	First woman (with co-researcher, Ellen Berscheid) to receive the Distinguished Scientist Award of the Society of Experimental Social Psychology. Pioneer in social psychology, in the study of passionate love and desire, the passionate beginnings of relationships, and how people fall in and out of love. Pioneering investigator of equity in relationships and emotional contagion. Broadened range of psychological research by moving scholarship beyond Western perspectives through cross-cultural studies of love and sex. Integrated historical studies of marriage, love, sex, and emotions over the past 500 years.
P. A. Katz	Founder and editor of first scientific academic journal, *Sex Roles: A Journal of Research*, devoted to publishing research and theoretical articles on women's issues. Founded the Institute for Research on Social Problems. Pioneer also in developmental and social psychology. Researched perceptual and cognitive factors in race bias and how children acquire concepts and attitudes about race and gender. Pioneering theoretical writings on gender with a positive focus on females and gender–role flexibility. Research on origins of race and gender learning within a longitudinal, cross-ethnic context.

TABLE 22.4
(continued)

Eminent Woman	Innovations and 'Firsts'
L. M. Bartoshuk	First to receive the Association for Chemoreception Sciences Award for Outstanding Achievement in the Chemical Senses. Innovative researcher who discovered that water acts to remove an inhibitory tastant, the independence of the four taste qualities, and that genetic variation involves more than one group of chemically related bitter compounds. Discovered supertasters (individuals with large numbers of taste buds) providing a kind of "Rosetta Stone" to evaluate psychophysical scales. Characterized taste phantoms; discovered inhibitory interactions among taste nerves cause one type of phantom. Discovered laboratory models of some taste phantoms and interactions between taste and oral somatosensation.
P. Keith-Spiegel	Co-authored landmark *Ethics in Psychology*. Instrumental in developing first APA ethics code on prohibition of sexual contact between psychologist and client. Initiated the statement "Sexual intimacies with clients is unethical." Innovator in instructional design/technology, developed the Multimedia Integrity Teaching Tool, a U.S. Department of Education funded multimedia program in CD-ROM for first offenders of a college or university honesty code. Wrote *The Complete Guide to Graduate School Admission*. Innovative teacher and facilitator of professional development.
K. Deaux	Landmark research on pervasiveness and persistence of gender beliefs and biases. Early and important contributor to social psychology of gender with her book, *The Behavior of Women and Men*. Innovative exploration of steel industry and impact of hiring women in blue-collar positions in her book, *Women of Steel*. Provided (with Brenda Major) a framework for examining similarities and differences between women and men and the contextual influences on behavior. Contributor to amicus brief filed by APA in Price Waterhouse v. Hopkins case.

TABLE 22.4
(continued)

Eminent Woman	Innovations and 'Firsts'
J. E. N. Albino	The first woman to serve as President of the four-campus University of Colorado System. Professional leader. First woman elected Chair of Presidents Commission of National Collegiate Athletics Association. Innovator in field of health psychology and dental behavioral sciences. Longitudinal studies of adolescents clarified impact of dental–facial appearance on self-perception and social adjustment. Developed measures for assessment of psychological need for treatment. Studied prevention behavior of adolescents within context of mental health and provided cognitive/behavioral change strategies used successfully in various health areas.
M. W. Matlin	Distinguished award-winning teacher and author of five highly regarded undergraduate psychology textbooks in a wide variety of specialties: *Human Experimental Psychology; Cognition; Sensation & Perception; Psychology of Women;* and *Psychology* (an introductory textbook where more than half of the examples concern the lives of women and girls). Presented innovative workshops and talks on the teaching of psychology of women and gender at national and regional conferences.
P. T. Reid	Innovative researcher on the impact of gender, race, ethnicity, and class and leader in psychological organizations. First African American hired at University of Tennessee–Chattanooga, first African American to chair the Psychology Department at that university, first African American academic administrator at the Graduate Center of City University, the first African American woman to head the APA Office of Social and Ethical Responsibility and serve on APA Council, and the first woman of color to be elected President of APA Division 35. Noted for ability to motivate students, particularly women and men of color in the study of social issues from a feminist perspective.
J. Brooks-Gunn	Founding Director of the Center for Children and Families and of the Columbia University Institute on Child and Family Policy. Pioneer in conducting policy-oriented, multidisciplinary research on family and community influences on the well being of children and youth; and on the interaction between behavior and biology. Cutting edge life-span developmental research led to groundbreaking national prevention programs. Prolific and highly respected researcher on a wide range of topics.

TABLE 22.4
(continued)

Eminent Woman	Innovations and 'Firsts'
D. F. Halpern	Distinguished award-winning teacher and author of important, widely-read, thought-provoking textbooks. *Thought and Knowledge: An Introduction to Critical Thinking* helps readers apply the principles and research of cognitive psychology to become more effective thinkers and *Sex Differences in Cognitive Abilities* is an integrated view of the controversial nature and nature research. Highly respected researcher in cognitive psychology and gender differences.
J. S. Hyde	Innovator in meta-analyses of research on psychological gender differences that have impacted the field's perception of gender differences. Research supported conclusions of gender similarities and great overlap of the male and female distributions. Author of widely-read textbooks on human sexuality, gender differences, and on the psychology of women. Professional leader and highly respected researcher.
L. Comas-Díaz	Founder and editor of the interdisciplinary journal, *Cultural Diversity and Mental Health/Cultural Diversity and Ethnic Minority Psychology*, the official journal of the APA Society for the Psychological Study of Ethnic Minority Issues; founder of the Transcultural Mental Health Institute; and founder of the Puerto Rican Psychological Association of Connecticut. Pioneer in integrating ethnicity and gender in mental health and in culturally relevant psychological treatment. Leader in women and people of color issues in psychology.

prestigious awards (Linda Bartoshuk and Elaine Hatfield). All were pioneers and groundbreakers.

As evident in the autobiographies, as delineated in Chapter 1 (subfields) and Tables 22.3 (interests) and 22.4 (innovations), the prolific, pioneering, landmark work of these women spans a wide, diverse range. The diverse contributions of each woman are interconnected by unifying themes that are expressed in multiple ways. They are leaders, academicians, researchers, therapists, policymakers, consultants, and entrepreneurs. In addition, they identify themselves as activists and advocates (Albino, Bricklin, Brooks-Gunn, Comas-Díaz, Cantor, Halpern, Horowitz, Katz, Keith-Spiegel, Matlin, Reid, and Willis).

When asked to identify their most significant contributions to psychology, many in this volume as in the earlier volumes refer not to their outstanding and varied accomplishments, but to their roles as teachers and mentors. These distinguished women are extraordinary not only in their accomplishments, but in their sense of generativity as they mentor students toward their own unique contributions. They truly are exemplars of high-level professionals who have integrated achievement and affiliation for optimal functioning (O'Connell, 1988).

PROFESSIONAL DEVELOPMENT

These women often held multiple positions, sometimes simultaneously, in various combinations of academe, industry, and the media as president (Albino and Horowitz), provost (Albino, Hyde, and Reid), dean (Albino, Horowitz, and Reid), chair (Halpern, Hatfield, Hyde, Katz, Reid, and Scarr), professor (Albino, Bartoshuk, Bricklin, Culbertson, Deaux, Halpern, Hatfield, Horowitz, Hyde, Katz, Keith-Spiegel, Matlin, Reid, Scarr, and Willis), chief executive officer (Scarr), director (Brooks-Gunn, Cantor, Comas-Díaz, Culbertson, Hyde, Katz, and Scarr), researcher (Bartoshuk, Brooks-Gunn, and Culbertson), therapist (Bricklin, Cantor, Comas-Díaz, Culbertson, Hatfield, Johnson, and Willis), media psychologist (Bricklin), consultant (Johnson, Katz, and Willis), and entrepreneur (Bricklin, Brooks-Gunn, Cantor, Comas-Díaz, Johnson, and Katz). The positions they held, the institutions that employed them, and the years of employment are shown in Table 22.5.

A consistent finding is that neither marital pattern (single, married, or divorced) nor the presence or absence of children excluded the possibility of attaining the highest ranks for the 53 eminent women. The routes to the highest ranks and positions include one or more of the following: (a) a strong, almost continuous commitment to academe (Albino, Bartoshuk, Bricklin, Culbertson, Deaux, Halpern, Hatfield, Horowitz, Hyde, Katz, Keith-Spiegel, Matlin, Reid, Scarr, and Willis); (b) significant work as a researcher (Albino, Bartoshuk, Brooks-Gunn, Culbertson, Deaux, Hatfield, Horowitz, Hyde, Katz, Reid, and Scarr); and (c) an established reputation as a psychologist in positions allied to or outside academe (Bricklin, Brooks-Gunn, Cantor, Comas-Díaz, Culbertson, Johnson, and Scarr). For the 53 eminent women in the three volumes, the movement between academe and other settings is overlapping, sequential, and in both directions.

Recurrent threads through the employment histories of these women are the ability to integrate interests with opportunities and the flexibility to shift employment settings and direction. The variety of employment patterns of these 19 and the earlier group of 34 women provide many valuable lessons and an instructive model for current and future generations.

TABLE 22.5

Major Professional Patterns

Eminent Women	Institution	Title	Dates
F. M. Culbertson	Children's Hospital, Washington, DC	Research Psychologist	1957
	Central Wisconsin Colony and Training School	Research Psychologist	1958–1959
	Wisconsin Diagnostic Center, Madison	Clinical Psychologist	1962–1965
	University of Wisconsin Medical School	Acting Chief Clinical Psychologist	1965–1966
	NIH, Berkeley, CA	Research Psychologist	1966–1967
	Madison, WI Public Schools	School Psychologist	1967–1968
	University of Wisconsin Whitewater	Associate Professor to Professor	1968–1988
		School Psychologist	1968–1971
		Director, Graduate Program in School Psychology	1977–1983; 1985–1988
	Mental Health Associates	Licensed Clinical/School Psychologist	1988–present
P. M. Bricklin	Columbia Broadcasting System	"Radio and TV Personality"	1965–1981
	Hahnemann University	Assistant to Full Professor	1967–1989
	Bricklin Associates	Psychologist– Educational Consultant	1964–present
	Johns Hopkins University	Adjunct Professor	1985–1990
	Widener University	Professor	1989–present

TABLE 22.5
(continued)

Eminent Women	Institution	Title	Dates
F. D. Horowitz	Southern Oregon College	Assistant Professor	1959–1961
	University of Kansas	Assistant to Full Professor	1961–1991
		Vice Chancellor for Research, Graduate Studies and Public Service and Dean of Graduate School	1978–1991
	City University of New York Graduate School and University Center	President	1991–present
N. G. Johnson	Kennedy Memorial Hospital for Children	Director of Psychology/ Psychology Training	1970–1988
	Boston University Medical School	Clinical Assistant Professor	1976–present
	ABCS Psychology Resources	President	1977–present
	Boston College	Adjunct Associate Professor	1978–1981
	Massachusetts School of Professional Psychology	Adjunct Faculty Member	1978–1988
	Westwood Pembrooke Health System	Specialist in Psychology	1991–1997
	Access for Change	Owner	1997–present
	JPP Consultants: Business Practices for Professionals	Consultant	1997–present
	W2W	Principal	1997–present

TABLE 22.5
(continued)

Eminent Women	Institution	Title	Dates
S. Scarr	Institute of Child Study, University of Maryland	Assistant Professor	1965–1966
	University of Pennsylvania	Visiting Lecturer, Department of Psychology	1966–1967
	William T. Carter Foundation for Child Development, University of Pennsylvania	Acting Director	1967–1970
	Graduate School of Education, University of Pennsylvania	Lecturer/Assistant Professor/Associate Professor	1967–1971
	Institute of Child Development, University of Minnesota	Associate Professor Professor	1971–1974 1974–1977
	Department of Psychology, Yale University	Professor	1977–1983
	University of Virginia, Charlottesville	Fellow Center for Advanced Studies	1983–1984; 1987–1988
		Chair, Psychology Department	1984–1989
		Commonwealth Professor	1983–1996
		Professor Emerita	1996–present
	Kindercare Learning Centers, Inc.	Board of Directors Chair Chair & CEO	1990–present 1994–1997 1995–1997

378

TABLE 22.5
(continued)

Eminent Women	Institution	Title	Dates
D. W. Cantor	Westfield, New Jersey	Private Practice	1976–present
	Rutgers University	Visiting Assistant Professor; Director of Continuing Education	1979–1986
	New Jersey Psychological Association	Director of Professional Affairs	1987–1991
	The Leadership Equation Institute	Principal	1994–present
D. J. Willis	University of Oklahoma Health Sciences Center	Assistant Professor Associate Professor Professor	1971–1977 1977–1982 1982–1999
	University of Oklahoma American Indian Institute	Consultant	1999–2000
E. Hatfield	University of Minnesota	Assistant/Associate Professor	1963–1966
	University of Rochester	Associate Professor	1966–1967
	University of Wisconsin	Associate Professor/Professor	1967–1981
	University of Hawaii	Chair and Professor	1981–1983
		Professor	1981–present

TABLE 22.5 (continued)

Eminent Women	Institution	Title	Dates
P. A. Katz	Institute for Development Studies, New York	Senior Associate	1962–1963
	Queens College, Queens, NY	Instructor	1962–1963
	New York University	Assistant/Associate Professor	1963–1969
	City University of New York, Graduate Center	Chair, Developmental Psychology Section	1969–1975
		Associate Professor/Professor	1969–1976
	Institute for Behavior Research, Boulder CO	Senior Associate	1976–1977
	Institute for Research on Social Problems	Director	1976–present
L. M. Bartoshuk	Natick Army Labs	Research Psychologist	1966–1970
	J. B. Pierce Foundation	Assistant to Full Fellow	1970–1989
	Yale University School of Medicine	Assistant to Full Professor	1971–1989
		Full Professor Surgery and Psychology	1989–present
P. Keith-Spiegel	California State University, Northridge	Assistant/Associate/Full Professor	1966–1991
	Ball State University	Voran Distinguished Professor of Social and Behavioral Sciences	1991–present

TABLE 22.5 *(continued)*

Eminent Women	Institution	Title	Dates
K. Deaux	Wright State University	Assistant Professor	1967–1970
	Purdue University	Assistant/ Associate/ Full Professor	1970–1987
	City University of New York Graduate School and University Center	Professor of Psychology and Women's Studies	1987–present
		Executive Officer of Psychology	1994–1997
		Distinguished Professor of Psychology	1995–present
J. E. N. Albino	School of Dental Medicine, State University of New York at Buffalo	Assistant/ Associate/Full Professor	1973–1990
	State University of New York at Buffalo	Associate Provost	1984–1987
	School of Architecture and Planning, State University of New York at Buffalo	Associate Provost and Interim Dean	1987–1988
	Graduate School, State University of New York at Buffalo	Associate Provost and Dean of the Graduate School	1989–1990
	University of Colorado at Boulder and University of Colorado Health Sciences Center at Denver	Professor	1990

381

TABLE 22.5 *(continued)*

Eminent Women	Institution	Title	Dates
J. E. N. Albino *(Continued)*	University of Colorado	Vice President for Academic Affairs and Research and Dean of System Graduate School	1990–1991
		President	1991–1995
	University of Colorado Health Sciences Center and University of Colorado at Boulder	Professor	1995–1997
	University of Colorado	President Emerita	1997
	California School of Professional Psychology	President	1997–2000
	California School of Professional Psychology at Alliant University	President	2000–present
M. W. Matlin	State University of New York at Genesco	Assistant Professor	1971–1979
		Coordinator, Women's Studies	1977–1995
		Associate Professor	1979–1982
		Professor	1982–1987
		Distinguished Teaching Professor	1987–present

TABLE 22.5 *(continued)*

Eminent Women	Institution	Title	Dates
P. T. Reid	Howard University, Washington, D.C.	Assistant Professor	1976–1979
	University of Tennessee at Chattanooga, Department of Psychology	Associate Professor	1979–1985
		Professor	1985–1990
	City University of New York Graduate School and University Center	Chair, Department of Psychology	1988–1990
		Professor of Psychology	1990–1998
		Acting Head of Ph.D. Program in Developmental Psychology	1991–1992
		Associate Provost and Dean for Academic Affairs	1992–1998
		Interim Provost and Senior Vice President for Academic Affairs	1998
	University of Michigan	Professor of Psychology and Research Scientist	1998–present

TABLE 22.5 *(continued)*

Eminent Women	Institution	Title	Dates
J. Brooks-Gunn	Barnard College	Adjunct Faculty	1975–1984
	Institute for the Study of Exceptional Children, Educational Testing Service and St. Luke's-Roosevelt Hospital Center	Associate Director	1977–1982
	Center for Research in Human Development, Educational Testing Service	Research Scientist	1978–1983
	Columbia University	Assistant Professor of Clinical Pediatrics	1978–1985
	Educational Testing Service and Columbia University	Director, Adolescent Study Program	1982–1993
	Division of Education Policy Research, Princeton, NJ	Senior Research Scientist	1983–1993
	University of Pennsylvania	Adjunct Faculty	1985–1990
	Teachers College, Columbia University	Founding Director, Center for Children and Families	1991–present

TABLE 22.5 *(continued)*

Eminent Women	Institution	Title	Dates
J. Brooks-Gunn *(Continued)*		Virginia and Leonard Marx Professor of Child Development and Education	1991–present
	Columbia University	Member, Graduate School of Arts and Sciences	1993–present
		Founding Director, Child and Family Policy	1998–present
	Harvard University	National Fellow, Graduate Training Program, Inequality and Social Policy	1998–present
D. F. Halpern	University of California, Riverside	Lecturer	1979–1981
	California State University, San Bernardino	Assistant/ Associate Professor	1981–1986
		Professor	1986–present
		Chair, Department of Psychology	1996–present
J. S. Hyde	Bowling Green State University	Assistant Professor	1972–1976
		Associate Professor	1976–1979
	Denison University	Associate Professor	1979–1983
		Professor of Psychology	1983–1986
		Acting Provost	1985–1986

TABLE 22.5 *(continued)*

Eminent Women	*Institution*	*Title*	*Dates*
J. S. Hyde *(continued)*	University of Wisconsin-Madison	Director, Women's Studies Research Center	1986–1990
		Professor of Psychology and Women's Studies	1986–present
		Associate Vice Chancellor for Academic Affairs	1990–1992
		Director, Women Faculty Mentoring Program	1996–present
		Evjue-Bascom Professor of Women's Studies	1996–present
		Chair, Department of Psychology	1998–present
		Helen Thompson Woolley Professor of Psychology and Women's Studies	1999–present
L. Comas-Díaz	Yale University Department of Psychiatry	Assistant Professor	1979–1984
	Hill Mental Health Clinic, Connecticut Mental Health Center (affiliated with Yale University)	Assistant Director	1981–1983

TABLE 22.5 *(continued)*

Eminent Women	*Institution*	*Title*	*Dates*
L. Comas-Díaz *(Continued)*	American Psychological Association	Director of Ethnic Minority Affairs and Associate Director of Minority Fellowship Program	1984–1986
	George Washington University School of Medicine	Assistant/Associate Clinical Professor of Psychology in Psychiatry and Behavioral Sciences	1986–1993
	Washington, DC	Private Practice, clinical	1986–present
	Transcultural Mental Health Institution	Executive Director	1986–present

A long-standing topic of study in lifespan developmental psychology is the relationship between age and achievement. The women in these three volumes provide strong evidence that age is not a barrier to creative scientific achievement (O'Connell, 1983, 1988). Dorothy Cantor, who earned her doctorate at age 39, subsequently became the eighth woman to serve as president of the American Psychological Association (APA) and is renowned for her continuing contributions to the field of psychology. Judith Albino became President Emerita then went on to serve as President of the California School of Professional Psychology; Sandra Scarr became Professor Emerita and continued her life of high achievement in the venue of the corporate world serving as Chair of the Board of Directors and as Chief Executive Officer of Kindercare Learning Centers. Lillian Troll (Volume 2) who earned her doctorate at age 52 is an exemplar of the possibilities of career change in mid-life and is highly respected for her many innovative contributions to the field of adult development. Anne Anastasi and Leona Tyler (Volume 2), who earned their college degrees at 19 years-old, served as presidents of APA and made notable lifelong contributions to the field of psychology, exemplify the association among precocity, longevity, and achievement and demonstrate that age is not a barrier to achievement. Lois Meek Stolz (Volume 2) had a professional life that spanned over 70 years; she continued to be professionally productive into her 90s. Mary Ainsworth, Myrtle McGraw, and Lois Murphy (Volume 1) are just three additional examples of productivity at advanced ages. The continuation of high achievement after "retirement" is a recurrent phenomena among these 53 eminent women. Their lives illustrate lifelong achievement. Other researchers studying chiefly male populations support the view that the picture for creativity in the later years of life is an optimistic one (Csikszentmihalyi, 1996; Simonton, 2000).

LIFE-SPAN DEVELOPMENT: BARRIERS

As the historical and social context becomes more contemporary with each succeeding generation of women, it might be expected that there would be less overt discrimination and fewer restrictions on educational and professional opportunities. To a limited extent, this is true, but the overt discrimination and restrictions that were experienced by these women were significant (Table 22.6). Their definite contributions were made in environments that ranged from benign to hostile, from accepting to rejecting. They faced barriers of sexism and racism.

They were denied admission to math and science classes (Bartoshuk) and doctoral programs (Bricklin and Johnson); scholarships, advancement, and grant opportunities were denied (Bartoshuk, Brooks-Gunn, and Johnson). They were denied employment opportunities (Hatfield) or employed but underpaid (Bartoshuk, Brooks-Gunn, and Katz) because they were women. In some instances, the women were employed reluctantly because of their race or ethnicity (Comas-Díaz and Reid). In addition to discrimination, the women suffered sexual harassment and other manifestations of sexism and racism (Bartoshuk, Bricklin, Comas-Díaz, Deaux, Hatfield, Johnson, Katz, Keith-Spiegel, Reid, and Scarr). Some mentioned not being taken seriously as a scholar (Albino, Hatfield, Johnson, and Keith-Spiegel), the lack of mentors (Albino, Comas-Díaz, and Katz), and financial concerns during their education and in the years beyond (Culbertson, Bricklin, Halpern, Hatfield, Katz, and Keith-Spiegel).

Marital status was sometimes related to restriction of educational and employment opportunities. Dorothy Cantor was able to pursue her doctorate when a new program opened near her marital home. Some were denied employment at the same institutions as their husbands because of anti-nepotism rules (Culbertson and Horowitz). Several mention the difficulties in balancing multiple roles (Bricklin, Brooks-Gunn, Culbertson, Halpern, Hyde, Johnson, Keith-Spiegel, Matlin, and Reid). Yet, despite institutional barriers and other restrictions, the women in this and the earlier volumes made extraordinary contributions to psychology.

LIFE-SPAN DEVELOPMENT: COPING STRATEGIES

The development of coping strategies for these and other barriers reflected a variety of approaches and some commonalities.

Personality, Intelligence, Motivation

Recurring themes in these autobiographies are the persistence, resourcefulness, and cognitive and behavioral flexibility of these women in the face of obstacles. They showed strength, determination, optimism, and commitment. When one pathway was blocked, they chose another (Albino, Bartoshuk, Bricklin, Brooks-Gunn, Comas-Díaz, Culbertson, Halpern, Hatfield, Horowitz, Johnson, and Katz). They took risks, changed direction, and relocated. When advancement was delayed, they changed to more receptive institutions or persisted until advancement came (Bartoshuk, Hatfield, Katz, and Reid). They were multi-talented and used these talents well in a variety of settings and in a variety of capacities. They relocated with spouses and, despite limited opportunities, worked at the most interesting position they could obtain (Albino, Culbertson, Horowitz,

TABLE 22.6

Barriers and Coping Strategies of Eminent Women in Psychology

Eminent Woman	Barriers	Coping Strategies
F. M. Culbertson	Lack of money.	Applied for scholarship.
	Finishing thesis with birth of twins—couldn't afford paid help.	Typed thesis while neighbors baby-sat for children.
	Finding employment with four children at home.	Set up a co-share job with a friend.
P. M. Bricklin	Lack of money or support due to mother's negative attitude about higher education and a woman's chance of marriage.	Won academic scholarships, earned money, graduate assistantships to proceed with my educational goals.
	Limited role of women.	Saw barriers and problems as challenges.
	Opportunities for graduate school; as a woman, denied admission to Hopkins doctoral program.	Attended doctoral program at Temple. Strong believer in the "act as if" philosophy. Doors that seemed closed, opened.
	Balancing roles of wife, mother, and professional psychologist.	Gradual awareness that I can be all three and not neglect any one.
F. D. Horowitz	None mentioned.	
N. G. Johnson	Sexual harassment.	Avoidance, silence, and learning to discourage further contact.
	Discrimination when applying to graduate school—"You'll just take the place of a man, have a baby, and leave the field."	To respond simply, "No, I won't; I will persist."

TABLE 22.6 *(continued)*

Eminent Woman	Barriers	Coping Strategies
S. Scarr	Being a female in 1950s wanting a career.	Plowed ahead with lots of disapproval from family and friends.
	Being sexually harassed in every job until the 1980s.	Cried a lot and said "no."
	Research on genetic differences was highly controversial and sometimes led to abusive and threatening treatment in the 1970s.	Called on colleagues and university police to protect me.
D. W. Cantor	Assumption that paid employment would stop after children were born. Husband said I was "bored" and "boring."	Returned to school and gradually took on work.
	No nearby doctoral programs where I could combine motherhood and training.	Applied to new GSAPP at Rutgers University as soon as it opened.
	Advent of managed care, interfering with practice of psychotherapy.	Refused to join managed care panels and worked outside of their system.
D. J. Willis	None mentioned.	
E. Hatfield	Finances.	Always worked full time.
	Psychology Department wouldn't hire women.	Worked at Student Activities Bureau and volunteered to teach and do research in the Psychology Department.
	Not taken seriously as scholar.	Stayed focused and persevered.

TABLE 22.6 (*continued*)

Eminent Woman	Barriers	Coping Strategies
P. A. Katz	Lack of sophistication about educational institutions.	Trial and error.
	Financial needs.	Scholarship aid and work in college; trainee and research assistant funds in graduate school.
	Sex discrimination at two places of employment.	Changed jobs; confrontation.
L. M. Bartoshuk	Women were not allowed in advanced high school math and science classes.	Agreed to take typing and bookkeeping for permission to take math and science.
	Strong resistance to female students in lab at Brown University.	Proved seriousness and work ethos.
	Bias against working women with children; denied opportunity to submit grant proposal (had no research funds), promotion was withheld, and salary kept low.	Decided to leave position; interviewed with Provost of Sciences at Yale. Allowed to submit grant proposal (awarded), promoted, and salary raised.
	Continued to suffer abuse. Abuse of women was endemic; attitudes at top supported prejudice at lower levels.	Decided to leave once again. Medical School Dean found Yale appointment as tenured Full Professor in Department of Surgery. Support from other women.

TABLE 22.6 *(continued)*

Eminent Woman	Barriers	Coping Strategies
	Senior researcher but paid lowest salary.	Questioned salary discrepancy; received $25,000 raise for parity with other researchers.
P. C. Keith-Spiegel	Finances.	Lived very frugally.
	Sexual harassment.	The term did not exist then; suffered in silence.
	Not always taken seriously as a scholar.	Tried harder.
	Assumption that much of early work, coauthored with husband (Spiegel), was mostly his work.	Vigorous documentation to contrary (husband publicly stated that I did work).
	Being mother and professor. Wanting to succeed in both. Feeling so tired all the time.	Strict time management, paying others to assist, maintaining a good relationship with ex-husband (during single motherhood and beyond).
	Told that I couldn't achieve something.	Proved them wrong.
K. Deaux	Parents' (particularly mother's) lack of understanding and valuing of advanced education (marriage seen as goal of good undergraduate education!).	Independently supported advanced education.
	Sexism in the academy.	Obliviousness; then stubborn (naïve?) persistence.

TABLE 22.6 *(continued)*

Eminent Woman	Barriers	Coping Strategies
J. E. N. Albino	Graduate school professors not supportive; assumed a woman would not be productive scholar.	Worked independently.
	Absence of women colleagues/role models in early career.	Became "one of the boys"; modeled behavior of male role models.
	Opposition of strong "Old Boys" network to rapid move into top leadership.	Tried to stay focused on important issues; ignored personal attacks (not very successful strategy).
		Developed own support.
M.W. Matlin	No training as teacher in graduate school. Lacked confidence in teaching ability.	Told myself that life involved taking moderate risks; in a couple of years liked teaching, then loved it.
	Initially hesitant about taking risk of writing college textbooks.	Decided to be daring and risk writing books.
	Not enough time to do everything.	Learned to be extremely efficient, say "no" when over-committed, and take time for vacations and leisure activities.
P. T. Reid	Stress of working on two dissertations with two babies and managing the demands of dual career family.	Child care and maintaining mutually supportive marital relationship using honest communication, mutual respect, support, and shared family responsibility.

TABLE 22.6 *(continued)*

Eminent Woman	Barriers	Coping Strategies
	Racism/sexism	Perseverance. Maintaining own standards, staying connected to family and friends for reality checks, and keeping grounded in true values.
J. Brooks-Gunn	Coordinating graduate school with husband's choices.	Took turns.
	As research scientist, paid less although brought in more grants.	Federal Affirmative Action raised salary 35% when institution started using standard formula.
	Denied NIH grant after positive review. Article with positive reviews rejected for publication because editor did not believe premise.	Submitted slightly changed grant to another study section for funding. Submitted article to another journal that published it.
D. F. Halpern	Family opposed to college for females.	Supported self and pursued education.
	Balancing children and graduate school.	Worked very hard.
J. Hyde	Dual-earner couple finding two jobs in the same area.	Took turns. Got the best first job and husband followed. Later husband got better job and I followed.
L. Comaz-Díaz	Language (birth defect—cleft palate).	Focused on non-verbal communication.
	Lack of mentors.	Searched for areas of identification with potential mentors.
	Racism/sexism.	Became political; became an expert.

Hyde, Johnson, and Reid). They faced isolation and exclusion with determination and dedication (Comas-Díaz, Reid, and Scarr). They were open to change and to new experiences; learning was an integral part of their lives. These women and the women in the earlier volumes strongly valued achievement in education and occupation; they were very highly motivated to be productive.

Mentors and Professional and Social Networks

The availability of mentors and role models is extremely important in the development of achievement and creativity (O'Connell, 1983, 1988). Mentors and role models help advance the development of achievement through such forces as identification, modeling, inspiration and, ultimately, the incentive for unique contributions. These remarkable women were aided by both male and female mentors. The ratio of identified mentors is 1.3 men to 1 woman, slightly less than the 3 men to 2 women in Volume 2. Thus, in all volumes, men outnumbered women as mentors due to their larger numbers in the field. With the increasing percentage of women earning their doctorates in psychology, it is likely that in future decades the percentage of women mentors will increase accordingly. Some of the male mentors mentioned were Donald Campbell, Leon Festinger, Bill Greiner, Nicholas Hobbs, Leonard Horowitz, Michael Lewis, Norman Maier, Boyd McCandless, Wilbert McKeachie, Steve Sample, Logan Wright, Robert Zajonc, and Edward Zigler; role models included fathers, grandfathers, and uncles. Some of the female mentors mentioned include Dorothy Cantor, Susan Gray, Mavis Hetherington, Bernice Lott, Eleanor Maccoby (mentioned by 2 of the women and the only female professor Margaret Matlin ever had), Helen Peak, Julie Richmond, Donna Shalala, Helen Strauss, Bonnie Strickland, and Adele Youtz; role models included mothers, grandmothers, aunts, nuns, and the mythical figures of Wonder Woman, Brenda Starr, and Nancy Drew.

Professional socialization and the formation of critical links in professional and social networks so necessary to reaching eminence in psychology and other fields were facilitated by the mentors (Clawson, 1980; Levinson, 1978). Lillian Comas-Díaz writes that intellectual mentors are important for "inspiration, courage, and wisdom." The mentor relationship provides credibility and shortens the time needed to prove oneself. The mentors provided access, information, advice, support, knowledge, challenge, guidance, and visibility for the aspiring professionals. Recommendations for education programs, assistantships, and positions often came from mentors, professors, or members of a woman's professional network.

In times of crisis, the women depended on their own inner resources, their flexibility, adaptability, persistence, and strength, but they also vigorously employed their social and professional networks. These networks provided effective coping strategies and worked well to accomplish various goals (O'Connell, 1983).

AWARDS, HONORS, AND PROFESSIONAL LEADERSHIP

Exceptional achievement is a culturally-valued behavior and exceptional achievers often find themselves honored with awards, honors, and other forms of acclaim (Simonton, 1998, 1999). All 19 women have been recognized as Fellows by APA and various divisions within APA for "outstanding and unusual contributions" to the field of psychology. Some have been recognized with fellow status in other professional organizations as well; for example, Kay Deaux, Frances Horowitz, and Sandra Scarr are Fellows of the American Association for the Advancement of Science; and Bartoshuk, Brooks-Gunn, Comas-Díaz, Deaux, Hatfield, Katz, Matlin, Reid, and Scarr are Fellows of APS.

These eminent women have won many APA awards for distinguished contributions, too numerous to include here except for a few examples. Culbertson won the Distinguished Contribution to International Advancement of Psychology Award; Bricklin, the Distinguished Contribution to Practice and State Leadership Awards; Horowitz, the Distinguished Contribution to Science Award; Halpern, the Distinguished Contribution to Education and Teaching Award; Scarr, the Distinguished Contribution to Research in Public Policy Award; Cantor, the Distinguished Contribution to Applied Psychology as a Professional Practice Award; Comas-Díaz, the Distinguished Contributions to the Public Interest Award. The APA Karl F. Heiser Award for Advocacy was won separately by Cantor and Willis. The APA National Book Award was won by Scarr. Linda Bartoshuk, Lillian Comas-Díaz, and Diane Halpern had the distinction of being APA G. Stanley Hall Lecturers. Diane Halpern, Patricia Keith-Spiegel, and Margaret Matlin won the Distinguished Teaching Award of the American Psychological Foundation (APF); Elaine Hatfield had the distinction of winning the APF National Media Award not once but twice for her books.

In addition, these eminent women have won awards from national, state, and regional associations, from the divisions of APA, from universities, and professional societies for their achievements, their books, research, leadership, and their contributions to policy, practice, and advocacy. They have served as presidents of one or more prestigious professional societies—Albino, Brooks-Gunn, Cantor, Culbertson, Deaux, Hatfield, Horowitz (2), Hyde, Johnson, Scarr (3),

TABLE 22.7
Selected Awards, Honors, and Professional Leadership Positions of Eminent Women in Psychology

F. M. Culbertson

Diplomat, School Psychology, 1972

Honorary President, Second Congresso (Brasil) Regional Latino Americano de Psicologia, Porte Allegro, Brasil, 1979

President, International Council of Psychologists, 1979–1980

Fellow, APA Divisions 12, 16, 30, 35, 42, 52, 1980

Chair, APA Committee on International Relations, 1981–1982

APA Distinguished Contribution to the International Advancement of Psychology Award, 1984

Outstanding Contributions to Research and Professionalism, APA Division 12, Section 4 Clinical Psychology of Women, 1986

APA Board of Convention Affairs, 1992–1995

Chair, APA Membership Committee, 1996

APA Council Representative, 1998–2000

P. M. Bricklin

Honorary Doctoral Degree (Ll.D.), St Joseph College, 1972

Pennsylvania Psychological Association Award, 1975–1977

President, Philadelphia Society of Clinical Psychologists Award, 1976–1977

Distinguished Service Award, Philadelphia Society of Clinical Psychologists, 1979

Chair, APA Committee on Structure and Function of Council, 1980–1981

Distinguished Service Award, Pennsylvania Psychological Association, 1983

APA Board of Professional Affairs Award, 1983

Chair, APA Board of Professional Affairs, 1983

APA Board of Directors, 1987–1989

American Association of State Psychology Boards Recognition, 1988

American Psychological Association Recognition, 1988

TABLE 22.7 *(continued)*

Selected Awards, Honors, and Professional Leadership Positions of Eminent Women in Psychology

National Academy of Practice (Distinguished Practitioner), 1989

Fellow, APA Divisions 1, 16, 29, 31, 37, 42, 43, 1990

APA Council Representative, 1990–present

AASPB Morton Berger Award, 1991

APA Presidential Citation, 1992

Association for State and Provincial Licensing Boards Roger C. Smith Award, 1995

Honorary Doctor of Humane Letters Degree, Chicago School of Professional Psychology, 1996

APA Award for Distinguished Contributions to Practice, 1996

APA State Leadership Award, 1999

Chair, APA College of Professional Psychology, 1999

F. D. Horowitz

Trustees Award Medal, Board of Trustees, Cherry Lawn School, Darien, Connecticut, 1971

Outstanding Educator in America Award, 1973

University of Kansas—Women's Hall of Fame, 1974

Fellow, APA Divisions 1 and 7, 1975

President, APA Division 7, 1977–1978

President, American Psychological Foundation (APF), 1991–1994

President, CUNY Graduate School and University Center, 1991–present

APA Centennial Award for Sustained Contribution to Science Directorate, 1992

Society for Psychologists in Management Award, 1993

New York Women's Forum Board of Directors, 1995–1997

Rebecca Rice Award for Lifetime Achievement, Antioch College, 1996

President, Society for Research in Child Development, 1997–1999

Femmy Award, The Feminist Press, 1998

Fellow, American Association for the Advancement of Science

TABLE 22.7 *(continued)*
Selected Awards, Honors, and Professional Leadership Positions of Eminent Women in Psychology

N. G. Johnson

President, Massachusetts Psychological Association, 1981–1983

APA Council Representative, 1985–1988, 1995–1997

Finance Committee Co-chair, APA, 1987–1988

Fellow, APA Divisions 12, 29, 35, 42, 51, 1991

Board of Directors, APA Division 29, 1992–1998

President, APA Division 35, 1994–1995

APA Presidential Task Force Co-chair: Adolescent Girls: Strengths and Stresses, 1995–1997

APA Board of Directors, 1997–1999

Distinguished Practitioner in the National Academy of Practice in Psychology, 1998

Distinguished Leader for Women in Psychology Recognition Award, the Committee on Women in Psychology, 1998

Career Contribution Award, Massachusetts Psychological Association, 1999

President, American Psychological Association, 2001

S. Scarr

Fellow, APA Divisions 7, 9, 15, 37, 1973

Fellow, American Association for the Advancement of Science, 1973

President, APA Division 7, 1981–1983

Chair, APA Council of Editors, 1982–1983

APA National Book Award for *Mother Care Other Care*, 1985

President, Behavior Genetics Association, 1985–1986

APA Council Representative, 1985–1988

Founding Fellow, American Psychological Society, 1988

APA Distinguished Contributions to Research in Public Policy Award, 1988

TABLE 22.7 *(continued)*
Selected Awards, Honors, and Professional Leadership Positions of Eminent Women in Psychology

APA Board of Directors, 1988–1991

Chair, Executive Committee, Council of Graduate Departments of Psychology, 1988–1989

Elected to American Academy of Arts and Sciences, 1989

President, Society for Research in Child Development, 1989–1991

Chair, APS Publications Committee, 1989–1991

James McKeen Cattell Award for Distinguished Contributions to Applied Research, American Psychological Society, 1993

President, American Psychological Society, 1996–1997

D. W. Cantor

Chair, Executive Board, New Jersey Association for the Advancement of Psychology, 1981

President, New Jersey Psychological Association, 1985

Psychologist of the Year—New Jersey Psychological Association, 1988

APA Council of Representatives, 1988–1991

Distinguished Practitioner, National Academy of Practice, 1989

Fellow, American Psychological Association Divisions 29, 31, 35, 42, 51, 1989

APA Board of Director, 1991–1994

APA Karl F. Heiser Award for Advocacy, 1993

Doctor of Humane Letters, Honoris Causa, Massachusetts School of Professional Psychology, 1994

Outstanding Sustaining Advocacy Award, Association for the Advancement of Psychology, 1994

Distinguished Graduate Alumni Award, Kean College of NJ, 1995

Psychologist of the Year - APA Division of Independent Practice, 1996

President, American Psychological Association, 1996

Peterson Prize, Graduate School of Applied & Professional Psychology, Rutgers University, 1997

APA Committee on Women in Psychology Leadership Citation, 1997

TABLE 22.7 *(continued)*
Selected Awards, Honors, and Professional Leadership Positions of Eminent Women in Psychology

Ann Klein Advocate Award—New Jersey Community Health Law Project, 1997

APA Award for Distinguished Contributions to Applied Psychology as a Professional Practice, 1999

Chair, APA Insurance Trust, 1999

D. J. Willis

Founding Editor, *Journal of Pediatric Psychology*, 1976–1977

President, Society for Pediatric Psychology, 1976–1977

Editor, *Journal of Clinical Child Psychology*, 1976–1981

President, APA Division 12, section on Child Clinical Psychology, 1982–1983

Distinguished Professional Contributions Award, Society of Pediatric Psychology, APA Division 12, 1982–1983

President, APA Division 37, 1984–1985

APA Council Representative, 1985–1986, 1987–1990, 1997–2000

Fellow, APA Divisions 12, 29, 37, 42 and 45, 1987

Faculty Award, Sciences Center for the Interdisciplinary Training Program in Child Abuse and Neglect, 1987–1991, 1995

Distinguished Psychologist Citation, Oklahoma Psychological Association, 1989

Presidential Award for Exceptional Scholarly Contributions, APA Division 12, 1989

Outstanding Achievement for Advocating for Psychology Award, Association for the Advancement of Psychology, 1990

APA Karl F. Heiser Presidential Award for Advocacy, 1992

Nicholas Hobbs Award for Distinguished Child Advocacy, APA Division 37, 1993

Distinguished Professional Contributions Award, APA Division 12, 1996

Outstanding Indian Woman of the Year, Oklahoma Federation of Indian Women, 1999–2000

President, APA Division 29, 2000–2001

TABLE 22.7 *(continued)*
Selected Awards, Honors, and Professional Leadership Positions of Eminent Women in Psychology

E. Hatfield

Fellow, APA Division 8, 1970

APF National Media Award, 1979 and 1986

Most Cited Social Psychologist, 1984–1988

Fellow, American Psychological Society, 1988

University of Hawaii - Distinguished Scientific Award, 1989

Society of Experimental Social Psychology Distinguished Scientific Award, 1993

Society for the Scientific Study of Sex Award, 1994

Alfred C. Kinsey Award, Society for the Scientific Study of Sex, 1998

President, Society for the Scientific Study of Sexuality, 1999

P. A. Katz

Fellow, APA Divisions 7, 8, 9, 35, 45, 1972

Founding Editor, *Sex Roles: A Journal of Research*, 1976–1991

APA Council of Representative, 1979–1986

President, APA Division 9, 1986–1987

Charter Fellow, American Psychological Society, 1988

Leadership Citation of the APA Committee of Women in Psychology, 1989

Media Award, APA Division 46, 1992

Carolyn Wood Sherif Award, APA Division 35, 1994

Outstanding Service Award, APA Division 9, 1996

Editor, *Journal of Social Issues*, 1997–2000

President, APA Division 35, 1999–2000

TABLE 22.7 *(continued)*
Selected Awards, Honors, and Professional Leadership Positions of Eminent Women in Psychology

L. M. Bartoshuk

Scientific Director's Silver Key Award for Research, Natick Army Labs, 1970

Chair, Association for Chemoreception Sciences, 1980–1981

Fellow, APA Divisions 1, 3, 6, and 25, 1982

M. A. Prizatim Honorary Yale Degree, 1985

Charter Fellow, American Psychological Society, 1988

President, APA Division 6, 1988–1989

APA G. Stanley Hall Lecturer, 1989

Manheimer Award for Research, Monell Chemical Senses Institute, 1990

Kreshover Award for Research, National Institute of Dental Research, 1990

President, Eastern Psychological Association, 1990–1991

Leah Lowenstein Award for Non-Sexist Teaching, Yale University School of Medicine, 1991

APA Distinguished Scientist Lecturer, 1992

Elected to American Academy of Art and Sciences, 1995

Society of Experimental Psychology, 1995

Association for Chemoreception Sciences Outstanding Achievement Award, 1998

P. Keith-Spiegel

Outstanding Service Award, Los Angeles County Psychological Association, 1972 and 1974

Distinguished Humanitarian Award, California State Psychological Association, 1976

National Vice President, Psi Chi Western Region, 1975–1976, 1977–1979

APA Council Representative, 1975–1977, 1978–1980

Fellow, APA Divisions 2, 7, 9, 34, 35, 37, 38, 1977

TABLE 22.7 *(continued)*
Selected Awards, Honors, and Professional Leadership Positions of Eminent Women in Psychology

Chair, Committee on Scientific and Professional Ethics and Conduct, 1977–1979, 1980–1981

President, Western Psychological Association, 1981

Trustee's Outstanding Teaching Award, California State University System (19 campuses), 1989

President, APA Division 2, 1990–1991

Award for Outstanding Service, APA Division 2, 1993

APF Distinguished Teaching Award, 1994

APA G. Stanley Hall Scholar, 1996

K. Deaux

APF Media Awards Honorable Mention, Book Category, 1976

Fellow, APA Divisions 8, 9 and 35, 1977

Chair, National Science Foundation Postdoctoral Fellowship Review Panel, 1981

President, Midwestern Psychological Association, 1981–1982

Fellow, Center for Advanced Study in the Behavioral Sciences, Stanford, CA, 1983–1984, 1986–1987

Chair, National Institute of Mental Health Research Education Review Committee, 1985–1986

Gordon Allport Intergroup Relations Prize (with B. Major), APA Division 9, 1987

Carolyn Wood Sherif Award, APA Division 35, 1987

Chair, APA Publication and Communications Board, 1987–1988

Fellow, American Psychological Society, 1988

Fellow, American Association for the Advancement of Science

President, APA Society of Personality and Social Psychology, 1990–1991

Heritage Research Award, APA Division 35, 1993

President, Eastern Psychological Society, 1994–1995

President, American Psychological Society, 1997–1998

TABLE 22.7 *(continued)*
Selected Awards, Honors, and Professional Leadership Positions of Eminent Women in Psychology

J. E. N. Albino

Fellow in Higher Education Administration, American Council on Education, 1983–1984

Fellow, APA Divisions 27 and 38, 1985

Fellow, World Health Organization Collaborating Center for Research on Health in Housing, 1988–1992

President, Behavioral Sciences Group, American Association for Dental Research, 1983–1984

Treasurer, APA Board of Directors, 1990–1994

Chair, APA Finance Committee, 1990–1995

President, University of Colorado, 1991–1995

Honorary Doctor of Science Degree, Manhattan College, 1994

Susan B. Anthony Award, Colorado Women's Political Caucus, 1994

Women of the Year Award, Boulder Business and Professional Women, 1995

Colorado Psychological Association Achievement Award, 1996

President, California School of Professional Psychology, 1997–2000

President, California School of Professional Psychology at Alliant University, 2000–present

M. W. Matlin

Chancellor's Award for Excellence in Teaching, State University of New York, 1977

Teaching of Psychology Award for 4-year Colleges/Universities, APA Division 2, 1985

Distinguished Teaching Professorship, State University of New York, 1987

Fellow, APA Divisions 1, 2, 35 and 48, 1988

Fellow, American Psychological Society, 1988

APF Distinguished Teaching in Psychology Award, 1995

TABLE 22.7 *(continued)*
Selected Awards, Honors, and Professional Leadership Positions of Eminent Women in Psychology

Fellow, Canadian Psychological Association, 1995

Chair, Psychology Graduate Record Examination Committee, 1998

P. T. Reid

Chair, Black Women's Concerns, APA Division 35, 1978–1980

Outstanding Professor, Student Government Association, University of Tennessee at Chattanooga, 1983–1985

Chair, Committee on Women in Psychology, 1984

APA Council Representative, 1985–1986

Fellow, APA Divisions 9, 35, 45, 1987

Charter Fellow, American Psychological Society, 1988

Outstanding Department Head, College of Arts and Sciences, University of Tennessee–Chattanooga, 1989

APS Board of Directors, 1989

Outstanding Services to Adult Students, University of Tennessee–Chattanooga, 1990

President, APA Division 35, 1991–1992

APA Distinguished Centennial Speaker, 1992

Ralph Speilman Lecturer, Bucknell University, 1992

Distinguished Publication Award, Association of Women in Psychology, 1994

Distinguished Professionals and Educators Award, Mid-Brooklyn Civic Association, 1995

APA Committee on Women in Psychology Leadership Citation, 1996

J. Brooks-Gunn

Fellow, APA Divisions 7, 35, and 37, 1988

William Goode Book Award for *Adolescent Mothers in Later Life*. American Sociological Association, 1988

TABLE 22.7 *(continued)*
Selected Awards, Honors, and Professional Leadership Positions of Eminent Women in Psychology

Charter Fellow, APS

President, Society for Research on Adolescence, 1994–1996

John T. Hill Award for Excellence in Theory Development and Research on Adolescents, Society for Research on Adolescence, 1996

Nicholas Hobbs Award for Policy Research on Children, APA Division of Children, Youth, and Families, 1997

Hammer Award, Vice President Gore's National Performance Review Award, 1998

Gallagher Lectureship, Society for Adolescent Medicine, 1999

W. T. Grant Foundation 2000 Lecturer, American Psychosomatic Society

D. F. Halpern

Outstanding Research Award, California State University, 1985

Silver Medal Winner, Council for the Advancement and Support of Education, 1986

Professor of the Year Award, Chamber of Commerce, 1986

Outstanding Professor Award, California State University System (19 campuses), 1986

Educational Equity Award, Association of Black Faculty and Staff, 1987

Fellow, APA Divisions 1, 2, 3 and 35, 1989

Professional Growth Award, CSUSB, 1990

APA G. Stanley Hall Lecturer, 1991

APA Council Representative, 1992–1995

Fulbright Scholar Award, 1994

President, APA Division 1, 1996–1997

APA Distinguished Career Contributions to Education and Teaching, 1996–97

Arthur Moorefield Memorial Award, 1997

President, APA Division 2, 1997–1998

APF Distinguished Teaching Award, 1998

Distinguished Visiting Scholar Award, James Madison University, 1998

TABLE 22.7 *(continued)*

Selected Awards, Honors, and Professional Leadership Positions of Eminent Women in Psychology

President, Western Psychological Association, 1998–1999

Wang Family Excellence Award, California State University system, 1999

J. S. Hyde

Academic Excellence Award, Bowling Green University, 1975

Fellow, APA Divisions 1, 8, 35, 1985

Women Educators Award, American Educational Research Association, 1988

Outstanding Teaching Award, Wisconsin Students Association, 1991

Outstanding Teaching Award, Wisconsin Panhellenic/Interfraternity Council, 1991

Kinsey Award, Society for the Scientific Study of Sex, 1992

President, APA Division 35, 1993–1994

Chancellor's Award for Teaching, University of Wisconsin, 1996

Heritage Award, APA Division 35, 1996

Honorary Doctorate of Social Sciences, Denison University, 1996

Chair, APA PsycINFO Advisory Board, 1997

Carolyn Sheriff Award, APA Division 35, 1998

President, Society for the Scientific Study of Sexuality, 1999–2000

Chair, APA Publication and Communications Board, 2000

L. Comas-Díaz

Fellow, APA Divisions 12, 35, 42, 45, 46, 1989

APA Committee on Women Leadership Citation Award, 1989

APA Council Representative, 1989–1992, 1998

Chair, APA Committee on International Relations in Psychology, 1990

Board of Directors, American Orthopsychiatric Association, 1990–1993

Fellow, American Psychological Society, 1991

TABLE 22.7 *(continued)*
Selected Awards, Honors, and Professional Leadership Positions of Eminent Women in Psychology

Chair, APA National Media Awards Committee, 1993

Founding Editor, *Cultural Diversity and Mental Health*, 1993; renamed *Cultural Diversity and Ethnic Minority Psychology*, 1998

APA G. Stanley Hall Lecturer, 1994

Distinguished Humanitarian Award, American Association of Applied and Preventive Psychology, 1994

Women of Color Distinguished Publication Award, Association for Women in Psychology, 1995

Distinguished Publication Award, Association for Women in Psychology, 1995

Frantz Fanon Award and Lecture, Postgraduate Center for Mental Health, 1995

Board of Directors, American Society of Hispanic Psychiatry, 1997–1998

APA Distinguished Contributions in the Public Interest Award, 2000

---

and Willis—of APA divisions—Bartoshuk, Deaux, Halpern (2), Horowitz, Hyde, Johnson (2), Katz (2), Keith-Spiegel, Reid, Scarr, and Willis (2)—and of regional professional societies—Bartoshuk, Bricklin, Cantor, Deaux (2), Halpern, and Johnson.

DEVELOPMENTAL CONTEXT: HISTORICAL AND SOCIAL EVENTS

Although most of the women in this volume were not yet born or were children during the major historical events of the first half of the 20th century, some of the women wrote of the effects these events had on their lives. In response to the inquiry about the influence of historical events on their education and career, several women wrote about the Great Depression: "My parents, particularly my mother, were very influenced by the Great Depression—I learned to respect money" (Norine Johnson). "The depression was very significant in our family life. We were often without food, relied on social services and public health for many basic needs. Awareness of the importance of money was no doubt seeded at that time. Family always stressed education as the means to meet financial obligations and gain financial status ..." (Frances Culbertson). "... parents' attitudes related to thrift times are still with me" (Judith Albino).

About World War II, they wrote "... strong values developed around not depending too much on men" (Judith Albino). "The model of a country working together, teamwork, optimism had a profound effect on my late childhood and early adolescence" (Patricia Bricklin). "Fewer men on campus opened up research opportunities for me as an undergraduate research assistant in experimental psychology sophomore year" (Frances Culbertson). "Expanding and expansive higher education milieu followed the second world war" (Frances Horowitz). For some World War II was a "difficult life period [as the] child of a single mother with a younger sister. Mom said, 'Get a good education so that you don't have to be poor'" (Patricia Keith-Spiegel). "My dad was in WWII—the separation was difficult" (Norine Johnson).

The events of the second half of the century had a much more direct impact on their development. War protests, peace through negotiation, civil rights, racial integration, women's rights, and college student unrest fueled the demonstrations of this period. The events and social activism of the 1960s and 1970s brought major philosophical changes that had a lasting impact on the lives and careers of many of these women. The women describe their participation, their thinking, and the effects of the Vietnam War and the Civil Rights Movement in their own words. "Vietnam was a period of great turmoil in universities, and I was part of the protests.... We lost a lot of academic time but gained a lot of self-respect" (Sandra Scarr). "Vietnam—the pain of losing faith in one's leaders—that we as a country could be wrong" (Patricia Bricklin). "The Vietnam War certainly influenced my thoughts about politics, power, ethnocentrism, etc." (Margaret Matlin). "The Civil Rights Movement and the challenge to the Mississippi Democratic Party in summer of 1964 gave me a clearer picture of class differences, politics, and racism" (Pamela Reid). "Martin Luther King and the racial struggles of the 60s raised my conscience and radicalized me" (Norine Johnson). Some wrote about the Civil Rights Movements and the Women's Movement. "The Women's Movement, Civil Rights Movement, and the Civil Rights Movement for Persons with Disabilities affected all aspects of my life" (Patricia Bricklin).

Many of the women wrote of the impact of the Women's Movement and the opportunities afforded by it. "Probably the most significant event was the Women's Movement which opened my eyes to the possibilities for me" (Dorothy Cantor). "The Women's Movement made more opportunities available" (Kay Deaux). "I finished my PhD in 1972, just when Women's Movement was rolling. Opportunities were just opening up for women, including me" (Janet Hyde). "The Women's Movement of the 1970s validated my voice" (Norine Johnson). Historical and social influences of the times played a significant role in shaping the lives of these women and those of the women in the earlier volumes. In Volume 1, the women witnessed the Great Depression and two major wars, World Wars I and II. The impact of these significant historical events on career patterns varied with the woman's stage of professional attainment. For some, the Great Depression interrupted their education; for others, World War II brought career opportunities; for still others, significant involvement in the wartime effort. For the women in Volume 2, World War II brought some increase in job opportunities for positions vacated by men, but the aftermath of the war had a very significant impact on career and family life. "The aftermath of World War II, and the decade of the 1950s brought the emphasis on the family—fostered by a 'togetherness' zeitgeist—to a new realization" (O'Connell, 1988, p. 361). Some of the women in Volume 2 wrote of the impact Betty Friedan's work (1963) on the "crisis in women's identity" and the "forfeited self" had on them. For them, role conflict was a challenge to achievement, a challenge they met and resolved. Although the sets of events and influences varied, the impact of the historical and social moment was felt by the women in all three volumes.

TRANSHISTORIC ASPECTS OF CREATIVITY AND ACHIEVEMENT

Creativity and achievement are rarely the outcome of a single variable, more often the result of a multitude of variables. The lives and careers of these eminent women demonstrate that creativity and achievement involve developmental, personal, professional, cognitive, motivational, and sociohistorical processes and influences. Perhaps the broadest influence, and the most universal, is the sociohistorical. It is consistent with this research on 53 eminent women, and the research of others, that the sociocultural environment and the zeitgeist can influence creative production in various ways. Under conditions of cultural diversity and enrichment of the environment, creative activity tends to increase. The aftermath of periods of crisis, war, turmoil, or unrest can nurture the creative environment with diversity and cultural enrichment (Csikzentmihalyi, 1996; Simonton, 2000). The occurrence and aftermath of these events can generate awareness of gaps in the culture and scientific domain and stimulate efforts toward relevant new ideas, insightful problem-solving, theoretical formulations, and creative productions. Although the zeitgeist can enhance or decrease the general level of creative activity, it is unlikely that it can account for individual differences in development and manifestation of creativity because of the multitude of variables involved in the creative process and the achievement of eminence.

It is clear from the autobiographies and my own and others' research that, at the least, achieving eminence requires true enjoyment of the work (Johnson writes, "I love being a psychologist.") and being energized by challenging and complex tasks (Brooks-Gunn writes, "I continued my fascination with social cognition of infants" and "The new millennium presents innovative and exciting research opportunities."). Achieving eminence also requires intelligence, motivation, exposure to intellect–nurturing stimuli, cognitive style (which includes divergent thinking and the capacity for remote associations), systematic training and practice in a specific domain or discipline, a rich body of discipline-relevant knowledge and well-developed skills, professional and social networks, influential mentors, and, of course, social and historical context among other variables. It is also clear that creativity and achievement do not occur in a vacuum; they occur in a social context, but they also follow a substantial and laborious period of practice or apprenticeship (Csikszentmihalyi, 1996; Ericsson, 1996; Simonton, 1987, 1991a, 1991b).

Creative ideas, creative production and achievement, for the most part, are the outcome of a strong well-developed knowledge basis and a diverse, enriched sociocultural environment. As the 53 autobiographies demonstrate, creativity and achievement develop in complex dynamic interaction between the person, the domain, the gatekeepers in the field, and the sociocultural milieu. Eminence within a domain occurs when the creativity and achievement are recognized and valued by others in the field or society. Awards, honors, and leadership positions are the outcome of achievement and testimony to eminent status.

TRANSHISTORIC AND TIME-SPECIFIC PROFILES AND PATTERNS

The interplay between the transhistoric aspects of creativity and achievement for eminent women and others raises questions about what we can learn from the 53 eminent women in these three volumes. Is it possible to develop transhistoric or time–specific profiles and patterns of achievement for eminent women in psychology? Are there variables that are related to eminence across time? Are there variables that are influenced by historical and social context? Is there a single profile for eminent women in psychology? Is it transhistoric or time–specific?

Analyses of the lives and careers of the eminent women in these three volumes reveal that the variables related to eminence for women born early in the 20th century are birth order and family of origin; educational institutions, graduate support, and years from baccalaureate to doctorate; marital status and marital partners; coping strategies toward barriers; mentors and colleagues; and awards and honors. A definitive profile begins to emerge, a profile that may be transhistorical. The women who fit this profile come from privileged, well-educated, middle-class families that valued high levels of achievement in education and occupation. They were firstborn into families that were professional or entrepreneurial. The women attended prestigious colleges (Ivy League or Seven Sisters institutions), remained single, or married professional men and remained childless. They went from baccalaureate to doctorate in less time than others in the doctorate population, received financial graduate support, had an impressive list of mentors, colleagues, and good professional and social networks.

To fulfill their individual potential, their identities stretched beyond accepted gender role prescriptions. They saw creativity and achievement as purposeful work. They persisted in the face of discrimination and other barriers to contribute ideas, approaches, and definitive work in psychology and allied fields. They were often pioneers and groundbreakers, and were recognized by election to leadership positions and by honors and awards. Although this profile is descriptive of the women born early in the century, there are substantial deviations and other variables to consider before the profile can be considered transhistorical.

Time–specific historical and social forces contributed to changes in educational opportunities in the 20th century. For women born between 1891 and 1914, choices for graduate training were limited. Few institutions offered degrees in the new science of psychology, and the institutions that did tended to be Ivy League or Seven Sisters institutions. For women born between 1915 and 1950, the sites of formal education included a widening range of colleges and universities, including state institutions. In Volume 1, 65% of the women attended an Ivy League or Seven Sisters institution for all or part of their doctoral education; in Volume 2 and the present volume, the comparable percentages are 41% and 32%. Although Ivy League and Seven Sisters institutions continued to be good choices and affiliations with distinguished institutions or sites of employment facilitated creativity and eminence, other choices and other routes became available and feasible. For 53% of the women in Volume 1, the sites of employment at some point in their careers included Ivy League or Seven Sister institutions although tenure was elusive; the comparable percentages for Volumes 2 and the present volume are 29% and 26%, respectively. For the younger women, there was a wider variation in degree-awarding institutions and sites of employment. These are important variations indicative of the changing educational and occupational context for women.

The increase in the number of degree-awarding institutions provided greater access to professional training. For women whose families of origin were not privileged, professional training came into reach. Although being born into an educated, professional, and/or wealthy family continued to be very advantageous in achieving eminence, achievement now became accessible to women who were not from a family privileged in at least one of these ways. It became possible to achieve eminence when educational and occupational achievement for women was not a family value due to cultural, religious, or other beliefs or circumstances. In the last half of the 20th century, professional training came into reach and achievement became attainable regardless of family privilege or values.

At the same time, the marital status of these women began to reflect the changing social context of the 20th century. Marriage and parenthood were more likely to become part of the texture of life for eminent women born later rather than earlier. For the 18 women born between 1891 and 1914, 78% (14) married; of these, 21.4% became parents. After 1915, the pattern changed significantly in favor of marriage and parenthood. For the 35 women born between 1915 and 1950, 91.4% (32) married, and of these, 75% became parents. More specifically, for the 18 women born between 1915 and 1932, 94% (17) married, of these, 76% became parents; for the 17 women born between 1933 and 1950, 88% (15) married and 73% became parents. Analyzing the data for the three volumes, 55% (29) of the 53 women became parents. In Volume 1, 29% (5) of the 17 women became parents; in Volume 2, 53% (9) of the 17 women became parents; in the present volume, 79% (15) of the 19 women became parents. With each succeeding volume, this very dramatic increase in percentage of eminent women engaged in parenting reflects the demise of the perception that women must choose career or marriage and parenthood; it also reflects the demise of the sanctions against employed women with children. It is appropriate to conclude that historical and societal influences contributed to this change and expansion in role definition. These women include single, married-without-children, married-with-children, and single parents. Marital pattern did not exclude achieving the highest professional ranks or the mantle of eminence for these women.

Time–specific historical and social changes were manifest. The importance of highly educated, professional, and affluent families of origin for achieving eminence diminished, but did not disappear, as the century progressed, from 88% of fathers and 47% of mothers who were professional or entrepreneurial in Volume 1, to 58% of both fathers and mothers in the present volume. In the early years of the century, well-positioned families supportive of achievement were crucial for educational and occupational distinction and the attainment of eminence. As the century progressed, educational and occupational opportunities made the attainment of eminence possible for increasing numbers without the benefit of well-positioned, supportive families of origin. In a similar vein, prestigious educational institutions and sites of employment became less crucial to the attainment of eminence, and designated marital or parental statuses virtually disappeared as the century progressed. All these time–specific variables changed in significant ways during the 20th century. These time–specific historical and social changes necessitated some modifications in the original profile based on the women born early in the century.

A transhistoric profile that best portrays the majority of the 53 eminent women in these three volumes emerges—a profile that contains variables that are related to eminence across time. This transhistoric profile represents most of the eminent women, and parts of the profile fit all the women. As a group, the 53 predominantly firstborn women went from baccalaureate to doctorate in less time than others; received financial graduate support; had an impressive list of mentors and colleagues and good professional and social networks; married professional men; developed their own gender role prescriptions; valued creativity and achievement and saw them as purposeful work; and persisted in the face of discrimination and other barriers to contribute ideas, approaches, and definitive work to psychology and allied fields. They were often first as pioneers and groundbreakers, and were recognized by election to leadership positions and by honors and awards.

A modification for 21% of the 53 women relates to interruption in educational attainment. For example, these women took more than a decade to go from baccalaureate to doctorate: Thelma Alper, Katherine M. Banham, Patricia Bricklin, Dorothy Cantor, Diane Halpern, Ruth Howard, Norine Johnson, Carolyn Payton, Carolyn Sherif, Leona Tyler, and Lillian Troll. The years of birth for these women encompass a 50-year period and their marital patterns represent 4 marital categories. The reasons for the extended period of time include financial circumstances, family consideration, and lack of opportunity. Some women suffered from a paucity of mentors and colleagues. Although earning the doctorate in a brief period of time is a predictor of later achievement and the presence of mentors, colleagues, and social and professional networks important to achievement, the absence of these markers did not deter these women from the highest levels of professional achievement and leadership. There does not seem to be any one insurmountable variable in the face of talent, ability, resourcefulness, flexibility, determination, perseverance, and strong motivation.

Several of the eminent women write of their struggles but also of their belief that the chance to succeed exists alongside the challenge to overcome obstacles. Lillian Comas-Díaz writes, "I know the burdens and gifts of the wounded healer. Although pain can be sublimated into healing, it can only be done after facing our demons. Searching for who I am, while making sense out of dislocation, I have been fortunate to alchemize adversity into opportunity. As an illustration, my speech problems fostered a gift for storytelling, while socioeconomic barriers ignited my drive for achievement." Patricia Keith-Spiegel writes, "My first memories from childhood in Los Angeles are painted in bleak tones. I even recall food as gray. The occasional splash of color was from a rare meat dish or a piece of fruit. The meat was almost always Spam and the fruit was usually an orange.... A minuscule two-room apartment over a garage on my grandmother's property housed my mother, little sister, and me. The only sanctuary where I could be completely alone was inside my own head."

The women in Volume 2 also wrote of their struggles. Bonnie Strickland wrote, "Few of my friends went to college, and my family was in no position to support me financially. Scholarships, waiting tables, lifeguarding, and delivering newspapers and movie theater programs all combined to provide my tuition, housing costs, and spending money." Leona Tyler wrote "... we were on the verge of poverty most of the time." Martha Bernal wrote, "Throughout my life, however critical I might be of this country, I have felt grateful for the opportunities of which I availed myself. They would most likely not have existed had I lived in Mexico." Carolyn Payton wrote, "I learned, as all children in public school, that I was an American and as such was guaranteed the pursuit of happiness, equality, and justice. I learned that lesson well and have continuously struggled to achieve these rights as a minority and as a woman."

As a group, these 53 women persevered despite professional and personal obstacles, learned from their experiences, focused on the tasks at hand, and brought their considerable talents to bear. These talents seem to echo the correlates of wisdom-related performance. These correlates involve a quadruple interplay of intelligence (e.g., reasoning ability, memory, and complex problem-solving), personality (e.g., openness to experience, personal growth, and psychological mindedness), the interface between personality and intelligence (e.g., creativity, cognitive style, and social intelligence), and life experiences (e.g., general life and specific professional experiences).

The autobiographies and the commonalities and differences among the women reveal that the superior levels of knowledge, insight, and judgment exhibited can be identified as wisdom. In an interaction of multiple characteristics, interests, and environmental contexts (Sternberg, 1985, 1998), they used the extraordinary breadth and depth of their intelligence, knowledge, creativity, motivation, insight, and judgment to achieve goals that benefited the field of psychology and society at large. It is appropriate to conclude that the excellence of their behavior fits the pattern of predictive correlates of wisdom-related performance and the definition of wisdom (Baltes & Staudinger, 2000; Staudinger, Lopez, & Baltes, 1997; Sternberg, 1990) and that they not only exhibited wisdom in their lives and careers, but their lives contain remarkable wisdom for others to share.

These women were risk-takers, self-reliant, courageous, energetic, and flexible. They made optimal use of their intelligence, creativity, and insights—going beyond existing knowledge to make new discoveries. They had great curiosity following their interests and inclinations into new subdisciplines and new opportunities. They found that solving one problem uncovered others. They saw the world as it was and as it might be. Their lives were marked by a complexity of purpose, by a weaving and reweaving of endeavors. They made wide use of support systems, professional and social, but were not afraid to be pioneers and go it alone. Their lives resound with integration, complexity, and wisdom (O'Connell, 1983, 1988).

The 19 women in this volume, like the 34 women before them, are innovators continuing in the pioneering spirit that women have shown from the very beginning. These women are younger and more contemporary, but pioneers nonetheless. The world has undergone major transformations in the 20th century, bringing equal access to education, employment, and advancement into reach. There is still much that needs to be done in this 21st century.

The thorough and complex integration of women into the history of psychology is essential. If the history of psychology is to be accurate, it must integrate the formidable contributions made by women in the evolution and development of the field as a science since its inception. These women, like their many predecessors, have brought us to the forefront of knowledge with their innovative and pioneering work. They have helped shape the science and profession of psychology, the history of the 20th century, and the quality of our lives. They are inspirational and wise role models of achievement for now and for the future. For our own well-being and that of others, we need to understand the strengths, experiences, and contexts of these eminent women and to be empowered by our knowledge, insights, and understanding of their lives, careers, and extraordinary achievements.

NOTE

This chapter is indebted to O'Connell (1983, 1988).

REFERENCES

Baltes, P. B., & Staudinger, U. M. (2000). Wisdom: A metaheuristic (pragmatic) to orchestrate mind and virtue toward excellence. *American Psychologist, 55,* 122–136.
Bryson, R. B., Bryson, J. B., Licht, M. H., & Licht, B. G. (1976). The professional pair: Husband and wife psychologists. *American Psychologist, 31,* 10–16.
Clawson, J. G. (1980). Mentoring in managerial careers. In C. B. Dear (Ed.), *Work, family and the career: New frontiers in theory and research* (pp. 144–165). New York: Praeger.
Cole, J. R., & Zuckerman, H. (1987, February). Marriage, motherhood and research performance in science. *Scientific American,* pp. 119–125.
Csikszentmihalyi, M. (1996). *Creativity: Flow and the psychology of discovery and invention.* New York: HarperCollins.
Eisenstadt, J. M. (1978). Parental loss and genius. *American Psychologist, 33,* 211–223.
Ericsson, K. A. (Ed.). (1996). *The road to expert performance: Empirical evidence from the arts and sciences, sports, and games.* Mahwah, NJ: Lawrence Erlbaum Associates.
Featherman, D. (1978). *Schooling and occupational careers: Constancy and change in worldly success.* Madison: University of Wisconsin, Center for Demography and Ecology.
Friedan, B. (1963). *The feminine mystique.* New York: Norton.
Furumoto, L., & Scarborough, E. (1986). Placing women in the history of psychology: The first American women psychologists. *American Psychologist, 41,* 35–42.
Hennig, M., & Jardim, A. (1977). *The managerial woman.* New York: Anchor-Doubleday.
Kluckhohn C., & Murray, H. A. (1953). Personality formation: The determinants. In C. Kluckhohn, H. A. Murray, & D. Schneider (Eds.), *Personality in nature, society and culture* (p. 53). New York: Knopf.
Levinson, D. J. (1978). *The seasons of a man's life.* New York: Knopf.
Mellilo, D. (1983). Birth order, perceived birth order, and family position of academic women. *Individual Psychology, 39,* 57–62.
O'Connell, A. N. (1983). Synthesis: Profiles and patterns of achievement. In A. N. O'Connell & N. F. Russo (Eds.), *Models of achievement: Reflections of eminent women in psychology* (pp. 298–326). New York: Columbia University Press.
O'Connell, A. N. (1988). Synthesis and resynthesis: Profiles and patterns of achievement 2. In A. N. O'Connell & N. F. Russo (Eds.), *Models of achievement: Reflections of eminent women in psychology,* Vol. 2 (pp. 317–366). Hilldale, NJ: Lawrence Erlbaum Associates.
O'Connell, A. N., & Russo, N. F. (Eds.). (1980). Eminent women in psychology [Special issue]. *Psychology of Women Quarterly, 5*(1).

O'Connell, A. N., & Russo, N. F. (Eds.). (1990). *Women in psychology: A bio-bibliographic sourcebook.* Westport, CT: Greenwood.
Roe, A. (1952). *The making of a scientist.* New York: Dodd, Mead.
Runyan, W. M. (1984). *Life histories and psychobiography: Explorations in theory and method.* New York: Oxford University Press.
SAUS. (1985). *Statistical abstracts of the United States* (105th ed.). Washington, DC: Bureau of the Census.
SAUS. (1986). *Statistical abstracts of the United States* (106th ed.). Washington, DC: Bureau of the Census.
Simonton, D. K. (1987). Developmental antecedents of achieved eminence. *Annals of Child Development, 5,* 131–169.
Simonton, D. K. (1991a). Career landmarks in science: Individual differences and interdisciplinary contrasts. *Developmental Psychology, 27,* 119–130.
Simonton, D. K. (1991b). Emergence and realization of genius: The lives and works of 120 classical composers. *Journal of Personality and Social Psychology, 61,* 829–840.
Simonton, D. K. (1992). Leaders of American psychology, 1879–1967: Career development, creative output, and professional achievement. *Journal of Personality and Social Psychology, 62,* 5–17.
Simonton, D. K. (1994). *Greatness: Who makes history and why.* New York: Guilford.
Simonton, D. K. (1998). Fickle fashion versus immortal fame. *Journal of Personality and Social Psychology, 75,* 198–210.
Simonton, D. K. (1999). Talent and its development. *Psychological Review, 106,* 435–457.
Simonton, D. K. (2000). Creativity: Cognitive, personal, developmental, and social aspects. *American Psychologist, 55,* 151–158.
Staudinger, U. M., Lopez, D. E., & Baltes, P. B. (1997). The psychometric location of wisdom-related performance: Intelligence, personality, and more? *Personality and Social Psychology Bulletin, 23,* 1200–1214.
Sternberg, R. J. (1985). Implicit theories of intelligence, creativity, and wisdom. *Journal of Personality and Social Psychology, 49,* 607–627.
Sternberg, R. J. (Ed.). (1990). *Wisdom: Its nature, origins, and development.* New York: Cambridge University Press.
Sternberg, R. J. (1998). A balance theory of wisdom. *Review of General Psychology, 2,* 347–365.
U. S. Bureau of the Census. (1995). *Current Population Reports. Series P20–482.* Washington, DC: U. S. Government Printing Office.

Index

A

ABCS Psychological Services, 86–88
Abrams, J. C., 60
Academe, women in, xiii, 6, 21–22
  women presidents, 369–370, 373
Access for Change, 88–89
Achievement, 370–374, 398–410, 412–413
  longevity, 22, 388
  see also Creativity, Profiles and patterns
Adolescent Study Program, 281
Ainsworth, M., xvii, 22, 388
Albino, J., 8–9, 20, 22, 219–237, 347, 351–352, 356–358, 369, 374–375, 388–389, 397, 411
Albright, M., 18
Alliant University, 233, *see also* California School of Professional Psychology
Allport, G., 102
Alper, T., 416

American Academy of Arts and Sciences, 108, 180, 397, 401, 404
American Association for the Advancement of Science, 397, 399–400, 405
American Federation of Indian Women, 128
American Indian children and families, 128
American Men of Science, 19
American Orthopsychiatry Association, 337
American Psychological Association, xx, 39–40, 57, 93, 302, 337, 398–410
Association for the Advancement of Psychology (formerly Committee for the Advancement of Psychology), 122, 131, 401–402
Board of Convention Affairs, 398
Board of Directors, 20, 92, 107, 118, 398, 400–401, 406

Note: Thanks to David H. Kelly, Montclair State University, and Beatrice Truica, Pace University, for their assistance in reading the page proofs and preparing the index.

421

422 Index

Board of Education and Training, 232, 263
Board of Ethnic Minority Affairs, xx
Board of Professional Affairs, 131, 398
Board of Social and Ethical Responsibility, xx, 263, 269
Boards and committees, xiii
Carolyn Wood Sherif Award, 163, 324, 403, 405, 409
Committee for the Advancement of Professional Practice, 118
Committee on Accreditation, 91
Committee on Children, Youth, and Families, 122
Committee on Women in Psychology, xx, 19–20, 92, 118, 163, 263–268, 400–401, 403, 407, 409
Council of Representatives, 20, 92, 107, 118, 160, 195, 263, 398–401, 403–404, 407–409
Distinguished Career Contribution to Education and Teaching Award, 408
Distinguished Contribution to Applied Psychology as a Professional Practice Award, 122, 397, 402
Distinguished Contribution to the International Advancement of Psychology Award, 42, 397–398
Distinguished Contribution to Practice Award, 399
Distinguished Contribution to Psychology in the Public Interest Award, 337, 397, 410
Distinguished Contribution to Research in Public Policy Award, 108, 397, 400
Distinguished Professional Contributions Award, 131, 402
Distinguished Scientific Contributions Award, 19, 139
Division of Behavioral Neuroscience and Comparative Psychology (formerly Physiological and Comparative Psychology), Division 6, 178, 404
Division of Child, Youth, and Family Services, Division 37, 131, 136–137, 402, 404, 407
Division of Counseling Psychology, Division 17, 21
Division of Developmental Psychology, Division 7, xix, 20, 106–107, 399–400, 403–404, 407
Division of Experimental Psychology, Division 3, 404

Division of Health Psychology, Division 38, 404, 406
Division of International Psychology, Division 52, 41, 398
Division of Media Psychology, Division 46, 20, 403, 409
Division of Population and Environmental Psychology, Division 34, 404
Division of Psychoanalysis, Division 39, 20–21, 118
Division of Psychologists in Independent Practice, Division 42, 21, 91, 118, 401–402, 409
Division of Psychotherapy, Division 29, 21, 400–402
Division of School Psychology, Division 16, 40, 398–399
Division of State Psychological Association Affairs, 401
Division of the History of Psychology, Division 26, xx
Ethics Committee, 192
Fellow Status, 20, 92, 122, 397–410
G. Stanley Hall Lecturer, 397, 404–405, 408–410
Gordon Allport Intergroup Relations Award, 405
Heritage Award, 324, 405, 409
Insurance Trust, 58, 122, 401–402
Karl F. Heiser Award for Advocacy, 122, 131, 397, 401
Lifetime Career Contributions to Education Award, 302
Membership, 18–20, 398
National Book Award, 397, 400
Nicholas Hobbs Award, 131, 402, 408
Office of Ethnic Minority Affairs, 335
Office of Social and Ethical Responsibility, 263–269
PsycINFO Advisory Board, 409
Publications and Communications Board, 208–212, 405, 409
Society for Community Research and Action, Division 27, 406
Society for General Psychology, Division 1, xix, 399, 404, 406, 408–409
Society for Personality and Social Psychology, Division 8, xx, 208, 403, 405, 409
Society for the Psychological Study of Ethnic Minority Issues, Division 45, 20, 336, 409
Society for the Psychological Study of Social Issues, Division 9, xx, 400, 403–405, 407

Index **423**

Society for the Psychology of Women (formerly Division on the Psychology of Women), Division 35, xiii, xvii, xx, 19–20, 89–91, 122, 160, 163, 260, 262–263, 324, 338, 398, 400–401, 403–407, 409
Society for the Psychological Study of Men and Masculinity, Division 51, 401
Society for the Study of Peace, Conflict & Violence, Division 48, 406
Society for the Teaching of Psychology, Division 2, xix, 196, 249–250, 404–406, 408
Society of Clinical Psychology (formerly Clinical Psychology), Division 12, 20–21, 131, 402, 409
Society of Pediatric Psychology, Division 54, 20, 129–130, 402
Symposium on Eminent Women in Psychology, xvii, xix
Task Force on Adolescent Girls, 122
Task Force on Women Doing Research, xvii
Task Force on the Changing Gender Composition of Psychology, 6, 118
Women presidents of, 7–8, 19, 90–91, 115, 121, 359, 369, 388, 400–401
American Psychological Foundation, 122, 195, 250, 397, 399, 401, 403, 406, 408
Distinguished Teaching Award, 195, 250, 302, 397, 405–406
James McKeen Cattell Award for Distinguished Contributions to Applied Research, 108, 401
National Media Award, 141, 145, 397, 403, 405, 409
American Psychological Society, xiii, 8, 21, 106–108, 214, 369, 397, 400, 403, 407
Fellows, 397–410
Presidents, 107, 369, 401, 403, 405
Publications Committee, 401
Anastasi, A., 8, 20, 23, 358–359, 388
Anthony, S., 16
Anti-nepotism, xiii, 16, 206–207, 389
Antioch College, 65, 74, 207, 222
Association for the Advancement of Psychology, *see* American Psychological Association
Association for Chemoreception Sciences, 176, 404

Association for Women in Psychology (formerly Association for Women Psychologists), 19, 338, 407, 410
Association of State and Provincial Psychology Boards, 57
Auld, F., 84–85
Authorship credit, 191–192
Awards, 19–20, 92, 122, 131, 139, 163, 180, 195, 246–247, 250, 302, 324, 335, 337–338, 397–410, 413

B

Babledelis, G., xiii, xx
Ball State University, 194–196
Baltes, P., 418
Bandura, A., 267
Banham, K., 353, 416
Bardon, J., 117
Barriers, 388–397
Barron, R., 85
Bartoshuk, L., 8, 22, 169–183, 347, 352, 357, 374–375, 388–389, 397, 410
Bayley, N., 19, 22–23
Bayley Scales of Mental and Motor Development, 22
Benjamin, L., xviii
Berkowitz, L., 38
Berman, P., 262
Bernal, M., 21, 23, 417
Bernay, T., 119–121
Berscheid, E., 139–141
Bethune, M., 16
Bieri, J., 206
Birth order, 347–350
Block, J., 316
Boston University, 87
Bowling Green University, 315–317, 409
Brazelton, T. B., 71
    Neonatal Behavioral Assessment Scale (also known as the Brazelton Scale), 71
Brewer, M., 8, 369
Bricklin, B., 8, 50–52, 55, 60
Bricklin, P., 8–9, 20–21, 45–62, 346, 351–352, 358, 369, 374–375, 388–389, 397, 410, 411, 416
Brim, O., 282
Brooklyn College, 153
Brooks-Gunn, J., 8, 22, 275–292, 347, 356, 369, 374–375, 389, 397, 413
Brown University, 173, 229–232

424   *Index*

Brown v. Board of Education, 17
Buhler, C., 18, 23, 188

C

California School of Professional Psychology (at Alliant University), 232–233, 369, 388, 406
California State University, 302, 408
California State University-Northridge, 194
Calkins, M., 8, 19, 23, 359
Campbell, A., 36
Campbell, D., 205–206, 396
Canadian Psychological Association, 407
Cantor, D., 7–9, 20–21, 90, 113–124, 346, 353, 357–358, 369, 374–375, 388–389, 396–397, 410–411, 416
Capaldi, E., 8, 369
Carleton College, 172
Catterall, C., 40
Center for Advanced Study in the Behavioral Sciences, 212, 405
Center for Children and Families, 285
Children and parenthood, 354–355, 357–358
City College of New York (CCNY), 115–116
City University of New York, Graduate Center, 158–159, 206, 212–213, 215, 269, 369
Civil Rights Act, 17
Civil Rights Movement, xii, 7, 16, 334, 411
Claremont Graduate University, 189
Clark, K., 17
Clark, M., 17, 23, 353
College of New Jersey (formerly Trenton State College), 262
Columbia University, 205–206, 284–286
Comas-Díaz, L., 8, 21, 23, 329–342, 347, 351, 353, 369, 374–375, 389, 396–397, 417
Commission on the Status of Women, 17
Committee on Women in Psychology
 see American Psychological Association
Connecticut College, 278
Contributions, 8–9, 22–23, 40–43, 57–61, 72, 74–75, 89, 93, 122–123, 130–131, 144–146, 161–163, 178–180, 193, 195–197, 209–210, 214–215, 225–227, 230, 232–234, 249–250, 252–253, 263, 266–269, 280–282, 285–287, 299–300, 317–318, 320, 322–323, 336, 359, 369–375

Coping strategies, 389–397
Creativity, 412–413, 417–418
 see also Achievement, Profiles and patterns
Crosby, F., 163
Cross-cultural psychology, 23, 142–145, 300, 335–337
Culbertson, F., 8, 19, 21, 29–44, 347, 351, 356–357, 359, 375, 389, 397, 411
Cummings, N., 232
Curie, M., 16
Czikszentmihalyi, M., 388, 412–413

D

Deaux, K., 8, 21–22, 201–218, 347, 351, 369, 375, 397, 410–411
DeBeauvoir, S., 16
Denison University, 319, 321
Denmark, F., xviii, 8, 20, 22, 359
Dentistry
 see Health psychology
DePauw University, 83
Depression
 see Great Depression
Discrimination
 see Racial/ethnic/religious discrimination, Sex/gender discrimination
Douvan, E., 6, 20
Drake, E., 119
DreamTracks, 117
Dual careers, 37–39, 50–55, 60–61, 65, 68–69, 83–86, 93, 102–103, 105, 144–146, 156–157, 159, 174–176, 178, 194, 196, 207, 212–213, 224–225, 228, 245, 247, 252, 260–261, 264–265, 269–270, 279, 283–284, 287, 296, 298, 313–315, 318, 320–321, 335–336, 338–339, 390, 394–395
Duck, S., 142
Duke University, 99

E

Eastern Psychological Association, 178, 404–405
Editors, founders of professional journals, 106, 158, 162, 369–374, 402–403
Educational patterns, 7, 358–368, 414–416

Index

Educational Testing Service, 279, 282, 284
Eichorn, D., xviii. 20–21
Eminence, selection criteria, 6–7
Eminent Women in Psychology, xviii, 8
Eminent Women
  see Achievement, Awards, Barriers, Birth order, Children and parenthood, Contributions, Dual Careers, Educational patterns, Families of origin, Innovations, Interests, Leadership, Marital partners, Marital patterns, Professional and social networks, Professional positions, Profiles and patterns, Siblings
Empathy Power, 120–121
Employed women, 17–18, 21–22
Equal Pay Act, 17
Ericsson, K., 413
Ethics, 51–55, 57, 107–108, 191–193, 197

F

Families of origin, 7, 346–353, 413–417
Faust, M., 189
Feminism, xii, 89, 93, 158, 268, 298–299, 311, 316, 334, 336–337
Ferraro, G., 18
Festinger, L., 139, 396
Fiske, S., 212
Florida State University, 222
Forbes, 223
Fowler, R., 121
Frenkel-Brunswik, E., 23
Freud, A., 23, 188
Friedan, B., 17, 412
Fromm, E., 21, 353
Furstenberg, F., 282
Furumoto, L., xviii

G

Gender composition of psychology, 19–21
Gender discrimination
  see Sex/gender discrimination
Gender stereotypes, 48, 211–212
George Peabody College, 128–129
Gibson, E., 19, 22, 180
Gilbreth, L., 22
Gilmore, R., 142
Ginsburg, R., 18
Glickman, S., 204

Glucksberg, S., 212
Goldwater, B., 141
Goodenough, F., 23
Goodnow, J., 22
Goodson, F., 83
Gottesman, I., 101
Goucher College, 66
Gough, H., xviii
Graham, F., 22, 359
Gray, S., 129, 396
Gray-Shelberg, L., 197
Great Depression, 7, 16–17, 81–82, 99, 137, 410–412
Greiner, B., 396
Greiner, W., 227–228
Gruber, H., xviii
Grushka, M., 179
Guthrie, R. V., 262

H

Hahnemann University, 59
Halpern, D., 8, 22, 293–305, 347, 351–353, 356–357, 374–375, 389, 397, 410, 416
Hardy, J., 175
Harrower, M., xvii
Harvard University, 87, 34–35, 101, 191, 279
Hatfield, E., 8–9, 22, 135–147, 346, 358, 374–375, 389, 397
Health psychology, 225–227
Hebb, D., 74
Heiderbreder, E., 18, 23
Helson, R., 23, 316
Henle, M., xvii, 353
Hetherington, M., 396
Historical events, impact of, 6–7, 9, 15–16, 410–418
Hobbs, N., 129
  see also American Psychological Association
Hollingworth, L., 18, 22
Honors
  see Awards, Leadership
Horner, M., 224
Horney, K., 18, 23
Horowitz, F., 8–9, 22, 63–77, 346, 356, 358–359, 369, 374–375, 389, 397, 410–411
Horowitz, L., 243–244, 396
Howard (Beckham), R., 23, 416
Howard University, 260–263, 265
Hyde, J., 8–9, 20, 23, 249, 307–327, 347, 351, 353, 356–359, 375, 389, 396–397, 410–411

I

Inhelder, B., 22
Innovations, 8–9, 18–19, 22–23, 359, 368–375, 418
Institute for Child and Family Policy, 286
Institute for Research on Social Problems, 159
Institute for the Study of Exceptional Children, 282–283
Interests, of eminent women, 360–368
International Association of Applied Psychology, 40–41
International Council of Psychologists (formerly the International Council of Women Psychologists; formerly the National Council of Women Psychologists), 19, 36, 39–41, 398
International School Psychology Association, 40
Interpersonal attraction, 141–142
Iowa Child Welfare Station, 67
Ives, M., 353

J

Jacklin, C., 244
Jahoda, M., 22
John B. Pierce Foundation, 175–176, 178
Johns Hopkins University, 49
Johnson, N., 8–9, 20–21, 79–96, 118, 122, 346, 351, 353, 356–357, 369, 388–389, 396–397, 410–411, 413, 416
Jones, M., xvii
Journal of Clinical Child Psychology, 130–131, 402
Journal of Pediatric Psychology, 130–131, 402
JPP Consultants: Business Practices for Professionals, 88–89

K

Karrer, T., 179
Katz, P., xiii, 8–9, 20, 22, 149–167, 346, 351–352, 356–358, 369, 374–375, 389, 397, 410
Kean University of New Jersey, 116, 401
Keita, G., 263
Keith-Spiegel, P., 8–9, 23, 185–199, 347, 357, 374–375, 389, 397, 410–411, 417

Kindercare Learning Centers, 108–109, 388
King, M. L., 411
Kiowa Tribe, 128
Kohlberg, L., 155
Koocher, G., 191, 193
Korean War, 16

L

Ladd-Franklin, C., 22
LaFrance, M., 211
Leadership, 7–8, 21, 40–41, 57–60, 73–74, 86–92, 106, 109, 115, 118–121, 130–131, 144–145, 158–159, 163, 178–179, 193, 214–215, 228–234, 263–264, 269, 285–287, 302, 317–318, 320–324, 336–337, 397–410
Leavitt, H. S., 172
Lewin, K., 36, 206
Lewis, M., 279, 282, 396
Likert, R., 36
Lindzey, G., 206
Lipsitt, L., xviii
Loevinger, J., 23
Loftus, E., 8, 369
Lopez, D., 418
Lott, B., 91, 396

M

Maccoby, E., 22, 244, 314, 396
Maier, N., 396
Maier, R. F., 35–36
Major, B., 211, 213
Malloy, J., 88
Marino, S., 177
Marital partners, 354–357
Marital patterns, 7, 353–356, 375, 414–416
Mary Louis Academy, Queens, New York, 259
Maslow, A., 18
Massachusetts School of Professional Psychology, 87
Matlin, M., 8–9, 22, 239–254, 347, 351, 353, 356–358, 374–375, 389, 396–397, 411
Matthews, H., 49
McCandless, B., 67–68, 396
McCullough, C., 312
McCormick, M., 283–284
McGraw, M., 22, 388
McKeachie, W., 396

Mead, G. H., 213–214
Mead, M., 153
Media psychology, 50–55
Mednick, M., 22, 262, 266
Mentors, 396–397
Meredith, W., 314
Midwestern Psychological Association, 208, 405
Milgram, S., 155
Miller, I., 177
Miller, N., 154–155
Minority women, 21, 23, 125–131, 255–273, 329–342
Mitchell, M., 21
Models of Achievement: Reflections of Eminent Women in Psychology, xiv, xviii–xix, 5
  Vol. 1, xvii–xix, 352–353, 356–358, 368, 412, 414–415
  Vol. 2, xviii–xix, 8, 351–353, 356–358, 368–369, 412, 414–415, 417
Moscow State University, 300
Mullen, F., 39–40, 42
Multimedia, 196–197
Murphy, L., 22, 388

N

Nadoolman, W., 179
Natick Army Labs, 174, 404
National Academy of Practice in Psychology, 92, 122, 401
National Academy of Sciences, 131
National Collegiate Athletics Association, 232
National Conference on Education and Training in Feminist Practice, 89
National Council of Negro Women, 16
National Council of Schools and Programs in Professional Psychology, 60
National Institute of Child Health and Human Development, 281, 298
National Institute of Health, 101, 175–176, 232, 269
National Institute of Mental Health, 84–85, 101, 154, 280, 322, 405
National Science Foundation, 140, 176, 405
Nature–nurture controversy, 8, 71, 73, 299–300
Neonatal behavior, 71
Neonatal Behavioral Assessment Scale
  see Brazelton, T. B.
Nepotism, 38, 68–69, 206–207, 231
Nettles, S. R. M., 263

Neugarten, B., 22
New Jersey Psychological Association, 118, 122, 401
New York University, 156–158
Newcomb, T., 36
Noller, P., 142
Northeastern State University, 128
Northwestern University, xiii, 204

O

O'Connell, A., xiv, xvii–xxi, 5–10, 13–26, 343–420
  Biographical Information Forms–Version E, 3, 346
O'Connor, S., 18
Oberlin College, 311–313
Occidental College, 188–190
Oklahoma Federation of Indian Women, 128, 402
Oklahoma House of Representatives, 127
Oklahoma Psychological Association, 131, 402
Orzack, M., 38

P

Parents of eminent women
  see Families of origin
Parks, R., 16–17
Parsons, O., 129
Paul, A., 16
Payton, C., 21, 23, 263, 416–417
Peak, H., 36, 42, 396
Pfaffmann, C. 173–175, 179
Phil Donahoe Show, 224
Philadelphia Society of Clinical Psychologists, 57
Piaget, J., 22
Piliavin, J., 139
Pregnancy Discrimination Act, 17
Price Waterhouse v. Hopkins, 211–212, 372
Professional positions, 375–388
Profiles and patterns, 9, 413–418
Project Share, 40
Proshansky, H., 206
Proxmire, W., 140–141
Psi Chi, the National Honor Society in Psychology, xx, 196, 404
Psychology of Women Quarterly, xiii
Psychotherapy: Theory, Research, and Practice, 131
Purdue University, 207–208, 215

Q

Queens College, CUNY, 156

R

Racial/ethnic/religious discrimination, 265–268, 333–335, 389
Rapson, R. I., 142–144
Reid, P. T., 8–9, 19, 22–23, 347, 255–273, 351, 353, 356–357, 374–375, 389, 396–397, 410–411
Reston, J., 141
Richmond, J., 396
Rioch, M., 358
Robert Wood Johnson Foundation, 283
Roe, A., 352
Roosevelt, E., 17
Routh, D., 132
Ruble, D., 280
Russo, N. F., xviii, xx, 317
Rutgers University (GSAPP), xvii, 116–119, 401

S

Sample, S., 227, 396
Scarborough, E., xviii, xx
Scarr, S., 8, 20–22, 97–112, 279, 346, 353, 356, 358, 369, 375, 388, 397, 410–411
Schachter, S., 139
Selection criteria, xix, 6–7
Sex/gender discrimination, 17–19, 49, 56, 58, 83, 87, 102, 105, 121, 139, 154–155, 158–159, 163, 171–173, 175–176, 178, 180, 189, 205, 207, 209–210, 212, 230–231, 266, 316, 323, 333–334, 388, 390–393
Sex Roles, xiii, 158, 162, 403
Sexton, V., xx
Sexual harassment, 390–391, 393
Shalala, D., 322, 396
Shapiro, J., 143
Sherif, C., 22, 358, 416
Shields, S., xviii
Siblings, 347–351
Simonton, D., 347, 352, 388–389, 397, 412–413
Skinner, B. F., 83
Smith, M., xviii
Smith, P. C., 22, 359

Social and cultural environment, 17–18, 412–418
 see also Historical events
Social identity theory, 213–214
Social Science Research Council, 282
Society for Research on Adolescence, 408
Society for Research on Child Development, 107, 263, 267, 287, 399, 401
Society for the Scientific Study of Sexuality, 142, 145, 324, 403, 409
Society of Experimental Psychology, 180, 404
Society of Experimental Social Psychology, 145, 208, 371, 403
Southern Seminary, 128–129
Spence, J. T., xii–xiv, xx, 8, 20, 22, 206–207, 359, 369
Spiegel, D., 191
Stanford University, 138, 209, 243–244
Stanton, E., 16
State University of New York-Buffalo, 224–225, 227
State University of New York-Geneseo, 245–246, 250
Statistics
 APA memberships, 18–21
 doctorates awarded, 7, 21
 minorities, 21, 23
 salary gap, 17–18, 22
 subfields, 20–22
 tenure, 6, 21
Staudinger, U., 418
Stereotypes, 152–153, 160, 163, 210–212, 258
Sternberg, R., 418
Stevens, H, 38
Stevens, J., 175
Stevens, S. S., 176
Stolz, L., 347, 388
Strauss, H., 117, 396
Strickland, B., 8, 21–22, 334, 369, 396, 417
Suffragette movement, 16
Supertasters, 179
Syracuse University, 153

T

Tedesco, L., 225–227
Temple University, 49, 261–262
Texas Christian University, 223
Thompson, C., 18
Thorpe, M., xx
Thurstone, T., 23

Index

Transcultural Mental Health Institute, 336
Transhistoric and time-specific aspects, 413–418
  see also Achievement, Creativity, Profiles and patterns
Travis, C., 89
Troll, L., 22, 358, 388, 416–417
Truica, B., xx
Tyler, L., 8, 20–21, 23, 358–359, 388, 416

U

Uhlinger (Shantz), C., 83–84
University of California-Berkeley, 204, 314, 316
University of Cincinnati, 299
University of Colorado, 161, 229–232
University of Connecticut, 177
University of Delaware, 265
University of Florida, 178
University of Hawaii, 142, 145
University of Iowa, 69
University of Kansas, 69
University of Kent, Cambridge, England, 214
University of Maryland, 102–3
University of Massachusetts-Amherst, 334
University of Michigan, 35, 138, 244, 270
University of Minnesota, 104, 139, 177
University of Oklahoma, 128–129
University of Pennsylvania, 103, 262, 279–280, 297
University of Puerto Rico, 333
University of Tennessee-Chattanooga, 266–267, 269, 407
University of Texas, xiii, 206–207, 223–224
University of Virginia, 106, 108
University of Wisconsin-Madison, 37–39, 139, 321–324
University of Wisconsin-Whitewater, 39
US Advisory Board on Child Abuse and Neglect, 131
US Congress, 131

V

Vassar College, 101, 106
Vetter, L., xviii
Vietnam War, 16, 174, 209, 245, 250, 313, 316, 411

W

Walker, L., 92, 120
Walsh, M. R., 249
Washburn, M., 8, 19, 359
Wayne State University, 84–85
Weinberg, R., 105
Wertheimer, M., xviii
Western Psychological Association, 196, 405, 409
Widener University, 59
Willis, D., 8, 21–23, 125–134, 346, 369, 374–5, 397, 410
Wisdom, 6, 9, 417–418
Witmer, L., 49
Woman to Woman (W2W), 88
Women in Psychology: A Bio-bibliographic Sourcebook, xviii, 8
Women in Psychology for Legislative Action (WPLA), 120
Women, in the 20th century, 16
Women's Educational Equity Act, 17
Women's Heritage in Psychology, xviii
Women's Movement, 7, 16–17, 159, 209, 411
Women's Rights Convention, 16
Woolley, H., 18, 23, 324
Worell, J., 89
World War I, 7, 48, 171, 412
World War II, 7, 16–17, 19, 48–49, 100, 137, 139, 187–188, 277, 309, 411, 412
Wright State University, 207
Wright, L., 85, 129–130, 396
Wrightsman, L., 208

Y

Yale University, 106, 154–155, 174–175, 177–178, 404
Yanagisawa, 178–179
Youtz, A., 396

Z

Zager, K., 122
Zajonc, R., 244–245, 396
Zigler, E., 155, 160, 396
Zimbardo, P., 156

BF
109
A1
M62
2001

Reinsch Library
Marymount University
2807 N Glebe Road
Arlington, VA 22207